EDUGORILLA
PUBLICATION

Indian Navy

Senior Secondary Recruits (SSR)

Latest Edition
Practice Kit

20 Tests

12 Sectional Test

08 Mock Test

Based On Real Exam Pattern

✓ Thoroughly Revised and Updated

✓ Detailed Analysis of all MCQs

Title	: Indian Navy Senior Secondary Recruits (SSR)
Author Name	: Mr. Rohit Manglik
Published By	: EduGorilla Community Pvt. Ltd.
Publishers Address	: 12/651, First Floor Opp. Arvindo Park, Near Jama Masjid, Indira Nagar, Lucknow, Uttar Pradesh-226016, India

Copyright EduGorilla

Disclaimer EduGorilla

ROHIT MANGLIK
CEO, EduGorilla

Dear Applicants,

People say *"Success comes to those who work hard."* But I've seen people working hard for their exams day in and day out for marginal success. While others succeed in their examinations by putting in just half the work. So are they God Gifted? No! I believe that it's because they work *smart* and not just *hard*. Similarly, for your exams, you should strategize your preparation so as to increase the likelihood of success. Well with EduGorilla get ready to increase your *chances of selection* in your exam by *16x*.

EduGorilla helps you in not only working *hard* but also working in a *smart and strategic* manner. With EduGorilla's preparation package, you get a chance to make your exam preparation easy, and a fun learning path towards selection. Finding the right path to your preparations can be difficult if you don't know in which direction to head. Don't worry, we have you covered! EduGorilla will be your guide to success in your journey. With our Preparation Package, you can prepare strategically and beat the exam in just one attempt.

EduGorilla's Preparation Package includes-

• **Test Series**　　　　• **Books**

Our preparation package is handcrafted as per the latest changes, expert opinions, and students' discretion. Thus, enabling you to get through each stage of the selection process for your exam.

Our Books are designed by the teachers and experts of the respective exam with a combined 150+ years of experience; to provide you with easy, efficient, and effective learning. Our books are smart, in the sense that not only do they give you the answers to the questions but also provide similar questions for practice.

EduGorilla's competent Test Series gives you real-time experience and confidence through which you can clear your offline or online exam in just one attempt. We currently host 83,000+ mock tests for 1,440+ competitive and academic exams.

Thus, EduGorilla misses no chance to assist you in your preparation and covers all stages of the exam, so that you don't have to look anywhere else.

We provide complete preparation packages for defense, banking, teaching, and other National & State-Level exams. Hence, it doesn't matter which exam you aspire to because you will reach your success.

ALL THE BEST !
Let EduGorilla be your Guide to Success.

Rohit Manglik,
Founder and CEO, EduGorilla

INTRODUCTION

EduGorilla focuses on guiding students to succeed in their examinations. With that in mind, our book, titled "Indian Navy : Senior Secondary Recruits (SSR)", has been drafted through the collective efforts of our distinguished experts with 150+ years of combined experience. This book consists of questions that are created following the latest changes in the syllabus and exam pattern. We compiled the book on the basis of questions that are most likely to appear in the Indian Navy Senior Secondary Recruits (SSR). Through EduGorilla's "Indian Navy : Senior Secondary Recruits (SSR)" your chances of success will increase 16x.

EduGorilla does this through our Complete Preparation Package. This package consists of well-conceptualized and structured content in the form of questions that are tailor-made according to your needs and will help you practice for exams in a smart way by pinpointing all the necessary information. It also provides hints and solutions, along with a smart answer sheet for your self-evaluation. You can assess your shortcomings and work accordingly on areas that may require more of your attention.

EduGorilla promises to help you succeed in your examination and accomplish your dream goals. We believe in our aspirants and see them at the top of the merit list. And the first step towards the top is to start preparing with us. EduGorilla's "Indian Navy : Senior Secondary Recruits (SSR)" includes the following attributes.

➤ Well-Researched Content

➤ Top-Notch Quality

➤ Detailed Answers and Analysis

➤ Smart Answer Sheet

➤ Exam Relevant Questions

Therefore, EduGorilla fortifies your preparation and makes it durable enough to help you stand tall and beat the examination.

Indian Navy Senior Secondary Recruits (SSR)
Scan QR code for Eligibility, Exam Pattern, Syllabus and more.

Book ID: 0330

TABLE OF CONTENTS

Mock Test 01

English

Ques (1-5):Direction: Read the following passage and answer the question.

It is to progress in the human sciences that we must look to undo the evils which have resulted from a knowledge of the physical world hastily and superficially acquired by the population unconscious of the changes in themselves that the new knowledge has imperative. The road to a happier world than any known in the past lies open before us if atavistic destructive passions can be kept in the leash while the necessary adaptations are made. Fears are inevitable in time, but hopes are equally rational and far more likely to bear good fruit. We must learn to think rather less of the dangers to be avoided than of the good that will lie within our grasp if we can believe in it and let it dominate our thoughts. Science, whatever unpleasant consequences it may have, by the way, is in its very nature a liberator, a liberator of bondage to physical nature and in time to come, a liberator from the weight of destructive passions. We are on the threshold of utter disaster or unprecedentedly glorious achievement. No previous age has been fraught with problems so momentous, and it is to science that we must look to for a happy future.

Q.1 What does science liberate us from?

A. Fears and destructive passions

B. Slavery to physical nature and from passions

C. Bondage to physical nature

D. Idealistic hopes of glorious future

Q.2 Should human sciences be developed because they will:

A. Provide more knowledge of the physical word

B. Make us conscious of the changing world

C. Make us conscious of the changing in ourselves

D. Eliminate the destruction caused by a superficial knowledge of the physical world

Q.3 If man's bestial yearning is controlled:

A. The future will be tolerable

B. The future will be brighter than the present

C. The present will be brighter than the future

D. The present will become tolerable

Q.4 Fears and hopes according to the author:

A. Are closely linked with the life of modern man

B. Can bear fruit

C. Can yield good results

D. Are irrational

Q.5 To carve out a bright future man should:

A. Analyse dangers that lie ahead

B. Try to avoid dangers

C. Overcome fear and dangers

D. Cultivate a positive outlook

Q.6 Choose the correctly punctuated sentence.

A. However, David did not achieve his goal.

B. However; David did not achieve his goal.

C. However David did not achieve his goal!

D. However: David did not achieve his goal.

Q.7 Direction: Choose the correct alternative to correct the sentence.

In our country, women **have an opportunities to rise** to the top in every walk of life.

A. have been having opportunities

B. have had opportunities for a raise

C. have opportunities to rise

D. will be have opportunities to rise

Q.8 Direction: Choose the appropriate synonym of the word.

Hoarse

A. Noisy   B. Harmful   C. Pleasant   D. Harsh

Q.9 Direction: Choose the appropriate antonym of the word.

Capitulate

A. Conquer

B. Venerate

C. Destroy

D. Surrender

Q.10 Direction: Choose the correct Active / Passive sentence.

I had 500 INR in my wallet. I lost it.

A. I had 500 INR in my wallet, but I lost it.

B. I had 500 INR in my wallet, which has been lost by me.

C. I lost the 500 INR I had in my wallet.

D. The 500 INR in my wallet is lost.

Q.11 Direction: Change Active to Passive Voice or vice - versa as the case may be.

Has the work been completed by you?

A. Has you completed the work?

B. Have you completed the work?

C. Have you been completing the work?

D. Is the work complete?

Q.12 Direction: Change direct to indirect Speech or vice - versa as the case may be.

"Do you write a good hand?" the teacher said to the student.

A. The teacher asked the student if he would write a good hand.

B. The teacher asked the student if he can write a good hand.

C. The teacher asked the student if he has written a good hand.

D. The teacher asked the student if he wrote a good hand.

Q.13 Direction: Choose the most appropriate alternative to change a sentence from indirect to direct speech or vice - versa.

The customer asked the waiter if he could book a table for dinner that night.

A. The customer said to the waiter, "Can I book a table for dinner tonight?"

B. The customer said, "Can I book a table for dinner tonight?"

C. The customer said to the waiter, "Can I book a table tonight?"

D. The customer said to the waiter, "Could I book a table for dinner tonight?"

Q.14 Direction: Choose the most appropriate preposition to complete the sentence.

I bring fresh flowers _______ the lovely lady coming from the seas.

A. for   **B.** off   **C.** in   **D.** to

Q.15 Direction: Choose the most appropriate preposition to complete the sentence.

_______ the nine gods, he swore.

A. At   **B.** Of   **C.** By   **D.** Into

Q.16 Direction: Choose the most appropriate pronoun to complete the sentence.

Two gold jewellery sets were given to _______ by my grandmother.

A. them   **B.** our   **C.** me   **D.** I

Q.17 Direction: Choose the most appropriate verbs/tense to complete the sentence.

I was _______ to know that everybody was fine.

A. pleasant   **B.** pleased   **C.** pleasing   **D.** pleaseful

Q.18 Direction: Choose the most appropriate verbs/tense to complete the sentence.

The garden _______ sweet with flowers like the rose and the jasmine.

A. was smelling   **B.** had been smelling
C. smelled   **D.** None

Q.19 Direction: Choose the most appropriate determiners to complete the sentence.

_______ men must be punished.

A. An   **B.** Those   **C.** The   **D.** Each

Q.20 From the given four options choose the correct sentence.

A. I can't go out tonight because I have to prepare for my interview tomorrow.

B. I can't go out tonight because I has to prepare for my interview tomorrow.

C. I can't went out tonight because I have to prepare for my interview tomorrow.

D. I can't go out tonight because I have to prepare about my interview tomorrow.

Q.21 Direction: Select the correct adjective from the given options.

You can not grow cherries in these areas. They grow only in _______ conditions.

A. exceptional   **B.** specific
C. special   **D.** considerable

Q.22 Identify the adjective out of the given options.

A. Cowardly   **B.** Belly
C. Apply   **D.** Beautifully

Q.23 Direction: Fill in the blank with an appropriate determiner.

He had heard there were many beavers in _____ park.

A. No determiner   **B.** a
C. an   **D.** the

Q.24 Direction: Fill in the blank with a suitable phrasal verb.

Sandy just stood by and _________ my glass.

A. showed off   **B.** read out
C. gave up   **D.** filled up

Q.25 Direction: Fill in the blank with the most appropriate phrasal verb.

He _______ his grandfather.

A. takes off   **B.** takes to
C. takes after   **D.** takes for

Science

Q.26 The dimensions of planck's constant are the same as those of:

A. Energy   **B.** Power
C. Angular frequency   **D.** Angular momentum

Q.27 A tennis ball is thrown straight up and caught at the same height. Which of the following can describe the motion of the ball when it reaches the apex?

A. The velocity of the ball is zero.
B. The acceleration of the ball is zero.
C. The acceleration of the ball is 9.8 m/s^2 up.
D. None of these

Q.28 An object moving at constant velocity in an inertial frame must:

A. Have a net force acting on it
B. Have zero net fore acting on it
C. Not have any force of gravity on it
D. Stop after some time due to gravity

Q.29 A body of mass 3 kg is dropped from a height of 1 m. The kinetic energy of the body will be when it touches the ground:

A. 49 J   **B.** 29.4 J   **C.** 200 J   **D.** 150 J

Q.30 A water film is made between two straight parallel wires of length $10\ cm$ each and at a distance of $0.5\ cm$ from each other. If the distance between the wire is increased by $1\ mm$, how much work will be done? Surface tension of water $= 72\ dynes/cm$

A. 288 ergs   **B.** 72 ergs   **C.** 144 ergs   **D.** 216 ergs

Q.31 In a gas of diatomic molecules, the ratio of the two specific heats of gas $\dfrac{C_P}{C_V}$ is:

A. 7 : 6   **B.** 7 : 5   **C.** 6 : 5   **D.** 7 : 8

Q.32 A body has same temp as that of the surroundings. The ratio of radiations emitted and radiations received from the surroundings is:

A. Zero
B. One
C. Infinity
D. None of these

Q.33 Which of the following will not show the change in their time period when they are taken to moon?

A. A simple pendulum
B. A physical pendulum
C. A torsional pendulum
D. None of these

Q.34 If a wave's frequency doubles and its wavelength is:

A. Halved
B. Also doubled
C. Unhanged, as c is constant
D. Now 4 times longer

Q.35 A hollow metal sphere of radius 10 cm is charged such that the potential on its surface is 80 V. The potential at the centre of the sphere is:

A. Zero
B. 80 V
C. 800 V
D. 8 V

Q.36 In an electric current is passed through a nerve, the man:

A. Begins to laugh
B. Begins to weep
C. Is excited
D. None of these

Q.37 When a charged particle enters in a uniform magnetic field, its kinetic energy:

A. Remains constant
B. Increases
C. Decreases
D. Becomes zero

Q.38 Current in a circuit is wattles if:

A. Current is alternating
B. Resistance in circuit is zero
C. Inductance in circuit is zero
D. Resistance and inductance both are zero

Q.39 Maxwell's modified form of Ampere's circuital law is:

A. $\oint \vec{B} \cdot d\vec{S} = 0$
B. $\oint \vec{B} \cdot d\vec{l} = \mu_0 i$
C. $\oint \vec{B} \cdot d\vec{l} = \mu_0 i + \frac{1}{\epsilon_0} \frac{dq}{dt}$
D. $\oint \vec{B} \cdot d\vec{l} = \mu_0 i + \mu_0 \epsilon_0 \frac{d\phi_E}{dt}$

Q.40 A plant with green leaves placed in red light will appear:

A. Black
B. Green
C. Red
D. Violet

Q.41 A water drop is divided into 8 equal droplets. The pressure difference between the inner and outer side of the big drop will be:

A. Same as that for smaller droplet
B. $\frac{1}{2}$ of that for smaller droplet
C. $\frac{1}{4}$ of that for smaller droplet
D. Twice of that for smaller droplet

Q.42 Which of the following is not a mode of radioactive decay?

A. Positron emission
B. Electron capture
C. Fusion
D. Alpha decay

Q.43 A message signal of frequency ω_m is superimposed on a carrier wave of frequency ω_c to get an amplitude modulated wave (AM). The frequency of the AM wave will be:

A. ω_m
B. ω_c
C. $\left(\frac{\omega_m + \omega_c}{2}\right)$
D. $\left(\frac{\omega_m - \omega_c}{2}\right)$

Q.44 What is the number of hydrogen atoms present in the hydrocarbon formed by the hydrogenation of ethylene?

A. 4
B. 6
C. 8
D. 2

Q.45 _____ is a program that translated mnemonic statements into executable instructions.

A. Software
B. Assembler
C. Translator
D. None of these

Q.46 Calculate the work required to be done to stop a car of $1500 \, kg$ moving at a velocity of $60 kmh^{-1}$.

A. $-208333 \, J$
B. $208333 \, J$
C. $-209333 \, J$
D. $-207333 \, J$

Q.47 Metals react with oxygen to form:

A. Basic oxides
B. Acidic oxides
C. Both (A) and (B)
D. None of the above

Q.48 The major components of food which is required by the body for wear and tear is ________ .

A. vitamins
B. minerals
C. salt
D. protein

Q.49 The protozoan that causes malaria is:

A. Entamoeba histolytica
B. Euglena
C. Paramecium
D. Plasmodium

Q.50 VIRUS stands for:

A. Vital Information Recourse Under Siege
B. Vital Information Reason Under Siege
C. Vital Information Recourse Under System
D. Virus Information Recourse Under Siege

Mathematics

Q.51 Let O be the circumcentre, G be the centroid and O' be the orthocentre of a triangle ABC. Three vectors are taken through O and are represented by $\vec{a} = \vec{OA}, \vec{b} = \vec{OB}$ and $\vec{c} = \vec{OC}$, then $\vec{a} + \vec{b} + \vec{c}$ is:

A. $\vec{OG}$
B. $2\vec{OG}$
C. $\vec{OO}$
D. None of these

Q.52 There are four machines and it is known that exactly two of them are faulty. They are tested, one by one in a random order till both the faulty machines are identified. Then the probability that only two tests are needed, is:

A. $\frac{1}{3}$
B. $\frac{1}{6}$
C. $\frac{1}{2}$
D. $\frac{1}{4}$

Q.53 What is the value of $\lim\limits_{x\to 0}\dfrac{(1-\cos 2x)^2}{x^4}$?

A. 1 **B.** 8 **C.** 4 **D.** 0

Q.54 If n (X) = 300, n (Y) = 400 and n (X ∪ Y) = 500, then n (X - Y) is equal to:

A. 120 **B.** 140 **C.** 150 **D.** 100

Q.55 Let $f: R \to R$ be the function defined by $f(x) = 2x - 3, \forall x \in R$. Then $f^{-1}(x) =$?

A. $2x + 3$ **B.** $\dfrac{x}{2} + 3$ **C.** $\dfrac{1}{2x-3}$ **D.** $\dfrac{x+3}{2}$

Q.56 What is the sum of all natural numbers between 300 and 500 which are divisible by 7?

A. 29334 **B.** 11527 **C.** 12572 **D.** 11571

Q.57 The expression $\dfrac{\sin 4x - \sin 2x}{\cos 4x + \cos 2x}$ is equal to:

A. $\cot x$ **B.** $\tan x$
C. $\tan 2x$ **D.** None of these

Q.58 Find the value of cos 3x.

A. 3 cos x - 4cos³ x **B.** 4 cos³ x - 3 cos x
C. 4 cos x - 3 cos³ x **D.** None of these

Q.59 What is the value of $\int_{-2}^{2}|x|\,dx$?

A. 0 **B.** 1 **C.** 2 **D.** 4

Q.60 What is the degree of the differential equation $\left(\dfrac{d^3y}{dx^3}\right)^{\frac{3}{2}} = \left(\dfrac{d^2y}{dx^2}\right)^2$?

A. 1 **B.** 2 **C.** 3 **D.** 4

Q.61 Evaluate $\int \cos^2 x\,dx$.

A. $\dfrac{x}{2} + \dfrac{\sin 2x}{2} + c$ **B.** $\dfrac{x}{2} + \dfrac{\sin 2x}{4} + c$
C. $\dfrac{x}{2} - \dfrac{\sin 2x}{4} + c$ **D.** $\dfrac{x}{2} + \dfrac{\cos 2x}{4} + c$

Q.62 What is the modulus of $\dfrac{4+2i}{1-2i}$ where $i = \sqrt{-1}$?

A. $2\sqrt{5}$ **B.** 4 **C.** 3 **D.** 2

Q.63 If p and q are the roots of the equation $x^2 - 30x + 221 = 0$, what is the value of $p^3 + q^3$?

A. 7010 **B.** 7110 **C.** 7210 **D.** 7240

Q.64 If a, b, c, d, e, f are in A.P., then e – c is equal to:

A. 2 (c - a) **B.** 2 (d - c) **C.** 2 (f - d) **D.** (d - c)

Q.65 Find the angle between two vectors $\vec{a} = 2\hat{\imath} + \hat{\jmath} - 3\hat{k}$ and $\vec{b} = 3\hat{\imath} - 2\hat{\jmath} - \hat{k}$.

A. −160° **B.** −60° **C.** 160° **D.** 60°

Q.66 If the straight line, $2x - 5y + 4 = 0$ is perpendicular to the line passing through the points $(1,5)$ and $(\alpha, 3)$, then α equals:

A. $\dfrac{6}{5}$ **B.** $\dfrac{9}{5}$ **C.** $\dfrac{7}{8}$ **D.** 2

Q.67 The equation of the ellipse whose vertices are at $(\pm 5, 0)$ and foci at $(\pm 4, 0)$ is:

A. $\dfrac{x^2}{25} + \dfrac{y^2}{9} = 1$ **B.** $\dfrac{x^2}{9} + \dfrac{y^2}{25} = 1$
C. $\dfrac{x^2}{16} + \dfrac{y^2}{25} = 1$ **D.** $\dfrac{x^2}{25} + \dfrac{y^2}{16} = 1$

Q.68 A bag contains 7 red and 4 blue balls. Two balls are drawn at random with replacement. The probability of getting the balls of different colors is:

A. $\dfrac{28}{121}$ **B.** $\dfrac{56}{121}$
C. $\dfrac{1}{2}$ **D.** None of these

Q.69 Find $2X - Y$ matrix such as $X + Y = \begin{bmatrix} 7 & 5 \\ 3 & 4 \end{bmatrix}$ and $X - Y = \begin{bmatrix} 1 & -3 \\ 3 & 0 \end{bmatrix}$.

A. $\begin{bmatrix} 3 & 4 \\ 0 & -2 \end{bmatrix}$ **B.** $\begin{bmatrix} 5 & -2 \\ 6 & 2 \end{bmatrix}$
C. $\begin{bmatrix} 5 & 4 \\ 3 & -2 \end{bmatrix}$ **D.** $\begin{bmatrix} -3 & 4 \\ 0 & -2 \end{bmatrix}$

Q.70 What is the value of the determinant $\begin{vmatrix} x+2 & x+3 & x-1 \\ x+6 & x+8 & x+4 \\ x+9 & x+11 & x+7 \end{vmatrix}$?

A. $-x + 32$ **B.** 32
C. 12 **D.** 16

Q.71 If parabola $y^2 = 4kx$ passes through point $(-2,1)$, then the length of latus rectum is:

A. $\dfrac{1}{2}$ **B.** $\dfrac{1}{3}$
C. $\dfrac{1}{4}$ **D.** None of these

Q.72 The distance between the parallel planes $3x + y + 3z = 8$ and $9x + 3y + 9z = 15$ is:

A. $\dfrac{5}{\sqrt{19}}$ **B.** $\dfrac{7}{\sqrt{19}}$ **C.** $\dfrac{3}{\sqrt{19}}$ **D.** $\dfrac{9}{\sqrt{19}}$

Q.73 If the planes $2x - y - 3z - 7 = 0$ and $4x - 2y + 5kz + 9 = 0$ are parallel, then $5k + 7$ is:

A. 4 **B.** 5 **C.** 3 **D.** 1

Q.74 A line passes through $(1,1)$ and is perpendicular to the line $3x + y = 7$. Its x-intercept is:

A. −2 **B.** 2 **C.** $\dfrac{2}{3}$ **D.** $-\dfrac{2}{3}$

Q.75 The radius of the circle $x^2 + y^2 + x + c = 0$ passing through the origin is:

A. $\dfrac{1}{4}$ **B.** $\dfrac{1}{2}$ **C.** 1 **D.** 2

General Awareness

Q.76 Which country has signed a $ 2.25 billion deal with a Russian state-run nuclear energy company 'ASE' in August 2022?

[RBI Assistant, 2020], [UPSSSC Rajasva Lekhpal, 2015]

A. India **B.** China
C. Japan **D.** South Korea

Q.77 Who among the followings has been elected as the 15 th President of India in July 2022 ?

A. Nirmala Sitharaman   **B.** Swati Piramal
C. Hima Kohli   **D.** Droupadi Murmu

Q.78 What is the contribution of India to the UN Women Core budget in 2022?

[Delhi Forest Guard, 2021], [HSSC Canal Patwari, 2021]

A. USD 10,000   **B.** USD 50,000
C. USD 100,000   **D.** USD 500,000

Q.79 Who was the founder of the Gupta dynasty?
A. Sri Gupta   **B.** Chandragupta II
C. Samudragupta   **D.** Skandgupta

Q.80 In banking, ATM stands for _______.
A. Automated Tallying Machine
B. Automated Teller Machine
C. Automated Totalling Machine
D. Automated Transaction of Money

Q.81 Which region is often called "The Land of 5 Rivers"?
A. Punjab   **B.** Maharashtra
C. Andhra Pradesh   **D.** Himachal Pradesh

Q.82 The author of the book "To Kill A Mockingbird" is ______.
A. Amitav Ghosh   **B.** Alice Munro
C. Harper Lee   **D.** Patrik Modiano

Q.83 The Capital of Argentina is _______.
A. Havana   **B.** Canberra
C. Buenos Aires   **D.** Ottawa

Q.84 Which among the following is a martial dance?
A. Kathakali
B. Bamboo dance in Meghalaya
C. Mayurbhanj Chhau
D. Bhangra of Punjab

Q.85 Direction: Which number will complete the given series?
0, 5, 22, 57, ?, 205
A. 198   **B.** 116   **C.** 172   **D.** 92

Q.86 If OUT is coded as 152120, IN will be coded as:
A. 1015   **B.** 819   **C.** 1813   **D.** 914

Q.87 The New Kwanza is the currency of _______.
A. Cuba   **B.** Angola   **C.** Bahamas   **D.** Chad

Q.88 Which scientist discovered the 'Penicillin'?
A. Alexander Fleming   **B.** Robert Koch
C. Louis Pasteur   **D.** Ernst Chain

Q.89 Who is the founder and CEO of SpaceX?
A. James   **B.** Tim Cook
C. James Sophia   **D.** Elon Musk

Q.90 With which sports "Formula-1" is associated?
A. Motor racing   **B.** Cricket
C. Ice Hockey   **D.** Polo

Q.91 What was the importance of the Lucknow Pact of 1916?
A. Muslim leaders agreed to join the noncooperation movement led by Mahatama Gandhi.
B. British agreed to the partition of India, so that Muslims can get their separate land.
C. It built friendly relations between Muslim League and Indian National Congress (INC) and also the groups between INC.
D. Noncooperation movement was halted and British agreed to grant autonomy to all provinces.

Q.92 Direction: In question from the given alternatives select the word which cannot be formed using the letters of the given word.(Repetition is not allowed)
DISBURSEMENT
A. BURST   **B.** DISTURB
C. SISTER   **D.** SENTIMENT

Q.93 Which one of the following languages is not widely spoken in Meghalaya?
A. English   **B.** Garo   **C.** Khasi   **D.** Hindi

Q.94 How many languages are recognized as scheduled languages?
A. 21   **B.** 22   **C.** 23   **D.** 24

Q.95 'Dandia' is a popular dance of:
A. Punjab   **B.** Gujarat
C. Tamil Nadu   **D.** Maharashtra

Q.96 Baisakhi is usually celebrated on:
A. 14th April   **B.** 25th April
C. 1st May   **D.** 31st December

Q.97 How many numbers of players are there in the game of Handball?
A. 4   **B.** 5   **C.** 6   **D.** 7

Q.98 Which nation is referred to as the " Giant of Africa "?
A. Egypt   **B.** Nigeria
C. South Africa   **D.** Scotland

Q.99 Bangladesh has a land border with_______.
A. only India   **B.** India and Myanmar
C. India and Bhutan   **D.** India and China

Q.100 Name the capital of Pakistan.
A. Rawalpindi   **B.** Islamabad
C. Karachi   **D.** Lahore

// Smart Answer Sheet //

Correct — Percentage of students who answered correctly. **Skipped** — Percentage of students who skipped.

Q.	Ans.	Correct / Skipped	Q.	Ans.	Correct / Skipped	Q.	Ans.	Correct / Skipped	Q.	Ans.	Correct / Skipped	Q.	Ans.	Correct / Skipped	Q.	Ans.	Correct / Skipped
1	B	76.81 % / 15.14 %	18	C	84.1 % / 15.48 %	35	B	76.18 % / 10.17 %	52	B	80.45 % / 10.46 %	69	B	87.17 % / 12.67 %	86	D	89.99 % / 10.01 %
2	D	83.52 % / 10.75 %	19	B	81.73 % / 18.09 %	36	C	79.16 % / 13.57 %	53	C	86.02 % / 10.13 %	70	C	53.39 % / 42.17 %	87	B	87.77 % / 10.81 %
3	B	88.54 % / 10.21 %	20	A	89.87 % / 10.04 %	37	A	62.96 % / 31.29 %	54	D	82.97 % / 10.47 %	71	A	63.67 % / 32.81 %	88	A	66.68 % / 31.77 %
4	A	88.13 % / 11.23 %	21	B	76.24 % / 11.49 %	38	B	47.79 % / 44.39 %	55	D	78.15 % / 20.17 %	72	C	40.69 % / 56.66 %	89	D	48.49 % / 35.54 %
5	D	80.1 % / 19.44 %	22	A	50.22 % / 44.3 %	39	D	42.85 % / 49.07 %	56	D	42.83 % / 32.01 %	73	D	68.76 % / 30.4 %	90	A	85.36 % / 14.14 %
6	A	81.63 % / 16.32 %	23	D	67.5 % / 30.16 %	40	A	78.55 % / 15.4 %	57	B	67.08 % / 31.74 %	74	A	41.61 % / 49.71 %	91	C	87.26 % / 10.39 %
7	C	77.01 % / 21.62 %	24	D	54.7 % / 33.52 %	41	B	43.22 % / 39.27 %	58	B	63.13 % / 30.77 %	75	B	55.59 % / 39.01 %	92	D	84.43 % / 10.89 %
8	D	83.39 % / 16.55 %	25	C	60.82 % / 38.95 %	42	C	51.72 % / 33.62 %	59	D	86.21 % / 11.91 %	76	D	89.19 % / 10.39 %	93	D	86.48 % / 12.72 %
9	A	80.97 % / 16.36 %	26	D	40.03 % / 52.79 %	43	B	86.79 % / 13.05 %	60	C	68.82 % / 31.09 %	77	D	89.86 % / 10.08 %	94	B	48.75 % / 49.41 %
10	C	82.24 % / 13.87 %	27	C	88.82 % / 10.66 %	44	B	53.13 % / 41.73 %	61	B	41.48 % / 42.56 %	78	D	77.94 % / 13.73 %	95	B	79.45 % / 18.19 %
11	B	82.68 % / 13.09 %	28	B	45.4 % / 42.89 %	45	B	83.75 % / 13.99 %	62	D	87.14 % / 10.92 %	79	A	81.93 % / 17.53 %	96	A	78.99 % / 12.32 %
12	D	81.82 % / 16.23 %	29	B	63.06 % / 30.25 %	46	A	55.63 % / 40.43 %	63	B	48.52 % / 37.47 %	80	B	84.16 % / 13.67 %	97	D	86.99 % / 12.44 %
13	A	79.79 % / 18.81 %	30	C	66.8 % / 32.39 %	47	A	88.34 % / 10.12 %	64	B	87.55 % / 11.81 %	81	A	85.07 % / 11.57 %	98	B	84.55 % / 15.25 %
14	A	87.87 % / 11.9 %	31	B	41.05 % / 51.86 %	48	D	52.7 % / 43.63 %	65	D	62.16 % / 35.61 %	82	C	79.0 % / 13.06 %	99	B	80.81 % / 10.01 %
15	C	79.63 % / 17.15 %	32	B	59.91 % / 32.07 %	49	D	49.5 % / 37.31 %	66	B	47.92 % / 47.04 %	83	C	86.7 % / 12.41 %	100	B	87.67 % / 11.2 %
16	C	87.85 % / 11.71 %	33	C	78.71 % / 16.82 %	50	A	51.47 % / 34.57 %	67	A	67.36 % / 32.18 %	84	C	88.47 % / 10.56 %			
17	B	76.53 % / 20.73 %	34	A	78.58 % / 16.83 %	51	C	68.5 % / 31.18 %	68	B	80.64 % / 15.02 %	85	B	79.4 % / 11.39 %			

//Hints and Solutions//

1. Acccording to the passage, "Science, whatever unpleasant consequences it may have, by the way, is in its very nature a liberator, a liberator of bondage to physical nature and in time to come, a liberator from the weight of destructive passions." **So, science liberates us from bondage or slavery to physical nature and from destructive passions**.

Hence, the correct option is (B).

2. According to the passage, "It is to progress in the human sciences that we must look to undo the evils which have resulted from a knowledge of physical world hastily and superficially acquired by population unconscious of the changes in themselves that the new knowledge has imperative." This means that the **population is unable to recognize the changes that the new knowledge has brought in** them which they have superficially acquired from the physical world. **Only, progress in human sciences can eliminate the destruction which is caused by this knowledge.**

Hence, the correct option is (D).

3. According to the passage, "The **road to a happier world**, than any known in the past, lies open before us **if atavistic destructive passions can be kept in leash**" which means that if man's bestial (cruel) or destructive passions or yearnings are kept under control, we will have happier and brighter future than the present or the past.

Hence, the correct option is (B).

4. According to the passage, "Fears are inevitable in time, but hopes are equally rational and far more likely to bear good fruit." This statement means that **more than fear, hope can bear good fruit**. Therefore, option (A) is correct as it can be concluded from the passage how hopes and fears are closely linked with the life of modern man. Options (B) and (C) are incorrect. Also, it is mentioned that hopes are rational which means option (D) is incorrect.

Hence, the correct option is (A).

5. According to the passage, "We must learn to think less of the dangers to be avoided than of the good that will lie within our grasp if we can believe in it and let it dominate our thoughts." This means that **instead of thinking and getting worried about how to avoid the dangers** that are unavoidable, a man **must think about the good and have a positive outlook** to carve out a bright future.

Hence, the correct option is (D).

6. However, David did not achieve his goal.

The comma (,) is used to separate ideas or elements. Also, it is used after the salutation, or when a brief pause is required after a word or phrase.

For example; Thanks for your help, Tom.

In the question, we require a brief pause after however as it is the introductory adverb.

A semicolon (;) is used when we need to separate independent clauses and to show a close relationship between them.

For example; She was hurt; she knew he had said that to upset him.

A colon (:) is used to provide a pause before introducing related information, or when we want to define or introduce something and join unequal parts of sentences.

For example; He missed only one person: Advik.

An exclamation mark (!) is used to denote a sudden outcry or emphasis.

For example; His behaviour made me furious!

Hence, the correct option is (A).

7. In our country, women **have opportunities to rise** to the top in every walk of life.

In the given question 'an' cannot be used because 'an' is used with singular and countable nouns.

In option (A), instead of 'have been having', 'have had' should be used in order to make the sentence simple. Also, in general statements, we use the simple present tense or past tense form.

In option (B), 'raise' is incorrect because we use 'raise' when we talk about a transitive verb (it has a direct object).

In the given sentence, 'rise' will be used because we do not have any direct object i.e., we are talking about 'the top of every walk of life'.

For example; Raise your hand. (Object is hand)

In option (D), 'have' is incorrect. Whenever we use 'will be' i.e., the action is to be performed in the future, we use the 'ing' form of the verb. In the present tense, 'have' cannot be used with 'will be'.

For example; She will be having a party tomorrow.

Hence, the correct option is (C).

8. Hoarse means (of a person's voice) sounding rough and harsh, typically as the result of a sore throat or of shouting.

For example; I heard a hoarse whisper.

Harsh means unpleasantly rough or jarring to the senses.

For example; I cannot bear his harsh voice.

It is clear from the examples that hoarse and harsh are synonyms.

Noisy means making or given to making a lot of noise.

Harmful means causing or likely to cause harm.

Pleasant means giving a sense of happy satisfaction or enjoyment.

Hence, the correct option is (D).

9. Capitulate means cease to resist an opponent or an unwelcome demand; yield.

For example; The king had to capitulate to the enemy forces.

Conquer means overcome and take control of (a place or people) by military force.

For example; We need to conquer poverty.

It is clear from the examples that the antonym of capitulate is conquer.

Venerate means regard with great respect; revere.

Destroy means end the existence of (something) by damaging or attacking it.

Surrender means stop resisting an enemy or opponent and submit to their authority.

Hence, the correct option is (A).

10. I lost the 500 INR I had in my wallet.

In the passive voice, we make the subject of the sentence as the object of the passive sentence and use the past participle form of the verb.

So, in option (C), 500 INR which is the subject becomes the object and wallet which is the object becomes the subject. Also, we use the past participle form 'had'.

The verb generally comes in between the subject and the object.

Accordingly, options (A) and (B) are incorrect because the verb had come before the subject i.e 500 INR.

'Is' is used with third person singular nouns like he/she/it.

Hence, the correct option is (C).

11. Have you completed the work?

The subject of the sentence should be in agreement with the pronoun used. Usually, we use 'has' with pronouns like he/she/it whereas we use 'have' with pronouns like I/you/we. So, in the given sentence 'have' should be used.

Also, the given question is in the past tense which is identified by the word completed so, the correct transformation of the sentence should also be in the past tense. Accordingly, the present continuous tense 'been completing' in option (C) is incorrect.

Option (D) has missing information as there is no mention of the subject you.

Hence, the correct option is (B).

12. The teacher asked the student if he wrote a good hand.

The given sentence: Do you write a good hand? the teacher said to the student is in the present tense. When a sentence in present and future tense is converted to indirect speech, the tense does not change. So, we simply change the pronoun from the first person to the third person i.e., from 'you' to 'he' and change 'write' to 'wrote'.

Option (A) uses the past tense of the word 'will' i.e., 'would'. While converting a sentence from direct to indirect speech, 'will' changes to 'would', but the given sentence does not contain will.

Option (B) contains 'can' which is incorrect because 'can' always changes to 'could' in indirect speech.

Option (C) contains 'has' which is incorrect as 'has' changes to 'had' in indirect speech.

Hence, the correct option is (D).

13. The customer said to the waiter, "Can I book a table for dinner tonight?"

Option (B) is incorrect because the customer is asking the waiter and the statement has no mention of the waiter.

Option (C) is incorrect because it has missing information i.e., for dinner so it is not the correct conversion of the given sentence to the direct speech.

Option (D) is incorrect because whenever we change a sentence from indirect to direct speech could changes to can. [from past tense to present tense]

Hence, the correct option is (A).

14. I bring fresh flowers for the lovely lady coming from the seas.

Both to and for are used to describe a motive or a reason but the difference is, 'to' is always used before a verb whereas 'for' is used before a noun. In the given sentence, the motive is for the lovely lady. Clearly, lady is a noun. So, we should use 'for' before the lovely lady.

Use of 'to' - For example; He came here to work. (Work is a verb)

'Off' is used when we have to convey a separation or disconnection.

For example; The dog ran off the street.

'In' is used to define a resting place or to denote something within an area.

For example; He lives in Europe.

Hence, the correct option is (A).

15. By the nine gods, he swore.

'By' is used when a particular thing is done with the help of another thing or with reference to another thing.

For example; I"ll send this by email.

In the given question, the subject 'he' is doing an action with reference to the nine gods. So, 'by' will be used in the sentence.

'At' is used when we refer to a particular time or place.

For example; Meet me at midnight.

'Of' is used to indicate relating to, belonging to someone, for reference or to indicate a number or amount.

For example; This is a picture of my dog.

'Into' is used to express movement generally with a verb that expresses movement.

For example; She came into my room.

Hence, the correct option is (C).

16. Two gold jewellery sets were given to me by my grandmother.

Me is used when the person speaking is receiving the action of the verb in some way.

For example; She smiled at me.

Them is used in place of plural nouns in the third person.

For example; The kids are playing. I will not disturb them.

Our is a first-person plural possessive pronoun. It specifies ownership by the speaker.

For example; This is our school.

I is used when the person speaking is doing the action.

For example; I am going to rest.

In the given question, me should be used as clearly the speaker of the statement which is identified by my grandmother is the object. Them can also be used but the most appropriate word is me.

Hence, the correct option is (C).

17. I was pleased to know that everybody was fine.

Since the sentence is in simple past tense which is recognized by the word was, past tense form of the word please i.e., pleased will be used to make the sentence grammatically correct.

Pleasant is used in the simple present tense.

Pleasing is the present participle form.

Pleaseful is an incorrect form of the word please.

Hence, the correct option is (B).

18. The garden smelled sweet with flowers like the rose and the jasmine.

Option (C) is correct because when we give a general statement or a fact we use the third form of the verb i.e., verb+ed.

Option (A) uses the past continuous tense i.e., an action happening in the past.

For example; She was going to a party.

Option (B) is in the past perfect continuous tense i.e., the action which started at a point in the past and is still continuing in the present. Usually, an adverb of time is used with them.

For example; At that time, she had been preparing for 2 months.

In the given question, there is no adverb of time.

Hence, the correct option is (C).

19. Those men must be punished.

Those is used to demonstrate subjects which are in plural form.

For example; Those are my shirts.

In the given sentence, those will be used to point towards a subject in the plural form i.e., men.

An is used before vowels.

For example; An apple a day keeps a doctor away.

The is used to refer to a particular thing or person. It is never used at the beginning of the sentence before 'man'.

For example; He is the same man I saw yesterday. (Correct because it used to refer to a specific person)

Each is used before singular nouns.

For example; Each student must have their card.

Hence, the correct option is (B).

20. The correct formation of sentence is:

'I can't go out tonight because I have to prepare for my interview tomorrow', because the preposition 'for' is used after the verb prepare.

I can't go out tonight because I has to prepare for my interview tomorrow is incorrect because the verb after 'I' should be 'have'.

I can't went out tonight because I have to prepare for my interview tomorrow is incorrect because the basic form of the verb i.e., go should be used after can't.

I can't go out tonight because I have to prepare about my interview tomorrow is incorrect because the preposition about is used after the verb prepare.

Hence, the correct option is (A).

21. 'Specific' means 'particular'. The context of the given sentence is that cherries grow in some particular conditions only. Therefore, the adjective 'specific' is suitable to describe 'condition'.

'Exceptional' means 'uncommon or extra-ordinary'.

'Special' means 'uncommon or unusual'.

'Considerable' means 'substantial, remarkable'.

None of these adjectives are suitable to describe the noun 'condition' to grow cherries.

The completed sentence, thus, becomes: You can not grow cherries in these areas. They grow only in specific conditions.

Hence, the correct option is (B).

22. Adjectives are words that modify nouns or pronouns to make them more specific.

Option (A) cowardly is an adjective that means 'lacking courage'.

Option (B) belly is a noun which is the term given to the front part of the human trunk consisting of the stomach. It is also used to describe the undersurface of a ship or an aircraft.

Option (C) apply is a verb that means to make a formal request.

Option (D) beautifully is an adverb that means in a way that is pleasing.

Hence, the correct option is (A).

23. It is stated that there are many beavers in the park. This suggests that the sentence is talking about a particular park. So, the definite determiner 'the' should be used.

Hence, the correct option is (D).

24. The context refers to pouring something in a glass. Here, the phrasal verb "filled up" is correct as it means to complete something completely.

Option (A) is incorrect as "to show off" is to behave in a way that is intended to attract attention or admiration.

Option (B) is incorrect as "to read out" is to read aloud.

Option (C) is incorrect as "to give up" is to stop trying to do something before you have finished.

Hence, the correct option is (D).

25. To "take after" someone is to be like them. The context refers to him being like someone.

To "take off" is to leave.

To "take to" someone is to begin to like them.

To "take for" something is to regard as something.

Hence, the correct option is (C).

26. Planck's constant: It is a physical constant that is the quantum of electromagnetic action. It relates the energy carried by a photon to its frequency by, $E = hv$.

$$\therefore h = \frac{E}{v}$$

Where, $E =$ energy, $v =$ frequency and $h =$ Planck's constant

Now,

Dimensional formula of energy $(E) = [ML^2\ T^{-2}]$

Dimensional formula of frequency $(v) = [T^{-1}]$

$$h = \frac{ML^2 T^{-2}}{T^{-1}}$$

$$\therefore h = ML^2\ T^{-1}$$

$\therefore$ Dimensional formula of Planck's constant h is $[ML^2\ T^{-1}]$.

Angular momentum: It is the rotational equivalent of linear momentum.

$$L = I \times \omega$$

$$\therefore L = r \times p$$

Where, $L =$ angular momentum, $I =$ moment of inertia, $\omega =$ angular momentum, $r =$ distance and $p =$ linear momentum

Now,

Dimensional formula of distance $(r) = [L]$

Dimensional formula of inear momentum $(p) = [MLT^{-1}]$

Therefore, the dimensional formula of $L = [L] \times [MLT^{-1}]$

$$\therefore L = [ML^2\ T^{-1}]$$

$\therefore$ Dimensional formula of angular momentum L is $[ML^2\ T^{-1}]$.

Hence, the correct option is (D).

27. When the ball is at the top, it becomes stationary due gravitational pull of the earth and then returns back, thus it's velocity becomes zero as it can't go further anymore. Unfortunately, this moment of zero velocity is hardly visible, since it occurs in a very short amount of time. When the tennis ball is at the peak possible, acceleration due to gravity is acting upon the ball which is equal to 9.8 m/s².

Hence, the correct option is (C).

28. According to the second law of motion,

Force $(F) = K\dfrac{p_2 - p_1}{t} = K\dfrac{m(v-u)}{t} = K\dfrac{m(v-v)}{t} = 0$ [As velocity is constant]

$$\therefore F = 0$$

As there is constant velocity, therefore acceleration will be zero. So the force will be zero.

Hence, the correct option is (B).

29. Given,

Mass of a body (m) = 3 kg and height (h) = 1m

The potential energy of the body,

PE = mgh

$\Rightarrow$ PE = 3 × 9.8 × 1

$\Rightarrow$ PE = 29.4 J

As the body falls, its kinetic energy increases at the expense of potential energy.

When the body touches the ground, it's potential energy becomes zero and because of the conservation of energy, the potential energy gets converted into kinetic energy.

So, the kinetic energy of the object at the ground = potential energy of the body at 1 m = 29.4 J

Hence, the correct option is (B).

30.

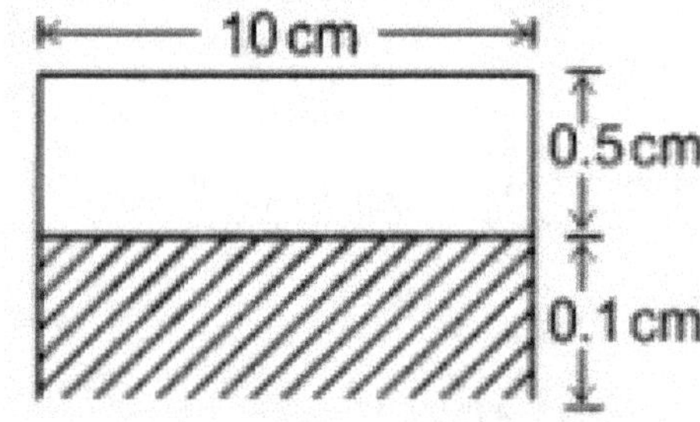

Given,

Length of wires is $10\ cm$, distance between the wire is $0.5\ cm$ and surface tension of water is $72\ dynes/cm$.

Since this is a water film so it has two surfaces therefore increment in area $= \Delta S = 2(A_1 - A_2)$

Where, ΔS is the change in the surface area and A is the area.

$$\Rightarrow \Delta S = 2(10 \times 0.6 - 10 \times 0.5)$$

$$\Rightarrow \Delta S = 2(6 - 5) = 2\ cm^2$$

Therefore, Work done $=$ Surface tension $\times$ Surface area

$$W = T \times \Delta S$$

Where, T is the surface tension of the water.

$W = 72 \times 2 = 144$ ergs

Hence, the correct option is (C).

31. The total number of molecules is nN_A where N_A is the Avogadro number. If the gas is diatomic, the internal energy of the gas is-

$$U = nN_A\left(\frac{5}{2}kT\right) = n\frac{5}{2}RT$$

If molecules do not vibrate. In this case,

$$C_v = \frac{1}{n}\frac{dU}{dT} = \frac{5}{2}R$$

And,

$$C_p = C_v + R = \frac{5}{2}RT + R = \frac{7}{2}R$$

Then,

$$\gamma = \frac{C_p}{C_v} = \frac{\frac{7}{2}R}{\frac{5}{2}R} = \frac{7}{5} = 7:5$$

$\therefore$ In a gas of diatomic molecules, the ratio of the two specific heats of gas is $7:8$.

Hence, the correct option is (B).

32. Suppose a body is kept in a room for a long time. We find that the temperature of the body remains constant and is equal to the room temperature. The body is still radiating thermal radiation. But at the same of point, it is also absorbing part of radiation emitted by the surrounding objects.

We thus conclude that when the temperature of a body is equal to the temperature of its surroundings, it radiates at the same rate as it absorbs. So the ratio will be one.

Hence, the correct option is (B).

33. Time Period of the torsional pendulum is given by the Relation,

$$T = 2\pi\sqrt{\frac{I}{C}}$$

Where $I =$ moment of inertia

$C =$ restoring couple of the string

But, the time period of a torsional pendulum does not depend upon the acceleration due to gravity and thus they will not vary on other planets.

Hence, the correct option is (C).

34. Let,

$v_1 =$ the original wave frequency $= v$

$\lambda_1 =$ the original wavelength

$\lambda_2 =$ the new wavelength

$v_2 =$ the new wave frequency $= 2v$

Then,

Relation between velocity, frequency and wavelength : $c = v \times \lambda$

$$\therefore c = v_1 \times \lambda_1 = v \times \lambda_1 \dots (1)$$

$$c = v_2 \times \lambda = 2v \times \lambda_2 \dots (2)$$

Divide equation (1) and (2), we get

$$\frac{c}{c} = \frac{v \times \lambda_1}{2v \times \lambda_2}$$

$$\Rightarrow \lambda_2 = \frac{\lambda_1}{2}$$

$\therefore$ If a wave's frequency doubles and its wavelength is halved.

Hence, the correct option is (A).

35. In the case of a hollow metal sphere (spherical shell), the electric field inside the shell is zero. This means that the potential inside the shell is constant. Therefore the potential at the centre of the sphere is the same as that on its surface, i.e. 80 V as no work is done in moving a charge inside the shell.

Hence, the correct option is (B).

36. If an electric current is passed through a nerve, it interferes the conduction of the impulses in the nerves and the man will become insensitive to pain. The nerves will get numb and weakened due to the electric force. The nerves tissue provides some resistance to the current but not much. This can result in the severe damage, amnesia, seizure or even a respiratory arrest. Therefore a man gets excited.

Hence, the correct option is (C)

37. When a charged particle enters a magnetic field B its kinetic energy remains constant as the force exerted on the particle is:

$$F = q\vec{V} \times \vec{B}$$

This force is perpendicular to $\vec{V}$, so the work done by $\vec{B} = 0$. This does not cause any change in kinetic energy.

Hence, the correct option is (A).

38.

- Component $I_{rms}\sin\phi$ is normal to E_{rms}. As the phase angle between $I_{rms}\sin\phi$ and E_{rms} is $\frac{\pi}{2}$.

$$P_{av} = E_{rms}(I_{rms}\sin\phi)\cos\frac{\pi}{2} = 0$$

- We call the component $I_{rms}\sin\phi$ as the idle or wattles current because it does not consume any power in a.c. circuit. This happens in a purely inductive or capacitive circuit in which current and voltage differ by a phase difference of $\frac{\pi}{2}$.

- It is possible in a circuit where resistance is zero.

Hence, the correct option is (B).

39.

- To modify Ampere's law, Maxwell followed a symmetry consideration.

- By Faraday's law, a changing magnetic field induces an electric field, hence a changing electric field must induce a magnetic field. As currents are the usual sources of the magnetic field, a changing electric field must be associated with the current. Maxwell called that current as displacement current.

- To maintain the dimensional consistency, the displacement current is added in ampere's law:

$$\oint \vec{B} \cdot \vec{dl} = \mu_0 I + \mu_0 \epsilon_0 \left(\frac{d\Phi_E}{dt} \right)$$

Where, $\epsilon_0 \left(\dfrac{d\Phi_E}{dt} \right)$ is the displacement current.

Hence, the correct option is (D).

40. Green plants are green because they contain a pigment called chlorophyll. Chlorophyll absorbs a certain amount of wavelengths of light within the visible light spectrum. As chlorophyll absorbs light in longer wavelength regions of the visible light spectrum (like red color) and the shorter wavelength regions of the visible light spectrum (like blue color). Greenlight is not absorbed but reflected, making the plant appear green.

A plant appears green in sunlight, it should appear black or grey in red light as it will not have green wavelengths to reflect in order to appear green.

Hence, the correct option is (A).

41. Let R and r be the radii of the bigger droplet and smaller droplets respectively.

Volume is conserved when the water droplet is divided into 8 smaller droplets.

From volume conservation,

$$\frac{4}{3}\pi R^3 = 8 \times \frac{4}{3}\pi r^3$$

$$\Rightarrow r = \frac{R}{2}$$

Pressure difference between surfaces $= \Delta p = \dfrac{4\sigma}{R}$ (Since there are two surfaces for water, it is multiplied by an extra factor of 2)

Pressure difference from bigger droplet $= p_b = \dfrac{4\sigma}{R}$

Pressure difference from smaller droplet $= p_s = \dfrac{4\sigma}{r}$

$$= \frac{4\sigma}{\frac{R}{2}} = \frac{8\sigma}{R} = 2 \times \frac{4\sigma}{R} = 2p_b$$

$$\therefore p_b = \frac{1}{2}p_s$$

Hence, the correct option is (B).

42.

- No radiation like alpha, beta or gamma is emitted in a fusion reaction, so it is not a radioactive decay. Therefore option (C) is incorrect.

- Beta-decay is a type of radioactive decay in which a beta particle (fast energetic electron or positron) is emitted from an atomic nucleus. Therefore option (A) and (B) is correct.

- The process in which two light nuclei combine (at extremely high temperature) to form a single heavier nucleus is called nuclear fusion.

- The mass of a single nucleus so formed is less than the sum of the masses of parent nuclei. This difference in mass results in the release of a tremendous amount of energy.

- Alpha decay or α-decay is a type of radioactive decay in which an atomic nucleus emits an alpha particle and thereby transforms into a different atomic nucleus, with a mass number that is reduced by four and an atomic number that is reduced by two.

Hence, the correct option is (C).

43. According to the question, the frequency of the carrier wave is ω_c. Thus the amplitude-modulated wave also has frequency ω_c.

Hence, the correct option is (B).

44.

- Ethylene $\left(C_2H_4 \right)$ is a chemical compound with four hydrogen atoms bound to a pair of carbon atoms which are connected with a double bond.

- It's a colorless gas and extremely flammable.

- Hydrogenation means addition of hydrogen, thus complete hydrogenation of ethyne gives ethane.

$$C_2H_6 = C_2H_6 + H_2 \rightarrow CH_3 - CH_3$$

- The number of hydrogen atoms present in the hydrocarbon formed by the hydrogenation of ethylene is 6.

Hence, the correct option is (B).

45. Assembler is a program that translated mnemonic statements into executable instructions. Assembler is used to convert the assembly language into machine code because machine code is only a code that is understood by the computer system.

Hence, the correct option is (B).

46. Given,

Mass of car, $(m) = 1500 \; kg$

Velocity of car $(v) = 60 kmh^{-1} = 60 \times \dfrac{5}{18} = \dfrac{50}{3} \; m/s$

Work done $=$ Change in kinetic energy of the car

$$W = \frac{1}{2}mv^2 - \frac{1}{2}mu^2 = \frac{1}{2} \, m(v^2 - u^2)$$

$$\Rightarrow W = \frac{1}{2}(1500) \left[(0)^2 - \left(\frac{50}{3} \right)^2 \right]$$

$$\Rightarrow W = \frac{1}{2} \times 1500 \times \frac{2500}{9} = -208333 \; J$$

Hence, the correct option is (A).

47. Metals react with oxygen to form basic oxides. Metallic oxides are basic in nature because they react with dilute acids to form salt and water. They also react with water to form metal hydroxides which are alkaline in nature because these metal hydroxides release OH^- ions in solution.

Hence, the correct option is (A).

48. Proteins are called the building blocks of body. They are needed for growth and development and to repair the normal wear and tear of the body. The body needs to digest proteins to make them available to fulfill these functions. Protein is the important part of the diet as it helps in building muscles. So, proteins are the major components of food which is required by the body for wear and tear.

Hence, the correct option is (D).

49. The protozoan that causes malaria is Plasmodium which spreads from one infected person to another through the bite of female Anopheles mosquito.

Hence, the correct option is (D).

50. VIRUS stands for Vital Information Recourse Under Siege.

A computer virus is actually a malicious software program or "malware" that, when infecting your system, replicates itself by modifying other computer programs and inserting its own code. Infected computer programs may also include a data file or the "boot" sector of a hard drive.

Hence, the correct option is (A).

51. Given,

O is the circumcentre, G is the centroid and O' is the orthocentre of a triangle ABC.

We know that, the centroid divides the distance from the orthocentre to the circumcentre in the ratio $2:1$ i.e G divides the line segment joining O and O' in the ratio of $2:1$.

According to the question,

$$\Rightarrow \vec{a} + \vec{b} + \vec{c} = \overrightarrow{OA} + \overrightarrow{OB} + \overrightarrow{OC} = (\vec{A} - \vec{O}) + (\vec{B} - \vec{O}) + (\vec{C} - \vec{O})$$

$$\Rightarrow \vec{a} + \vec{b} + \vec{c} = \left(\vec{A} + \vec{B} + \vec{C}\right) - 3 \times \vec{O}$$

$$\Rightarrow \vec{a} + \vec{b} + \vec{c} = 3 \times \left[\left(\frac{\vec{A} + \vec{B} + \vec{C}}{3}\right) - \vec{O}\right]$$

$$\Rightarrow \vec{a} + \vec{b} + \vec{c} = 3 \times [\vec{G} - \vec{O}]$$

$$\Rightarrow 3 \times \vec{G} = 2 \times \vec{O} + \vec{O'}$$

$$\Rightarrow \vec{O'} - \vec{O} = 3 \times \left(\vec{G} - \vec{O}\right)$$

$$\Rightarrow \overrightarrow{OO'} = 3 \times \left(\vec{G} - \vec{O}\right)$$

$$\Rightarrow \overrightarrow{OO'} = \vec{a} + \vec{b} + \vec{c}$$

Hence, the correct option is (C).

52. Let,

Event A = Selecting the faulty machine in the first test.

Event B = Selecting the faulty machine in the second test.

Event $A \cap B$ = Selecting the faulty machine in 2 tests.

Given, there are 4 machines out of two are faulty.

$$\therefore P(A) = \frac{n(A)}{n(S)} = \frac{2}{4} = \frac{1}{2}$$

$$P(B) = \frac{n(B)}{n(S)} = \frac{1}{3}$$

$\Rightarrow P(A \cap B) = P(A) \times P(B) = \frac{1}{2} \times \frac{1}{3} = \frac{1}{6}$ ($\because A$ and B are independent events)

Hence, the correct option is (B).

53. Given,

$$\lim_{x \to 0} \frac{(1 - \cos 2x)^2}{x^4}$$

$$= \lim_{x \to 0} \frac{\left(2\sin^2 x\right)^2}{x^4} \quad (1 - \cos 2\theta = 2\sin^2 \theta)$$

$$= \lim_{x \to 0} \frac{4\sin^4 x}{x^4}$$

$$= \lim_{x \to 0} 4 \times \left(\frac{\sin x}{x}\right)^4$$

$$= 4 \times 1 = 4$$

Hence, the correct option is (C).

54. Given,

n (X) = 300, n (Y) = 400 and n (X ∪ Y) = 500

As we know that, for any two finite sets A and B,

n (A ∪ B) = n (A) + n (B) - n (A ∩ B)

∴ n (X ∪ Y) = n (X) + n (Y) - n (X ∩ Y)

⇒ 500 = 300 + 400 - n (X ∩ Y)

⇒ n (X ∩ Y) = 200

As we know that, for any two finite sets A and B,

n (A - B) = n (A) - n (A ∩ B)

∴ n (X - Y) = n (X) - n (X ∩ Y) = 300 - 200 = 100

Hence, the correct option is (D).

55. As we know,

For a given function $f(x) = y$, we say that $x = f^{-1}(y)$.

Let's say that $y = f(x) = 2x - 3$

$$\Rightarrow x = \frac{y + 3}{2} = f^{-1}(y)$$

Replacing y by x, we get

$$f^{-1}(x) = \frac{x + 3}{2}$$

Hence, the correct option is (D).

56. The numbers between 300 and 500 which are divisible by 7, are $301, 308, 315, \ldots, 497$.

This is an A.P with first term $= 301$.

Therefore from the nth term of A.P. $= a + (n - 1)d$

We have,

$$497 = 301 + (n - 1)7$$

$$\Rightarrow 196 = (n - 1)7$$

$$\Rightarrow n - 1 = \frac{196}{7} = 28$$

$$\Rightarrow \text{Number of terms} = n = 28 + 1 = 29$$

Now, sum $= \frac{n}{2}(a + 1)$

$= \frac{29}{2}(301 + 497)$

$= \frac{29 \times 798}{2}$

$= 29 \times 399$

$= 11571$

Hence, the correct option is (D).

57. Given,

$\frac{\sin 4x - \sin 2x}{\cos 4x + \cos 2x}$

$= \frac{2\cos\left(\frac{4x+2x}{2}\right)\sin\left(\frac{4x-2x}{2}\right)}{2\cos\left(\frac{4x+2x}{2}\right)\cos\left(\frac{4x-2x}{2}\right)}$

$= \frac{\sin x}{\cos x}$

$= \tan x$

So, the expression $\frac{\sin 4x - \sin 2x}{\cos 4x + \cos 2x}$ is equal to tan x.

Hence, the correct option is (B).

58. Let,

cos 3x = cos (2x + x)

⇒cos 3x = cos 2x. cos x - sin 2x. sin x

= (2cos²x - 1). cos x - (2sin x. cos x). sin x

= 2cos³ x - cos x - 2sin² x. cos x

= cos x (2cos² x - 1 - 2sin² x)

= [cos x (2cos² x - 1 - 2 (1 - cos² x)]

= [cos x (4cos² x -3)]

= 4 cos³ x - 3 cos x

Hence, the correct option is (B).

59. $\int_{-2}^{2}|x|\,dx = \int_{-2}^{0}|x|\,dx + \int_{0}^{2}|x|\,dx$

$= \int_{-2}^{0} -x\,dx + \int_{0}^{2} x\,dx$

$= -\frac{1}{2}[x^2]_{-2}^{0} + \frac{1}{2}[x^2]_{0}^{2}$

$= \frac{-1}{2}[0^2 - (-2)^2] + \frac{1}{2}[2^2 - 0^2]$

$= 2 + 2 = 4$

Hence, the correct option is (D).

60. Given,

$\left(\frac{d^3y}{dx^3}\right)^{\frac{3}{2}} = \left(\frac{d^2y}{dx^2}\right)^2$

Squaring both the sides, we get

$\left(\frac{d^3y}{dx^3}\right)^3 = \left(\frac{d^2y}{dx^2}\right)^4$

Here highest derivative is $\left(\frac{d^3y}{dx^3}\right)^3$.

$\therefore$ Degree $=$ power of $\left(\frac{d^3y}{dx^3}\right)^3 = 3$

Hence, the correct option is (C).

61. As we know,

$1 + \cos 2x = 2\cos^2 x$

$1 - \cos 2x = 2\sin^2 x$

$\int \cos x\,dx = \sin x + c$

Let $I = \int \cos^2 x\,dx$

$= \int \frac{1+\cos 2x}{2}\,dx$

$= \frac{1}{2}\int (1 + \cos 2x)\,dx$

$= \frac{1}{2}\left[x + \frac{\sin 2x}{2}\right] + c$

$= \frac{x}{2} + \frac{\sin 2x}{4} + c$

Hence, the correct option is (B).

62. Let $z = x + iy = \frac{4+2i}{1-2i}$

$= \frac{4+2i}{1-2i} \times \frac{1+2i}{1+2i}$

$= \frac{4+10i+4i^2}{1-4i^2}$

As we know,

$i^2 = -1$

$= \frac{4+10i-4}{1+4}$

$x + iy = \frac{10i}{5} = 0 + 2i$

As we know that if $z = x + iy$ be any complex number, then its modulus is given by,

$|z| = \sqrt{x^2 + y^2}$

$\therefore |z| = \sqrt{0^2 + 2^2} = 2$

Hence, the correct option is (D).

63. Given,

p and q are the roots of the equation $x^2 - 30x + 221$. By comparing the given equation with the standard quadratic equation $ax^2 + bx + c = 0$, we get $a = 1, b = -30$ and $c = 221$.

As we know that, if α and β are the roots of the quadratic equation, $ax^2 + bx + c = 0$. Then

$\alpha + \beta = -\frac{b}{a}$ and $\alpha \times \beta = \frac{c}{a}$

$\Rightarrow p + q = 30$ and $pq = 221$

$\Rightarrow p^3 + q^3 = (p + q) \times (p^2 - pq + q^2) = (p + q) \times [(p + q)^2 - 3pq$

$\Rightarrow p^3 + q^3 = (p + q) \times [(p + q)^2 - 3pq] = 30 \times [900 - 663] = 7110$

Hence, the correct option is (B).

64. Let x be the common difference of the A.P., a, b, c, d, e, f...

$\therefore$ e = a + (5 - 1)x [∵ an = a + (n - 1)d]

⇒ e = a + 4x and d = a + 3x

∴ c = a + 2x

⇒ (e − c) = 2x

$\Rightarrow (d - c) = x$

$\Rightarrow (e - c) = 2(d - c)$

Hence, the correct option is (B).

65. Given:

$$\vec{a} = 2\hat{\imath} + \hat{\jmath} - 3\hat{k} \text{ and } \vec{b} = 3\hat{\imath} - 2\hat{\jmath} - \hat{k}$$

$$\vec{a} \cdot \vec{b} = (2\hat{\imath} + \hat{\jmath} - 3\hat{k}).(3\hat{\imath} - 2\hat{\jmath} - \hat{k})$$

$$\Rightarrow \vec{a} \cdot \vec{b} = 6 - 2 + 3 = 7 \quad \dots (1)$$

$$\left|\vec{a}\right| = \sqrt{2^2 + 1^2 + (-3)^2} = \sqrt{14} \quad \dots (2)$$

$$\left|\vec{b}\right| = \sqrt{3^2 + (-2)^2 + (-1)^2} = \sqrt{14} \quad \dots (3)$$

$$\cos\theta = \frac{\vec{a} \cdot \vec{b}}{\left|\vec{a}\right| \cdot \left|\vec{b}\right|}$$

Put the values from $(1), (2)$ and (3) in above equation,

$$= \frac{7}{\sqrt{14} \cdot \sqrt{14}}$$

$$= \frac{1}{2}$$

$$\cos\theta = \cos 60°$$

$$\Rightarrow \theta = 60°$$

Hence, the correct option is (D).

66. Let the slope of the line $2x - 5y + 4 = 0$ be m_1 and the slope of the line joining the points $(1,5)$ and $(\alpha, 3)$ be m_2.

$$m_2 = \frac{3-5}{\alpha-1} = \frac{-2}{\alpha-1}$$

Now, the slope of the line $= m_1 = \frac{2}{5}$

Given,

Lines are perpendicular to each other,

$$\therefore m_1 m_2 = -1$$

$$\Rightarrow \frac{-2}{\alpha-1} \times \frac{2}{5} = -1$$

$$\Rightarrow -4 = -5 \times (\alpha - 1)$$

$$\Rightarrow (\alpha - 1) = \frac{4}{5}$$

$$\Rightarrow \alpha = \left(\frac{4}{5}\right) + 1 = \frac{9}{5}$$

Hence, the correct option is (B).

67. As we know,

$$\text{Equation of ellipse} = \frac{x^2}{a^2} + \frac{y^2}{b^2} = 1$$

$$\text{Eccentricity } (e) = \sqrt{1 - \frac{b^2}{a^2}}$$

Where, vertices $= (\pm a, 0)$ and focus $= (\pm ae, 0)$

Given,

Vertices of ellipse $(\pm 5, 0)$ and foci $(\pm 4, 0)$

So, $a = \pm 5$

$$\Rightarrow a^2 = 25 \text{ and}$$

$$ae = 4$$

$$\Rightarrow e = \frac{4}{5}$$

Now, $\frac{4}{5} = \sqrt{1 - \frac{b^2}{5^2}}$

$$\Rightarrow \frac{16}{25} = \frac{25-b^2}{25}$$

$$\Rightarrow 16 = 25 - b^2$$

$$\Rightarrow b^2 = 9$$

$$\therefore \text{Equation of ellipse} = \frac{x^2}{25} + \frac{y^2}{9} = 1$$

Hence, the correct option is (A).

68. There are a total of 7 red $+4$ blue $= 11$ balls

Probability of drawing 1 red ball $= \frac{^7C_1}{^{11}C_1} = \frac{7}{11}$

Probability of drawing 1 blue ball $= \frac{^4C_1}{^{11}C_1} = \frac{4}{11}$

Probability of drawing $(1$ red $)$ And $(1$ blue $)$ ball $= \frac{7}{11} \times \frac{4}{11} = \frac{28}{121}$

Similarly, Probability of drawing $(1$ blue $)$ And $(1$ red $)$ ball $= \frac{4}{11} \times \frac{7}{11} = \frac{28}{121}$

Probability of getting the balls of different colors $= \frac{28}{121} + \frac{28}{121} = \frac{56}{121}$

Hence, the correct option is (B).

69. Given,

$$X + Y = \begin{bmatrix} 7 & 5 \\ 3 & 4 \end{bmatrix} \dots\text{(i)}$$

$$X - Y = \begin{bmatrix} 1 & -3 \\ 3 & 0 \end{bmatrix} \dots\text{(ii)}$$

Adding the 2 equations, we get

$$2X = \begin{bmatrix} 8 & 2 \\ 6 & 4 \end{bmatrix}$$

$$\Rightarrow X = \begin{bmatrix} 4 & 1 \\ 3 & 2 \end{bmatrix}$$

Substracting (ii) from (i), we get

$$2Y = \begin{bmatrix} 6 & 8 \\ 0 & 4 \end{bmatrix}$$

$$\Rightarrow Y = \begin{bmatrix} 3 & 4 \\ 0 & 2 \end{bmatrix}$$

Let $A = 2X - Y$

$$A = 2 \times \begin{bmatrix} 4 & 1 \\ 3 & 2 \end{bmatrix} - \begin{bmatrix} 3 & 4 \\ 0 & 2 \end{bmatrix}$$

$$\Rightarrow A = \begin{bmatrix} 8 & 2 \\ 6 & 4 \end{bmatrix} - \begin{bmatrix} 3 & 4 \\ 0 & 2 \end{bmatrix}$$

$$\Rightarrow A = \begin{bmatrix} 5 & -2 \\ 6 & 2 \end{bmatrix}$$

Hence, the correct option is (B).

70. Let $\Delta = \begin{vmatrix} x+2 & x+3 & x-1 \\ x+6 & x+8 & x+4 \\ x+9 & x+11 & x+7 \end{vmatrix}$

By applying $C_2 \to C_2 - C_1, C_3 \to C_3 - C_1$

$$= \begin{vmatrix} x+2 & 1 & -3 \\ x+6 & 2 & -2 \\ x+9 & 2 & -2 \end{vmatrix}$$

By applying $C_3 \to C_3 + C_2$

$$= \begin{vmatrix} x+2 & 1 & -2 \\ x+6 & 2 & 0 \\ x+9 & 2 & 0 \end{vmatrix}$$

Expanding along C_3, we get

$$= -2[2(x+6) - 2(x+9)]$$
$$= -4[x+6-x-9]$$
$$= 12$$

Hence, the correct option is (C).

71. As we know,

The length of the latus rectum of the parabola $y^2 = 4ax$ is $4a$.

Given,

The parabola $y^2 = 4kx$ passes through point $(-2,1)$.

The point $(-2,1)$ is satisfying the equation of parabola $y^2 = 4kx$.

$$\Rightarrow (1)^2 = 4k(-2)$$

$$\Rightarrow k = \frac{-1}{8}$$

Now, the length of the latus rectum $= 4k$

The length of latus rectum $= 4\left(\frac{-1}{8}\right)$

The length of latus rectum $= \frac{-1}{2}$

The length of latus rectum can not be negative.

$\therefore$ The length of latus rectum $= \frac{1}{2}$

So, if parabola $y^2 = 4kx$ passes through the point $(-2,1)$, then the length of the latus rectum is $\frac{1}{2}$.

Hence, the correct option is (A).

72. As we know,

Distance between two parallel plane $ax + by + cz + d_1 = 0$ and $ax + by + cz + d_2 = 0$ is $\left| \frac{d_1 - d_2}{\sqrt{a^2+b^2+c^2}} \right|$.

Given,

$3x + y + 3z = 8$ and $9x + 3y + 9z = 15$

On dividing $9x + 3y + 9z = 15$ by 3, we get

$3x + y + 3z = 5$

Now, distance between $3x + y + 3z = 8$ and $3x + y + 3z = 5$

$$= \left| \frac{8-5}{\sqrt{3^2+1^2+3^2}} \right|$$

$$= \frac{3}{\sqrt{19}}$$

Hence, the correct option is (C).

73. As we know,

If plane $a_1 x + b_1 y + c_1 z + d_1 = 0$ and $a_2 x + b_2 y + c_2 z + d_2 = 0$ are a parallel i.e. $\frac{a_1}{a_2} = \frac{b_1}{b_2} = \frac{c_1}{c_2} \neq \frac{d_1}{d_2}$

Given,

The planes $2x - y - 3z - 7 = 0$ and $4x - 2y + 5kz + 9 = 0$ are parallel.

We know that if plane are parallel than ratio of coefficient of x, y and z are equal.

$$\frac{2}{4} = \frac{-1}{-2} = \frac{-3}{5k}$$

$$\Rightarrow \frac{1}{2} = \frac{-3}{5k}$$

$$\Rightarrow 5k = -6$$

So, $k = \frac{-6}{5}$

Now,

$$5k + 7 = 5 \times \left(\frac{-6}{5}\right) + 7 = 1$$

Hence, the correct option is (D).

74. Given,

$3x + y = 7$

$\Rightarrow y = -3x + 7$

The slope of line $= m = -3$

Then the slope of a line perpendicular to it is $\frac{-1}{m} = \frac{1}{3}$

The equation of line passing through $(1,1)$ with slope $\frac{1}{3}$ is

$$y - 1 = \left(\frac{1}{3}\right)(x-1).$$

$$\Rightarrow 3y - 3 = x - 1$$

$$\Rightarrow 3y = x + 2$$

$$\Rightarrow 3y - x = 2$$

For x-intercept, $y = 0$

$\therefore x = -2$

So, the x-intercept of line is -2.

Hence, the correct option is (A).

75. Let $x^2 + y^2 = r^2$ is the equation of circle. then $(0,0)$ is the origin and r is the radius of the circle.

We know that, $x^2 + y^2 = r^2$ is the equation of circle. then $(0,0)$ is the origin and r is the radius of the circle.

Given,

Equation of circle is $x^2 + y^2 + x + c = 0,$ which is passing through the origin. i.e. $c = 0$

$\Rightarrow x^2 + y^2 + x = 0$

$\Rightarrow x^2 + x + \frac{1}{4} - \frac{1}{4} + y^2 = 0$

$\Rightarrow x^2 + x + \frac{1}{4} + y^2 = \frac{1}{4}$

$\Rightarrow \left(x + \frac{1}{2}\right)^2 + y^2 = \left(\frac{1}{2}\right)^2$

which is equation of circle with radius is $\frac{1}{2}$.

So, the radius of the circle $x^2 + y^2 + x + c = 0$ passing through the origin is $\frac{1}{2}$.

Hence, the correct option is (B).

76. South Korea has signed a $ 2.25 billion deal with a Russian state-run nuclear energy company 'ASE'in August 2022.

- It has been signed to provide components for Egypt's first nuclear power plant.
- ASE is a subsidiary of Rosatom, a state-owned Russian nuclear conglomerate.
- South Korea has also signed a $ 20 billion contract to build nuclear power reactors in the UAE.

Hence, the correct option is (D).

77. Former Jharkhand Governor and National Democratic Alliance candidate Droupadi Murmu has been elected as the 15th President of India on 21 July 2022.

She is the first tribal woman to be elected to the position & the youngest as well.

She defeated opposition candidate Yashwant Sinha by bagging 64.03% of the electoral college votes.

Hence, the correct option is (D).

78. India has contributed USD 500,000 to the UN Women, the United Nations agency for gender equality and women empowerment for their core budget.

India's Permanent Representative to the United Nations T.S.Tirumurti announced that India reaffirmed its partnership of women-led development and gender parity. UN Women Executive Director, Sima Bahous thanked India for its contribution.

Hence, the correct option is (D).

79. The Gupta Empire was an ancient Indian empire existing from the mid-to-late 3rd century CE to 543 CE. At its zenith, from approximately 319 to 467 CE, it covered much of the Indian subcontinent. This period is considered the Golden Age of India by historians. The ruling dynasty of the empire was founded by king Sri Gupta.

Hence, the correct option is (A).

80. ATM (Automated Teller Machine) is a computerized machine placed by local banks in various parts of a city or town to enable customers to access their bank accounts and perform certain banking operations like balance enquiry and cash withdrawal.

Hence, the correct option is (B).

81. Punjab is a state in North India, forming a part of the larger Punjab region. The word Punjab is a compound of the Persian words Panj (five) and āb (water). Thus, Panjāb roughly means "the land of five rivers". The five rivers are the Sutlej, Beas, Ravi, Chenab and Jhelum.

Hence, the correct option is (A).

82. Harper Lee, whose first novel, "To Kill a Mockingbird," about racial injustice in a small Alabama town, sold more than 40 million copies, died at the age of 89. Harper Lee, the famously reclusive author of To Kill a Mockingbird, spent most of her life out of the spotlight.

Hence, the correct option is (C).

83. Buenos Aires is the capital of Argentina.

Following a long period of unrest and a power struggle, Buenos Aires emerged even stronger and was named the federal capital of Argentina in 1880.

Hence, the correct option is (C).

84. Mayurbhanj Chhau dance was originally a tribal dance, which originated from the forests of Mayurbhanj, Odisha in the 18th century. It got the status of a martial art form in the 19th century. It slowly left its martial character and mellowed.

Hence, the correct option is (C).

85. Pattern followed is:

$1^3 - 1 = 0$

$2^3 - 3 = 5$

$3^3 - 5 = 22$

$4^3 - 7 = 57$

$5^3 - 9 = 116$

$6^3 - 11 = 205$

Hence, the correct option is (B).

86.

Alphabets	A	B	C	D	E	F	G	H	I	J	K	L	M
Positional value	1	2	3	4	5	6	7	8	9	10	11	12	13
Positional value	26	25	24	23	22	21	20	19	18	17	16	15	14
Alphabets	Z	Y	X	W	V	U	T	S	R	Q	P	O	N

OUT → O = 15, U = 21, T = 20 → 152120

Similarly,

IN → I = 9, N = 14 → 914

Hence, the correct option is (D).

87. The New Kwanza is the currency of Angola. The currency has its name derived from the Kwanza River. The Cuanza (Kwanza)

River is the longest river at 966 kilometers, situated in the central part of the country. The time zone of Angola in West Africa Time(WAT) is 1 hour ahead of Coordinated Universal Time(UTC). Luanda is the capital and largest city of Angola.

Hence, the correct option is (B).

88. Sir Alexander Fleming was a Scottish physician and microbiologist, best known for discovering the enzyme lysozyme and the world's first broadly effective antibiotic substance which he named penicillin.

Hence, the correct option is (A).

89. Space Exploration Technologies Corp. (SpaceX) is an American aerospace manufacturer and space transportation services company headquartered in Hawthorne, California. It was founded in 2002 by Elon Musk with the goal of reducing space transportation costs to enable the colonization of Mars Elon Musk-led space exploration startup SpaceX successfully launched its Falcon 9 rocket.

Hence, the correct option is (D).

90. Formula-1 also called F1 in short, is an international auto racing sport. F1 is the highest level of single-seat, open-wheel, and open-cockpit professional motor racing contest.

Hence, the correct option is (A).

91. The Lucknow Pact of 1916 built friendly relations between the Muslim League and Indian National Congress (INC) and also the groups between INC. It was for the first time that the Hindus and the Muslims came together on common ground. It sowed the seed of belief among the British that India could get a government of Self. The extremist and moderate faction of the INC also got united.

Hence, the correct option is (C).

92. 1) BURST → This can be formed as DISBURSEMENT

2) DISTURB → This can be formed as DISBURSEMENT

3) SISTER → This can be formed as DISBURSEMENT

4) SENTIMENT → This cannot be formed as there is only 1 'N' and 1 'T' in DISBURSEMENT

So, word SENTIMENT cannot be formed from the word DISBURSEMENT.

Hence, the correct option is (D).

93. People of Meghalaya, which is one of the north-eastern states of India, do not speak Hindi widely. The languages like Garo, Pnar, Khasi, and English are spoken widely in this state. English is the official language of Meghalaya.

Hence, the correct option is (D).

94. Official languages of India are listed in the Eighth Schedule to the Constitution of India. As per Article 344(1) and 351 of the Indian Constitution, Eighth Schedule recognizes 22 languages. States and Union Territory can adopt an official language that is used locally for carrying out administrative duties.

Hence, the correct option is (B).

95. Dandia is a folk dance of Gujarat. It is also known as Dandiya raas or Raas. The folk dance is performed at the Navaratri festival. The dance is also performed in the Marwar region of Rajasthan. Dandiya Ras, Garba, Tippani Juriun, and Bhavai are the major folk dances of Gujarat.

Hence, the correct option is (B).

96. Baisakhi usually celebrated on the 13th or 14th of April every year. It is an important day for the Sikhs. It is the birthday of Khalsa. On this day farmers offer their harvest to God and pray for a good harvest and blessings.

Hence, the correct option is (A).

97. Handball which is also known as 'team handball' or Olympic handball or European team handball or European handball or Borden ball, is a team sport in which two teams consisting of seven players each.

Hence, the correct option is (D).

98. Nigeria is referred to as the " Giant of Africa ". Nigeria is regarded as the most populous black nation in the world hence called the "Giant of Africa". Egypt is called the Gift of the Nile. Scotland is called the Land of Cakes.

Hence, the correct option is (B).

99. Bangladesh has a land border with India and Myanmar. India shares a 4,096-km-long border with Bangladesh. It is the fifth-longest land border in the world. India shares its longest boundary with Bangladesh.

Hence, the correct option is (B).

100. Newly-independent Pakistan had chosen Karachi as its capital in 1947. However, a decade later, President Ayub Khan chose to move the capital nearly 1,500 kilometres to the north, to the new city of Islamabad.

Hence, the correct option is (B).

Mathematics

Q.1 The symmetric difference of sets $A = \{1,2,3,4,5,6,7,8\}$ and $B = \{1,3,5,6,7,8,9\}$ is:

A. $\{1,3,5,6,7,8\}$

B. $\{2,4,9\}$

C. $\{2,4\}$

D. $\{1,2,3,4,5,6,7,8,9\}$

Q.2 What is modulus of $\dfrac{1}{1+5i} - \dfrac{1}{1-5i}$?

A. $\dfrac{7}{15}$ B. $\dfrac{2}{9}$ C. $\dfrac{3}{17}$ D. $\dfrac{5}{13}$

Q.3 If 8 points out of 15 are in the same straight line, then what is the number of triangles formed?

A. 428 B. 399 C. 287 D. 370

Q.4 Find the coefficient of x^2 in $\left(3x - \dfrac{1}{x^2}\right)^6$

A. 0 B. $\dfrac{-3}{2}$ C. $\dfrac{3}{2}$ D. $\dfrac{5}{8}$

Q.5 Evaluate $\dfrac{\log 256}{\log 16} = \log x$

A. 1000 B. 100 C. 200 D. 500

Q.6 If $\Delta = \begin{vmatrix} 115 & 106 & 97 \\ 10 & 1 & -8 \\ 106 & 97 & 88 \end{vmatrix}$ then value of Δ is:

A. 0 B. 1572 C. 1648 D. 2421

Q.7 If the matrix $\begin{bmatrix} \cos\theta & \sin\theta & 0 \\ \sin\theta & \cos\theta & 0 \\ 0 & 0 & 1 \end{bmatrix}$ is singular, then $\theta =$

A. $\dfrac{\pi}{4}$ B. $\dfrac{\pi}{2}$ C. π D. 0

Q.8 If $A = \begin{bmatrix} 1 & 1 \\ 0 & 1 \end{bmatrix}$ then $A^n =$?

A. $\begin{bmatrix} 1 & n \\ 0 & 1 \end{bmatrix}$ B. $\begin{bmatrix} n & n \\ 0 & n \end{bmatrix}$ C. $\begin{bmatrix} n & 1 \\ 0 & n \end{bmatrix}$ D. $\begin{bmatrix} 1 & 1 \\ 0 & n \end{bmatrix}$

Q.9 Find the equation of the straight line parallel to the line x + 2y + 4 = 0 and passing through the point (2, 5)

A. x + 2y + 4 = 0 B. x + 2y - 11 = 0

C. x + 2y + 5 = 0 D. x + 2y - 12 = 0

Q.10 The value of $\tan^{-1}\left(\dfrac{1}{7}\right) + \tan^{-1}\left(\dfrac{1}{13}\right)$ is:

A. $\tan^{-1}\left(\dfrac{1}{7}\right) + \tan^{-1}\left(\dfrac{1}{13}\right)$

B. $\tan^{-1}\left(\dfrac{2}{7}\right)$

C. $\tan^{-1}\left(\dfrac{2}{9}\right)$

D. $\tan^{-1}\left(\dfrac{1}{9}\right)$

Q.11 Find the type of one - one function f : {1, 2, 3} → {1, 2, 3}

A. Into B. Onto

C. Both onto and into D. None of the above

Q.12 Find, $\displaystyle\lim_{x\to\infty}\left(\dfrac{x}{x+1}\right)$

A. 0 B. ∞ C. 1 D. -1

Q.13 If $s = \sin\theta(1 + \sec\theta); \dfrac{ds}{d\theta} =$?

A. $\cos\theta + \sec^2\theta$ B. $\cos^2\theta + \sec^2\theta$

C. $\cos^2\theta + \sec\theta$ D. $\tan\theta + \tan\theta\sec^2\theta$

Q.14 Which of the following is an equation of the line tangent to the graph of $h(x) = x^4 - 2x^2 + 2x$ at the point where $x = 1$?

A. $y = 2x + 1$ B. $y = x - 1$

C. $y = x + 1$ D. $y = 2x - 1$

Q.15 If $A = \{1,2\}, B = \{1,2,3,4\}, C = \{5,6\}$ and $D = \{5,6,7,8\}$ then state which of the following statement is true.

A. $(A \times C) \subset (B \times D)$

B. $(B \times D) \subset (A \times C)$

C. $(A \times B) \subset (A \times D)$

D. $(D \times A) \subset (B \times A)$

Q.16 The solution of $\int \dfrac{1}{\sqrt{x^2-6x+1}} dx$

A. $\log|(x - 3) + |\sqrt{(x^2 - 6x + 1)}| + c$

B. $\log|(x - 9) - |\sqrt{(x^2 - 4x + 1)}| + c$

C. $\log|(x - 3) - |\sqrt{(x^2 - 6x + 1)}| + C$

D. $\log|(x - 9) + |\sqrt{(x^2 - 4x + 1)}| + C$

Q.17 Evaluate $\displaystyle\int_{-1}^{1} 5x^4\sqrt{x^5 + 1}\, dx$

A. $\dfrac{6\sqrt{2}}{5}$ B. $\dfrac{5\sqrt{3}}{4}$ C. $\dfrac{4\sqrt{2}}{3}$ D. $\dfrac{3\sqrt{2}}{4}$

Q.18 The union of the sets { $1,2,5$} and { $1,2,6$} is the set _______

A. { 1,2,6,1} B. { 1,2,5,6}

C. { 1,2,1,2} D. { 1,5,6,3}

Q.19 The intersection of the sets { $1,2,5$} and { $1,2,6$} is the set -

A. { 1,2} B. { 5,6} C. { 2,5} D. { 1,6}

Q.20 Average of $x, x + 2, x + 5$ is A and average of $y, y + 3, y + 7$ is B. What is the mean of A and B in terms of x if $y = x - 2$?

A. $x + \dfrac{14}{6}$ B. $x + \dfrac{13}{6}$ C. $x + \dfrac{11}{6}$ D. None

Q.21 A coin is tossed and a dice is rolled. The probability that the coin shows the head and the dice shows 6 is

A. $\dfrac{1}{2}$ B. $\dfrac{1}{6}$ C. $\dfrac{1}{12}$ D. $\dfrac{1}{24}$

Q.22 The difference of {1,2,3} and {1,2,5} is the set_________.

A. {1}   **B.** {5}   **C.** {3}   **D.** {2}

Q.23 If $\log 2 = 0.3010$ and $\log 3 = 0.4771$, the value of $\log_5 512$ is:

A. 2.870   **B.** 2.967   **C.** 3.876   **D.** 3.912

Q.24 A survey determines that in a locality, 33% go to work by Bike, 42% go by Car, and 12% use both. The probability that a random person selected uses neither of them is-

A. 0.29   **B.** 0.37   **C.** 0.61   **D.** 0.75

Q.25 A coin is biased so that the head is 3 times as likely to occur as the tail. If the coin is tossed twice, find the probability distribution of the number of tails:

A. $P(T = 0) = \frac{11}{16}$ **B.** $P(T = 1) = \frac{6}{16}$

C. $P(T = 2) = \frac{13}{16}$ **D.** None of these

English

Q.26 Direction: Choose the correct antonym of the given word:

Undermine

A. Assist   **B.** De-emphasize

C. Strengthen   **D.** Sabotage

Q.27 Direction: Choose the correct antonym of the given word:

Rancid

A. Abominable   **B.** Fresh

C. Polite   **D.** Putrid

Q.28 Direction: In the following question, choose the word opposite in meaning to the given bold word.

Born in **squalid** surroundings of the slums she rose to stardom overnight.

A. Dirty   **B.** Clean

C. Disorderly   **D.** Mean

Q.29 Direction: Choose the correct synonym of the given word:

Tactile

A. Brittle   **B.** Compelling

C. Intangible   **D.** Palpable

Q.30 Direction: Choose the correct synonym of the given word:

Atone

A. Dull   **B.** Monochromatic

C. Repent   **D.** Augment

Ques (31-35):Direction: In the following question, a sentence is divided into three parts (a), (b) and (c). Find out which part of the sentence has an error and choose that as your answer. If there is no error, then choose (d) as your answer.

Q.31 The risk of death from multiple fears or another strong emotion are greater (a)/ for individuals with preexisting heart conditions, but people (b)/ who are perfectly healthy in all other respects can also fall victim. (c)/ No error (d).

A. (a)   **B.** (b)   **C.** (c)   **D.** (d)

Q.32 When we tell somebody about a statement we heard a few days earlier and have to fill a couple (a)/ of the plot holes with our own embellishments to make sure (b)/ everything makes sense and we're not crazy. (c)/ No error (d).

A. (a)   **B.** (b)   **C.** (c)   **D.** (d)

Q.33 The therapy involved a therapist putting a client at a trancelike state (a)/ where she was encouraged to root out (b)/ and re-experience forgotten childhood memories. (c)/ No error (d).

A. (a)   **B.** (b)   **C.** (c)   **D.** (d)

Q.34 I don't see how (a)/ that's any different as (b)/ you trying to protect me. (c)/ No error (d).

A. (a)   **B.** (b)   **C.** (c)   **D.** (d)

Q.35 Many a man are harassed to death to pay the (a)/ rent of a larger and more luxurious box (b)/ who would not have frozen to death in such a box as this. (c)/ No error (d).

A. (a)   **B.** (b)   **C.** (c)   **D.** (d)

Ques (36-40):Direction: Read the following passage to answer the given questions based on it.

The University Grant Commission's directive to college and University lecturers to spend a minimum of 22 hours a week in direct teaching is the product of budgetary cutbacks rather than pedagogik wisdom. It may seem odd, at first blush, that teachers should protest about teaching a mere 22 hours. However, if one considers the amount of time academics require to prepare to lectures of good quality as well as the time they need to spend doing research, it is clear that most conscientious teachers work more than 40 hours a week. In University system around the world lecturers rarely spend more than 12 to 15 hours in directing teaching activities a week. The average college lecturer in India does not have any office space. If computers are available, internet connectivity is unlikely. Libraries are poorly stocked. Now the UGC says universities must implement a complete **freeze** on all permanent recruitment, abolish all posts which have been vacant for more than a year, and cut staff strength by 10 per cent. And it is an order to ensure that these cutbacks do not affect the quantum of teaching that existing lecturers are being asked to work longer. Obviously, the quality of teaching and academic work in general will decline. While it is true that in some college teachers do not take their classes regularly, the UGC and the institution concerned must find a proper way to hold them accountable. An absentee teacher will continue to play truant even if the number of hours he is required to teach goes up.

All of us are well aware of the unsound state that the Indian higher education system is in today. Thanks to years of **sustained** financial neglect, most Indian universities and colleges do no research worth the name. Even as the number of students entering colleges has increased dramatically, public investment in higher education has actually declined in relative terms. Between 1985 and 1997, when public expenditure on higher education as percentage of outlays on all levels of education grew by more than 60 per cent in Malaysia and 20 per cent in Thailand, India showed a decline of more than 10 percent. Throughout the world, the number of teachers in higher education per million populations grew by more than 10 per cent in the same period; in India it fell by one per cent. Instead of transferring the burden of government apathy on to the backs of the teachers, the UGC should insist that the need of the country's university system be adequately catered to.

Q.36 Why does the UGC want to increase the directing teaching hours of university teachers?

A. UGC feels that the duration of contact between the teacher and the taught should be more.

B. UGC wants teachers to spend more time in their departments

C. UGC does not have money to appoint additional teachers

D. All of above

Q.37 Which of the following is the reason for the sorry state of affairs of the Indian Universities as mentioned in the passage?

A. The poor quality of teachers

B. Politics within and outside the departments

C. Heavy burden of teaching hours on the teachers

D. Not getting enough financial assistance

Q.38 Besides direct teaching, University teachers spend considerable time in/on

A. Administrative activities such as admission

B. Supervising examination and correction of answer papers

C. Carrying out research in the area of their interest

D. None of these

Q.39 Which of the following statement is NOT TRUE in the context of the passage?

A. UGC wants teachers to spend minimum 40 hours in a week in teaching

B. Some college teachers do not conduct their classes regularly

C. None

D. All are true

Q.40 Which of the following statements is/are TRUE in the context of the passage?

1. Most colleges do not carry out research worth the name.

2. UGC wants lecturers to spend minimum 22 hours a week in direct teaching

3. Indian higher education system is in unsound state

A. Only 1 and 2
B. Only 2
C. Only 1 and 3
D. All 1, 2 and 3

Q.41 Which of these is not a punctuation mark?

A. Full stop
B. Comma
C. Colon
D. Hashtag

Q.42 Which of these is used after a nominative absolute?

A. Colon
B. Comma
C. Full stop
D. Question mark

Q.43 Which of these is used to separate short co-ordinate clauses of a compound sentence?

A. Semicolon
B. Comma
C. Full stop
D. Colon

Q.44 Direction: Fill in the blanks with suitable prepositions:
Defeat never comes ____ any man until he admits it.

A. into
B. to
C. on
D. from

Q.45 Direction: Fill in the blanks with suitable prepositions:
A lamp is hung ____ my head.

A. on
B. above
C. in
D. by

Q.46 Direction: Fill in the blanks with suitable prepositions:
____ the given diagram, We can see the black box.

A. to
B. in
C. from
D. by

Q.47 Direction: In the following question, a sentence has been given in Direct & Indirect Speech. Out of the four alternatives suggested, select the one which best expresses the same sentence in Direct & Indirect Speech?
Kiran asked me, "Did you see the Cricket match on television last night?"

A. Kiran asked me whether I saw the Cricket match on television the earlier night.

B. Kiran asked me whether I had seen the Cricket match on television the earlier night.

C. Kiran asked me did I see the Cricket match on television the last night.

D. Kiran asked me whether I had seen the Cricket match on television the last night.

Q.48 Direction: In the following question, a sentence has been given in Direct & Indirect Speech. Out of the four alternatives suggested, select the one which best expresses the same sentence in Direct & Indirect Speech?
I said to him, "Why are you working so hard?"

A. I asked him why he was working so hard.

B. I asked him why was he working so hard.

C. I asked him why had he been working so hard.

D. I asked him why he had been working so hard.

Q.49 Direction: In the following question, a sentence has been given in Active/Passive Voice. Out of the four alternatives suggested, select the one which best expresses the same sentence in Passive/Active Voice?
He killed himself.

A. Himself was killed by him.

B. Killing himself was done by him.

C. He was killed by himself.

D. He had to kill himself.

Q.50 Direction: A sentence has been given in Active/Passive Voice. Out of the four alternatives suggested, select the one which expresses the same sentence in Passive/Active Voice and mark your answer.
People generally prefer wealth to health.

A. Wealth to health is generally preferred.

B. Wealth to health is preferred by people generally.

C. Generally people are preferred wealth to health.

D. Generally is preferred wealth to health.

Science

Q.51 A person holds a bucket by applying a $10n$ force. He then moves a horizontal distance of $5\ m$ and climbs up a vertical distance of $10\ m$. Find out the total work done by him?

A. 100J **B.** 150J **C.** 50J **D.** 200J

Q.52 A simple harmonic oscillator has an amplitude A and time period T. The time require by it to travel from $x = A$ to $x = \dfrac{A}{2}$ is_______

A. $\dfrac{T}{6}$ **B.** $\dfrac{T}{4}$ **C.** $\dfrac{T}{3}$ **D.** $\dfrac{T}{2}$

Q.53 The vapour of a carboxylic acid HA when passed over MnO_2 at $573\ K$ yields propanone. What is the acid HA?

A. Methanoic acid **B.** Ethanoic acid
C. Propanoic acid **D.** Butanoic acid

Q.54 Combine three resistors 5Ω,4.5Ω and 3Ω in such a way that the total resistance of this combination is maximum:

A. 12.5Ω **B.** 13.5Ω **C.** 14.5Ω **D.** 16.5Ω

Q.55 Which property of an electromagnetic wave, depends on the medium in which it is travelling?

A. Velocity **B.** Frequency
C. Time period **D.** Wave length

Q.56 There are two statements:
Statement A: Rate of change of momentum corresponds to force
Statement B: Rate of change of momentum corresponds to Kinetic Energy
Which one of the following is correct?

A. A only
B. B only
C. Both A and B are correct
D. Both A and B are wrong

Q.57 The value of acceleration due to gravity -

A. Is same on equator and poles
B. Is least on poles
C. Is least on equator
D. Increases from pole to equator

Q.58 The main fuse is connected in:

A. live wire
B. Neutral wire
C. Both the live and earth wires.
D. Both earth and neutral wire.

Q.59 The unit of linear acceleration is:

A. kg-m **B.** m/s **C.** m/s² **D.** rad/s²

Q.60 The relative density of mercury is 13.6. Its density in $S.I.$ unit is given as $X \times 10^3\ kgm^{-3}$. Find X?

A. 13 **B.** 14 **C.** 13.6 **D.** 14.6

Q.61 Match the following:

(A) Viral diseases	(i) Dengue, Malaria, Plague
(B) Bacterial diseases	(ii) Measles, Mumps, Swine flue, Chickenpox
(C) Diseases spread through insects	(iii) Tuberculosis, Diphtheria, Tetanus, Cholera, Typhoid
(D) Hereditary diseases	(iv) Diabetes Hypertension, Cancer

A. (A - iii), (B - i), (C - iv), (D - ii)
B. (A - ii), (B - iii), (C - i), (D - iv)
C. (A - i), (B - ii), (C - iii), (D - iv)
D. (A - iv), (B - iii), (C - ii), (D - ii)

Q.62 The number of protons in an atom of an element A is 19 then, the number of electron in its ion A^+ is:

A. 18 **B.** 19 **C.** 20 **D.** 21

Q.63 According to the MyPyramind food guidance system, a person should obtain most of their fat from __________.

A. beef, chicken, and fish
B. vegetables oils, nuts, and fish
C. fats, oils, and sweets
D. milk, yogurt, and cheese

Q.64 Widal test is carried out to test ______

A. HIV **B.** Typhoid **C.** Malaria **D.** Diabetes

Q.65 The flux linked with a coil at any instant t is given by $\Phi_B = 10t^2 - 50t + 250$. The induced emf at $t = 3s$ is:

A. $-190\ V$ **B.** $-10\ V$ **C.** $10\ V$ **D.** $190\ V$

Q.66 A diffraction pattern is obtained using a beam of red light. What happens if the red light is replaced by blue light?

A. Bands disappear
B. No change
C. Diffraction pattern becomes narrower and crowded together
D. Diffraction pattern becomes broader and further apart

Q.67 A cycle tyre bursts suddenly. What is the type of this process?

A. Isothermal **B.** Adiabatic
C. Isochoric **D.** Isobaric

Q.68 In an atom two electrons move around the nucleus in circular orbits of radii R and $4R$. The ratio of the time taken by them to complete one revolution is:

A. $1:4$ **B.** $4:1$ **C.** $1:8$ **D.** $8:7$

Q.69 Assertion
In adiabatic compression , the internal energy and temperature of the system get decreased .

Reason
The adiabatic compression is a slow process .

A. Both Assertion and Reason are correct and Reason is the correct explanation for Assertion
B. Both Assertion and Reason are correct but Reason is not the correct explanation for Assertion

C. Both Assertion and Reason are correct but Reason is not the correct explanation for Assertion

D. Both Assertion and Reason are incorrect

Q.70 If a cylinder containing a gas at high pressure explodes, the gas undergoes.
A. Reversible adiabatic change and fall of temperature
B. Reversible adiabatic change and rise of temperature
C. Irreversible adiabatic change and fall of temperature
D. Irreversible adiabatic change and rise of temperature

Q.71 The ratio of the electrostatic force of attraction to the gravitational force between the proton and electron of the hydrogen atom is of the order of:
A. 10^{39} **B.** 10^{-39} **C.** 10^{8} **D.** 10^{-8}

Q.72 The organic reaction represented by equation $CH_3 - CH = O + H_2 \, NOH$ gives $CH_3 - CH - NH + H_2O$ is an example of:
A. An addition reaction
B. A condensation reaction
C. An oxidation reaction
D. An elimination reaction

Q.73 Radiocarbon is produced in the atmosphere as a result of:
A. Collision between fast neutrons and nitrogen nuclei present in the atmosphere.
B. Action of ultraviolet light from the sun on atmospheric oxygen.
C. Action of solar radiations particularly cosmic rays on carbon dioxide present in the atmosphere.
D. Lightning discharge in atmosphere.

Q.74 The number of electrons presents in H^+ is:
A. Zero **B.** One **C.** Two **D.** Three

Q.75 The temperature coefficient of resistance of a semiconductor:
A. Is always positive
B. Is always negative
C. Is zero
D. May be positive or negative or zero

General Awareness

Q.76 In which of the following regions Passage Exercise between India and Russia was conducted in January 2022?
A. Red Sea **B.** Arabian Sea
C. South China Sea **D.** Mediterranean Sea

Q.77 Consider the following pairs of Indian embroidery?
(1) Kashida - Karnataka
(2) Phulkari - Punjab
(3) Kasuti - West Bengal
Choose the correct option using the codes given below-
A. 1 and 2 only **B.** 1 and 3 only
C. 2 only **D.** 1,2 and 3

Q.78 Which of the following pairs are correctly matched?

1. Mrichchakatikam - Shudraka
2. Buddhacharita - Vasuvandhu
3. Mudrarakshasa - Vishakhadatta
4. Harshacharita - Banabhatta
Select the correct answer using the codes given below:
A. 1, 2, 3 and 4 **B.** 1, 3 and 4
C. 1 and 4 **D.** 2 and 3

Q.79 Gandhara Art is the combination of -
A. Indo - Roman **B.** Indo – Greek
C. Indo – Islamic **D.** Indo – China

Q.80 How old is the Sitalsasthi festival?
A. approx 100 years **B.** Approx 200 years
C. Approx 300 years **D.** Approx 400 years

Q.81 Southern Part of Indian Eastern Coastal Plain is called:
A. North Circar **B.** Malabar Coast
C. Coromandal Coast **D.** Konkan Coast

Q.82 Among the following cities, which one is nearest to the Tropic of Cancer?
A. Delhi **B.** Kolkata **C.** Jodhpur **D.** Nagpur

Q.83 Sankosh river forms boundary between —.
A. Jharkhand and West Bengal
B. Assam and Arunachal Pradesh
C. Assam and West Bengal
D. Bihar and Jharkhand

Q.84 Where is the Palamau Tiger reserve located?
A. Rajasthan **B.** Jharkhand
C. Odisha **D.** Uttar Pradesh

Q.85 Which of the following international prizes/awards is given for outstanding contribution in the field of Journalism?
A. Oscar Award **B.** Booker Prize
C. Pulitzer Prize **D.** Sullivan Award

Q.86 33rd Moortidevi Award for the year 2019 was given to _________.
A. George Miller **B.** Mira kumar
C. Vishwanath Tiwari **D.** Satheesh Reddy

Q.87 What is the national currency of Jordan?
A. Jordanian down **B.** Jordanian shekel
C. Jordanian lira **D.** Jordanian dinar

Q.88 Who of the following has been awarded with the highest award of Palestine?
A. Narendra Modi **B.** Francis hollande
C. Barrack obama **D.** Donald trump

Q.89 Which of these Indians has not won a Nobel Award?
A. Rabindranath Tagore
B. C. V. Raman
C. Satyajit Ray
D. Amartya Sen

Q.90 Who wrote The book 'To Live or Not Live'?

A. Viren sourie   **B.** Kapil Ishapuri
C. Nirad C. Chaudhuri   **D.** Raghav Bahal

Q.91 The famous book 'Anandmath' was authored by:
A. Sarojini Naidu
B. Bankim Chandra Chottapadhya
C. Sri Aurobindo
D. Rabindrnath Tagore

Q.92 The Moplah Rebellion in 1921 in Malabar was Muslim Peasants Rebellion against:
A. Muslim Land Holders
B. The British Government Authority
C. The non-tribal outsiders
D. Hindu Land Holders

Q.93 Who among the following wrote the novel "Durgesnandini"?
A. Bipin Chandra Pal
B. Bankim Chandra Chattopadhyay
C. Gopal Krishna Gokhale
D. Sarojini Naidu

Q.94 The Indian Air Force celebrated its Golden jubilee in -
A. 1962   **B.** 1972   **C.** 1982   **D.** 1992

Q.95 What does the term IRBM stand for?
A. Intermediate Researched Ballistic Missile
B. Intermediate Resource Ballistic Missile
C. Intermediate Range Ballistic Missile
D. Intermediated Range Ballistic Missile

Q.96 Naval submarine INS Kalvari has been a partnership between India and which EU nation?
A. Italy   **B.** France
C. Germany   **D.** Spain

Q.97 The Indian Navy has inked a MoU with which port trust for utilizing the Port's berthing facility at Mattancherry wharf for Naval ships?
A. Kandla Port Trust   **B.** Kolkata Port Trust
C. Cochin Port Trust   **D.** Chennai Port Trust

Q.98 Which scheme was launched previous year as per Budget 2019 to improve the Health Sector of the country?
A. Suraksha Bima Pariyojana
B. Swachh Bharat Mission
C. Rashtriya Swasthya Bima Yojana
D. Ayushman Bharat scheme

Q.99 In which city International Training Centre for Operational Oceanography is stablised?
A. New Delhi   **B.** Hyderabad
C. Chennai   **D.** Lucknow

Q.100 Who fits with this description 'Indian Cotton merchant, Banker, Congressman, a close associate of Mahatma Gandhi'?
A. M. R. Jayakar   **B.** V. S. Sastri
C. G. D. Birla   **D.** Jamanlal Bajaj

// Smart Answer Sheet //

Correct — Percentage of students who answered correctly. **Skipped** — Percentage of students who skipped.

Q.	Ans.	Correct / Skipped	Q.	Ans.	Correct / Skipped	Q.	Ans.	Correct / Skipped	Q.	Ans.	Correct / Skipped	Q.	Ans.	Correct / Skipped	Q.	Ans.	Correct / Skipped
1	B	46.48 % / 50.75 %	18	B	77.05 % / 21.25 %	35	A	78.42 % / 14.26 %	52	A	44.48 % / 46.01 %	69	D	49.22 % / 40.9 %	86	C	13.87 % / 85.54 %
2	D	77.89 % / 15.63 %	19	A	85.28 % / 14.13 %	36	C	46.87 % / 45.51 %	53	B	50.32 % / 38.09 %	70	C	57.93 % / 41.69 %	87	D	61.53 % / 38.45 %
3	B	46.32 % / 36.64 %	20	C	89.86 % / 10.0 %	37	D	52.87 % / 37.7 %	54	A	58.32 % / 38.06 %	71	A	10.3 % / 70.78 %	88	A	49.14 % / 41.9 %
4	A	13.06 % / 76.27 %	21	C	42.89 % / 56.08 %	38	C	61.01 % / 38.4 %	55	A	78.25 % / 11.17 %	72	A	82.69 % / 11.51 %	89	C	81.05 % / 11.22 %
5	B	50.38 % / 42.43 %	22	C	88.68 % / 10.75 %	39	A	50.07 % / 34.29 %	56	A	78.99 % / 19.67 %	73	A	89.36 % / 10.36 %	90	C	84.92 % / 13.01 %
6	A	46.31 % / 44.47 %	23	C	45.21 % / 39.2 %	40	D	46.13 % / 33.56 %	57	C	48.98 % / 35.87 %	74	A	76.86 % / 20.53 %	91	B	57.25 % / 38.05 %
7	A	23.02 % / 75.43 %	24	B	42.36 % / 48.29 %	41	D	76.18 % / 18.49 %	58	A	86.97 % / 11.42 %	75	A	40.21 % / 37.37 %	92	D	85.81 % / 11.44 %
8	A	87.91 % / 11.28 %	25	B	67.88 % / 30.34 %	42	B	50.86 % / 45.28 %	59	C	51.61 % / 41.7 %	76	B	55.47 % / 35.97 %	93	B	62.37 % / 31.19 %
9	D	46.62 % / 40.88 %	26	C	48.43 % / 45.8 %	43	B	62.48 % / 31.29 %	60	C	16.35 % / 80.09 %	77	C	60.88 % / 38.69 %	94	C	65.26 % / 34.46 %
10	C	11.12 % / 70.59 %	27	B	24.96 % / 70.13 %	44	B	85.24 % / 12.91 %	61	B	56.44 % / 30.83 %	78	B	26.77 % / 69.97 %	95	C	78.7 % / 20.47 %
11	B	40.43 % / 57.99 %	28	B	68.22 % / 31.29 %	45	B	58.77 % / 35.59 %	62	A	40.73 % / 33.31 %	79	B	41.95 % / 57.44 %	96	B	87.19 % / 10.33 %
12	C	62.91 % / 34.74 %	29	D	67.11 % / 30.59 %	46	B	41.49 % / 57.05 %	63	B	81.99 % / 17.24 %	80	D	79.62 % / 19.52 %	97	C	87.61 % / 12.28 %
13	A	23.46 % / 75.29 %	30	C	64.58 % / 31.7 %	47	B	47.33 % / 35.36 %	64	B	45.19 % / 49.98 %	81	C	82.73 % / 15.98 %	98	D	66.95 % / 30.82 %
14	D	49.62 % / 39.74 %	31	A	64.95 % / 33.46 %	48	A	83.04 % / 13.86 %	65	B	76.53 % / 21.16 %	82	B	41.85 % / 40.78 %	99	B	13.43 % / 80.25 %
15	A	64.94 % / 35.0 %	32	A	76.14 % / 14.11 %	49	C	64.43 % / 32.39 %	66	C	68.05 % / 31.22 %	83	B	63.05 % / 31.88 %	100	C	61.86 % / 37.31 %
16	A	49.09 % / 48.72 %	33	A	60.61 % / 34.7 %	50	A	68.46 % / 30.63 %	67	B	17.56 % / 78.46 %	84	B	88.81 % / 10.8 %			
17	C	14.77 % / 83.48 %	34	B	87.73 % / 12.24 %	51	A	61.02 % / 38.64 %	68	C	16.91 % / 78.16 %	85	C	53.15 % / 40.47 %			

//Hints and Solutions//

1. Symmetric difference of two sets is a set which contains elements which are in exactly one set.

$$A \oplus B = (A - B) + (B - A)$$

$$= \{2,4,9\}$$

Hence, the correct option is (B).

2. Let $z = \dfrac{1}{1+5i} - \dfrac{1}{1-5i}$

We know that,

$$z = \dfrac{z_2 - z_1}{z_1 z_2}$$

$$z_2 = (1 - 5i), z_1 = (1 + 5i)$$

$$\Rightarrow \dfrac{(1-5i)-(1+5i)}{(1+5i)(1-5i)}$$

$$\Rightarrow \dfrac{-10i}{(1)^2 - (5i)^2}$$

$$\Rightarrow -\dfrac{10i}{26} = -\dfrac{5}{13}i$$

The modulus of z is $\therefore |z| = \sqrt{(0)^2 + \left(\dfrac{5}{13}\right)^2}$

$$\Rightarrow \sqrt{\dfrac{25}{169}} = \dfrac{5}{13}$$

Hence, the correct option is (D).

3. Number of triangles formed from 15 point $= {}^{15}C_3 - {}^{8}C_3$

Since 8 parts are collinear, then ${}^{8}C_3$ triangles will not be formed so,

$${}^{15}C_3 - {}^{8}C_3$$

$$= \dfrac{15!}{3!12!} - \dfrac{8!}{3!5!}$$

$$= \dfrac{15 \times 14 \times 13}{3 \times 2} - \dfrac{8 \times 7 \times 6}{3 \times 2}$$

$$= 455 - 56 = 399$$

Hence, the correct option is (B).

4. $T_n = {}^{n}C_r (a)^{n-r}$

$$= \left(3x - \tfrac{1}{x^2}\right)^6 = {}^{6}C_0(3x)^6 \cdot \left(\tfrac{1}{x^2}\right)^0 + {}^{6}C_1(3x)^5 \cdot \left(\tfrac{1}{x^2}\right)^1$$
$$+ {}^{6}C_2(3x)^4\left(\tfrac{1}{x^2}\right)^2$$
$$+ {}^{6}C_3(3x)^3\left(\tfrac{1}{x^2}\right)^3 + {}^{6}C_4(3x)^2 \cdot \left(\tfrac{1}{x^2}\right)^4 + {}^{6}C_5(3x)^1 \cdot$$
$$\left(\tfrac{1}{x^2}\right)^5 + {}^{6}C_6(3x)^0\left(\tfrac{1}{x^2}\right)^6$$

We can see that there is no term of x^2 so the coefficient is 0.

Hence, the correct option is (A).

5. $\dfrac{\log 256}{\log 16} = \log x$

$$\dfrac{\log(16)^2}{\log(16)} = \log x$$

$$\dfrac{2\log(16)}{\log(16)} = \log x$$

$$\Rightarrow 2 = \log x$$

$$\Rightarrow x = 10^2$$

$$\Rightarrow x = 100$$

Hence, the correct option is (B).

6. By operating $C_2 \rightarrow C_2 - \dfrac{1}{2}(C_1 + C_3)$ we get,

$$\Delta = \begin{vmatrix} 115 & 0 & 97 \\ 10 & 0 & -8 \\ 106 & 0 & 88 \end{vmatrix} = 0$$

Hence, the correct option is (A).

7. A matrix is said to be singular if its determinant is zero

i.e. for matrix A to be singular, $|A| = 0$

For a singular matrix, the inverse doesn't exist

Given that, matrix $\begin{bmatrix} \cos\theta & \sin\theta & 0 \\ \sin\theta & \cos\theta & 0 \\ 0 & 0 & 1 \end{bmatrix}$ is singular

Then, $\begin{vmatrix} \cos\theta & \sin\theta & 0 \\ \sin\theta & \cos\theta & 0 \\ 0 & 0 & 1 \end{vmatrix} = 0$

$$\Rightarrow \begin{vmatrix} \cos\theta & \sin\theta \\ \sin\theta & \cos\theta \end{vmatrix} = 0$$

$$\Rightarrow \cos^2\theta - \sin^2\theta = 0$$

$$\Rightarrow \cos 2\theta = \cos\dfrac{\pi}{2}$$

$$\therefore \theta = \dfrac{\pi}{4}$$

Hence, the correct option is (A).

8. Given,

$$A = \begin{bmatrix} 1 & 1 \\ 0 & 1 \end{bmatrix}$$

$$A^2 = A.A = \begin{bmatrix} 1 & 1 \\ 0 & 1 \end{bmatrix}\begin{bmatrix} 1 & 1 \\ 0 & 1 \end{bmatrix}$$

$$= \begin{bmatrix} 1+0 & 1+1 \\ 0 & 1 \end{bmatrix} = \begin{bmatrix} 1 & 2 \\ 0 & 1 \end{bmatrix}$$

$$A^3 = A^2.A = \begin{bmatrix} 1 & 2 \\ 0 & 1 \end{bmatrix}\begin{bmatrix} 1 & 1 \\ 0 & 1 \end{bmatrix}$$

$$= \begin{bmatrix} 1 & 2+1 \\ 0 & 1 \end{bmatrix} = \begin{bmatrix} 1 & 3 \\ 0 & 1 \end{bmatrix}$$

Seeing the pattern here,

$$A^n = \begin{bmatrix} 1 & n \\ 0 & 1 \end{bmatrix}$$

Hence, the correct option is (A).

9. Given,

Equation of the straight line parallel to x + 2y + 4 = 0 is x + 2y + k = 0.

Since equation is passing through the points (2, 5)

2 + 2(5) + k = 0

2 + 10 + k = 0

12 + k = 0

k = - 12

So,

The required equation of the line is x + 2y - 12 = 0

Hence, the correct option is (D).

10. We know that,

$$\Rightarrow \tan^{-1}x + \tan^{-1}y$$

$$= \tan^{-1}\left(\frac{x+y}{1-xy}\right),$$

We have,

$$\tan^{-1}\left(\frac{1}{7}\right) + \tan^{-1}\left(\frac{1}{13}\right)$$

$$= \tan^{-1}\left(\frac{\frac{1}{7}+\frac{1}{13}}{1-\frac{1}{7}\times\frac{1}{13}}\right)$$

$$= \tan^{-1}\left(\frac{20}{90}\right)$$

$$= \tan^{-1}\left(\frac{2}{9}\right)$$

Hence, the correct option is (C).

11. Since f is one - one, three elements of {1, 2, 3} must be taken to 3 different elements of the co - domain {1, 2, 3} under f. So, f has to be onto.

Hence, the correct option is (B).

12. At $x = \infty$, the value is $\frac{\infty}{\infty}$, so limit is of an indeterminate form $\left(\frac{0}{0}, \frac{\infty}{\infty}, 0 \times \infty, 00, 1\infty, \infty0\right)$

To avoid indeterminate form

$$\lim_{x\to\infty}\left(\frac{x}{x+1}\right)$$

$$= \lim_{x\to\infty}\left(\frac{1}{1+\frac{1}{x}}\right)$$

$$= \frac{1}{1+0} = 1$$

Hence, the correct option is (C).

13. According to quotient Rule:

$$(\cos\theta)' = -\sin\theta$$

$$\Rightarrow (\sin\theta)' = \cos\theta$$

$$\Rightarrow (\sec\theta)' = \sec\theta\tan\theta$$

$$\Rightarrow \tan\theta' = \sec^2\theta$$

$$s = \sin\theta(1 + \sec\theta) = \sin\theta + \tan\theta$$

$$\frac{ds}{d\theta} = (\sin\theta)' + (\tan\theta)' = \cos\theta + \sec^2\theta$$

Hence, the correct option is (A).

14. Equation of a line is given as $y - y_1 = m(x - x_1)$ where m is the slope. So to find the tangent line, we need its slope and a point on the line. Tangent of the line is given by $h'(x)$.

$$h(x) = x^4 - 2x^2 + 2x$$
$$h'(x) = 4x^3 - 4x + 2$$
$$h'(1) = 4(1)^3 - 4(1) + 2 = 2$$

Slope of the tangent line is, 2 i.e. $m = 2$.

At $x = 1$

$$h(1) = (1)^4 - 2(1)^2 + 2(1) = 1$$

So, the intersection point is $(1,1)$

Equation of line: $y - y_1 = m(x - x_1)$

$$y - 1 = 2(x - 1)$$
$$y = 2x - 1$$

Hence, the correct option is (D).

15. $A \times C = \{1,2\} \times \{5,6\}$
$$= \{(1,5)(1,6)(2,5)(2,6)\}$$
$$B \times D = \{1,2,3,4\} \times \{5,6,7,8\}$$
$$= \{(1,5)(1,6)(1,7)(1,8)(2,5)(2,6)(2,7)$$
$$(3,5)(3,6)(3,7)(3,8)(4,5)(4,6)(4,7)(4,8)\}$$
$$(A \times C) \subset (B \times D)$$

Hence, the correct option is (A).

16. $l = \int \frac{1}{\sqrt{x^2-6x+1}}dx = \int \frac{1}{\sqrt{x^2-6x+9-9+1}}dx = \int \frac{1}{\sqrt{(x-3)^2-\sqrt{8}^2}}dx$

$$l = \log | (x - 3) + \sqrt{((x - 3)^2 - \sqrt{8}^2)} | +c$$

$$l = \log|(x - 3) + |\sqrt{(x^2 - 6x + 1)} | +c$$

Hence, the correct option is (A).

17. Put, $t = x^5 + 1$, then $dt = 5x^4dx$

$$\int 5x^4\sqrt{x^5 + 1}dx$$

$$\Rightarrow \int \sqrt{t}dt = \frac{2}{3}t^{\frac{3}{2}}$$

$$\Rightarrow \frac{2}{3}(x^5 + 1)^{\frac{3}{2}}$$

Hence, $\int_{-1}^{1} 5x^4\sqrt{x^5 + 1}dx$

$$\Rightarrow \frac{2}{3}\left[(x^5 + 1)^{\frac{3}{2}}\right]_{-1}^{1}$$

$$\Rightarrow \frac{2}{3}\left[(1^5 + 1)^{3/2} - ((-1)^5 + 1)^{\frac{3}{2}}\right]$$

$$\Rightarrow \frac{2}{3}\left[2^{\frac{3}{2}} - 0^{\frac{3}{2}}\right]$$

$$\Rightarrow \frac{2}{3}\left(2\sqrt{2}\right)$$
$$\Rightarrow \frac{4\sqrt{2}}{3}$$

Hence, the correct option is (C).

18. The union of the sets A and B is the set that contains those elements that are either in A or in B.
Let, $A = \{1,2,5\}$ and $B = \{1,2,6\}$
So, $A \cup B = \{1,2,5,6\}$
Hence, the correct option is (B).

19. The intersection of the sets A and B is the set that contains those elements that are both in A and B.
Let, $A = \{1,2,5\}$ and $B = \{1,2,6\}$
So, $A \cap B = \{1,2\}$
Hence, the correct option is (A)

20. $A = \dfrac{(x+x+2+x+5)}{3}$
$= \dfrac{(3x+7)}{3}$
$B = \dfrac{(y+y+3+y+7)}{3}$
$= \dfrac{(3y+10)}{3}$
Mean of A and B
$= \dfrac{(A+B)}{2}$
$= \dfrac{\left[\frac{(3x+7)}{3}+\frac{(3y+10)}{3}\right]}{2}$
$= \dfrac{(3x+3y+17)}{6}$
$= \dfrac{(3x+3x-6+17)}{6}$
$= \dfrac{(6x+11)}{6}$
$= \dfrac{x+11}{6}$

Hence, the correct option is (C).

21. The probability of getting a head on tossing a coin $(P_1) = \dfrac{1}{2}$

The probability of getting a six on rolling a dice $(P_2) = \dfrac{1}{6}$
These two events are independent.
So, the probability that the coin shows the head and the dice shows 6 is given by-
$$P = P_1 x P_2 = \frac{1}{2} x \frac{1}{6} = \frac{1}{12}$$

Hence, the correct option is (C).

22. The difference of the sets A and B denoted by $(A - B)$ is the set containing those elements that are in A not in B.
Let, $A = \{1,2,3\}$ and $B = \{1,2,5\}$
So, $A - B = \{3\}$
Hence, the correct option is (C)

23. $\log_5 512$
$\Rightarrow \dfrac{\log 512}{\log 5}$
$\Rightarrow \dfrac{\log 2^9}{\log\left(\frac{10}{2}\right)}$
$\Rightarrow \dfrac{9\log 2}{\log 10 - \log 2}$
$\Rightarrow \dfrac{9\times 0.3010}{1-0.3010}$
$\Rightarrow \dfrac{2.709}{0.699}$
$\Rightarrow \dfrac{2709}{699}$
$\Rightarrow 3.876$
Hence, the correct option is (C).

24. Let, go to work by bike $= P(B)$.
By car $= P(C)$
And, By both $= P(B \cap C)$
Given, $P(B) = 0.33, P(C) = 0.42$
$P(B \cap C) = 0.12$
$P(B \cap C) = ?$
$P(B \cap C) = 1 - P(B \cup C)$
$= 1 - P(B) - P(C) + P(B \cap C)$
$= 1 - 0.22 - 0.42 + 0.12$
$= 0.37$
Hence, the correct option is (B).

25. Given a biased coin such that heads is 3 times as likely as tails. The coin is tossed twice.
$$P(H) = \frac{3}{4} \text{ and } P(T) = \frac{1}{4}$$
Let T be the random variable for the number of tails.
$$P(T = 0) = P(HH) = \frac{3}{4} \times \frac{3}{4} = \frac{9}{16}$$
$$P(T = 1) = P(HT, TH) = \frac{3}{4} \times \frac{1}{4} + \frac{3}{4} \times \frac{1}{4} = \frac{3}{16} + \frac{3}{16} = \frac{3}{8} = \frac{6}{16}$$
$$P(T = 2) = P(TT) = \frac{1}{4} \times \frac{1}{4} = \frac{1}{16}$$
Hence, the correct option is (B)

26. Undermine – to make something weaker, undermine is to weaken the position, goals, or success of something.

Strengthen - to become stronger or to make something stronger.

Assist- to give support or help.

De-emphasize- to remove emphasis from something.

Sabotage - damage that is done on purpose and secretly in order to prevent an enemy or a competitor from being successful.

Hence, the correct option is (C).

27. Rancid – (of foods containing fat or oil) smelling or tasting unpleasant as a result of being old and stale.

Fresh - (used especially about food) produced or picked very recently; not frozen or in a tin.

Hence, the correct option is (B).

28. Squalid means extremely dirty or unpleasant. Therefore, the opposite is clean.

Hence, the correct option is (B).

29. Tactile – Perceptible by touch, connected with the sense of touch.

Palpable - Capable of being touched or felt.

Hence, the correct option is (D).

30. Atone – To show that one is sorry for doing something wrong.

Repent - To cause to feel regret or contrition.

Hence, the correct option is (C).

31. Replace 'are' with 'is'. The verb in an 'or', 'either/or', or 'neither/nor' sentence agrees with the noun or pronoun closest to it which in this case is 'emotion'.

Hence, the correct option is (A).

32. The flaw is in the first part of the sentence.

The sentence implies that we need to add some details to the statement to make it more acceptable. The preposition 'in' is missing in the first part of the sentence. The phrasal verb 'fill in' means 'to act as a substitute for something' and in the given sentence, it suggests that we have to fill in the gaps with our own ideas to make sure everything makes sense. So, the correct sentence is: When we tell somebody about a statement we heard a few days earlier and have to fill **in** a couple of the plot holes with our own embellishments to make sure everything makes sense and we're not crazy.

Hence, the correct option is (A).

33. The error is in the first part of the sentence.

The sentence implies that the therapy involved a therapist putting a client into a half-conscious state where she was encouraged to find her forgotten childhood memories.

The error is due to the wrong usage of the preposition 'at'. 'At' means 'expressing location or arrival in a particular place or position'. The correct preposition which suits the context of the sentence is 'into' as it means 'expressing movement or action with the result that someone or something becomes enclosed or surrounded by something else'.

So, the correct sentence is: The therapy involved a therapist putting a client into a trance-like state where she was encouraged to root out and re-experience forgotten childhood memories.

Hence, the correct option is (A).

34. The error is in the second part of the sentence.

The error is due to the wrong usage of the preposition 'as'. We use the preposition 'than' after 'different' if it is followed by a noun or a pronoun.

In the above sentence, a different is followed by a pronoun 'you'. Therefore, 'as' must be replaced with 'than'.

The correct sentence is: I don't see how that's any different than you trying to protect me.

Hence, the correct option is (B).

35. The error lies in part 1 of the given sentence as the fixed expression "many a/an" is more formal than the single word "many" and it is much less common. Like the adjective and the pronoun, 'many a/an' is used for indicating a large number of something and it takes a singular countable noun followed by a singular verb while 'many' is used with countable plural nouns followed by plural verb.

Hence, the correct option is (A).

36. Kindly refer to the 1st sentence of the 1st paragraph.

The University Grant Commission's directive to college and University lecturers to spend a minimum of 22 hours a week in direct teaching is the product of budgetary cutbacks rather than pedagogik wisdom.

Hence, the correct option is (C).

37. The answer to this question can also be inferred from the 1st sentence of the 1st paragraph.

Hence, the correct option is (D).

38. The answer can be inferred from the 3rd sentence of the 1st paragraph. If one considers the amount of time academics require to prepare to lectures of good quality as well as the time they need to spend doing research, it is clear that most conscientious teachers work more than 40 hours a week.

Hence, the correct option is (C).

39. In the given context of the passage, option A is not true.

Hence, the correct option is (A).

40. In the given context of the passage, all the statements are true. Kindly refer to the 1st and 2nd sentences of the 1st paragraph and first few sentences of the 2nd paragraph.

Hence, the correct option is (D).

41. The main punctuation marks are full stop, comma, colon, semicolon, question mark, exclamation mark, hyphen, dash, brackets, apostrophe. Hashtag isn't a punctuation mark. It is a symbol used in social networks, and it has no relevance in English Grammar.

Hence, the correct option is (D).

42. The comma is used after a nominative absolute. For example, " Once over, she returned home in complete peace."

Hence, the correct option is (B).

43. The comma is used to separate short co-ordinate clauses of a compound sentence. For example, " She came, she stooped, she conquered."

Hence, the correct option is (B).

44. Defeat never comes **to** any man until he admits it.

Hence, the correct option is (B).

45. A lamp is hung **above** my head.

Hence, the correct option is (B).

46. In the given diagram, We can see the black box.

Hence, the correct option is (B).

47. Kiran asked me whether I had seen the Cricket match on television the earlier night.

Hence, the correct option is (B).

48. I asked him why he was working so hard.

Hence, the correct option is (A).

49. He was killed by himself.

The subject of active voice becomes the object in passive voice and vice-versa. Moreover, the subject and the object interchange their placements in the sentence in active and passive voices and third form of verb is used. Case of past indefinite: In such cases, we use auxiliary 'was/were' + 'third form of the verb'.

Hence, the correct option is (C).

50. Wealth to health is generally preferred.

In case of present simple tense takes the third form of the verb with 'is/am/are'. Subject and object are inter changed.

Hence, the correct option is (A).

51. Given,

$$s = 5m, F = 10N, \text{ and } \theta = 90°$$

Work done is given by,

$$W1 = F\cos\theta = 10 \times 5 \times \cos90° = 0$$

In the case of vertical motion, the angle between force and displacement is $0°$.

Here, $F = 10\,N$, $s = 10\,m$, and $\theta = 0°$

So, work done, $W_2 = 10 \times 10 \times \cos0 = 100\,J$

Therefore, the total work done $= W1 + W2 = 100j$

Hence, the correct option is (A).

52. As the oscillator starts from $x = A$, we can take,

$$x = a\cos\omega t$$
$$\frac{A}{2} = a\cos\left(\frac{2\pi t}{T}\right)$$
$$\cos\left(\frac{2\pi t}{T}\right) = \frac{1}{2}$$
$$= \cos\left(\frac{\pi}{6}\right)$$
$$\frac{2\pi t}{T} = \frac{\pi}{6}$$
$$\text{or } t = \frac{T}{6}$$

Hence, the correct option is (A).

53. The vapour of ethanoic acid (HA) when passed over MnO_2 at $573\,K$ yields propanone.

$$2CH_3COOH \xrightarrow[573\,K]{MnO} CH_3COCH_3 + CO_2 + H_2O$$

Hence, the correct option is (B).

54. The maximum resistance will be in the series arrangement.

Thus,

R=5Ω+4.5Ω+3Ω=12.5Ω

Hence, the correct option is (A).

55. The frequency, wavelength and time period can all vary according to the wave producing source. But, the velocity of an electromagnetic wave depends upon the medium through which it is travelling. The velocity of wave in a vacuum is termed as speed of light, which is assumed to be 3 x 108 m/s.

Hence, the correct option is (A).

56. We know that F=dp/dt which is the rate of change of momentum with time and KE=p²/2m and hence rate of change of momentum does not corresponds to kinetic energy. So, choice (a) is correct.

Hence, the correct option is (A).

57. The value of acceleration due to gravity is least on equator because distance between surface of the earth and its centre is more on equator than in poles.

Hence, the correct option is (C).

58. The live wires coming out from the output terminals of kWh meter has another fuse in it called the main fuse.

The fuse is connected in series with the live wire before it enters the household circuit. This is done so because it is only the live wire which has a high potential of 220 volts unlike the neutral wire which carries zero potential. The fuse has a high rating of about 50 amperes. Thus it prevents any damage such as fire to the entire electrical wiring entering the house due to short-circuit or overloading.

Hence, the correct option is (A).

59. Linear acceleration is defined as the rate of change of linear velocity of a body with respect to the time.

i.e, a = v/t and unit of velocity is m/s.

So, unit of linear acceleration becomes m/s².

Hence, the correct option is (C).

60. $RD = \dfrac{\text{density of mercury}}{\text{density of water}}$

$13.6 = \dfrac{\text{density of mercury}}{1\,gcm^{-3}}$

So, Density of mercury in $CGS = 13.6\,gcm^{-3}$

So, Density of mercury in Sl unit,

$= \dfrac{13.6 \times 100 \times 100 \times 100}{1000}\,kgm^{-3}$

$\Rightarrow 13.6 \times 10^3\,kgm^{-3}$

Hence, the correct option is (C).

61.

(A) Viral diseases	(ii) Measles, Mumps, Swine flue, Chickenpox
(B) Bacterial diseases	(iii) Tuberculosis, Diphtheria, Tetanus, Cholera, Typhoid

(C) Diseases spread through insects	(i) Dengue, Malaria, Plague
(D) Hereditary diseases	(iv) Diabetes Hypertension, Cancer

Hence, the correct option is (B).

62. In the neutral atom of an element,

Number of protons $=$ Number of electrons

$\therefore$ Number of electrons in element $A = 19$

Now, in A^+ ion, the positive charge is acquired by the loss of one electron.

$\therefore$ Number of electrons in ion $A^+ = 19 - 1 = 18$

Hence, the correct option is (A).

63. According to the MyPyramind food guidance system, a person should obtain most of their fat from **vegetables oils, nuts, and fish.**

Hence, the correct option is (B).

64. Widal test is carried out to test Typhoid. It is a common agglutination test employed in the serological diagnosis of enteric fever.

Hence, the correct option is (B).

65. $e = -\dfrac{d\phi}{dt} = -\dfrac{d}{dt}\left(10t^2 - 50t + 250\right)$

$= (20t - 50) = -(20(3) - 50)$

$= -(60 - 50) = -10\ V$

Hence, the correct option is (B).

66. The width of the fringe in diffraction pattern is given as $\dfrac{D\lambda}{d}$,

So, when the red light is replaced by blue light, the wavelength decreases which means that the fringe width decreases and pattern becomes narrower and crowded together.

Hence, the correct option is (C).

67. Any process is adiabatic is rapid such that there should not be any heat transfer between the system and it's surroundings. When a tyre bursts suddenly, the expansion takes place instantly. This leads to decrease in temperature inside. As such, the higher temperature air outside will transfer heat to it. This heat transfer is not rapid and doesn't take place instantly, unlike the expansion, which is instantaneous. Heat transfer takes place after the bursting, due to which one can consider that there is almost no energy exchange during the actual process. Thus process is adiabatic.

Hence, the correct option is (B).

68. Time period, $T \propto (R)^{\frac{3}{2}}$

$\therefore \dfrac{T_1}{T_2} = \left(\dfrac{R_1}{R_2}\right)^{\frac{3}{2}} = \left(\dfrac{1}{4}\right)^{\frac{3}{2}} = \dfrac{1}{8}$

Thus the ratio of time period is $1:8$

Hence, the correct option is (C).

69. When a process takes place very rapidly so that the heat does not find time to flow in or out then the process is adiabatic. Adiabatic compression is a rapid action and both the internal energy and the temperature increase.

Hence, the correct option is (D).

70. Gas cylinder suddenly explodes is an irreversible adiabatic change and work done against expansion reduces the temperature. An adiabatic process is a type of thermodynamic process which occurs without transferring heat or mass between the system and its surroundings

Hence, the correct option is (C).

71. Electrostatic force of attraction $= \dfrac{kq_1q_2}{r^2}$

$= \dfrac{9\times10^9\times\left(1\cdot6\times10^{-19}\right)^2}{r^2}$

Gravitational force of attraction $= \dfrac{Gm_e m_p}{r^2}$

$= \dfrac{\left(6\cdot67\times10^{-11}\right)\left(9\cdot1\times10^{-31}\right)\left(1\cdot67\times10^{-27}\right)}{r^2}$

Ratio $\dfrac{F_e}{F_g} = \dfrac{9\times10^9\times\left(1\cdot6\times10^{-19}\right)^2}{\left(6\cdot67\times10^{-11}\right)\left(9\cdot1\times10^{-31}\right)\left(1\cdot67\times10^{-27}\right)}$

$= \dfrac{23\cdot04\times10^{-29}}{101\cdot36\times10^{-69}}$

$= 2\cdot27 \times 10^{39}$

Hence, the correct option is (A).

72. The organic reaction represented by equation $CH_3 - CH = O + H_2NOH$ gives $CH_3 - CH - NH + H_2O$ is an example of a condensation reaction.

Hence, the correct option is (A).

73. Radiocarbon is produced in the atmosphere as result of collision between fast neutrons and nitrogen nuclei present in the atmosphere.

Nuclear reaction is given as :

$_7N^{14} + _0n^1 \rightarrow _6C^{14} + _1H^1$

Hence, the correct option is (A).

74. H$^+$ is a hydrogen ion, and it is an ion because it lost an electron. Electrons are negatively charged. When an atom gains electrons it will have NEGATIVE charges. So, it has zero electron.

Hence, the correct option is (A).

75. At given temperature, resistivity of any material depends on number of free electrons and drift speed of electrons in the material. The drift speed of electrons is determined by how often electrons collide with each other and other atoms in the material.

For semiconductors, resistivity decreases with increase in temperature because more free charge carriers (electrons and/ or holes) are available for conduction. Therefore, they have negative temperature coefficient.

Whereas, as temperature increases resistivity increases as electrons collide more frequently with vibrating atoms in conductor. This reduces drift speed of electrons (and thus current reduces) and gives them positive temperature coefficient of resistance.

Hence, the correct option is (A).

76. The Navies of India and Russia conducted a passing exercise in the Arabian Sea on 14 January 2022.

Indian Navy's indigenously designed and built guided-missile destroyer INS Kochi exercised with Russian Federation Navy's destroyer Admiral Tributs. A passing exercise is done to ensure that two navies participating in it are able to smoothly coordinate and communicate in times of a disaster or war.

Hence, the correct option is (B).

77. Designs in Indian embroidery are formed on the basis of the texture and the design of the fabric and the stitch. The dot and the alternate dot, the circle, the square, the triangle and permutations and combinations of these constitute the design. Kashida is of Jammu Kashmir, while Kasuti is of Karnataka. Phulkari is of Punjab.

Hence, the correct option is (C).

78. Buddhacharita was written by Ashvaghosh whereas the other three are correctly matched.

It is known from several references in the **Mrichchakatikam** that Shudraka was a South Indian and had good knowledge of Prakrit and Apabhramsa languages. He believed in the varna system and had special respect for cows and brahmins. The time of Shudraka was in the 6th century. Apart from Mrichhakatikam, he also composed Vasavadatta, Padmaprabhritaka etc.

Mudrarakshasa is a Sanskrit historical drama composed by Vishakhadatta. It was composed in the fourth century. In this, a unique analysis of the political successes of Chanakya is found on the basis of the famous accounts of Chanakya and Chandragupta Maurya.

Harshacharita is a Sanskrit text composed by Banabhatta. In this the biography of the Indian emperor Harshavardhana is described. This is the oldest Sanskrit text related to the historical story.

Hence, the correct option is (B).

79. Gandhara art also known as Greco-Buddhist art, it developed when artistic influences from Greek and Rome mixed with Buddhist traditions of Afghanistan. Under patronising of Kushan kings, Gandhara Art new heights. At the same time, a different style of art was developing at Mathura in India.

Hence, the correct option is (B).

80. The marriage of Shiva and Parvati is celebrated as Sitalsasthi, a major festival of Utkal Brahmins since ages. It was started 400 years ago in Sambalpur after the king of Sambalpur brought Utkal Srotriya Vaidika Brahmins from Brahmin sasana villages of Puri district.

Hence, the correct option is (D).

81. North Circar-Coastal plain from Odisha to Andhra Pradesh.

Malabar Coast-Coastal plain from Mangalore to Kanyakumari.

Coromandal Coast-Coastal plain from Andhra Pradesh to Tamil Nadu.

Konkan Coast-coastal plain from Gujarat to Goa.

Hence, the correct option is (C).

82. Kolkata is the nearest city to the Tropic of Cancer (23 ½° North latitude). It is located just below the Tropic of Cancer.

Hence, the correct option is (B).

83. Sankosh river forms the boundary between Assam and Arunachal Pradesh.

Sankosh is a river that rises in northern Bhutan and empties into the Brahmaputra in the state of Assam in India. In Bhutan, it is known as the Puna Tsang Chu below the confluences of several tributaries near the town of Wangdue Phodrang.

Hence, the correct option is (B).

84. The Palamau Tiger Reserve is one of the nine original tiger reserves in India and the only one in the state of Jharkhand, India. It forms part of Betla National Park and Palamau Wildlife Sanctuary.

Hence, the correct option is (B).

85. Pulitzer Prize is given in the field of Journalism.

- Oscar is given in film industry.
- Booker prize is given in the field of books.
- Sullivan award is given in the field of sports.

Hence, the correct option is (C).

86. Poet-critic & Former President of Sahitya Akademi Dr Vishwanath Prasad Tiwari has been selected for the prestigious 33rd Moortidevi Award for the year 2019 for his work 'Asti Aur Bhavati'.

Hence, the correct option is (C).

87. Jordanian dinar has been the currency of Jordan since 1950. The Jordanian dinar is also widely used alongside the Israeli shekel in the West Bank.

Hence, the correct option is (D).

88. Narendra Modi during his recent visit to Palestine has been awarded the highest civilian award of Palestine.

Prime Minister Narendra Modi was conferred the 'Grand Collar of the State of Palestine' by President Mahmoud Abbas, recognising his key contribution to promote relations between India and Palestine.

Hence, the correct option is (A).

89. Satyajit Ray received numerous awards and honours, including India's highest award in cinema, the Dadasaheb Phalke Award (1984) and India's highest civilian award, Bharat Ratna (1992) but he never got nobel price.

Rabindra nath tagore got nobel price for literature in 1913. The Nobel Prize in Physics 1930 was awarded to Sir Chandrasekhara Venkata Raman "for his work on the scattering of light and for the discovery of the effect named after him". Amartya san was

awarded the Nobel Memorial Prize in Economic Sciences in 1998 and India's Bharat Ratna in 1999 for his work in welfare economics.

Hence, the correct option is (C).

90. Nirad C. Chaudhuri wrote The book 'To Live or Not Live'. Nirad Chandra Chaudhuri was an Indian Bengali–English writer and man of letters. Bengali author and scholar who was opposed to the withdrawal of British colonial rule from the Indian subcontinent and the subsequent rejection of Western culture in independent India.

Hence, the correct option is (C).

91. 'Anandamath', the famous Bengali novel written by Bankim Chandra Chattopadhyay in 1882. The novel and film are set in the events of the Sannyasi Rebellion, which took place in the late 18th century in eastern India, especially Bengal.

Hence, the correct option is (B).

92. Hindu Land Holders. The Malabar rebellion (also known as the Moplah rebellion and Māppila Lahaḷa in Malayalam) was an armed uprising in 1921 against British authority in the Malabar region of Southern India by Mappilas and the culmination of a series of Mappila revolts that recurred throughout the 19th century and early 20th century.

Hence, the correct option is (D).

93. Durgesnandini was the first novel of Bankim Chandra Chattopadhyay, which was published in 1864. He also wrote the national song of India.

Bankim Chandra Chattopadhyay was a famous Bengali novelist, poet, prose writer and journalist. The national anthem of India 'Vande Mataram' is his own composition, which became the source of inspiration for the revolutionaries during the Indian freedom struggle.

Hence, the correct option is (B).

94. Indian air force was officially established on 8th October 1932.Golden jubilee celebrate after the completion of 50 years of existence. so In 1982 Indian Air Force celebrated its golden jubilee.

Hence, the correct option is (C).

95. An intermediate-range ballistic missile (IRBM) is a ballistic missile with a range of 3,000–5,500 km (1,864–3,418 miles), between a medium-range ballistic missile (MRBM) and an intercontinental ballistic missile (ICBM).

Hence, the correct option is (C).

96. The Prime Minister, Shri Narendra Modi dedicated the naval submarine INS Kalvari to the nation, at a function in Mumbai.INS Kalvari is described as a prime example of "Make in India." The Prime Minister said that the 21st century is described as Asia's century. He added that it is also certain that the road to development in the 21st century goes through the Indian Ocean.

Hence, the correct option is (B).

97. The Indian Navy has inked a Memorandum of Understanding (MoU) with the Cochin Port Trust (CPT) for utilizing the Port's berthing facility at Mattancherry wharf for Naval ships. As per the MoU, Cochin Port's Q2 and Q3 berths at Mattancherry wharf, totaling 228 metre quay length, would be handed over to the Indian Navy for five years for berthing their ships.

Hence, the correct option is (C).

98. The government launched Ayushman Bharat scheme last year(2019) that aims to provide medical care coverage to about 50 crore Indians. Envisioning a healthy India and taking a step towards it will have a far-reaching positive effect in the years to come on the country's healthcare delivery system.

Hence, the correct option is (D).

99. The Union Cabinet chaired by Prime Minister Shri Narendra Modi was approved the establishment of International Training Centre for Operational Oceanography, as a Category-2 Centre (C2C) of UNESCO, in Hyderabad. The purpose of this Agreement is to establish a training centre towards development of capacity for the countries on the Indian Ocean Rim (IOR), African countries bordering the Indian and Atlantic Oceans, small island countries under the framework of UNESCO.

Hence, the correct option is (B).

100. A close associate of Mahatma Gandhi who was an Indian Cotton merchant, Banker, and Congressman, was G. D. Birla.

Hence, the correct option is (C).

English

Ques (1-5):Direction: Read the passage and answer the question that follows.

The concept of 'creative society' refers to a phase of development of a society in which a large number of potential contradictions become articulate and active. This is most evident when oppressed social groups get politically mobilized and demand their rights. The upsurge of the peasants and tribals, the movements for regional autonomy and self-determination, the environmental movements, and the women's movements in the developing countries are signs of the emergence of a creative society in contemporary times. The forms of social movements and their intensity may vary from country to country and place to place within a country. But the very presence of movements for social transformation in various spheres of a society indicates the emergence of a creative society in a country.

Q.1 How do social groups justify the concept of 'creative society'?
A. By protesting
B. By demanding their rights
C. By raising issues
D. Both (B) and (C)

Q.2 How can we describe 'creative society'?
A. The phase in which a large number of potential contradictions become articulate and active.
B. The phase in which a large number of creative thoughts become articulate and active.
C. The phase in which people contradict the law.
D. Both (A) and (B)

Q.3 Which of these does not show the emergence of the creative society?
A. Rise of peasants and tribals
B. Environmental movements
C. Women's movements
D. None of these

Q.4 Social movements can occur in:
A. Various spheres of society
B. Places in the country
C. Government organizations
D. Both (A) and (B)

Q.5 Which word from the passage can substitute the phrase 'belonging to the present'?
A. Contemporary
B. Autonomy
C. Potential
D. Upsurge

Q.6 Direction: In the question, a sentence has been given in an active/passive voice. Out of the given four alternatives, suggest the one which best expresses the given sentence in passive/active voice.

An amendment in the bill was being demanded by the farmers.
A. The farmers demanded an amendment in the bill.
B. The farmers were demanding an amendment in the bill.
C. The farmers had been demanding an amendment in the bill.
D. The farmers demand an amendment in the bill.

Q.7 Direction: In the question, a sentence has been given in an active/passive voice. Out of the given four alternatives, suggest the one which best expresses the given sentence in passive/active voice.

John has placed an order for a piano.
A. An order for a piano has been placed by John.
B. A piano is being ordered by John.
C. An order for a piano had been placed by John.
D. John was placing the order for a piano.

Q.8 Direction: Select the correct direct form of the given sentence.

She asked me how much I had paid for the mangoes.
A. She said to me, "How much did you pay for the mangoes?"
B. She said to me, "How much I paid for the mangoes?"
C. She said to me, "How I paid for the mangoes?"
D. She said to me, "How much did I pay for the mangoes?"

Q.9 Directions: Select the correct indirect form of the given sentence.

The traveler inquired, "Will there be a shelter for strangers?"
A. The traveler inquired if would there be a shelter for strangers.
B. The traveler inquired if there will be a shelter for strangers.
C. The traveler inquired if there would be a shelter for strangers.
D. The traveler inquired whether will there be a shelter for strangers.

Q.10 Choose the correct punctuated sentence.
A. The words, The Prohibited Area, made me return from there.
B. The words, 'The Prohibited Area', made me return from there.
C. The words "The Prohibited Area, made me return from there".
D. The words, "The Prohibited Area", made me return from there.

Q.11 Direction: Fill in the blank with the correct preposition.
Lady Sri Ram college is affiliated _____ the Delhi University.
A. to
B. from
C. with
D. None of the above

Q.12 Direction: Fill in the blank with the correct preposition.
You are requested to fill the form _____ black ink.

A. with   **B.** in   **C.** within   **D.** under

Q.13 Direction: Fill in the blank with the most appropriate pronoun.

The man _____ book you are reading is my father.

A. who   **B.** whose   **C.** whom   **D.** that

Q.14 Direction: Fill in the blank with a suitable pronoun.

My son and my daughter are very fond of _____.

A. herself   **B.** each other

C. themselves   **D.** himself

Q.15 Direction: Fill in the blank with the correct form of Verbs / Tense.

Raman saw that the clock _______.

A. stop   **B.** will stop

C. have been stopped   **D.** had stopped

Q.16 Direction: Choose the correct form of Verbs / Tense for the given sentence.

Man _____ how to reach the most distant planets.

A. hasn't knew   **B.** do not know

C. didn't knew   **D.** does not know

Q.17 Direction: Choose the correct form of Verbs / Tense for the given sentence.

She generally ________ her breakfast at 7 a.m.

A. takes   **B.** took

C. has taken   **D.** is taking

Q.18 Direction: In the following question, out of the four alternatives, select the alternative which will improve the underlined part of the sentence. In case No correction is needed, select "No correction required".

I saw him in the park <u>last Monday</u>.

A. on last Monday

B. at last Monday

C. on the last Monday

D. No correction required

Q.19 Direction: Select the most appropriate synonym of the given word.

Deference

A. Compliance   **B.** Dishonor

C. Disregard   **D.** Complication

Q.20 Direction: Choose the antonym of the given word.

Repulsive

A. Abhorrent   **B.** Attractive

C. Intolerant   **D.** Offensive

Q.21 Direction: Select the most appropriate synonym of the given word.

Altruist

A. Philanthropist   **B.** Impressionist

C. Nutritionist   **D.** Individualist

Q.22 From the given four options choose the correct sentence.

A. Have you ever watched a film in English?

B. Were John reading the book last night?

C. How long have you being waiting for me?

D. What is you doing here?

Q.23 Direction: Fill in the blank with an appropriate article.

I'm afraid of _____ dogs.

A. A   **B.** An

C. The   **D.** No article

Q.24 Direction: Fill in the blank by selecting the appropriate phrasal verb from the given options.

Have you any idea which son of his will ______ when he retires?

A. take up   **B.** take along

C. take over   **D.** take in

Q.25 Direction: Fill in the blank by selecting the appropriate phrasal verb from the given options.

He is _______ the trees with an electric saw.

A. cutting down   **B.** carrying on

C. bringing up   **D.** putting down

Science

Q.26 A certain capacitor of plate area A is separated by a distance d. If the separation distance is reduced to $\frac{d}{3}$ then the ratio of capacitance before and after is:

A. $1:2$ **B.** $3:2$ **C.** $1:\sqrt{2}$ **D.** $1:3$

Q.27 The SI unit of electric field intensity is-

A. C **B.** $C.m$ **C.** V **D.** $\frac{V}{m}$

Q.28 The frequency of AC in India is:

A. 50 Hz   **B.** 60 Hz   **C.** 220 Hz   **D.** 110 Hz

Q.29 Upon catching a ball, a cricket fielder swings his hands backwards. The concept behind this is explained by:

A. Newton's first law of motion

B. Newton's second law of motion

C. Newton's third law of motion

D. The law of inertia

Q.30 Two thin lenses of focal lengths f_1 and f_2 are in contact and coaxial. The power of the combination is -

A. $\frac{f_1+f_2}{2}$ **B.** $\frac{f_1+f_2}{f_1 f_2}$ **C.** $\sqrt{\frac{f_1}{f_2}}$ **D.** $\sqrt{\frac{f_2}{f_1}}$

Q.31 Kilo-Watt-Hour is the unit of-

A. Electric power   **B.** Energy

C. Impulse   **D.** Rate of Power

Q.32 The intensity and frequency of the incident light is increased by two times. Then which of the following statement is true?

A. Photoelectric current will be increased by two times.

B. Photoelectric current will be decreased by four times.

C. Photoelectric current remains the same.

D. Photoelectric current increases and then decreases.

Q.33 A lens has focal length $+20cm$. Its power will be:

A. $\frac{1}{20}$ dioptre   **B.** $\frac{1}{500}$ dioptre

C. $\frac{1}{5}$ dioptre   **D.** 5 dioptre

Q.34 Water is flowing inside a tube of a uniform radius ratio of radius of entry and exit terminals of the tube is $3:2$. Then the ratio of velocities at entry and exit terminals will be:

A. $4:9$ **B.** $9:4$ **C.** $8:27$ **D.** $1:1$

Q.35 The restriction on application of Bernoulli theorem is that the fluids _________.

A. should have high viscosity
B. be of unit density
C. must be incompressible
D. be at atmospheric pressure

Q.36 Work done by a simple pendulum in one complete oscillation is:

A. Zero   **B.** $2\pi\sqrt{\frac{l}{g}}$

C. Infinity   **D.** None of these

Q.37 The wave having compression and rarefaction is known as:

A. Transverse wave   **B.** Longitudinal wave
C. Light wave   **D.** Ultraviolet rays

Q.38 The rate of heat transfer in a conducting rod will increase by-

A. Decreasing temperature difference across ends
B. Decreasing the cross sectional area of the rod
C. Increasing the length of the rod
D. Decreasing the length of the rod

Q.39 The internal energy change for a system is + 20 Cal and the work done is – 200 Cal. Find the heat exchanged between the system and the surrounding.

A. 220 Cal   **B.** - 220 Cal
C. - 180 Cal   **D.** + 180 Cal

Q.40 The surface of a spherical shell is uniformly charged. Then what is the electric field inside the spherical shell?

A. Zero
B. Constant
C. Infinite
D. Proportional to the distance from the center

Q.41 The number of turns in the secondary coil and primary coil of a transformer are 200 and 500 respectively. If the electric current in the primary coil is $48\ A$ then find the current in the secondary coil.

A. $148\ A$ **B.** $130\ A$ **C.** $120\ A$ **D.** $100\ A$

Q.42 The magnetic field strength associated with a current-carrying solenoid is:

A. Uniform along the length of the solenoid
B. Magnetic field outside the solenoid is zero
C. Increased if the number of loops of coil is increased
D. All of the above

Q.43 Which one among the following waves are called waves of heat energy?

A. Radio waves   **B.** Infrared waves
C. Ultraviolet waves   **D.** Microwaves

Q.44 Light wavelength in air is $6000 \overset{\circ}{A}$ and refractive index of glass is 1.5, the wavelength of same light entering glass is:

A. $12000 \overset{\circ}{A}$ **B.** $4000 \overset{\circ}{A}$ **C.** $9000 \overset{\circ}{A}$ **D.** $6000 \overset{\circ}{A}$

Q.45 The number of neutrons in an atom is equal to the:

A. Mass number - atomic number
B. Atomic number
C. Number of electrons
D. Mass number

Q.46 Which of the following is true for Alkanes?

A. Alkanes are saturated hydrocarbon.
B. The general formula of alkanes is C_nH_{2n+2}.
C. Methane is an example of an Alkane.
D. All of the above

Q.47 The molecular formula of Propane is _______.

A. CH_4 **B.** C_4H_{10} **C.** C_3H_8 **D.** C_2H_6

Q.48 What is the height at which acceleration due to gravity becomes $\frac{1}{4}^{th}$ the acceleration due to gravity on the surface of the earth in terms of $'R'$, the radius of the earth?

A. $3R$ **B.** $\frac{R}{3}$ **C.** $2R$ **D.** R

Q.49 What would be the acceleration due to gravity (in m/s^2) of a planet of radius $6000\ km$ if escape velocity from it is $12\ km/s$?

A. 14 **B.** 9 **C.** 12 **D.** 6

Q.50 A computer cannot "boot" if it does not have the _____.

A. Compiler   **B.** Loader
C. Operating system   **D.** Assembler

Mathematics

Q.51 Find the maximum and minimum value of $17\sin\theta + 5\cos\theta$.

A. $\sqrt{314}, \sqrt{264}$ **B.** $\sqrt{314}, -\sqrt{314}$
C. $-\sqrt{314}, \sqrt{314}$ **D.** $\sqrt{23}, \sqrt{12}$

Q.52 $\sec^4\theta - \sec^2\theta$ is equal to:

A. $\tan^2\theta - \tan^4\theta$ **B.** $\tan^2\theta + \tan^4\theta$
C. $\cos^4\theta - \cos^2\theta$ **D.** $\cos^2\theta - \cos^4\theta$

Q.53 A bag contains 5 red, 8 black balls and 7 blue balls. A ball is drawn at random from the bag. Find the probability that the ball is drawn is not red.

A. $\frac{1}{5}$ **B.** $\frac{3}{5}$ **C.** $\frac{3}{4}$ **D.** $\frac{4}{5}$

Q.54 If $\frac{56}{54}P_{r+3} = 30800:1$, Find r.

A. 40 **B.** 41 **C.** 42 **D.** 43

Q.55 n (A) = 50, n (B) = 20 and n (A∩B) = 10, then n [(A - B) ∪ (B - A)] is:

A. 40   **B.** 50   **C.** 60   **D.** 70

Q.56 What is the value of $\left[(i)^{25} + \left(\frac{1}{i}\right)^{27}\right]^2$, where $i = \sqrt{-1}$?

A. 2   **B.** $\frac{1}{i}$ **C.** $-i$ **D.** -4

Q.57 If α, β are the roots of the equation $x^2 + 6x + 4 = 0$, then what is $\frac{\alpha^4 + \beta^4}{\alpha^{-4} + \beta^{-4}}$ equal to ?

A. 1024   **B.** 256   **C.** 64   **D.** 16

Q.58 If the sum of n numbers in the GP $4, 8, 16, \ldots$ is 2044 then n is:

A. 6   **B.** 7   **C.** 8   **D.** 9

Q.59 If x, y, z are three consecutive positive integers, then $\log(1 + xz)$ is:

A. $\log y$ **B.** $\log\frac{y}{2}$ **C.** $\log(2y)$ **D.** $2\log(y)$

Q.60 Find the value of $\log_6\sqrt{2} + \log_6\sqrt{3}$.

A. $\frac{1}{2}$ **B.** $\frac{1}{4}$ **C.** 1   **D.** 2

Q.61 What is the value of λ for which the vectors $2\hat{\imath} - 5\hat{\jmath} - \hat{k}$ and $-\hat{\imath} + 4\hat{\jmath} + \lambda\hat{k}$ are perpendicular?

A. 21   **B.** -18 **C.** -22 **D.** 22

Q.62 What is the value of m if the vectors $2\hat{\imath} - \hat{\jmath} + \hat{k}, \hat{\imath} + 2\hat{\jmath} - 3\hat{k}$ and $3\hat{\imath} + m\hat{\jmath} + 5\hat{k}$ are coplanar?

A. -2 **B.** 2   **C.** -4 **D.** 4

Q.63 If $A = \begin{bmatrix} -1 & 4 \\ 5 & 8 \end{bmatrix}$, then trace of matrix A is:

A. 6   **B.** 7   **C.** 8   **D.** 9

Q.64 What is the value of the determinant $\begin{vmatrix} i & i^2 & i^3 \\ i^4 & i^6 & i^8 \\ i^9 & i^{12} & i^{15} \end{vmatrix}$ where $i = \sqrt{-1}$?

A. 0   **B.** -2 **C.** $4i$ **D.** $-4i$

Q.65 If the direction cosines of a line are $\left(\frac{1}{k}, \frac{2}{k}, \frac{-2}{k}\right)$ then k is:

A. $\pm\left(\frac{1}{\sqrt{3}}\right)$ **B.** $\frac{1}{3}$ **C.** $\pm\sqrt{3}$ **D.** 3

Q.66 Find the radius of the circle which passes through the points $(1,2)$ and $(3,4)$ and the centre lies on the straight line $y - 3x + 2 = 0$.

A. 3   **B.** $\sqrt{3}$ **C.** 5   **D.** $3\sqrt{2}$

Q.67 $\lim\limits_{x \to 0} \dfrac{\sqrt{\left(\frac{1}{2}(1 - \cos 2x)\right)}}{x}$ is equal to:

A. 1   **B.** -1

C. 0   **D.** None of these

Q.68 What is the arithmetic mean of first 16 natural numbers with weights being the number itself?

A. $\frac{17}{2}$ **B.** $\frac{33}{2}$ **C.** 11   **D.** $\frac{187}{2}$

Q.69 The perpendicular distance between the straight lines $6x + 8y + 15 = 0$ and $3x + 4y + 9 = 0$ is:

A. $\frac{3}{2}$ **B.** $\frac{3}{10}$ **C.** $\frac{3}{4}$ **D.** $\frac{2}{7}$

Q.70 What is $\int_0^1 \dfrac{e^{\tan^{-1}x}dx}{1+x^2}$ equal to?

A. $e^{\frac{\pi}{4}} - 1$ **B.** $e^{\frac{\pi}{4}} + 1$ **C.** $e - 1$ **D.** e

Q.71 $\int \dfrac{(\log x)^2}{x} dx$ is equal to?

A. $\frac{(\log x)^2}{2} + c$ **B.** $\frac{(\log x)^3}{x} + c$

C. $\frac{(\log x)^3}{3} + c$ **D.** None of the above

Q.72 The sum of the focal distance of a point on the ellipse $\dfrac{x^2}{4} + \dfrac{y^2}{9} = 1$ is:

A. 4 units   **B.** 6 units   **C.** 8 units   **D.** 10 units

Q.73 The length of latus rectum of the ellipse $3x^2 + y^2 - 12x + 2y + 1 = 0$ is:

A. $2\sqrt{3}$ **B.** 12   **C.** $\frac{4}{\sqrt{3}}$ **D.** $\frac{3}{\sqrt{2}}$

Q.74 The length of the latus rectum of the parabola $y^2 - 8x + 6y + 1 = 0$ is:

A. 4   **B.** 8   **C.** 12   **D.** 2

Q.75 The arithmetic mean of 9 observations is 100 and that of 6 is 80, the combined mean of all the 15 observations will be:

A. 100   **B.** 80   **C.** 90   **D.** 92

General Awareness

Q.76 What was the theme of International Girls in ICT Day 2022 which is observed annually on the fourth Thursday in April?

A. Access and safety

B. Inspiring the Next Generation

C. Case For Change, Connected Women, IoT and Tech4Girls

D. Powering Change: Women in Innovation and Creativity

Q.77 Which medal did Devendra Jhajharia win in World Para Athletics Grand Prix 2022?

A. Gold   **B.** Silver

C. Bronze   **D.** None of the above

Q.78 Which was the last battle of Ashoka?

A. Battle of Plassey   **B.** Battle of Kalinga

C. Battle of Calicut   **D.** Battle of Panipat

Q.79 In which year was the Harappan civilization first discovered?

A. 1905   **B.** 1921   **C.** 1926   **D.** 1932

Q.80 Pin Valley National Park is located in which state of India?
A. Himachal Pradesh   **B.** Jammu & Kashmir
C. Punjab   **D.** Gujarat

Q.81 On which river is the Bhakra Nangal Dam situated?
A. Sutlej   **B.** Ghaggar   **C.** Ravi   **D.** Chenab

Q.82 The main crop of Uttar Pradesh is _____.
A. Maize   **B.** Rice
C. Wheat   **D.** None of these

Q.83 The Hornbill Festival is one of the important festivals celebrated in _______.
A. Arunachal Pradesh   **B.** Nagaland
C. Mizoram   **D.** Meghalaya

Q.84 'Ottamthullal' is a dance associated with the state of:
A. Kerala   **B.** Tamil Nadu
C. Andhra Pradesh   **D.** Manipur

Q.85 Hindi written in _____ script is the official language of India.
A. Pali   **B.** Sanskrit
C. Dogri   **D.** Devanagari

Q.86 _______ is the capital of South Africa.
A. London   **B.** New York
C. Moscow   **D.** Cape Town

Q.87 Manat is the currency of which country?
A. Azerbaijan   **B.** Armenia
C. Albania   **D.** Andorra

Q.88 Which among the following books was written by Barack Obama?
A. What happened
B. The audacity of hope
C. Hard Choices
D. Living History

Q.89 The book 'Wings of Fire' is authored by:
A. Salman Rushdie   **B.** A.P.J. Abdul Kalam
C. R.K. Narayan   **D.** Vikram Seth

Q.90 Who won the Booker Prize 2020 for Shuggie Bain?
A. Douglas Stuart   **B.** Margaret Busby
C. Margaret Atwood   **D.** Bernardine Evaristo

Q.91 Who among the following discovered electromagnetic induction?
A. Joule   **B.** Faraday   **C.** Ohm   **D.** Kepler

Q.92 Which scientist discovered the radioactive element, radium?

[UPTET Science and Maths, 2018]

A. Albert Einstein   **B.** Benjamin Franklin
C. Isaac Newton   **D.** Marie Curie

Q.93 Direction: Which will come in place of the X in the below table?

7	3	6
5	4	7
8	X	2

A. 9   **B.** 6   **C.** 5   **D.** 3

Q.94 Direction: Which will come in place of the question mark in the below table?

A	D	G
D	?	N
I	P	W

A. I   **B.** H   **C.** J   **D.** O

Q.95 If in a certain code language, ROUTINE is written as TLYOOGM, then how is "TICKET" written in that code language?
A. VFGFKM   **B.** VGFFKM
C. VFGKFM   **D.** VFGFKN

Q.96 If in a code 'SUBHAM' is written as 'TVCIBN' then 'SATYAM' will be written as–
A. TBVZBN   **B.** TBUBZN
C. TBUZBM   **D.** TBUZBN

Q.97 Direction: From the given alternatives, select the word which cannot be formed using the letters of the given word.
FORENSIC
A. SENIOR   **B.** FERNS
C. SINCE   **D.** CROWN

Q.98 Where is the Headquarters of the International Cricket Council located?
A. Melbourne   **B.** Dubai
C. New Delhi   **D.** London

Q.99 With which of the following sports is Manika Batra associated?
A. Cricket   **B.** Table Tennis
C. Badminton   **D.** Gymnastics

Q.100 What is the full form of "PSLV"?
A. Polarised Source Laser Viewing
B. Polar Survey Landing Vehicle
C. Polar Satellite Launch Vehicle
D. Precise Source Locating Vision

// Smart Answer Sheet //

Correct — Percentage of students who answered correctly. **Skipped** — Percentage of students who skipped.

Q.	Ans.	Correct / Skipped	Q.	Ans.	Correct / Skipped	Q.	Ans.	Correct / Skipped	.Q.	Ans.	Correct / Skipped	Q.	Ans.	Correct / Skipped	Q.	Ans.	Correct / Skipped
1	B	79.1 % / 15.83 %	18	D	76.85 % / 18.43 %	35	C	59.55 % / 31.43 %	52	B	63.0 % / 31.83 %	69	B	41.38 % / 42.6 %	86	D	85.99 % / 13.37 %
2	A	85.03 % / 12.45 %	19	A	76.5 % / 20.24 %	36	A	81.01 % / 10.76 %	53	C	85.2 % / 13.67 %	70	A	57.2 % / 38.43 %	87	A	49.67 % / 49.81 %
3	D	76.42 % / 10.35 %	20	B	86.61 % / 12.88 %	37	B	54.05 % / 45.25 %	54	B	89.05 % / 10.88 %	71	C	78.57 % / 19.18 %	88	B	76.12 % / 17.66 %
4	D	86.4 % / 11.91 %	21	A	78.68 % / 18.71 %	38	D	89.05 % / 10.46 %	55	B	86.17 % / 11.34 %	72	B	78.0 % / 16.1 %	89	B	63.87 % / 30.47 %
5	A	86.51 % / 13.15 %	22	A	51.17 % / 41.91 %	39	C	77.74 % / 18.92 %	56	D	48.63 % / 34.59 %	73	C	78.19 % / 16.96 %	90	A	67.45 % / 31.76 %
6	B	85.39 % / 11.12 %	23	D	76.79 % / 23.01 %	40	A	65.39 % / 32.57 %	57	B	85.36 % / 13.05 %	74	B	50.72 % / 43.54 %	91	B	49.41 % / 50.09 %
7	A	76.54 % / 21.04 %	24	C	47.75 % / 30.29 %	41	C	58.63 % / 37.87 %	58	D	43.0 % / 31.42 %	75	D	79.6 % / 10.08 %	92	D	82.67 % / 16.61 %
8	A	86.18 % / 12.29 %	25	A	79.94 % / 19.54 %	42	D	58.57 % / 37.18 %	59	D	85.42 % / 10.59 %	76	A	85.76 % / 13.17 %	93	B	87.71 % / 10.72 %
9	C	83.0 % / 15.33 %	26	D	76.95 % / 19.09 %	43	B	77.51 % / 21.63 %	60	A	56.88 % / 38.15 %	77	B	87.38 % / 10.01 %	94	A	41.5 % / 51.66 %
10	D	78.23 % / 19.29 %	27	D	80.48 % / 17.76 %	44	B	46.96 % / 38.05 %	61	C	82.57 % / 11.18 %	78	B	83.85 % / 14.0 %	95	A	89.35 % / 10.38 %
11	A	76.36 % / 14.92 %	28	A	56.72 % / 37.4 %	45	A	88.9 % / 10.64 %	62	C	77.55 % / 18.54 %	79	B	77.54 % / 20.78 %	96	D	77.91 % / 21.28 %
12	B	82.86 % / 11.7 %	29	B	86.04 % / 12.78 %	46	D	82.94 % / 12.83 %	63	B	89.44 % / 10.07 %	80	A	77.05 % / 14.02 %	97	D	86.39 % / 12.97 %
13	B	83.84 % / 10.12 %	30	B	85.57 % / 13.17 %	47	C	76.52 % / 17.9 %	64	D	87.52 % / 10.36 %	81	A	87.42 % / 12.45 %	98	B	82.7 % / 11.6 %
14	B	85.27 % / 14.54 %	31	B	88.33 % / 10.05 %	48	D	79.17 % / 18.97 %	65	D	88.98 % / 10.59 %	82	B	47.45 % / 41.78 %	99	B	55.36 % / 38.26 %
15	D	77.64 % / 12.32 %	32	A	82.34 % / 11.43 %	49	C	77.89 % / 12.95 %	66	A	43.99 % / 43.78 %	83	B	88.97 % / 10.65 %	100	C	83.86 % / 12.58 %
16	D	88.17 % / 11.45 %	33	D	88.35 % / 11.62 %	50	C	82.8 % / 12.47 %	67	D	83.19 % / 14.5 %	84	A	58.54 % / 32.89 %			
17	A	76.72 % / 20.25 %	34	A	68.1 % / 31.34 %	51	B	89.9 % / 10.06 %	68	C	79.62 % / 15.52 %	85	D	87.91 % / 11.05 %			

//Hints and Solutions//

1. According to the passage, "This is most evident when oppressed social groups get politically mobilized and demand their rights." Here 'this' means the concept of a 'creative society'.

Hence, the correct option is (B).

2. According to the passage, "The concept of 'creative society' refers to a phase of development of a society in which a large number of potential contradictions become articulate and active."

Hence, the correct option is (A).

3. According to the passage, "The upsurge of the peasants and tribals, the movements for regional autonomy and self-determination, the environmental movements, and the women's movements in the developing countries are signs of the emergence of a creative society in contemporary times."

Hence, the correct option is (D).

4. According to the passage, "The forms of social movements and their intensity may vary from country to country and place to place within a country. But the very presence of movements for social transformation in various spheres of a society indicates the emergence of a creative society in a country." There is no mention of government organizations.

Hence, the correct option is (D).

5. Contemporary means belonging to the present.

For example - There are so many problems in our contemporary society.

Autonomy means the right or condition of self-government.

Potential means having or showing the capacity to develop into something in the future.

Upsurge means an upward surge in the strength or quantity of something; an increase.

Hence, the correct option is (A).

6. The farmers were demanding an amendment in the bill.

While changing a sentence from passive form to active form we need to follow these instructions:

- Find the subject and object of the sentence and exchange their places; make changes in their cases as well if subject and object are pronouns.
- Use of 'was + being' indicates that the active form will be in the past continuous tense.
- Use 'was/were + V1+ing' according to the subject of the sentence.
- At last line up the remaining part.

Hence, the correct option is (B).

7. An order for a piano has been placed by John.

- In an active voice, a sentence emphasizes the subject, performing an action.
- In passive voice, a sentence emphasizes the action or the object of the sentence.
- The given sentence is in the active voice with present perfect tense and John is the subject and an order for a piano is the object.
- When we convert this sentence into passive voice, the subject 'John' becomes the object, and the object 'an order for piano' becomes the subject.
- The preposition 'by' is used before the subject 'John'.
- Always 3rd form of the main verb is used.
- Structure of passive present perfect: Object+ has/have+been+V3+by+Subject.

Hence, the correct option is (A).

8. She said to me, "How much did you pay for the mangoes?"

The given sentence is in Indirect Speech. As per the question we have to change it into Direct Speech.

The process of transformation is as follows:

- 'asked' will be changed into 'said to'.
- Comma and inverted commas will be added.
- The given sentence is an example of an interrogative sentence with a question word.
- 'How' will be used as a conjunction because we know that in an interrogative sentence with a question word the question word itself is used as a conjunction.
- 'I' will be changed into 'you'.
- 'Had paid' will be changed into 'did pay'. (indirect to direct speech)

Hence, the correct option is (A).

9. The traveler inquired if there would be a shelter for strangers.

The given sentence is a direct speech.

The basic rules for changing or converting direct speech into indirect speech:

- The commas and inverted commas are removed and the 'question mark' is replaced by 'full stop' and 'if' is included.
- The present simple tense format 'Subject + V1 (will) + Object' will be changed into the past simple tense format 'Subject + V2 (would) + Object'.

Hence, the correct option is (C).

10. The words, "The Prohibited Area", made me return from there.

- This sentence shows the importance of a written instruction which is very important to abide by.
- To show the importance of a particular thing, we put that inside double inverted comma if it contains more than one word.
- Here in the given sentence, we have an important instruction to follow.

- Therefore, we need to put that under an inverted comma.

Hence, the correct option is (D).

11. Lady Sri Ram college is affiliated to the Delhi University.

When we talk about a University or Board, we use affiliated to.

For example - They are national associations affiliated to larger organizations.

When you join a cause, you become affiliated with it and what it represents.

For example - I was not, however, affiliated with Outside Online in any capacity.

Considering the meaning of the sentence, as a University (Delhi University) is mentioned, we can use 'to' with 'affiliated.'

Hence, the correct option is (A).

12. You are requested to fill the form in black ink.

The preposition 'in' is used to show the language, material, etc., used.

For example - The student was writing in pencil.

For example - Please speak in English.

On the other hand, if we want to refer to the instrument used, we use the preposition 'with'.

For example - You should sign the papers with a blue pen.

In the given sentence, 'black ink' is a material, so, 'in' should be used.

Hence, the correct option is (B).

13. The man whose book you are reading is my father.

- The pronoun 'whose' is used to indicate that the following noun belongs to or is associated with the person or thing mentioned in the previous clause.

- The pronoun 'who' is used to introduce a clause giving further information about a person or people previously mentioned.

- The pronoun 'whom' is used to refer to the object of a verb or preposition.

- The pronoun 'that' is used to identify a specific person or thing observed or heard by the speaker.

Hence, the correct option is (B).

14. "My son and my daughter are very fond of each other."

- Since two people are being talked about in the sentence, option (A) and option (D) aren't correct.

- The pronoun 'each other' is used for two people whereas 'themselves' is used for more than two people.

Hence, the correct option is (B).

15. Raman saw that the clock had stopped.

If two actions take place in the past in succession, the structure is given below:

1st action - Past perfect tense i.e. Sub + had + V3 + Obj.

2nd action - Simple past tense i.e. Sub+ V2 + Obj.

For example - The patient had passed away before the surgeon arrived.

In the blank part of the given question, 'had stopped.' will be used as it is the 1st action in the given sentence.

Hence, the correct option is (D).

16. Man does not know how to reach the most distant planets.

Here, 'Man' is a singular noun so 'does' must be used. So, 'does not know' is the correct answer. The sentence is in the present tense because it talks about a fact that still applies. Perhaps in the future, we will be able to reach distant planets, and it will not be a fact anymore.

'hasn't knew' is wrong because 'knew' is the past tense of the verb 'know'. With 'has/have/had' we use the past perfect tense of the verb. So, 'known' would be correct.

'do not know' is in the present tense. 'Do' is used with plural nouns or with 'you/we/they'.

'didn't knew' is in the past tense but 'knew' is wrong because with 'did', verbs must in their base forms.

Hence, the correct option is (D).

17. She generally takes her breakfast at 7 a.m.

- The word 'generally' is used in the sentence. It shows that the sentence is in the Present Indefinite Tense.

- Structure of sentence with Present Indefinite Tense: Subject + V1 +s/es + Object

- So takes is the correct verb that will be used in the sentence.

Hence, the correct option is (A).

18. I saw him in the park last Monday.

- The given sentence says that somebody was seen in the park last Monday.

- When we use phrases beginning with this, that, next and last, we do not use any preposition before such phrases.

- On last Monday, at last Monday, and on the last Monday are grammatically incorrect because all these have the phrase last Monday which cannot be preceded with a preposition.

- But, in these expressions, the prepositions on and at are used which is inappropriate.

Hence, the correct option is (D).

19. Deference means respect and politeness.

For example - He treats her with such deference.

Compliance means the act of obeying an order, rule, or request.

For example - It is the job of the inspectors to enforce compliance with the regulations.

The most appropriate synonym of the given word 'Deference' is 'Compliance'.

Dishonor means a feeling of embarrassment and loss of people's respect or a situation in which you experience this.

Disregard means the fact of showing no care or respect for something.

Complication means something that makes a situation more difficult or the act of doing this.

Hence, the correct option is (A).

20. Repulsive means arousing intense distaste or disgust.

Attractive means pleasing or appealing to the senses.

Abhorrent means inspiring disgust and loathing; repugnant.

Intolerant means not tolerant of views, beliefs, or behavior that differ from one's own.

Offensive means causing someone to feel resentful, upset, or annoyed.

From the given options, we can say that the word 'Attractive' is the opposite in meaning.

Hence, the correct option is (B).

21. Altruist means a person who cares about others and helps them despite not gaining anything by doing this, altruists have a strong desire to help other people.

For example - She was an altruist and idealist.

Philanthropist means a person who seeks to promote the welfare of others, especially by the generous donation of money to good causes.

Therefore from the given meanings, we find that Altruist and Philanthropist are synonyms.

Impressionist means a painter, writer, or composer who is an exponent of impressionism

Nutritionist means a person who studies or is an expert in nutrition

Individualist means a person who is independent and self-reliant

Hence, the correct option is (A).

22. Have you ever watched a film in English?

The sentence is in 'Present Perfect Tense'.

Present Perfect Tense is used to express an event that started in the past and the impact of the event is now continuing (or a long-running event that started in the past and is still going on).

This tense is used to express actions completed in the recent past.

The present perfect tense in interrogative form has this structure: Have + Subject (I, You, We, You, They) + V3 (third form of main verb – past participle)

For example: Have they known about you?

The structure of the sentence in the first option is proper.

Hence, the correct option is (A).

23. No article is used before plural countable nouns used in a general sense as 'dogs' in the given sentence.

So, "I'm afraid of dogs" is the correct sentence.

Hence, the correct option is (D).

24. The context refers to assuming the role that the father played after his retirement. "To take over" in option (C) means to gain control of something. Here, it refers to gaining control of the father's position in the business. Thus, this is correct.

"To take up" is to start a new hobby.

"To take along" is to bring someone or something on location.

"To take in" is to give shelter to someone.

Hence, the correct option is (C).

25. He is cutting down the trees with an electric saw.

'Cutting down' means 'to reduce the amount/level of something'. In the given sentence, the context is that the trees are being cut with an electric saw. Therefore, the suitable phrasal verb is - 'cutting down'.

'Carrying on' means 'to continue doing something'.

'Bringing up' means 'to take care of the growth of something'.

'Putting down' means 'to criticize something'.

None of these are suitable as per the meaning of the given sentence.

Hence, the correct option is (A).

26. As we know,

The capacitance of a parallel plate capacitor is given by $C = \dfrac{kA\epsilon_0}{d}$.

Given,

Plate area $= A$

Separation distance $= d$

The new separation distance, $d' = \dfrac{d}{3}$

Before: $C = \dfrac{kA\epsilon_0}{d}$

After: $C' = \dfrac{kA\epsilon_0}{d'} = \dfrac{kA\epsilon_0}{\frac{d}{3}} = 3\dfrac{kA\epsilon_0}{d} = 3C$

Ratio $= \dfrac{C}{C'} = \dfrac{C}{3C} = \dfrac{1}{3}$

Hence, the correct option is (D).

27. As we know,

$$E = \dfrac{V}{r}$$

Where,

$E =$ electric field

V = electric potential

r = distance

The SI unit of $E = \dfrac{\text{SI unit of V}}{\text{SI unit of r}} = \dfrac{Volt}{meter} = \dfrac{V}{m}$

So, the SI unit of the electric field $(E) = \dfrac{V}{m}$

Hence, the correct option is (D).

28. As per Indian standard for domestic power supply we use AC current, which is also known as alternating current since they change its polarity at a certain interval of time. Now the two principal properties of the AC electric power supply are Voltage and frequency and we use 220 V and 50 Hz power supply for our common domestic use. Where 220 V is the potential difference and 50 Hz is its frequency.

Hence, the correct option is (A).

29. Upon catching the ball, the velocity of the ball is suddenly forced to become zero and stop moving. Due to momentum, the impact it will have on the hands of the fielder will be very high and can hurt his hands. On swinging his hands backwards, he increases the time in which the velocity of the ball will become zero. This decreases the rate of change of momentum and thus reduces the force acting on the fielder's hand. This avoids the chances of hurting hands. The relation between the rate of change of momentum and force applied is explained using Newton's second law of motion.

Hence, the correct option is (B).

30. Given,

Focal length of lens $1 = f_1$

Therefore, power of lens $1\ (P_1) = \dfrac{1}{f_1}$

Focal length of lens $2 = f_2$

Therefore, the power of lens $2\ (P_2) = \dfrac{1}{f_2}$

Power of the combination of lens $= P_1 + P_2 = \dfrac{1}{f_1} + \dfrac{1}{f_2} = \dfrac{f_1+f_2}{f_1 f_2}$

So, the power of the combination of lens is $\dfrac{f_1+f_2}{f_1 f_2}$.

Hence, the correct option is (B).

31. The commercial unit of electrical energy is a kilowatt-hour (kWh). The commercial unit of electric energy is the kilowatt or the Board of Trade (B.O.T) unit. One kilowatt-hour is defined as the electric energy consumed by the appliance of 1 kilowatt in one hour and it is also called one unit of energy.

Hence, the correct option is (B).

32. The intensity of light refers to the amount of photon energy per unit area. So, the greater the intensity of light more will be the number of photons, and as a result, more will be the number of ejected electrons. More electrons constitute more photocurrent. If the intensity is increased by two times, the photocurrent also increases by two times. The photocurrent is independent of the frequency of incident light.

Therefore, the photoelectric current will be increased by two times if the intensity and frequency of the incident light are increased by two times.

Hence, the correct option is (A).

33. Given,

$f = 20cm = 0.2m$

The power of the lens is written as

$P = \dfrac{1}{f(m)}$

$\Rightarrow P = \dfrac{1}{0.2}$

$\Rightarrow P = 5$ dioptre

Hence, the correct option is (D).

34. Given,

$\dfrac{r_1}{r_2} = \dfrac{3}{2}$

By equation of continuity:

$Q = A_1 v_1 = A_2 v_2$

Where v_1 = velocity at entry and v_2 = velocity at exit

$\Rightarrow \dfrac{v_1}{v_2} = \dfrac{A_2}{A_1}$

$\Rightarrow \dfrac{v_1}{v_2} = \dfrac{\pi r_2^2}{\pi r_1^2}$

$\Rightarrow \dfrac{v_1}{v_2} = \dfrac{2^2}{3^2}$

$\Rightarrow \dfrac{v_1}{v_2} = \dfrac{4}{9}$

Hence, the correct option is (A).

35. Bernoulli's principle states that the sum of pressure energy, kinetic energy, and potential energy per unit volume of an incompressible, non- viscous fluid in a streamlined irrotational flow remains constant along a streamline. This means that in steady flow the sum of all forms of mechanical energy in a fluid along a streamline is the same at all points on that streamline.

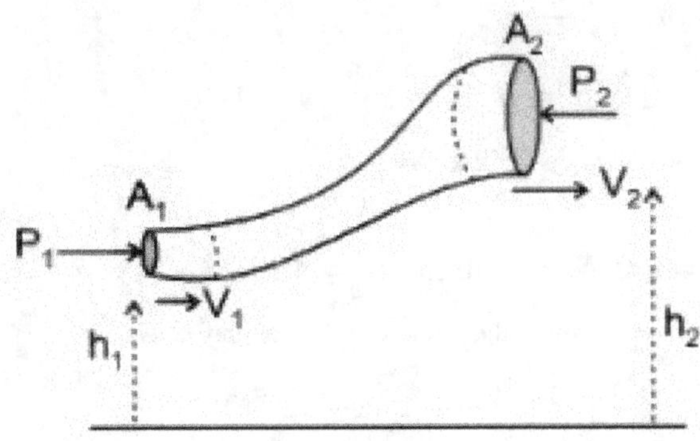

$P + \dfrac{1}{2}\rho V^2 + \rho g h = A$ constant

From above it is clear that, the restriction on application of Bernoulli theorem is that the fluids must be incompressible.

Hence, the correct option is (C).

36. Work done by a simple pendulum in one complete oscillation is zero.

One of the force is gravity. The force of gravity acts in a downward direction and does work upon the pendulum bob. At all points in the trajectory of the pendulum bob, the angle between the force of tension and its direction of motion is $90°$. Thus, the force of tension does not do work upon the bob.

Hence, the correct option is (A).

37. The wave having compression and rarefaction is known as a "Longitudinal wave".

Longitudinal wave motion is that wave motion in which individual particles of the medium execute simple harmonic motion about their mean position along the same direction, in which the wave is propagated.

Hence, the correct option is (B).

38. As the heat transfer rate is inversely proportional to length of the rod. By decreasing the length of the rod, the heat transfer rate will increase.

Hence, the correct option is (D).

39. Given,

ΔW = - 200 Cal and ΔU = + 20 Cal

According to the first law of Thermodynamics:

Heat exchanged (ΔQ) = ΔW + ΔU = - 200 + 20 = - 180 Cal

Hence, the correct option is (C).

40. From Gauss's law
$$\phi = \frac{q}{\epsilon_o}$$
$$\Rightarrow \phi = \int_s E \times ds$$
$$\Rightarrow \phi = E \times 4\pi r^2$$
Since the surface of the spherical shell is uniformly charged, so the charge inside a spherical shell is zero, the Gaussian Surface encloses no charge.
The Gauss's theorem gives
$$E \times 4\pi r^2 = \frac{q}{\epsilon_o} = 0$$

$$\therefore E = 0 \text{ for } r < R$$

Hence, the correct option is (A).

41. Given,

$$N_p = 500, N_s = 200 \text{ and } i_p = 48\ A$$

The ratio of current in the primary and secondary coil is

$$\frac{i_p}{i_s} = \frac{N_s}{N_p}$$

$$\Rightarrow i_s = i_p \left(\frac{N_p}{N_s}\right)$$

$$= 48 \times \left(\frac{500}{200}\right)$$

$$= 120\ A$$

Hence, the correct option is (C).

42.

- The magnetic field line is a straight line inside a solenoid. So, it remains uniform along its length.

- The magnetic field inside a solenoid is the sum of magnetic fields due to all loops. So, on increasing the number of loops, the number of electrons causing current increases. Thus magnetic field strength increases.

- The distance from the current-carrying conductor and the magnetic field are inversely proportional. Thus, towards the ends of the solenoid, the magnetic field strength reduces as they diverge.

- The magnetic field outside the solenoid is zero.

Hence, the correct option is (D).

43. The infrared waves present in the light ray coming from the sun is responsible for the heat energy. Thus infrared waves are called waves of heat energy.

Hence, the correct option is (B).

44. Given,

Wavelength of light in air $= 6000\overset{\circ}{A} = 6000 \times 10^{-10}\ m$
Refractive index, $\mu = 1.5$
From, $\mu = \frac{c}{v}$
$$\Rightarrow 1.5 = \frac{3 \times 10^8}{v}$$
$\Rightarrow$ Speed of light in glass, $v = 2 \times 10^8\ m/s$
From, $v = \lambda \times f$

Frequency of light in air, $f = \frac{c}{\lambda} = \frac{3 \times 10^8}{6000 \times 10^{-10}} = 5 \times 10^{14}\ Hz$
Frequency does not change when light enters from one medium to another.

The wavelength of the same light in the glass, $\lambda_{glass} = \frac{v}{f} = $

$\frac{2 \times 10^8}{5 \times 10^{14}} = 4 \times 10^{-7}\ m = 4000\overset{\circ}{A}$
Hence, the correct option is (B).

45. For neutral atom,

- Number of protons in an atom = Z
- Number of electrons in an atom = Z
- Number of nucleons in an atom = A
- Number of neutrons in an atom = N = A – Z

From above it is clear that the number of neutrons equal to the difference of a mass number and an atomic number.

Hence, the correct option is (A).

46. Alkanes are saturated open-chain hydrocarbons containing carbon-carbon single bonds. Alkanes belong to the group of aliphatic hydrocarbons. The general formula of alkanes is C_nH_{2n+2}, where n is the number of carbon atoms and 2n+2 is the number of hydrogen atoms. Methane is the first member of the alkane family.

Hence, the correct option is (D).

47. The molecular formula of propane is C_3H_8.

Alkanes are acyclic hydrocarbons in which carbon-carbon atoms have a single bond between them, i.e. they are saturated hydrocarbons. The general formula for alkanes is C_nH_{2n+2}, where 'n' is the number of carbon atoms. Propane is the third member of the alkane family with 3 carbon atom. If we put the number of carbon and hydrogen atoms present in propane in the above-mentioned formula, we will find that it holds true.

Hence, the correct option is (C).

48. Given,

Acceleration due to gravity at height h is $(g') = \dfrac{g}{4}$

As we know,

Acceleration due to gravity at height $(g') = \dfrac{g}{\left(1+\frac{h}{R}\right)^2}$

According to the question,

$$\dfrac{g}{\left(1+\frac{h}{R}\right)^2} = \dfrac{g}{4}$$

$$\Rightarrow \left(1+\frac{h}{R}\right)^2 = 4$$

$$\Rightarrow 1+\frac{h}{R} = 2$$

$$\Rightarrow \frac{h}{R} = 1$$

$$\Rightarrow h = R$$

Hence, the correct option is (D).

49. Given,

$V_e = 12\ km/s = 12 \times 10^3\ m/s$, and Radius $(R) = 6000\ km = 6 \times 10^6\ m$

The escape velocity on earth is given by:

$$V_e = \sqrt{\dfrac{2GM}{R}}$$

As we know, $GM = gR^2$

$$V_e = \sqrt{2gR}$$

By squaring both sides, we get

$$(V_e)^2 = 2\ gR$$

$$\Rightarrow g = \dfrac{V_e^2}{2R}$$

$$\Rightarrow g = \dfrac{\left(12 \times 10^3\right)^2}{2 \times 6 \times 10^6} = 12\ m/s^2$$

Hence, the correct option is (C).

50. An operating system is the system software that handles the software and hardware resources and provides services for computer programs. So, without an operating system, a computer cannot "boot".

Hence, the correct option is (C).

51. As we know,

Maximum value $= \sqrt{(m^2 + n^2)}$

Minimum value $= -\sqrt{(m^2 + n^2)}$

According to the question,

Maximum value of $17\sin\theta + 5\cos\theta = \sqrt{(m^2 + n^2)} = \sqrt{(17^2 + 5^2)}$

$$= \sqrt{(289 + 25)}$$

$$= \sqrt{314}$$

Minimum value of $17\sin\theta + 5\cos\theta = -\sqrt{(m^2 + n^2)} = -\sqrt{(17^2 + 5^2)}$

$$= -\sqrt{(289 + 25)}$$

$$= -\sqrt{314}$$

Hence, the correct option is (B).

52. $\sec^4\theta - \sec^2\theta$

$= \sec^2\theta\ (\sec^2\theta - 1)$

$= \sec^2\theta\ \tan^2\theta\quad [\because \tan^2\theta = \sec^2\theta - 1]$

$= (1 + \tan^2\theta)\ \tan^2\theta$

$= \tan^2\theta + \tan^4\theta$

Hence, the correct option is (B).

53. Given,

A bag contains 5 red, 8 black balls and 7 blue balls.

As we know,

$P(E) =$ Number of getting outcomes/Total number of all possible outcomes

Total outcomes $= 5 + 8 + 7 = 20$

Number of getting outcomes $=$ Number of black ball $+$ Number of blue ball $= 8 + 7 = 15$

$$P(E) = \dfrac{15}{20} = \dfrac{3}{4}$$

$\therefore$ Probability of getting not red ball $= \dfrac{3}{4}$

Hence, the correct option is (A).

54. Given,

$$\dfrac{^{56}P_{r+6}}{^{56}P_{r+3}} = 30800$$

$$\Rightarrow \dfrac{\frac{56!}{(56-r-6)!}}{\frac{54!}{(54-r-3)!}} = 30800$$

$$\Rightarrow \dfrac{56 \times 55 \times 54!}{(56-r-6)!} \times \dfrac{(54-r-3)!}{54!} = 30800$$

$$\Rightarrow \dfrac{(51-r)!}{(50-r)!} = \dfrac{30800}{56 \times 55}$$

$$\Rightarrow 51 - r = 10$$

$$\therefore r = 41$$

Hence, the correct option is (B).

55. Given,

n (A) = 50, n (B) = 20 and n (A∩B) = 10

As we know,

n (A Δ B) = n [(A - B) ∪ (B - A)] = n (A ∪ B) - n (A ∩ B)

Now,

n [(A - B) ∪ (B - A)] = n (A ∪ B) - n (A ∩ B)

= n (A) + n(B) - n (A∩B) - n (A∩B) [∵ n (A ∪ B) = n (A) + n(B) - n (A∩B)]

= n (A) + n(B) - 2n (A∩B)

= 50 + 20 - 2(10) = 50

Hence, the correct option is (B).

56. As we know,

$$(a^m \times a^n) = a^{m+n}$$
$$(a^m)^n = a^{mn}$$

Given,

$$\left[(i)^{25} + \left(\frac{1}{i}\right)^{27}\right]^2$$

$$= \left[(i)^{25} + \left(\frac{1}{i}\right)^{27}\right]^2 \ ... (\because \sqrt{-1} = i)$$

$$= \left[(i)^{24}i + \left(\frac{1}{i}\right)^{24}\left(\frac{1}{i}\right)^3\right]^2 \ ... (\because (a^m \times a^n) = a^{m+n})$$

$$= \left[((i)^6)^4 i + \left(\left(\frac{1}{i}\right)^6\right)^4 \left(\frac{1}{i}\right)^3\right]^2 \ ... (\because (a^m)^n = a^{mn})$$

$$= \left[i + \left(\frac{1}{i}\right)^3\right]^2 \ ... (\because i^4 = 1)$$

$$= \left[i - \frac{1}{i}\right]^2 \ ... (\because i^3 = -i)$$

$$= \left(\frac{i^2-1}{i}\right)^2 \ ... (\because i^2 = -1)$$

$$= \left(\frac{-1-1}{i}\right)^2$$

$$= \frac{(-2)^2}{i^2}$$

$$= -4$$

Hence, the correct option is (D).

57. As we know,

$$\text{Sum of roots} = -\frac{b}{a}$$

$$\text{Product of the roots} = \frac{c}{a}$$

Given,

$$x^2 + 6x + 4 = 0$$

Let α and β are roots, then

$$\alpha + \beta = -6, \alpha\beta = 4$$

Now,

$$\frac{\alpha^4 + \beta^4}{\alpha^{-4} + \beta^{-4}} = \frac{\alpha^4 + \beta^4}{\frac{1}{\alpha^4} + \frac{1}{\beta^4}}$$

$$= \frac{\alpha^4 + \beta^4}{\frac{(\alpha^4 + \beta^4)}{\alpha^4 \beta^4}}$$

$$= (\alpha\beta)^4$$

$$= (4)^4$$

$$= 256$$

Hence, the correct option is (B).

58. Given,

Series is $4, 8, 16, ...$

$$a = 4, r = 2$$

Sum of n numbers $= s_n = 2044$

As we know that,

Sum of n terms of GP $= s_n = \frac{a(r^n - 1)}{r - 1}$ (where $r > 1$)

$$\therefore 2044 = \frac{4(2^n - 1)}{2 - 1}$$

$$\Rightarrow 2044 = 4 \times (2^n - 1)$$

$$\Rightarrow 511 = (2^n - 1)$$

$$\Rightarrow 2^n = 512$$

$$\Rightarrow 2^n = 2^9$$

$$\therefore n = 9$$

Hence, the correct option is (D).

59. As we know,

$$\log m^n = n \log m$$

Let x, y, z are three consecutive positive integers.

$$\therefore y = x + 1 \text{ and } z = y + 1$$

$$\Rightarrow z = x + 2$$

$$\log(1 + xz)$$

$$= \log[1 + x(x + 2)]$$

$$= \log[1 + x^2 + 2x]$$

$$= \log(1 + x)^2$$

$$= 2\log(1 + x)$$

$$= 2\log y$$

So, If x, y, z are three consecutive positive integers, then $\log(1 + xz)$ is $2\log y$.

Hence, the correct option is (D).

60. $\log_6 \sqrt{2} + \log_6 \sqrt{3}$

$$= \log_6 (\sqrt{2} \times \sqrt{3}) \ (\because \log m + \log n = \log mn)$$

$$= \log_6 (\sqrt{6})$$

$$= \log_6 6^{\frac{1}{2}}$$

$= \frac{1}{2}\log_6 6 \; (\because \log m^n = n \log m)$

As we know,

$$\log_m n = \frac{\log_a n}{\log_a m}$$

If $m = n$,

$$\log_m m = \frac{\log_a m}{\log_n m} = 1$$

$\therefore \log_6 \sqrt{2} + \log_6 \sqrt{3} = \frac{1}{2}\log_6 6 = \frac{1}{2} \times 1 = \frac{1}{2}$

Hence, the correct option is (A).

61. Given,

$2\hat{\imath} - 5\hat{\jmath} - \hat{k}$ and $-\hat{\imath} + 4\hat{\jmath} + \lambda\hat{k}$ are perpendicular.

Let $\vec{a} = 2\hat{\imath} - 5\hat{\jmath} - \hat{k}$ and $\vec{b} = -\hat{\imath} + 4\hat{\jmath} + \lambda\hat{k}$.

We know that,

If vectors $\vec{a}$ and $\vec{b}$ are perpendicular then $\vec{a} \cdot \vec{b} = 0$

$\vec{a} \cdot \vec{b} = \left(2\hat{\imath} - 5\hat{\jmath} - \hat{k}\right) \cdot \left(-\hat{\imath} + 4\hat{\jmath} + \lambda\hat{k}\right) = 0$

$\Rightarrow -2 - 20 - \lambda = 0$

$\Rightarrow -22 - \lambda = 0$

$\therefore \lambda = -22$

Hence, the correct option is (C).

62. Let $\vec{a} = a_1\vec{i} + b_1\vec{j} + c_1\vec{k}, \vec{b} = a_2\vec{i} + b_2\vec{j} + c_2\vec{k}$

and $\vec{c} = a_3\vec{i} + b_3\vec{j} + c_3\vec{k}$ be the three vectors.

Condition for coplanarity $= \vec{a} \cdot \left(\vec{b} \times \vec{c}\right) =$

$$\begin{vmatrix} a_1 & b_1 & c_1 \\ a_2 & b_2 & c_2 \\ a_3 & b_3 & c_3 \end{vmatrix} = 0$$

$2\hat{\imath} - \hat{\jmath} + \hat{k}, \hat{\imath} + 2\hat{\jmath} - 3\hat{k}$ and $3\hat{\imath} + m\hat{\jmath} + 5\hat{k}$ are coplanar.

$$\therefore \begin{vmatrix} 2 & -1 & 1 \\ 1 & 2 & -3 \\ 3 & m & 5 \end{vmatrix} = 0$$

$\Rightarrow 2(10 + 3m) + 1(5 + 9) + 1(m - 6) = 0$

$\Rightarrow 20 + 6m + 14 + m - 6 = 0$

$\Rightarrow 7m + 28 = 0$

$\Rightarrow m = -4$

Hence, the correct option is (C).

63. Given,

$$A = \begin{bmatrix} -1 & 4 \\ 5 & 8 \end{bmatrix}$$

Trace of matrix $=$ sum of elements on the main diagonal

$= -1 + 8$

$= 7$

Hence, the correct option is (B).

64. Given,

Determinant is $\begin{vmatrix} i & i^2 & i^3 \\ i^4 & i^6 & i^8 \\ i^9 & i^{12} & i^{15} \end{vmatrix}$.

Since, we have,

$i = \sqrt{-1}$

$\therefore i^2 = -1, i^3 = -i, i^4 = 1, i^6 = -1, i^8 = 1, i^9 = i,$
$i^{12} = 1,$ and

$i^{15} = -i$

$= \begin{vmatrix} i & -1 & -i \\ 1 & -1 & 1 \\ i & 1 & -i \end{vmatrix}$

$= i(i - 1) + 1(-i - i) - i(1 + i)$

$= i^2 - i - 2i - i - i^2$

$= -4i$

Hence, the correct option is (D).

65. Given,

Direction cosines of a line are $\left(\frac{1}{k}, \frac{2}{k}, \frac{-2}{k}\right)$.

So, $l = \frac{1}{k}, m = \frac{2}{k}$ and $n = \frac{-2}{k}$

We know that,

Sum of squares of the direction cosines of a line is equal to unity.

$l^2 + m^2 + n^2 = 1$

$\Rightarrow \frac{1}{k^2} + \frac{4}{k^2} + \frac{4}{k^2} = 1$

$\Rightarrow \frac{9}{k^2} = 1$

$\Rightarrow k^2 = 9$

$\therefore k = \pm 3$

Hence, the correct option is (D).

66. Distance between two points (x_1, y_1) and (x_2, y_2) is given by,

$$d = \sqrt{(x_2 - x_1)^2 + (y_2 - y_1)^2}$$

Centre lies on the line $y - 3x + 2 = 0$

Let $x = h$

$y = 3h - 2$

So the center is of the form ($h, 3h - 2$).

Distance of centre from $(1,2)$ and $(3,4)$ will be equal.

$\Rightarrow (h - 1)^2 + (3h - 2 - 2)^2 = (h - 3)^2 + (3h - 2 - 4)^2$

$\Rightarrow h^2 - 2h + 1 + 9h^2 - 24h + 16 = h^2 - 6h + 9 + 9h^2 - 36h + 36$

$\Rightarrow -26h + 17 = -42h + 45$

$\Rightarrow 16h = 28$

$\Rightarrow h = \frac{7}{4}$

$\therefore y = \frac{21}{4} - 2 = \frac{13}{4}$

So, the centre is $\left(\frac{7}{4}, \frac{13}{4}\right)$.

Now, radius will be distance from any point say $(1,2)$ to the

centre of circle $\left(\frac{7}{4}, \frac{13}{4}\right)$.

$\therefore r^2 = \left(1 - \frac{7}{4}\right)^2 + \left(2 - \frac{13}{4}\right)^2$

$= \left(-\frac{3}{4}\right)^2 + \left(\frac{-5}{4}\right)^2$

$= \frac{9}{4} + \frac{25}{4}$

$= \frac{36}{4}$

$= 9$

$\therefore r = \sqrt{9} = 3$

Hence, the correct option is (A).

67. Given,

$\lim_{x \to 0} \dfrac{\sqrt{\left(\frac{1}{2}(1 - \cos 2x)\right)}}{x}$

$\lim_{x \to 0} \dfrac{\sqrt{\left(\frac{1}{2}(1 - \cos 2x)\right)}}{x} = \lim_{x \to 0} \dfrac{\sqrt{\left(\frac{1}{2}(2\sin^2 x)\right)}}{x}$

$= \lim_{x \to 0} \dfrac{\sqrt{(\sin^2 x)}}{x}$

$= \lim_{x \to 0} \dfrac{|\sin x|}{x} \quad \left(\because \left(\sqrt{x}^2\right) = |x|\right)$

Now, $LHL = \lim_{x \to 0^-} \dfrac{|\sin x|}{x} = \lim_{x \to 0^-} \dfrac{-\sin x}{x} = -1$

$RHL = \lim_{x \to 0^+} \dfrac{|\sin x|}{x} = \lim_{x \to 0^-} \dfrac{\sin x}{x} = 1$

Here $LHL \neq RHL$, so limit doesn't exist.

Hence, the correct option is (D).

68. Given,

Weights are $1, 2, 3, \ldots, 16$ and first natural numbers are $1, 2, 3, \ldots, 16$.

So, sum of observations $= (1 \times 1) + (2 \times 2) + (3 \times 3) + \cdots + (16 \times 16)$

$= 1^2 + 2^2 + \cdots + 16^2$

$= \dfrac{16(16+1)((2 \times 16) + 1)}{6}$

$= \dfrac{16 \times 17 \times 33}{6}$

Number of observation $= 1 + 2 + 3 + \cdots + 16$

$= \dfrac{16(16+1)}{2}$

$= \dfrac{16 \times 17}{2}$

Now, mean $= \dfrac{\text{Sum of observations}}{\text{Number of observation}}$

$= \dfrac{\frac{16 \times 17 \times 33}{6}}{\frac{16 \times 17}{2}}$

$= \dfrac{33}{3}$

$= 11$

Hence, the correct option is (C).

69. As we know,

The distance between the lines $y = mx + c_1$ and $y = mx + c_2$ is $\dfrac{|c_1 - c_2|}{\sqrt{1 + m^2}}$.

The distance between the lines $ax + by + c_1 = 0$ and $ax + by + c_2 = 0$ is $\dfrac{|c_1 - c_2|}{\sqrt{a^2 + b^2}}$.

Given,

Lines are $6x + 8y + 15 = 0$ and $3x + 4y + 9 = 0$.

$\Rightarrow 6x + 8y + 15 = 0$

Take 2 common from the above equation, we get

$\Rightarrow 3x + 4y + \dfrac{15}{2} = 0 \ldots (1)$

And $3x + 4y + 9 = 0 \ldots (2)$

Equations (1) and (2) are parallel to each other.

$\therefore$ The distance between the lines $= \dfrac{\left|\frac{15}{2} - 9\right|}{\sqrt{3^2 + 4^2}} = \dfrac{\left(\frac{3}{2}\right)}{5} = \dfrac{3}{10}$

Hence, the correct option is (B).

70. As we know,

$\int e^x dx = e^x + c$

$I = \int_0^1 \dfrac{e^{\tan^{-1} x} dx}{1 + x^2} \cdots (1)$

Let $\tan^{-1} x = t$

Differentiating both sides, we get

$\dfrac{dx}{1 + x^2} = dt$

Putting $\dfrac{dx}{1 + x^2} = dt$ in equation (1),

$I = \int_0^{\frac{\pi}{4}} e^t \, dt$

$\Rightarrow I = [e^t]_0^{\frac{\pi}{4}}$

$\Rightarrow I = e^{\frac{\pi}{4}} - e^0$

$\Rightarrow I = e^{\frac{\pi}{4}} - 1$

Hence, the correct option is (A).

71. As we know,

$\int x^n dx = \dfrac{x^{n+1}}{n+1} + c$

$I = \int \dfrac{(\log x)^2}{x} dx$

Let $\log x = t$

Differenatiating with respect to x, we get

$\dfrac{1}{x} dx = dt$

Now,

$I = \int t^2 dt$

$= \dfrac{t^3}{3} + c$

$= \dfrac{(\log x)^3}{3} + c$

Hence, the correct option is (C).

72. As we know,

The standard equation of an ellipse is $\dfrac{x^2}{a^2} + \dfrac{y^2}{b^2} = 1$

Given,

Equation of ellipse is $\dfrac{x^2}{4} + \dfrac{y^2}{9} = 1$.

Here $a^2 = 4$ and $b^2 = 9$

$\therefore a = 2$ and $b = 3$

$b > a$ so the major axis lies on y - axis with length $2b$.

Now, sum of the focal distance $= 2b = 2 \times 3 = 6$ units

Hence, the correct option is (B).

73. Standard Equation of ellipse $= \dfrac{x^2}{a^2} + \dfrac{y^2}{b^2} = 1$

Length of latus rectum $= \dfrac{2\,b^2}{a}$, when $a > b$ and $\dfrac{2a^2}{b}$, when $a < b$

$$3x^2 + y^2 - 12x + 2y + 1 = 0$$
$$\Rightarrow 3(x^2 - 4x + 4) - 12 + (y^2 + 2y + 1) = 0$$
$$\Rightarrow 3(x - 2)^2 - 12 + (y + 1)^2 = 0$$
$$\Rightarrow 3(x - 2)^2 + (y + 1)^2 = 12$$
$$\Rightarrow \dfrac{3(x-2)^2}{12} + \dfrac{(y+1)^2}{12} = 1 \text{ (Divide by } 12)$$
$$\Rightarrow \dfrac{(x-2)^2}{4} + \dfrac{(y+1)^2}{12} = 1$$
$$\Rightarrow \dfrac{(x-2)^2}{2^2} + \dfrac{(y+1)^2}{\left(2\sqrt{3}\right)^2} = 1$$

$\therefore a^2 = 2^2$ and $b^2 = \left(2\sqrt{3}\right)^2$

Here $a < b$

So, length of latus rectum $= \dfrac{2a^2}{b}$

$$= \dfrac{2(4)}{2\sqrt{3}}$$
$$= \dfrac{4}{\sqrt{3}} \text{ units}$$

Hence, the correct option is (C).

74. Given,

$$y^2 - 8x + 6y + 1 = 0$$
$$\Rightarrow y^2 + 6y + 9 - 9 - 8x + 1 = 0$$
$$\Rightarrow (y + 3)^2 - 8x - 8 = 0$$
$$\Rightarrow (y + 3)^2 = 8x + 8$$
$$\Rightarrow (y + 3)^2 = 8(x + 1)$$

Let new coordinate axes be X and Y,

Here $X = x + 1$ and $Y = y + 3$

$$\Rightarrow Y^2 = 4aX$$

Now comparing with above equation,

$\therefore 4a = 8$

So, length of the latus rectum of the parabola $= 4a = 8$

Hence, the correct option is (B).

75. Let x_1 and x_2 are the mean of the first and second group of data containing n_1 and n_2 items respectively.

Then the combined mean $= \dfrac{n_1 \bar{x}_1 + n_2 \bar{x}_2}{n_1 + n_2}$

Given,

Arithmetic mean of 9 observations is 100 and that of 6 is 80.

$n_1 = 9$ and $\bar{x}_1 = 100$

$n_2 = 6$ and $\bar{x}_2 = 80$

As we know,

Combined mean $= \dfrac{n_1 \bar{x}_1 + n_2 \bar{x}_2}{n_1 + n_2}$

$$= \dfrac{9 \times 100 + 6 \times 80}{9 + 6}$$
$$= \dfrac{1380}{15} = 92$$

Hence, the correct option is (D).

76. The theme of International Girls in ICT Day 2022 was Access and Safety. It is celebrated every year on the fourth Thursday in April. International Girls in ICT Day aims to inspire a global movement to increase the representation of girls and women in technology.

Hence, the correct option is (A).

77. Indian javelin thrower, Devendra Jhajharia has clinched a silver medal in the World Para Athletics Grand Prix 2022 in Morocco.

Paralympics gold medalist Devendra Jhajharia threw the javelin to a distance of 60.97 meters to capture the silver. He is a three-time Paralympics medalist.

Hence, the correct option is (B).

78. The last battle of Ashoka was the Battle of Kalinga. The Kalinga War (ended c. 261 BCE) was fought in ancient India between the Maurya Empire under Ashoka and the state of Kalinga, an independent feudal kingdom located on the east coast, in the present-day state of Odisha and north parts of Andhra Pradesh. He decided to give up fighting wars after the victory over Kalinga because he was horrified by the violence and bloodshed in that. He is the only king in the history of the world who gave up conquest after winning a war.

Hence, the correct option is (B).

79. Harappa was an Indus civilization urban centre. It lies in Punjab Province, Pakistan, on an old bank/bed of the River Ravi. Harappa was the first site of the civilization to be excavated in 1921. The excavation team was led by Daya Ram Sahni.

Hence, the correct option is (B).

80. Pin Valley National Park is a National park of India located within the Lahaul and Spiti district, in the state of Himachal Pradesh, in far Northern India. With its snow laden unexplored higher reaches and slopes, the Park forms a natural habitat for a number of endangered animals including the snow leopard and Siberian ibex.

Hence, the correct option is (A).

81. Bhakra Nangal Dam is a concrete gravity dam on the Sutlej River in Bilaspur, Himachal Pradesh in northern India. The dam forms the Gobind Sagar reservoir. The father of Bhakra Nangal dam is Sir Chaudhari Chhotu Ram. He conceived the Bhakra Dam way back in 1923, to rid the farmers of the so-called economic plague-spots of erstwhile Punjab state.

Hence, the correct option is (A).

82. The main crop of Uttar Pradesh is rice. It is cultivation is mainly concentrated in river valleys, deltas, and low-lying coastal areas. The main rice-producing states include West Bengal, Uttar Pradesh, Andhra Pradesh, Punjab, Tamil Nadu, Odisha, and Bihar. Shahjahanpur District is the top region by rice production in India. As of 2014, rice production in Shahjahanpur District was 545,993 tonnes that account for 10.48% of India's rice production.

Hence, the correct option is (B).

83. Hornbill Festival is one of the most important festivals of Nagaland. It takes place from 1st to 7th December every year. It is done by the Naga Troops.

Hence, the correct option is (B).

84. Ottamthullal is an art form performed only in Kerala. The meaning of Ottamthullal is 'poor man's Kathakali'. Kunchan Nambiar created this dance form, as an alternative to the Chakyar koothu. To protest against the prevalent socio-political structure and prejudices of the society, Kunchan Nambiar used it as a medium. Now it is a famous folk art presented in the temples of Kerala.

Hence, the correct option is (A).

85. The Constitution of 1950 recognized fourteen Indian languages of which Hindi was to be the first official language. English was to be a transitional language until 1965. On 14th September 1949, Hindi was adopted as the Official Language of the Union of India. Later in 1950, the Constitution of India declared Hindi in the Devanagari script as the official language of India.

Hence, the correct option is (D).

86. Cape Town is the legislative capital of South Africa. It is home to the country's legislative parliament, including the National Assembly and National Council of Provinces.

Hence, the correct option is (D).

87. Azerbaijani manat is the currency of Azerbaijan. Azerbaijan is a European country in the boundaries of Europe and Asia, with Baku as its capital. The majority of the population i.e more than 95 % of the people follow Islam. Ilham Aliyev is the president and Ali Asadov is the prime minister of the country.

Hence, the correct option is (A).

88. The audacity of hope is written by former President of the United States Barack Obama. This book was published in 2006. He served as the 44th president of the United States from 2009 to 2017. He was the first African American to be elected to the presidency. What happened, Hard Choices, Living History and It takes a village are written by Hillary Clinton.

Hence, the correct option is (B).

89. Wings of Fire is an Autobiography of A.P.J. Abdul Kalam. It covers his early life and his work in Indian space research and missile programs. World Students' Day is observed on 15 October to commemorate the birth anniversary of Dr A. P. J. Abdul Kalam.

Hence, the correct option is (B).

90. Douglas Stuart won the Booker Prize 2020 for Shuggie Bain. Douglas Stuart has won the Booker Prize his debut novel about a boy in 1980s Glasgow trying to support his mother as she struggles with addiction and poverty.

Hence, the correct option is (A).

91. Faraday discovered electromagnetic induction. On 29 August 1831, Michael Faraday discovered the induction of one current by another in his famous induction ring experiment familiar to every student of physics.

Hence, the correct option is (B).

92. Radium, known as radium chloride, was discovered by Marie Curie and Pierre Curie in 1898. He obtained the radium compound from uranite. Radium is found in nature in uranium ores. The amount of radium in one ton of uranite is very less, about one gram. equal to the seventh part.

Hence, the correct option is (D).

93. The pattern followed here is,

The sum of the elements of the row is 16.

Row 1:

$7 + 3 + 6 = 16$

Row 2:

$5 + 4 + 7 = 16$

Similarly,

Row 3:

$8 + X + 2 = 16$

$\therefore X = 6$

Hence, the correct option is (B).

94. The pattern followed here is,

Row 1: A + 3 = D, D + 3 = G

Row 2: D + 5 = I, I + 5 = N

Row 3: I + 7 = P, P + 7 = W

Hence, the correct option is (A).

95. The pattern for the code is as follows,

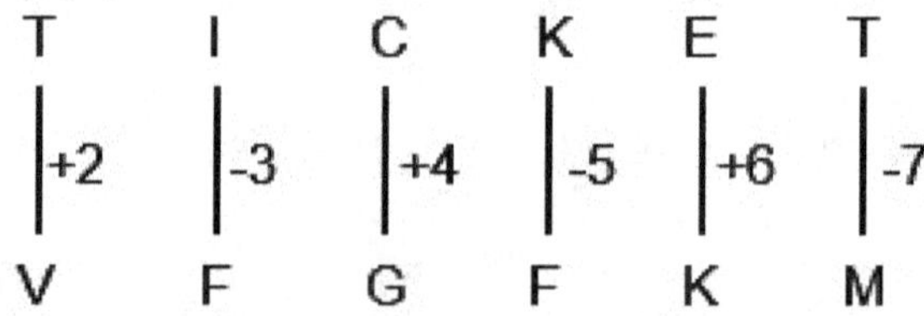

Similarly for the word "TICKET",

So, "TICKET" is coded as "VFGFKM".

Hence, the correct option is (A).

96.

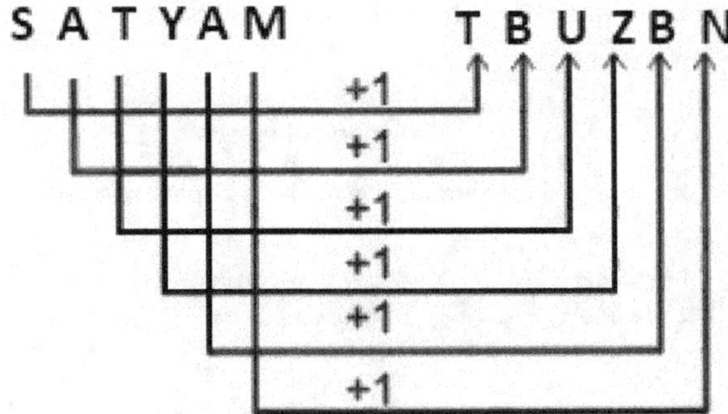

Similarly,

So, SATYAM will be written as TBUZBN.

Hence, the correct option is (D).

97. (A) SENIOR – FORENSIC (Can be formed)

(B) FERNS – FORENSIC (Can be formed)

(C) SINCE – FORENSIC (Can be formed)

(D) CROWN – FORENSIC (Cannot be formed because W is missing)

Hence, the correct option is (D).

98. The International Cricket Council (ICC) is headquartered in Dubai, United Arab Emirates. It is the international governing body of cricket. It was founded as the Imperial Cricket Conference in 1909 by representatives from England, Australia and South Africa, renamed the International Cricket Conference in 1965 and took up its current name in 1989.

Hence, the correct option is (B).

99. Manika Batra is associated with Table Tennis. She has been honoured with the Rajiv Gandhi Khel Ratna award in 2020. She has clinched the gold medal in the Commonwealth Games, 2018 in the Women's singles category. She won three gold medals at the 2016 South Asian Game.

Hence, the correct option is (B).

100. The full form of "PSLV" is Polar Satellite Launch Vehicle.

Polar Satellite Launch Vehicle (PSLV) is the third generation launch vehicle of India. It is the first Indian launch vehicle to be equipped with liquid stages.

Hence, the correct option is (C).

Mathematics

Q.1 Find the principal value of $\cos^{-1}\left(-\frac{1}{\sqrt{2}}\right)$:

A. $\frac{3\pi}{4}$ **B.** $\frac{3\pi}{3}$ **C.** $\frac{3\pi}{2}$ **D.** $\frac{3\pi}{1}$

Q.2 If $\sin^{-1}(x^2 - 7x + 12) = n\pi, \forall\, n \in I$, then x:

A. -2 **B.** 4 **C.** -3 **D.** 5

Q.3 There are 12 points in a plane out of which 5 are collinear. The number of triangles formed by the points as vertices is:

A. 185   **B.** 210   **C.** 220   **D.** 175

Q.4 Four dice are rolled. The number of possible outcomes in which at least one dice show 2 is:

A. 1296   **B.** 671   **C.** 625   **D.** 585

Q.5 Find the probability of throwing at most 2 sixes in 6 throws of a single die:

A. $\frac{35}{18}\left(\frac{5}{6}\right)^3$ **B.** $\frac{35}{18}\left(\frac{5}{6}\right)^7$ **C.** $\frac{35}{18}\left(\frac{5}{6}\right)^2$ **D.** $\frac{35}{18}\left(\frac{5}{6}\right)^4$

Q.6 How many types of remainder are there in $(12x + 5) \div 18$?

A. 1   **B.** 2   **C.** 3   **D.** 4

Q.7 A vector equally inclined to axes is :

A. $\hat{\imath} + \hat{\jmath} + \hat{k}$ **B.** $\hat{\imath} - \hat{\jmath} + \hat{k}$
C. $\hat{\imath} - \hat{\jmath} - \hat{k}$ **D.** $-\hat{\imath} + \hat{\jmath} - \hat{k}$

Q.8 A man walks 3 miles on the day he started and each day he walks one mile more than its previous day. Find the distance (in miles) he would walk in 15 days? (starting from Sunday) :

A. 150 miles   **B.** 60 miles
C. 84 miles   **D.** 88 miles

Q.9 If $\vec{a}$ and $\vec{b}$ are unit vectors, then what is the angle between $\vec{a}$ and $\vec{b}$ for $\sqrt{3}\vec{a} - \vec{b}$ to be a unit vector?

A. 30°   **B.** 45°   **C.** 60°   **D.** 90°

Q.10 If 5(4 - x) - 4 > 5x -2 > 2x - 6, then the value of x is:

A. -2   **B.** 2   **C.** -1   **D.** 3

Q.11 Write the set $A = \{1, 4, 9, 16, 25, \dots\}$ in set-builder form :

A. $A = \{x : x = n^2\}$ **B.** $A = \{x : x = n^3\}$
C. $A = \{x : x = n^4\}$ **D.** $A = \{x : x = n^5\}$

Q.12 Find the nature of roots of $x^3 + 7x^2 + 16x + 112$.

A. 1 real negative, 2 imaginary
B. 2 real negative, 1 imaginary
C. All imaginary
D. All real

Q.13 If
$A = \{3, 5, 7, 9, 11\}, B = \{7, 9, 11, 13\}, C = \{11, 13, 15\}$
Find $A \cap (B \cup C)$.

A. {7,9,11}   **B.** {7,9,13}
C. {5,9,13}   **D.** {5,7,13}

Q.14 Solve for x if $\log(x - 1) + \log(x + 1) = \log_2 1$:

A. $\sqrt{2}$ **B.** $\sqrt{3}$ **C.** $\sqrt{5}$ **D.** $\sqrt{7}$

Q.15 The locus of a point, whose abscissa and ordinate are always equal is

A. $x + y + 1 = 0$ **B.** $x - y = 0$
C. $x + y = 1$ **D.** none of these

Q.16 What can be said regarding if a line if its slope is negative

A. θ is an acute angle
B. θ is an obtuse angle
C. Either the line is x-axis or it is parallel to the x-axis.
D. None of these

Q.17 The equation of the line passing through the point $(2,3)$ with slope 2 is

A. $2x + y - 1 = 0$ **B.** $2x - y + 1 = 0$
C. $2x - y - 1 = 0$ **D.** $2x + y + 1 = 0$

Q.18 A jar contains 10 red marbles and 30 green ones. How many red marbles must be added to the jar so that 60% of the marbles will be red?

A. 25   **B.** 30   **C.** 35   **D.** 40

Q.19 Find all the points of local maxima and local minima of the function $f(x) = (x - 1)^3(x + 1)^2$

A. $1, -1, \frac{-1}{5}$ **B.** $1, -1$
C. $1, \frac{-1}{5}$ **D.** $-1, \frac{-1}{5}$

Q.20 The function f defined by $f(x) = x^3 - 6x^2 + 36x + 7$ is :

A. $x > 6,\ x > -2$ **B.** $x > 6,\ x > 2$
C. $x > -6,\ x > -2$ **D.** $x > -6,\ x > 2$

Q.21 Differentiate $f(x) = e^{3x}$ from first principles.

A. $3e^{2x}$ **B.** $2e^{3x}$ **C.** $2e^{2x}$ **D.** $3e^{3x}$

Q.22 Differentiate $f(x) = e^{ax+b}$ from first principles.

A. ae^{ax-b} **B.** ax^{ae+b} **C.** ae^{ax+b} **D.** ae^{ax-b}

Q.23 Evaluate $\int \dfrac{dx}{1+\cos x}$

A. $\tan\frac{x}{3} + C$ **B.** $\tan x + C$
C. $\tan\frac{x}{4} + C$ **D.** $\tan\frac{x}{2} + C$

Q.24 If A is a square matrix then $A - A'$ is a

A. diagonal matrix

B. skew symmetric matrix

C. symmetric matrix

D. None of these

Q.25 The locus of the point from which the tangent to the circles $x^2 + y^2 - 4 = 0$ and $x^2 + y^2 - 8x + 15 = 0$ are equal is given by the equation :

A. $8x + 19 = 0$ **B.** $8x - 19 = 0$

C. $4x - 19 = 0$ **D.** $4x + 19 = 0$

English

Q.26 Direction: In the following questions, choose the word opposite in meaning to the given word.

COUNTERFEIT

A. Fake   **B.** Dual

C. Genuine   **D.** Transient

Q.27 Direction: In the following questions, choose the word opposite in meaning to the given word.

CURB

A. Encourage   **B.** Endure

C. Abstain   **D.** Purge

Ques (28-31):Direction : Read the following passage and answer the questions that follow the passage. Your answers to these items should be based on the passage only.

The object underlying the rules of natural justice "is to prevent miscarriage of justice" and secure "fair play in action". As pointed out earlier the requirement about recording of reasons for its decision by an administrative authority exercising quasi-judicial functions achieves his object by excluding changes of arbitrariness and ensuring a degree of fairness in the process of decision making. Keeping in view the expanding horizon of the principle of natural justice which governs exercise of power by administrative authorities. The rules of natural justice are not embodied rules. The particularly statutory framework where under jurisdiction has been conferred on the administrative authority. With regard to the exercise of particular power by an administrative authority including exercise of judicial or quasi-judicial functions the legislature, while conferring the said power, may feel that it would not be in the larger public interest that the reasons for the order passed by the administrative authority be recorded in the order and be communicated to the aggrieved party and it may dispense with such a requirement.

Q.28 "The rules of the natural justice are not embodied rule" means that these rules.

A. are left deliberately vague

B. cannot be satisfactorily interpreted

C. are flexible

D. cannot be visualised

Q.29 From the passage it is clear that it is the legislature that-

A. invests the administrative authority with enormous powers

B. embodies rules

C. has the larger interests of public welfare

D. leaves administrative authority enough discretion to interpret rules.

Q.30 According to the passage, there is always a gap between-

A. Rules of natural justice and their application

B. Conception of a rule and its concretisation

C. Demand for natural justice and its realisation

D. Intention and execution

Q.31 "To dispense with a requirement" means -

A. to do without the demand

B. to drop the charge

C. to cancel all formal procedure

D. to alter the provisions of the case

Q.32 Direction : In the following questions a part of sentence is bold. Below are given alternatives to the bold part at (A), (B) and (C) and (D) which may improve the sentence. Choose the correct alternative. In case no improvement , your answer is (E).

He **has not and can never be** in the good books of his employer because he lacks honesty.

A. has not and cannot be

B. has not and can never been

C. has not been and can never be

D. No Improvement

Q.33 Direction: In the following questions a part of the sentence is bold. Below are given alternatives to the bold part at (A), (B), and (C) which may improve the sentence. Choose the correct alternative. In case No correction is required, your answer is (D).

When the examinations were over **Anil and me** went to our native town.

A. me and Anil

B. Anil and I

C. I and Anil

D. No correction required

Q.34 Direction: In the following questions a part of the sentence is bold. Below are given alternatives to the bold part at (A), (B), and (C) which may improve the sentence. Choose the correct alternative. In case No correction is required, your answer is (D).

Our office clock is not so **correct** as it should be it is usually five minutes fast.

A. right

B. regular

C. accurate

D. No correction required

Q.35 Direction: In the following questions a part of the sentence is bold. Below are given alternatives to the bold part at (A), (B), and (C) which may improve the sentence. Choose the correct alternative. In case No correction is required, your answer is (D).

I shall be grateful to you if you **are of** help to me now.

A. help

B. would help

C. helped

D. No correction required

Q.36 Direction : In the following question, a sentence is given with a blank to be filled in with appropriate word(s). Some alternatives are suggested for each question. Choose the correct alternative from the given alternatives.

Many leading members of the opposition party___to justify the party's decision.

A. having tried **B.** has tried

C. have been trying **D.** tries

Q.37 Direction : In the following question, a sentence is given with a blank to be filled in with appropriate word(s). Some alternatives are suggested for each question. Choose the correct alternative from the given alternatives.

The state-of-the art school is____with a medical clinic and fitness centre.

A. establish **B.** illustrative

C. having **D.** equipped

Q.38 Direction : Each sentence below has two blanks, each blank indicating that something has been omitted. Choose the set of words for each blank which best fits the meaning of the sentence as a whole.

The Bhagawad Gita is a part of the Mahabharata, but it stands____and is____in itself.

A. dependent, incomplete

B. together, justified

C. separate, diginified

D. apart, complete

Q.39 Direction : In the following questions, four/five alternatives are given for the meaning of the given Idiom/Phrase. Choose the alternative which best express the meaning of the Idiom/Phrase.

To be under someone's thumb.

A. To be found in a difficult or embarrassing

B. To be a part of one's experience

C. To be the result of someone's actions

D. To be under someone's control

Q.40 Direction : In the following questions, four/five alternatives are given for the meaning of the given Idiom/Phrase. Choose the alternative which best express the meaning of the Idiom/Phrase.

To be under arms.

A. To allow somebody to tell you what to do.

B. To learn to use various arms and ammunitions.

C. To be ready to fight in a war.

D. To manage to win

Q.41 Direction : In the following questions, four/five alternatives are given for the meaning of the given Idiom/Phrase. Choose the alternative which best express the meaning of the Idiom/Phrase.

To think on your feet

A. To be able to react quickly and effectively without

preparation

B. To think carefully before dooing anything

C. To form your own opinion about somebody

D. To try to solve a problem without anybody's help

Q.42 Direction : In the following questions, out of the given alternatives, choose the one which can be substituted for the given words/sentence.

A fixed orbit in space in relation to earth.

A. Geological **B.** Geo-synchronous

C. Geo-centric **D.** Geo-stationary

Q.43 Direction : In the following questions, out of the given alternatives, choose the one which can be substituted for the given words/sentence.

To issue a thunderous verbal attack.

A. Languish **B.** Animate

C. Fulminate **D.** Invigorate

Q.44 Direction : In the following questions, out of the given alternatives, choose the one which can be substituted for the given words/sentence.

Very pleasing to eat.

A. Appetizing **B.** Palatable

C. Tantalizing **D.** Sumptuous

Q.45 Find the correctly spelt word.

A. Entrepreneur **B.** Entrapreneur

C. Entrepraneur **D.** Enterprenuer

Q.46 Direction : In the following questions out of the four/five alternatives, choose the one which is best express the meaning of the given word.

NIMBLE

A. Weary **B.** Agile **C.** Inactive **D.** Clumsy

Q.47 Direction : In the following questions out of the four/five alternatives, choose the one which is best express the meaning of the given word.

MAROONED

A. Knotted **B.** Smooth **C.** Stranded **D.** Mended

Q.48 Direction : In the following questions, some of the sentences have errors and some have none. Find out which part of the sentence has an error. The number of that part is your answer. If there is no error, the answer would be (D).

It is unfortunate that(A)/ many youngsters get(B)/ addicted to gamble(C)./No error(D)

A. A **B.** B **C.** C **D.** D

Q.49 Direction : In the following questions, some of the sentences have errors and some have none. Find out which part of the sentence has an error. The number of that part is your answer. If there is no error, the answer would be (D).

Kamala's fountain-pen(A)/ is as expensive(B)/ as Shyama(C).No error(D)

A. A **B.** B **C.** C **D.** D

Q.50 Direction : In the following questions, some of the sentences have errors and some have none. Find out which part of the sentence has an error. The number of that part is your answer. If there is no error, the answer would be (D).

When we consider all the factors, which are many,(A)/ the number of school dropouts(B)/ are quite disturbing.(C)/No error(D)

A. A **B.** B **C.** C **D.** D

Science

Q.51 Highly branched chains of glucose units result in :

A. Starch **B.** Glycogen
C. Cellulose **D.** Galactose

Q.52 The gravitational force between two objects is F. If masses of both objects are halved without changing distance between them, then the gravitational force would become

A. $\frac{F}{4}$ **B.** $\frac{F}{2}$ **C.** F **D.** $2F$

Q.53 The speed of light in a certain material is 50% of its speed in a vacuum. What is the refractive index of this material?

A. 1 **B.** 2 **C.** 3 **D.** 4

Q.54 The shortest distance traveled by a particle executing SHM from the mean position in $2s$ is equal to $\frac{\sqrt{3}}{2}$ times its amplitude, determine its time period.

A. 11 sec **B.** 15 sec **C.** 16 sec **D.** 12 sec

Q.55 An electric oven of 2 kW power rating is operated in a domestic electric circuit 220 V that has a current rating of 5 A. What result do you expect? Explain.

A. Can catch fire. **B.** Will run normally
C. Will stop **D.** none of the above

Q.56 The loss of strength of a signal while propagation through a medium is ___________.

A. Noise **B.** Range
C. Attenuation **D.** Modulation

Q.57 The net force of the body is zero that means the force is not being applied to the body at all and hence the body is in equilibrium.

A. The first part of the statement is false and another part is true
B. The first part of the statement is false and another part is false too
C. The first part of the statement is true and another part is false
D. The first part of the statement is true and another part is true too

Q.58 Combine three resistors 5 Ω, 4.5 Ω, and 3 Ω, in such a way that the total resistance of this combination is maximum :

A. 12.5 Ω **B.** 13.5 Ω **C.** 14.5 Ω **D.** 16.5 Ω

Q.59 When a particle moves with a uniform velocity along a circular path, then the particle has:

A. Tangential acceleration only
B. Centripetal acceleration only
C. Both tangential and centripetal acceleration

D. None of the mentioned

Q.60 Most of animal fats are:

A. Saturated fats
B. Unsaturated fats
C. Monounsaturated fats
D. Monosaturated fats

Q.61 Which of the following oxide(s) of iron would be obtained on the prolonged reaction of iron with steam?

A. FeO **B.** Fe_2O_3
C. Fe_3O_4 **D.** Fe_2O_3 and Fe_3O_4

Q.62 The charge on positron is equal to the charge on:

A. Proton **B.** Electron
C. α –particle **D.** Neutron

Q.63 The frequency of ac mains in India is:

A. 30 Hz **B.** 50 Hz **C.** 60 Hz **D.** 120 Hz

Q.64 In a given atom, no two electrons can have the same value for all the four quantum number. This is called:

A. Hund's rule
B. Pauli's exclusion principle
C. uncertainty principle
D. Aufbau's principle

Q.65 Antibodies present in colostrum which protect the newborn from certain diseases is of:

A. IgG type **B.** IgA type **C.** IgD type **D.** IgE type

Q.66 A compass needle cannot be used to detect:

A. Magnetic North-South direction
B. Polarity of a magnet
C. Strength of a magnet
D. Direction of magnetic field

Q.67 Indicate the false statement about the resistance of a wire:

A. It depend on material of wire
B. It is unrectly proportional to the length of wire
C. It is directly proportional to the area of cross-section of wire
D. Resistance of metallic wire increases with increase in temperature

Q.68 For which of the following substances, the resistance decreases with increase in temperature:

A. Pure silicon **B.** Copper
C. Nichrome **D.** Platinum

Q.69 The ratio of intensity of magnetisation to the magnetisation force is known as:

A. flux density
B. susceptibility
C. relative permeability
D. none of the above

Q.70 The velocity of the most energetic electrons emitted from a metallic surface is doubled when the frequency (v) of incident radiation is double. What is the work function of this metal?

A. Zero   **B.** $\frac{hv}{3}$ **C.** $\frac{hv}{2}$ **D.** $\frac{2hv}{3}$

Q.71 One fermimete is equal to:

A. 10^{-9} m   **B.** 10^{-15} m   **C.** 10^{-18} m   **D.** 10^{-12} m

Q.72 SI unit of luminious intensity is:

A. Lumen   **B.** Lux   **C.** Candela   **D.** Watt

Q.73 The angular velocity (in rad/s) of a body rotating at N r.p.m. is:

A. $\frac{\pi N}{60}$ **B.** $\frac{2\pi N}{60}$ **C.** $\frac{\pi N}{120}$ **D.** $\frac{\pi N}{180}$

Q.74 What is the SI unit of Young's modulus of elasticity:

A. Dyne/cm   **B.** Newton/m
C. Newton/m^2 **D.** m^2/s

Q.75 When the milk is churned vigorously the cream from it is separated out due to:

A. Frictional force   **B.** Centrifugal force
C. Centripetal force   **D.** Gravitational force

General Awareness

Q.76 L&T collaborated with _____ to develop Green Hydrogen Technology.

A. IIT Bombay   **B.** IIT Delhi
C. IIT Kanpur   **D.** IIT Madras

Q.77 In which state, was India's first pure green hydrogen plant commissioned in April 2022?

A. Assam   **B.** Karnataka
C. Gujarat   **D.** Punjab

Q.78 The Prime Minister released a commemorative coin of Rs 100 denomination, to honour which personality?

A. Vijaya Raje Scindia
B. Syama Prasad Mukherjee
C. Deendayal Upadhyaya
D. M. S. Golwalkar

Q.79 In which of the following countries did Prime Minister Narendra Modi start 'Ramayana Circuit' on May 11, 2018?

[Super TET Paper - I, 2019]

A. Nepal   **B.** Indonesia
C. Sri Lanka   **D.** Myanmar

Q.80 Who wrote the book 'Reminiscences of the Nehru Age'?

A. C.D. Deshmukh
B. Dr. P.C. Alexander
C. M.O. Mathai
D. S.C. Rajagopalachari

Q.81 If LIGHT is coded as GILTH, find the code for RAINY.

A. IARYN   **B.** ARINY   **C.** NAIRY   **D.** RINAY

Q.82 What is the full form of "COBOL"?

[UPPCL Technician Electrical, 2021]

A. Computer and Business Language

B. Computer and Basic Operations Language
C. Common Business Oriented Language
D. Common Business Organised Language

Q.83 Jamini Roy was a famous :

A. Painter   **B.** Dancer   **C.** Producer   **D.** Actor

Q.84 According to the cultural history of India 'Panchayatan' is:

A. An assembly of elders of village
B. A religious sect
C. Temple construction style
D. Functionary of an administration

Q.85 What will come at the place of the question mark:

8,28,116,584, ?

A. 1752   **B.** 3504   **C.** 3508   **D.** 3502

Q.86 In a certain code, FIRE is coded as DGPC. What will be the last letter of the code word for SHOT?

A. Q   **B.** R   **C.** S   **D.** P

Q.87 On December 11, 1946 the Constituent Assembly elected its permanent chairman as :

A. Jawarharlal Nehru   **B.** Rajendra Prasad
C. B.R. Ambedkar   **D.** K.M. Munshi

Q.88 Jaydev Unadkat is the captain of which regional cricket team that won its maiden Ranji trophy?

A. Bengal cricket team
B. Saurashtra cricket team
C. Mumbai cricket team
D. Karnataka cricket team

Q.89 The Allahabad pillar Inscription is associated with which of the following?

A. Mahapadma Nanda
B. Chandragupta Maura
C. Ashoka
D. Bimbisar

Q.90 Who was the author of 'Gita Govinda' ?

A. Jayadeva   **B.** Mihir Bhoja
C. Kalidas   **D.** Magh

Q.91 Who among the following laid the foundation of Amritsar ?

A. Guru Amar Das   **B.** Guru Ram Das
C. Guru Arjun Dev   **D.** Guru Har Govind

Q.92 Who among the following founded the 'Independent Labour Party' in 1938?

A. B.R. Ambedkar   **B.** M.C. Rajah
C. Jagjivan Ram   **D.** Jayprakash Narayan

Q.93 Who is the head of the 11-member annual grant and affiliation committee constituted by the Indian Olympic Association?

A. Adille Sumariwala   **B.** D R Saini
C. Vagish Pathak   **D.** Abu Mehta

Q.94 The Bermuda triangle lies in:

A. North Atlantic Ocean
B. South Atlantic Ocean
C. North Pacific Ocean
D. South Pacific Ocean

Q.95 Which of the following pairs are correctly matched?
A. Kuchipudi – Madhya Pradesh
B. Kathakali – Kerala
C. Bharatnatyam – Andhra Pradesh
D. Kathak – Tamil Nadu

Q.96 Knesset is the Parliament of:
A. Denmark
B. Poland
C. Israel
D. Turkey

Q.97 The first summit of NAM was held at:
A. Cairo
B. Lusaka
C. Belgrade
D. New Delhi

Q.98 In the following options, out of the given group of wordings, choose one appropriately spelled.
A. Acquatance
B. Acquaintence
C. Acquaintance
D. Acquantance

Q.99 Which of the following rivers in India is shared by large number of states?
A. Mahanadi
B. Krishna
C. Cauvery
D. Godavari

Q.100 When was our National Anthem first sung and where?
A. 24 January 1950 in Calcutta
B. 24 January 1950 in Allahabad
C. 24 January 1950 in Delhi
D. 27 December 1911 in Calcutta

// Smart Answer Sheet //

Correct Percentage of students who answered correctly. **Skipped** Percentage of students who skipped.

Q.	Ans.	Correct / Skipped	Q.	Ans.	Correct / Skipped	Q.	Ans.	Correct / Skipped	Q.	Ans.	Correct / Skipped	Q.	Ans.	Correct / Skipped	Q.	Ans.	Correct / Skipped
1	A	85.32 % / 12.29 %	18	C	81.72 % / 13.99 %	35	B	60.64 % / 38.67 %	52	A	49.88 % / 46.67 %	69	B	51.3 % / 35.58 %	86	B	42.18 % / 53.96 %
2	B	43.88 % / 50.65 %	19	A	66.04 % / 32.33 %	36	C	63.76 % / 31.41 %	53	B	82.31 % / 11.91 %	70	D	61.0 % / 33.32 %	87	B	61.71 % / 31.56 %
3	B	49.02 % / 50.18 %	20	A	69.97 % / 30.0 %	37	D	79.58 % / 17.87 %	54	D	69.42 % / 30.55 %	71	B	52.21 % / 33.48 %	88	B	46.59 % / 31.92 %
4	B	68.91 % / 30.64 %	21	D	52.11 % / 47.52 %	38	D	83.98 % / 13.2 %	55	A	62.38 % / 33.07 %	72	C	49.25 % / 35.11 %	89	C	86.5 % / 13.46 %
5	D	31.67 % / 67.37 %	22	C	60.96 % / 33.66 %	39	D	78.83 % / 12.82 %	56	C	59.98 % / 31.74 %	73	B	43.53 % / 36.78 %	90	A	65.74 % / 33.66 %
6	C	77.99 % / 11.9 %	23	D	53.93 % / 45.61 %	40	C	89.08 % / 10.64 %	57	C	81.49 % / 16.02 %	74	C	84.51 % / 14.6 %	91	B	59.66 % / 31.5 %
7	A	69.73 % / 30.16 %	24	B	59.5 % / 35.3 %	41	A	87.28 % / 10.35 %	58	A	46.18 % / 38.55 %	75	B	67.83 % / 31.9 %	92	A	52.22 % / 30.98 %
8	A	67.56 % / 32.38 %	25	B	51.27 % / 39.91 %	42	D	59.18 % / 31.95 %	59	B	64.18 % / 35.37 %	76	A	59.48 % / 36.29 %	93	A	15.97 % / 83.16 %
9	A	56.83 % / 38.75 %	26	C	85.89 % / 12.96 %	43	C	88.6 % / 10.34 %	60	A	66.33 % / 32.76 %	77	A	46.98 % / 40.97 %	94	A	42.9 % / 33.32 %
10	C	62.54 % / 33.46 %	27	A	83.79 % / 10.75 %	44	B	79.93 % / 17.9 %	61	C	43.78 % / 41.05 %	78	A	59.2 % / 33.02 %	95	B	47.68 % / 36.98 %
11	A	61.88 % / 37.17 %	28	C	63.7 % / 34.48 %	45	A	86.6 % / 11.71 %	62	A	47.82 % / 37.45 %	79	A	48.69 % / 50.61 %	96	C	14.52 % / 77.95 %
12	A	10.86 % / 78.08 %	29	A	63.83 % / 35.07 %	46	B	80.85 % / 11.79 %	63	B	12.35 % / 71.07 %	80	C	23.26 % / 70.64 %	97	C	42.53 % / 45.12 %
13	A	63.14 % / 31.1 %	30	A	50.93 % / 36.23 %	47	C	78.68 % / 21.21 %	64	B	53.25 % / 46.64 %	81	A	54.85 % / 35.12 %	98	C	53.5 % / 34.0 %
14	A	64.96 % / 31.33 %	31	A	60.75 % / 31.65 %	48	C	53.83 % / 35.65 %	65	B	12.96 % / 86.35 %	82	C	10.31 % / 82.93 %	99	D	14.43 % / 78.07 %
15	B	61.73 % / 34.76 %	32	C	77.49 % / 10.7 %	49	C	85.44 % / 13.36 %	66	C	76.07 % / 13.67 %	83	A	19.26 % / 70.65 %	100	D	16.43 % / 70.09 %
16	B	65.97 % / 32.05 %	33	B	89.87 % / 10.07 %	50	C	82.31 % / 10.88 %	67	C	87.5 % / 10.96 %	84	C	21.41 % / 70.45 %			
17	C	78.41 % / 10.28 %	34	C	50.28 % / 32.42 %	51	B	68.12 % / 30.58 %	68	A	47.28 % / 43.53 %	85	C	69.19 % / 30.05 %			

//Hints and Solutions//

1. We have,

$$\cos^{-1}\left(-\frac{1}{\sqrt{2}}\right)$$

$$\cos^{-1}\left(-\cos\frac{\pi}{4}\right) \quad \because \frac{-1}{\sqrt{2}} = -\cos\frac{\pi}{4}$$

We know that,

$$\cos(\pi - \theta) = -\cos\theta$$

Therefore,

$$= \cos^{-1}\left(\cos\left(\pi - \frac{\pi}{4}\right)\right)$$

$$= \pi - \frac{\pi}{4}$$

$$= \frac{3\pi}{4}$$

Hence, the correct option is (A).

2. Given:

$$\sin^{-1}(x^2 - 7x + 12) = n\pi$$
$$\Rightarrow x^2 - 7x + 12 = \sin n\pi$$
$$\Rightarrow x^2 - 7x + 12 = 0 \quad (\because \sin n\pi = 0 \; \forall \; n \in I)$$
$$\Rightarrow (x - 4)(x - 3) = 0$$
$$\Rightarrow x = 4, 3$$

Hence, the correct option is (B).

3. Total number of triangles that can be formed with 12 points (if none of them are collinear).

$$= {}^{12}C_3$$

(this is because we can select any three points and form the triangle if they are not collinear).

With collinear points, we cannot make any triangle (as they are in straight line). Here 5 points are collinear. Therefore we need to subtract ${}^5C_3$ triangles from the above count.

So, required number of triangles, $= {}^{12}C_3 - {}^5C_3 =$

$$\frac{12!}{(12-3)!3!} - \frac{5!}{(5-3)!\times 3!} = \frac{9!\times 10 \times 11 \times 12}{1\times 2 \times 3 \times 9!} - \frac{5\times 4 \times 3!}{1\times 2 \times 3!} =$$

$$220 - 10 = 210$$

Hence, the correct option is (B).

4. Given:

No. of ways in which any number appearing in one dice $= 6$

No. of ways in which 2 appear in one dice $= 1$

No. of ways in which 2 does not appear in one dice $= 5$

There are 4 dice.

Getting 2 in at least one dice $=$ Getting any number in all the 4 dice $-$ Getting not 2 in any of the 4 dice.

$$= (6 \times 6 \times 6 \times 6) - (5 \times 5 \times 5 \times 5)$$

$$= 1296 - 625$$

$$= 671$$

Hence, the correct option is (B).

5. Let:

X: be the number six we get on 5 throws.

Throwing a pair of die is a Bernoulli trial.

So, X has binomial distribution.

$$P(X = x) = {}^nC_x q^{n-x} p^x$$

Where,

$n =$ number of times die is thrown $= 6$

$p =$ Probability of getting a six $= \frac{1}{6}$

$$q = 1 - \frac{1}{6} = \frac{5}{6}$$

Hence,

$$P(X = x) = {}^6C_x \left(\frac{1}{6}\right)^x \left(\frac{5}{6}\right)^{6-x}$$

We need to find probability of throwing at most 2 sixes in 6 throws of a single die.

$$P(X \le 2) = P(X = 0) + P(X = 1) + P(X = 2)$$

$$= {}^6C_0 \left(\frac{1}{6}\right)^0 \left(\frac{5}{6}\right)^6 + {}^6C_1 \left(\frac{1}{6}\right)^1 \left(\frac{5}{6}\right)^5 + {}^6C_2 \left(\frac{1}{6}\right)^2 \left(\frac{5}{6}\right)^4$$

$$= 1 \times 1 \times \left(\frac{5}{6}\right)^6 + 6 \times \frac{1}{6} \times \left(\frac{5}{6}\right)^5 + 15 \times \left(\frac{1}{6}\right)^2 \left(\frac{5}{6}\right)^4$$

$$= \left(\frac{5}{6}\right)^6 + \left(\frac{5}{6}\right)^5 + 15 \times \frac{1}{36} \times \left(\frac{5}{6}\right)^4$$

$$= \left(\frac{5}{6}\right)^6 + \left(\frac{5}{6}\right)^5 + \frac{5}{12} \times \left(\frac{5}{6}\right)^4$$

$$= \left(\frac{5}{6}\right)^4 \left(\left(\frac{5}{6}\right)^2 + \frac{5}{6} + \frac{5}{12}\right)$$

$$= \left(\frac{5}{6}\right)^4 \left(\frac{25}{36} + \frac{5}{6} + \frac{5}{12}\right)$$

$$= \left(\frac{5}{6}\right)^4 \left(\frac{25+30+15}{36}\right)$$

$$= \left(\frac{5}{6}\right)^4 \left(\frac{70}{36}\right)$$

$$= \frac{35}{18} \left(\frac{5}{6}\right)^4$$

So, the required Probability is $\frac{35}{18}\left(\frac{5}{6}\right)^4$

Hence, the correct option is (D).

6. (Let x = 1, 2, 3)

x=0, Remainder = 5

x=1, Remainder = 17

x=2, Remainder = 11

x=3, Remainder = 5

So, only 3 types of remainder.

Hence, the correct option is (C).

7. Given:

Direction ratios are $1,1,1$ and direction cosines $\frac{1}{\sqrt{3}}, \frac{1}{\sqrt{3}}, \frac{1}{\sqrt{3}}$

$$\Rightarrow \cos\alpha = \cos\beta = \cos\gamma$$
$$\Rightarrow \alpha = \beta = Y$$

so,

$$\Rightarrow \hat{\imath} + \hat{\jmath} + \hat{k}$$

Hence, the correct option is (A).

8. Given:

Given that the man walks 3 miles on Sunday

According to the question

So he will walk 4 miles on Monday

So he will walk 5 miles on Tuesday

So he will walk 6 miles on Wednesday

So he will walk 7 miles on Thursday

So he will walk 8 miles on Friday

So he will walk 9 miles on Saturday

and so on....

$\Rightarrow$ Hence he walks total miles in 15 Days = 3 + 4 + 5 + 6 + 7 + 8 + 9 + 10 + 11 + 12 + 13 + 14 + 15 + 16 + 17 = 150 miles

Short Trick:-

3 , 4, ...

$$l = a + (n-1)d$$

l = 3 + 14

$9l$ = 17

Sum of A.P = $\dfrac{n}{2}(a + l)$ = $\dfrac{15}{2} \times (20)$ = 150 miles

Hence, the correct option is (A).

9. Given:

$$1^2 = \left(\sqrt{3}\,\vec{a} - \vec{b}\right)^2$$

$$1 = 3a^2 + b^2 - 2\sqrt{3}\vec{a} \cdot \vec{b} \quad \left(a^2 = 1, b^2 = 1\right)$$

$$1 = 3 + 1 - 2\sqrt{3}\vec{a} \cdot \vec{b}$$

$$\Rightarrow \vec{a} \cdot \vec{b} = \dfrac{\sqrt{3}}{2}$$

$$\therefore \cos\theta = \dfrac{\vec{a} \cdot \vec{b}}{|\vec{a}||\vec{b}|} = \dfrac{\sqrt{3}}{2}$$

$$\Rightarrow \theta = 30°$$

Hence, the correct option is (A).

10. Given:

Solving first inequality, we get,

5(4 – x) – 4 > 5x – 2

$\Rightarrow$ 20 – 5x – 4 > 5x – 2

$\Rightarrow$ x > -1.8

Now, solving second inequality,

5x – 2 > 2x – 6

$\Rightarrow$ x > -1.33

Thus, x can take the value -1 from the given options.

Hence, the correct option is (C).

11. Given:

If we see the pattern here, the numbers are squares of natural numbers, such as:

$$1^2 = 1$$

$$2^2 = 4$$

$$3^2 = 9$$

$$4^2 = 16$$

And so on,

$$A = \{x : x \text{ is the square of a natural number}\}$$

Or we can write;

$$A = \{x : x = n^2, \text{where } n \in N\}$$

Hence, the correct option is (A).

12. In this type of question, we find out the nature of roots by putting the value.

Let $x = -7$

Put the value in equation

$$(-7)^3 + 7(-7)^2 + 16(-7) + 112$$
$$= -343 + 343 - 112 + 112$$
$$= 0$$

So, $x = -7$ will be the solution of equation.

Hence, $(x + 7)$ is a factor of this equation.

So, we can find out another factor by-

$$x + 7\ \overline{)\ x^3 + 7x^2 + 16x + 112\ }(x^2 + 16$$

$$\underline{x^3 + 7x^2}$$

$$0 \qquad 16x + 112$$

$$16x + 112$$

$$\underline{\qquad\qquad}$$

$$0$$

Hence, the $(x^2 + 16)$ is another factor

$x^2 + 16 = 0 \Rightarrow x^2 = \pm 4i$

So, the equation has 1 real negative and 2 imaginary roots.

Hence, the correct option is (A).

13. Given:

$A = \{3, 5, 7, 9, 11\}, B = \{7, 9, 11, 13\}, C = \{11, 13, 15\}$

we have to find the value of $A \cap (B \cup C)$

$A \cap (B \cup C) = (A \cap B) \cup (A \cap C)$

$(A \cap B) = \{7, 9, 11\}, \quad (A \cap C) = \{11\}$

$A \cap (B \cup C) = \{7, 9, 11\} \cup \{11\}$

$= \{7, 9, 11\}$

Hence, the correct option is (A).

14. Given:

$$\log(x - 1) + \log(x + 1) = \log_2 1$$

on comparing,

$$(x - 1)(x + 1) = 1$$
$$x^2 - 1 = 1$$
$$x^2 = 2$$
$$x = \pm\sqrt{2}$$

Since, log of negative number is not defined.

Therefore, $x = \sqrt{2}$

Hence, the correct option is (A).

15. Let the coordinate of the variable point P is (x, y)

Now, the abscissa of this point $= x$

and its ordinate $= y$

Given, abscissa = ordinate

$\Rightarrow x = y$

$\Rightarrow x - y = 0$

So, the locus of the point is $x - y = 0$

Hence, the correct option is (B).

16. Let θ be the angle of inclination of the given line with the positive direction of x -axis in the anticlockwise sense.

Then its slope is given by $m = \tan\theta$

Given, slope is positive.

$\Rightarrow \tan\theta < 0$

$\Rightarrow \theta$ lies between 0 and 180 degree.

$\Rightarrow \theta$ is an obtuse angle.

Hence, the correct option is (B).

17. Given, the point $(2,3)$ and slope of the line is 2

By, slope-intercept formula,

$y - 3 = 2(x - 2)$

$\Rightarrow y - 3 = 2x - 4$

$\Rightarrow 2x - 4 - y + 3 = 0$

$\Rightarrow 2x - y - 1 = 0$

Hence, the correct option is (C).

18. Let, x red marbles be added,

$\therefore \dfrac{10+x}{40+x} \times 100 = 60$

$\Rightarrow \dfrac{(10+x)\times 5}{40+x} = 3$

$\Rightarrow 50 + 5x = 120 + 3x$

$\Rightarrow 5x - 3x = 120 - 50$

$\Rightarrow 2x = 70$

$\Rightarrow x = \dfrac{70}{2} = 35$

Hence, the correct option is (C).

19. Let $y = f(x) = (x - 1)^3(x + 1)^2$. Then,

$\dfrac{dy}{dx} = 3(x - 1)^2(x + 1)^2 + 2(x + 1)(x - 1)^3$

$\Rightarrow \dfrac{dy}{dx} = (x - 1)^2(x + 1)\{3(x + 1) + 2(x - 1)\}$

$\Rightarrow \dfrac{dy}{dx} = (x - 1)^2(x + 1)(5x + 1)$

For local maximum or local minimum, we have

$\dfrac{dy}{dx} = 0 \Rightarrow (x - 1)^2(x + 1)(5x + 1) = 0$

$\Rightarrow x = 1$ or, $x = -1$ or

$x = -\dfrac{1}{5}$

Hence, the correct option is (A).

20. Given:

$f(x) = x^3 - 6x^2 + 36x + 7$
$f'(x) = 3x^2 - 12x + 36$
for incrising function,
$f'(x) = 3x^2 - 12x + 36 > 0$
$3x^2 - 12x + 36 > 0$
$x(x - 6) + 2(x - 6) > 0$
$(x + 2)(x - 6) > 0$
$x > 6, \ x > -2$

Hence, the correct option is (A).

21. Given:

$f(x) = e^{3x}$

$\Rightarrow \quad f(x + h) = e^{3(x+h)}$

$\dfrac{d}{dx}\big(f(x)\big) = \lim_{h \to 0} \dfrac{f(x+h)-f(x)}{h}$

$= \lim_{h \to 0} \dfrac{e^{3(x+h)}-e^{3x}}{h}$

$= \lim_{h \to 0} \dfrac{e^{3x}e^{3h}-e^{3x}}{h}$

$= \lim_{h \to 0} e^{3x} \left\{ \dfrac{(e^{3h}-1)}{3h} \right\} \times 3$

$= 3e^{3x} \qquad \left[\text{Since, } \lim_{x \to 0} \dfrac{e^x-1}{x} = 1 \right]$

Hence,

$\dfrac{d}{dx}(e^{3x}) = 3e^{3x}$

Hence, the correct option is (D).

22. Let

$f(x) = e^{3x+b}$

$\Rightarrow f(x + h) = e^{a(x+h)+b}$

$\dfrac{d}{dx}\big(f(x)\big) = \lim_{h \to 0} \dfrac{f(x+h)-f(x)}{h}$

$= \lim_{h \to 0} \dfrac{e^{3(x+h)+b}-e^{(2x+b)}}{h}$

$= \lim_{h \to 0} \dfrac{e^{ax+b}e^{ax}-e^{ax+b}}{h}$

$$= \lim_{h \to 0} e^{ax+b} \left\{ \frac{(e^{ah}-1)}{ah} \right\} \times a$$

$$= a e^{ax+b}$$

$$\left[\text{Since, } \lim_{x \to 0} \frac{e^x - 1}{x} = 1 \right]$$

So,

$$\frac{d}{dx}\left(e^{ax+b}\right) = a e^{ax+b}$$

Hence, the correct option is (C).

23. Given:

Integrate $\int \frac{dx}{1+\cos x}$

$$I = \int \frac{dx}{1+\cos x}$$

$$= \int \frac{1}{2\cos^2 \frac{x}{2}} dx$$

$$= \frac{1}{2} \int \sec^2 \frac{x}{2} dx = \frac{1}{2} \cdot \frac{1}{1/2} \tan \frac{x}{2} + C$$

$$= \tan \frac{x}{2} + C$$

Hence, the correct option is (D).

24. Consider,

$$(A - A')' = A' - (A')'$$

$$= A' - A$$

$$= -(A - A')$$

$$\Rightarrow (A - A')' = -(A - A')$$

So, $A - A'$ is skew-symmetric

Hence, the correct option is (B).

25. Given equation of circles are $x^2 + y^2 - 4 = 0$ and $x^2 + y^2 - 8x + 15 = 0$

Now, the required line is the radical axis of the two circles are

$$(x^2 + y^2 - 4) - (x^2 + y^2 - 8x + 15) = 0$$

$$\Rightarrow x^2 + y^2 - 4 - x^2 - y^2 + 8x - 15 = 0$$

$$\Rightarrow 8x - 19 = 0$$

Hence, the correct option is (B).

26. Counterfeit: made in exact imitation of something valuable with the intention to deceive or defraud.

Transient is to last for short time.

Genuine: truly what something is said to be; authentic.
Hence, the correct option is (C).

27. Curb is a check or restraint on something. Therefore, encourage is the opposite.

Endure is to remain in existence.

Purge is to get rid of unwanted feeling or condition.
Hence, the correct option is (A).

28. Embody means "be an expression of or give a tangible or visible form to (an idea, quality, or feeling)." Therefore, the rules are flexible as they are not embodied.
Hence, the correct option is (C).

29. These lines from the last part of the passage answer the question- "With regard to the exercise of particular power by an administrative authority including exercise of judicial or quasi-judicial functions the legislature, while conferring the said power".
Hence, the correct option is (A).

30. the answer is in the first few lines of the passage- "The object underlying the rules of natural justice "is to prevent miscarriage of justice" and secure "fair play in action". As pointed out earlier the requirement about recording of reasons for its decision by an administrative authority exercising quasi-judicial functions achieves his object by excluding changes of arbitrariness and ensuring a degree of fairness in the process of decision making."
Hence, the correct option is (A).

31. It can be concluded from the given lines of the passage "while conferring the said power, may feel that it would not be in the larger public interest that the reasons for the order passed by the administrative authority be recorded in the order and be communicated to the aggrieved party and it may dispense with such a requirement."
Hence, the correct option is (A).

32. Has/have/had + past participle

Here, past participle is missing, therefore "been" is to be used as third form of verb.
Hence, the correct option is (C).

33. "Anil and I" is the appropriate answer as a reference is made to the subject. When used as a subject 'Anil and I' will be correct and when used as an object 'Anil and me' will be correct.
Hence, the correct option is (B).

34. Accurate is correct in all details or precise. This is a better word as per the context.

Hence, the correct option is (C).

35. As per the context "would help" is appropriate as some sort of request is being made.

Hence, the correct option is (B).

36. The sentence demands for perfect continuous tense as the action started in past and is still in process, therefore, "have been trying".
Hence, the correct option is (C).

37. Equipped means supply with the necessary items for a particular purpose.

Illustrative: serving as an example or explanation.
Hence, the correct option is (D).

38. Apart means isolate or distant. And as the sentence says that Gita stands apart and is complete in itself.
Hence, the correct option is (D).

39. Example : They seem happy when they're out and about, but I hear that Johnny is under his husband's thumb at home.
Hence, the correct option is (D).

40. Example : The rebels now have thousands of people under arms.
Hence, the correct option is (C).

41. Example : I'd never heard about the company before, so I had to think on my feet.
Hence, the correct option is (A).

42. Geological is relating to the study of the earth's physical structure and substance.

Geo-synchronous is another term for synchronous(existing or occurring at the same time).

Geo-centric is having or representing the earth as the centre.
Hence, the correct option is (D).

43. Languish is weaken or deteriorate or grow weak.

Animate is to give appearance.

Invigorate is to give strength or energy to.
Hence, the correct option is (C).

44. Appetizing is tempting or inviting.

Tantalizing is to excite the senses of .

Sumptuous is lavish or grande or splendid.
Hence, the correct option is (B).

45. An Entrepreneur is a person who sets up a business or businesses, taking on financial risks in the hope of profit.
Hence, the correct option is (A).

46. Nimble is quick and light; agile.

Weary is exhausted or tired. Inactive is not working; inoperative. Clumsy is done awkwardly or without skill.
Hence, the correct option is (B).

47. Marooned is to leave trapped and alone and stranded also refers to same.

Mended is repaired.
Hence, the correct option is (C).

48. A preposition is followed by a "noun". It is never followed by a verb. If we want to follow a preposition by a verb, we must use the "-ing" form which is really a gerund or verb in noun form.

'Gambling' (used as a noun here) is the correct word. 'Gambling' can be used as a verb as well but 'gamble' is always a verb.
Hence, the correct option is (C).

49. It should be "as expensive as that of Shyama's".
Hence, the correct option is (C).

50. Instead of "are" it will be " is".

"The number of" follow singular verb whereas "A number of" takes plural verb.
Hence, the correct option is (C).

51. Highly branched chains of glucose units result in Glycogen.

Glycogen is a multibranched polysaccharide of glucose that serves as a form of energy storage in humans, animals, fungi, and bacteria. The polysaccharide structure represents the main storage form of glucose in the body.

Hence, the correct option is (B).

52. The gravitational force between two objects varies directly as their masses and inversely as the square of the distance between them. So, when the masses of both objects are halved without changing the distance, the gravitational force between them would become one-fourth of the original value.

Hence, the correct option is (C).

53. Given:

v= 50% c (c speed of light in vacuum)

Definition of refractive index (n).

$$n = \frac{c}{v}$$

$$\Rightarrow n = \frac{c}{50\%c}$$

$$\Rightarrow n = 2.0$$

Hence, the correct option is (B).

54. Given,
The shortest distance traveled by a particle executing SHM from the mean position in $2s$ is equal to $\frac{\sqrt{3}}{2}$ times its amplitude, determine its time period.
Displacement of a particle performing simple harmonic motion is given by,
$$x = a\sin(\omega t + a)$$
$$\frac{a\sqrt{3}}{2} = a\sin(\omega t + 0)$$
$$\frac{\sqrt{3}}{2} = \sin\omega t$$
$$\omega t = \sin^{-1}\left(\frac{-\sqrt{3}}{2}\right) = \frac{\pi}{3}$$
$$\left(\frac{2\pi}{T}\right)t = \frac{\pi}{3}$$
$$T = 2 \times 2 \times 3 = 12 \text{ sec}$$

Hence, the correct option is (D).

55. Given:
P = 2 kW ⇒ 2000 W
V = 220 V as , P = VI
I =5A
2000 W ≠ 220 × 5 = 1100
Here power and value of VI are not the same that means the current required for the oven is more than 5 A that the circuit can supply.
So, due to overloading, the circuit can break or catch fire.
Hence, the correct option is (A).

56. Attenuation is a general term that refers to any reduction in the strength of a signal. Attenuation occurs with any type of signal, whether digital or analog. Sometimes called loss, attenuation is a natural consequence of signal transmission over long distances.

Hence, the correct option is (C).

57. The net force of the body is zero that doesn't mean that the force is not being applied to the body at all and hence the body is in equilibrium. The equilibrium is only attained if the net force on the body tends to be equal to zero. Thus the forces cancel out. If this happens there is no motion of the body along any direction and hence the body is said to be in equilibrium.

Hence, the correct option is (C).

58. Given:

The maximum resistance will be in the series arrangement.

$$R = R_1 + R_2 + R_3$$

Thus, $\mathbf{R} = 5\Omega + 4.5\Omega + 3\Omega = 12.5\Omega$

Hence, the correct option is (B).

59. The acceleration of a particle at any instant moving along a circular path in a direction normal to the tangent at that instant and directed towards the centre of the circular path is known as the normal component of the acceleration or normal acceleration. It is also called radial or centripetal acceleration.

Hence, the correct option is (B).

60. Most of animal fats are Saturated fats, A saturated fat is a type of fat in which the fatty acid chains have all or predominantly single bonds.Saturated fat is mainly found in animal foods, but a few plant foods are also high in saturated fats, such as coconut, coconut oil, palm oil, and palm kernel oil.

Hence, the correct option is (A).

61. Iron is a metal that will not directly react with cold water or hot water but forms a metal oxide when steam is passed over it. When red hot iron reacts with steam it forms iron(II, III) oxide and hydrogen, and the reaction is reversible. $3Fe(s) + 4H_2O(g) \rightarrow Fe_3O_4(s) + 4H_2(g)$

Hence, the correct option is (C).

62. The charge on positron is equal to the charge on proton. The positron or antielectron is the antiparticle or the antimatter counterpart of the electron. The positron has an electric charge of +1e, a spin of, and has the same mass as an electron. When a low-energy positron collides with a low-energy electron, annihilation occurs, resulting in the production of two or more gamma ray photons.
Hence, the correct option is (A).

63. Frequency of AC mains in India is $50\ Hz$, similar to most European countries. Whereas the USA uses $60\ Hz$. The frequency of this alternating current varies from one country to another.

Hence, the correct option is (B).

64. The Pauli Exclusion Principle states that, in an atom or molecule, no two electrons can have the same four electronic quantum numbers. As an orbital can contain a maximum of only two electrons, the two electrons must have opposing spins.
Hence, the correct option is (B).

65. Antibodies present in colostrum are IgA which is also known as secretory immunoglobin. It is present in the mucosal lining of the gastrointestinal tract, the respiratory system and the urinogenital tract. Its role is to prevent pathogenic infection in these systems.

Hence, the correct option is (C).

66. A compass needle cannot be used to detect Strength of a magnet. The maximum energy product of a magnet is measured in Mega Gauss Oersteds (MGOe). This is the primary indicator of a magnets 'strength'. In general, the higher the maximum energy product value, the greater the magnetic field the magnet will generate in a particular application.
Hence, the correct option is (C).

67. The resistance of a current carrying conductor is inversely proportional to the area of cross section of the conductor. The reason is because the resistance occurs due to the collision of electrons/charged particles.So resistance is inversely proportional to area of cross section of the conductor.
Hence, the correct option is (C).

68. Pure Silicon at room temperature has perhaps one conduction electron for every 10^{13} (that's ten trillion) atoms. Increasing the temperature of intrinsic semiconductors provides more thermal energy for electrons to absorb, and thus will increase the number of conduction electrons. Voila – decreased resistance.
Hence, the correct option is (A).

69. In electromagnetism, the magnetic susceptibility is one measure of the magnetic properties of a material. The susceptibility indicates whether a material is attracted into or repelled out of a magnetic field.
Hence, the correct option is (B).

70. Using Einstein's photoelectric equation, we have

$$\frac{1}{2}mv^2 = h\nu - \phi_0 \text{....(i)}$$

According to the question, velocity (v) and frequency (ν) are doubled

$$\Rightarrow \frac{1}{2}m(2v)^2 = h2v - \phi_0$$

$$\Rightarrow 4\left(\frac{1}{2}mv^2\right) = 2h\nu - \phi_0$$

$$\Rightarrow 4(h\nu - \phi_0) = 2h\nu - \phi_0 \text{ (from equation (i))}$$

$$\Rightarrow 2h\nu = 3\phi_0 \quad \text{or} \quad \phi_0 = \frac{2h\nu}{3}$$

Hence, the correct option is (D).

71. One Fermi is a very small length. It is equal to 10^{-15} of a meter. Being such a small unit of length, Fermi is used in the measure of really small distances in nuclear science.
Hence, the correct option is (B).

72. The SI unit of luminous intensity is the candela (cd). The **candela** is the base unit of luminous intensity in the International System of Units; that is, luminous power per unit solid angle

emitted by a point light source in a particular direction.
Hence, the correct option is (C).

73. Angular velocity is defined as the rate of change of angular displacement with respect to time. It is usually expressed by the Greek letter ω (omega).
Mathematically, angular velocity,
$$\omega = \frac{d\theta}{dt}$$
If a body is rotating at the rate of N r.p.m. (revolutions per minute), then its angular velocity,
$$\omega = \frac{2\pi N}{60} \text{ rad/s}$$
Hence, the correct option is (B).

74. Young's modulus = stress/strain .This is a specific form of Hooke's law of elasticity. The units of Young's modulus in the English system are pounds per square inch (psi), and in the metric system newtons per square metre (N/m^2).
Hence, the correct option is (C).

75. A separator is a centrifugal device that separates milk into cream and skimmed milk. In Newtonian mechanics, the centrifugal force is an inertial force that appears to act on all objects when viewed in a rotating frame of reference.
Hence, the correct option is (B).

76. Larsen & Toubro (L&T) signed a pact with the Indian Institute of Technology in Bombay, Maharashtra to co-research and develop green hydrogen technology. Under this partnership, L&T will utilize its engineering expertise, product scale-up, and commercialization know-how, while IIT Bombay will use its cutting-edge research in hydrogen technologies and world-class technologists to develop indigenous globally-competitive technologies.

Hence, the correct option is (A).

77. Oil India Ltd commissioned India's first 99.999% pure green hydrogen pilot plant at its Jorhat Pump Station in Assam on 20 April 2022. It has an installed capacity of 10 kg per day and was commissioned in a record time of 3 months. The plant produces green hydrogen from the electricity generated by the existing 500kW Solar plant using a 100 kW Anion Exchange Membrane (AEM) Electrolyser array.

The use of AEM technology is being used for the first time in India. This plant is expected to increase its production of green hydrogen from 10 kg per day to 30 kg per day in the future. The company has initiated a detailed study in collaboration with IIT Guwahati on the blending of Green Hydrogen with Natural Gas and its effect on the existing infrastructure of OIL. The company also plans to study use cases for commercial applications of the blended fuel.

Hence, the correct option is (A).

78. The Indian Prime Minister Narendra Modi released a commemorative Rs 100 coin as part of the end of birth centenary celebrations of Vijaya Raje Scindia.

She was also called as the Rajamata of Gwalior and was born on the same day in the year 1919. Vijaya Raje Scindia started her political career from the Congress and later joined the

Swatantrata Party before becoming a member of the BJP's parent party, Jana Sangh.

Hence, the correct option is (A).

79. On May 11, 2018, Prime Minister Narendra Modi and Nepalese Prime Minister KP Sharma Oli jointly flagged-off a direct bus service between the two sacred cities Janakpur and Ayodhya, as part of the Ramayana Circuit.

The bus service seeks to promote religious tourism and built a strong foundation for people-to-people contact between the two countries. As per the mythological story 'Ramayana', Ayodhya is Lord Rama's birthplace, while, Janakpur is the birthplace of goddess Sita.

Hence, the correct option is (A).

80. M.O. Mathai wrote the book 'Reminiscences of the Nehru Age'. Mathai wrote the book about his experiences as the private secretary to Jawaharlal Nehru, in the brief span when the Janata alliance ousted Indira Gandhi from the Union Government.

Hence, the correct option is (C).

81. There are two groups LIG and HT each being reversed

LIG HT, GIL TH

Similarly,

RAI NY, IAR YN

Hence, the correct option is (A).

82. COBOL (common business-oriented language) is a compiled English-like computer programming language designed for business use. It is imperative, procedural and, since 2002, it is an object-oriented language. COBOL is primarily used in business, finance, and administrative systems for companies and governments. COBOL is still widely used in applications deployed on mainframe computers, such as large-scale batch and transaction processing jobs. However, due to its declining popularity and the retirement of experienced COBOL programmers, programs are being migrated to new platforms, rewritten in modern languages, or replaced with software packages. Most programming in COBOL is now purely to maintain existing applications; however, many large financial institutions were still developing new systems in COBOL as late as 2006 due to the mainframe processing speed.

Hence, the correct option is (C).

83. Jamini Roy (11 April 1887 – 24 April 1972) was an Indian painter. He was honored with the State award of Padma Bhushan in 1955. He was one of the most famous pupils of Abanindranath Tagore, whose artistic originality and contribution to the emergence of art in India remains unquestionable.

Hence, the correct option is (A).

84. Hindu temples are built in the Panchayatana layout: the main shrine is surrounded by four subsidiary shrines. The origin of the name are the Sanskrit words Pancha (five) et ayatana (containing).Generally, Hindu temples are built along a west-east axis. So the four subsidiary shrines are at the north-east, south-east, south-west, north-west.

Hence, the correct option is (C).

85. $8 \times 3 + 4 = 28$
$28 \times 4_{+4} = 116$
$116 \times 5 + 4 = 584$
$584 \times 6 + 4 = 3508$

Hence, the correct option is (C).

86. Given:

F	I	R	E
$-2\downarrow$	$-2\downarrow$	$-2\downarrow$	$-2\downarrow$
D	G	P	C

So,

S	H	O	T
$-2\downarrow$	$-2\downarrow$	$-2\downarrow$	$-2\downarrow$
Q	F	M	R

So the last letter will be R.

Hence, the correct option is (B).

87. On 11th December 1946, Prasad was unanimously elected as the Permanent Chairman of the Constituent Assembly under the temporary chairmanship of Dr. Sachchidananda Sinha.
Hence, the correct option is (B).

88. The Saurashtra cricket team led by an inspiring skipper Jaydev Unadkat recently won the maiden Ranji trophy of the team.

At the final clash on the fifth and final day at the Saurashtra Cricket Association Stadium, Rajkot, the team stopped the Bengal cricket team from clinching the trophy. There were several outstanding performers in the tournament including Arpita Vasavada, who scored a hundred in both semi-final and final, all-rounder Chirag Jani and Sheldon Jackson, who scored over 800 runs for the second successive season.

Hence, the correct option is (B).

89. The Allahabad pillar is an Ashoka Stambha, one of the pillars of Ashoka, an emperor of the Maurya dynasty who reigned in the 3rd century BC.
Hence, the correct option is (C).

90. The Gita Govinda (Song of Govinda) is a work composed by the 12th-century Indian poet, Jayadeva. The Gita Govinda (Sanskrit: गीत गोविन्दम्) (Song of Govinda) is a work composed by the 12th-century Hindu poet, Jayadeva. It describes the relationship between Krishna and the gopis (female cow herders) of Vrindavana, and in particular one gopi named Radha.
Hence, the correct option is (A).

91. Its foundation was laid by Ramdas ji, the fourth Guru of the Sikhs. It has been said in some sources that Guruji had laid the foundation of this gurudwara in December 1588 from Mian Mir, a Sufi saint of Lahore.The Golden Temple has been destroyed many times. But due to devotion and faith the Sikhs rebuilt it. It was rebuilt again in the 17th century by Maharaja Sardar Jassa Singh Ahluwalia. Every time it has been destroyed and every time it has been built, every incident of it is depicted in the temple. It was completely destroyed by the Afghan raiders in the 19th century. Then it was rebuilt by Maharaja Ranjit Singh and decorated with a layer of gold.The seventh Nizam of Hyderabad - Mir Osman Ali Khan used to donate annually towards this temple.
Hence, the correct option is (B).

92. The Independent Labour Party (ILP) was a political organization formed under the leadership of B. R. Ambedkar on 15 August 1936. It opposed the Brahmanical and capitalist structures in India, supported the Indian working class and sought to dismantle the caste system.
Hence, the correct option is (A).

93. The Indian Olympic Association has constituted an 11-member committee led by Adille Sumariwala, the President of the Athletics Federation of India.

The committee has been constituted to review and monitor the annual grant and affiliation fee of its members for the 2020-2021 cycle, in coordination with the finance department. The committee is also required to send a report on all pending issues regarding the previous year to IOA President.

Hence, the correct option is (A).

94. The Bermuda Triangle lies in a section of the North Atlantic Ocean, where a number of aircraft and ships are said to have disappeared under mysterious circumstances.
Hence, the correct option is (A).

95. Kathakali is a major form of classical Indian dance. It is a "story play" genre of art, but one distinguished by the elaborately colorful make-up, costumes and face masks that the traditionally male actor-dancers wear. Kathakali is a Hindu performance art in the Malayalam-speaking southwestern region of Kerala.

Hence, the correct option is (B).

96. The Knesset (Israel's unicameral parliament) is the country's legislative body. The Knesset took its name and fixed its membership at 120 from the Knesset Hagedolah (Great Assembly), the representative Jewish council convened in Jerusalem by Ezra and Nehemiah in the 5th century BCE.
Hence, the correct option is (C).

97. The First NAM(The Non-Aligned Movement) Summit Conference took place in Belgrade, Yugoslavia, in September 1961.
Hence, the correct option is (C).

98. Acquaintance means someone who is known but who is not a close friend. The state of being acquainted or casually familiar with someone or something.

Hence, the correct option is (C).

99. The Godavari River in India passes through the maximum number of States. The River Godavari passes through Maharashtra, Chhattisgarh, Telangana, Andhra Pradesh, Odisha, and Madhya Pradesh. The River Godavari starts in the 'Nashik district' of Maharashtra.

Hence, the correct option is (D).

100. The song Jana-Gana-mana, composed originally in Bengali by Rabindranath Tagore, was adopted in its Hindi version by the Constituent Assembly as the national anthem of India on 24

January 1950. It was first sung on 27 December 1911 at the Calcutta Session of the Indian National Congress.

Hence, the correct option is (D).

Mathematics

Q.1 If sin α + cos α = p, then what is cos² (2α) equal to?

[UPSC NDA, 2019]

A. p² **B.** p² - 1 **C.** p²(2- p²) **D.** p² + 1

Q.2 What is $\cos^{-1}\left(\frac{1-x^2}{1+x^2}\right)$ equal to?

A. $\sin^{-1}x$ **B.** $2\cot^{-1}x$
C. $2\tan^{-1}x$ **D.** $\tan^{-1}x$

Q.3 If $\left|\vec{a}\right| = 3, \left|\vec{b}\right| = 4$ and $\vec{a}\cdot\vec{b} = 6$, then find the value of $\left|\vec{a}\times\vec{b}\right|$.

A. $\sqrt{3}$ **B.** $8\sqrt{3}$ **C.** $6\sqrt{3}$ **D.** $4\sqrt{3}$

Q.4 If the roots of the equation $ax^2 + bx + c = 0$ are reciprocal to each other, then:

A. $a + c = 0$ **B.** $b = 0$
C. $a - c = 0$ **D.** None of these

Q.5 A bag contains 6 red, 5 blue balls and another bag contains 5 red and 8 blue balls. A ball is drawn from the first bag without noticing the colour is put in the second bag. A ball is drawn from the second bag. Find the probability that, the ball drawn is blue in colour.

A. $\frac{4}{7}$ **B.** $\frac{9}{14}$ **C.** $\frac{93}{154}$ **D.** $\frac{91}{154}$

Q.6 If the inverse of the matrix $A = \begin{bmatrix} 3 & 1 & 2 \\ 4 & 2 & 1 \\ 2 & a & 1 \end{bmatrix}$ does not exist then the value of a is:

A. $\frac{8}{7}$ **B.** $\frac{4}{5}$ **C.** $\frac{7}{9}$ **D.** $\frac{5}{7}$

Q.7 If 5, x, y, z, 80 are in GP then what is the value of x, y, and z?

A. x = 10, y = 20, z = 30
B. x = 10, y = 20, z = 40
C. x = 20, y = 30, z = 40
D. x = 5, y = 20, z = 30

Q.8 Find the conjugate of $\frac{i+3}{2i+1}$.

A. $1 - i$ **B.** $-i - 1$ **C.** $-i + 1$ **D.** $1 + i$

Q.9 The union of the two sets A = {1, 2, 7, 9, 12} and B = {x : x² - 10x + 16 = 0} is:

A. {} **B.** {2, 7}
C. {1, 2, 7, 8, 9, 12} **D.** {1, 8, 9, 12}

Q.10 What is the value of $\frac{dy}{dx}$, if $y^2 + x^2 + 3x + 5 = 0$ at $(0, -3)$?

A. 1 **B.** 1.5 **C.** 2 **D.** 0.5

Q.11 The value of $\cos^2 15° - \cos^2 75°$ is:

A. 1 **B.** $\frac{1}{2}$ **C.** $\frac{\sqrt{3}}{2}$ **D.** $\sqrt{3}$

Q.12 The value of $\begin{vmatrix} \sec^2 x & \tan^2 x & 1 \\ 2 & 1 & 1 \\ 10 & 8 & 2 \end{vmatrix}$:

A. $-2\sec^2 x - 6\tan^2 x$
B. $2\sec^2 x - 6\tan^2 x + 2$
C. 0
D. None of these

Q.13 If A = {x, y, z} and B = {1, 2}. Find the number of relations from A to B ?

A. 2^4 **B.** 2^6
C. 2^5 **D.** None of these

Q.14 Find the slope of the tangent of the curve $y^2 - 3x^3 + 2 = 0$ at $(1, -1)$.

A. -1.5 **B.** 2.5 **C.** 3.5 **D.** -4.5

Q.15 The mean of 8 observations is 25. The 7 observations are $30, 24, 27, 22, 18, 26, 32$. What is the 8th observation?

A. 20 **B.** 21 **C.** 22 **D.** 23

Q.16 $\lim\limits_{x\to 1} \frac{1-\sqrt{x}}{\cos^{-1}x}$ is equal to:

[UPSESSB TGT Mathematics, 2019]

A. 0 **B.** $\frac{1}{2}$ **C.** $\frac{1}{4}$ **D.** 1

Q.17 Find the harmonic mean, if the arithmetic mean is 27 and geometric mean is 9.

A. $9\sqrt{3}$ **B.** 9 **C.** 3 **D.** 27

Q.18 If the third term in the binomial expansion of $(1 + x)^m$ is $\left(\frac{-1}{8}\right)x^2$ then the rational value of m is:

A. 2 **B.** $\frac{1}{2}$
C. 3 **D.** None of these

Q.19 What is the value of λ for which the vectors $\hat{i} - \hat{j} + \hat{k}, 2\hat{i} + \hat{j} - \hat{k}, \hat{i}\lambda - \hat{j} + \hat{k}\lambda$ are coplanar?

A. 5 **B.** 4 **C.** 2 **D.** 1

Q.20 What is $\int_0^1 x(1 - x)^9 dx$ equal to?

A. $\frac{1}{110}$ **B.** $\frac{1}{132}$ **C.** $\frac{1}{148}$ **D.** $\frac{1}{140}$

Q.21 Evaluate $\int \frac{x}{3x^2+4} dx$.

A. $\frac{1}{3}\log(3x^2 + 4) + c$

B. $\frac{1}{6}\log(3x^2 + 4) + c$

C. $\frac{1}{6}\log(3x^2 + 4) + \tan^{-1}x + c$

D. None of the above

Q.22 Find the angle between the planes $x + 2y + z = 7$ and $2x - y + z = 13$.

A. $\theta = \cos^{-1}\left(\frac{1}{6}\right)$ **B.** $\theta = \cos^{-1}\left(\frac{1}{3}\right)$

C. $\theta = \cos^{-1}\left(\frac{2}{3}\right)$ **D.** $\theta = \cos^{-1}\left(\frac{3}{4}\right)$

Q.23 Find the equation of the hyperbola, the length of whose latus rectum is 4 and the eccentricity is 3.

A. $2x^2 - y^2 = 1$ **B.** $16x^2 - 2y^2 = 1$

C. $6x^2 - 2y^2 = 1$ **D.** None of these

Q.24 Find the eccentricity of the ellipse $\frac{x^2}{16} + \frac{y^2}{25} = 1$.

A. 1   **B.** $\frac{2}{3}$ **C.** $\frac{3}{5}$ **D.** $\frac{4}{5}$

Q.25 Equation of a line having slope 3 and the point (3, 2) lies on the line:

A. 3y - x - 3 = 0   **B.** y - 3x + 7 = 0

C. y + 3x - 11 = 0   **D.** 3y + x - 9 = 0

English

Ques (26-30):Direction: Read the following passage to answer the given question based on it.

Primitive man was probably more concerned with fire as a source of warmth and as a means of cooking food than as a source of light. Before he discovered less laborious ways of making fire, he had to preserve it, and whenever he went on a journey he carried a firebrand with him. His discovery that the firebrand, from which the torch may very well have developed, could be used for illumination was probably incidental to the primary purpose of preserving a flame.

Lamps, too, probably developed by accident. Early man may have had his first conception of a lamp while watching a twig or fibre burning in the molten fat dropped from a roasting carcass. All he had to do was to fashion a vessel to contain fat and float a lighted reed in it. Such lamps, which were made of hollowed stones or seashells, have persisted in identical form up to quite recent times.

Q.26 The firebrand was used to:

A. Prevent accidents   **B.** Provide light

C. Scare animals   **D.** Save labour

Q.27 Early lamps were made by:

A. Using a reed as a wick in the fat

B. Letting a reed soak the fat

C. Putting the fat in a shell and lighting it

D. Floating a reed in the seashell

Q.28 Lamps were probably developed through mere:

A. Hazard   **B.** Fate   **C.** Chance   **D.** Planning

Q.29 Primitive man's most important use for the fire was:

A. To provide warmth   **B.** To cook food

C. To provide light   **D.** Both (A) and (B)

Q.30 By 'primary' the author means:

A. Primitive   **B.** Fundamental

C. Elemental   **D.** Essential

Q.31 Direction: In the following question, a sentence is given in Active Voice. Out of the four options, select the one which best expresses the sentence in Passive Voice.

The little girl showed the visitor her drawing.

A. The little girl was shown her drawing by the visitor.

B. The visitor is being shown her drawing by the little girl.

C. The visitor was shown her drawing by the little girl.

D. The visitor is shown her drawing by the little girl.

Q.32 Direction: In the following question, a sentence is given in Active Voice. Out of the four options, select the one which best expresses the sentence in Passive Voice.

He bought a new car for the journey.

A. For the journey a new car bought by him.

B. A new car was bought for the journey by him.

C. His new car was bought for the journey.

D. He has bought a new car for the journey.

Q.33 Direction: Select the correct indirect form of the given sentence.

Kavya said, "I have made a new painting."

[SSC Selection Post Phase IX, 2020]

A. Kavya says that I make a new painting.

B. Kavya said that she have made a new painting.

C. Kavya said that she had made a new painting.

D. Kavya said that I have made a new painting.

Q.34 Direction: Select the option that is the direct form of the given sentence.

Brinda told her doctor that she was leaving for Boston the next day.

A. Brinda told to her doctor, "I will be leaving for Boston the next day".

B. Brinda told her doctor, "I was leaving for Boston tomorrow".

C. Brinda said to her doctor, "I am leaving for Boston tomorrow."

D. Brinda had told her doctor, "She was leaving for Boston the next day".

Q.35 Direction: Choose the word that is closest in meaning to the given word.

Erudite

A. Naive   **B.** Equivocate

C. Tireless   **D.** Scholarly

Q.36 Direction: Select the most appropriate antonym of the given word.

Worsen

A. Disappear   **B.** Leave

C. Command   **D.** Improve

Q.37 Direction: Select the most appropriate antonym of the given word.

Placate

A. Propitiate	**B.** Enrage

C. Appease	**D.** Conciliate

Q.38 Direction: Select the most appropriate synonym of the given word.

Gaudy

A. Simple	**B.** Plain	**C.** Proper	**D.** Flashy

Q.39 Direction: Choose the adjective in the given sentence.

No other team is _______ our team.

A. stronger	**B.** strongest than

C. as strong as	**D.** None of the above

Q.40 Direction: Choose the adjective in the given sentence.

I like ________ pop music but not all.

A. little	**B.** less	**C.** some	**D.** any

Q.41 Direction: Choose the preposition in the given sentence.

We've got this jumper ____ red.

A. in	**B.** to	**C.** with	**D.** at

Q.42 Direction: Choose the preposition in the given sentence.

Tell us _______ your holiday.

A. with	**B.** of

C. about	**D.** None of these

Q.43 Direction: Selecting the appropriate phrasal verb from the given options.

He <u>looks for</u> his grandfather with wide eyes and a quiet disposition.

A. brings up	**B.** takes after

C. backs out	**D.** No improvement

Q.44 Direction: Selecting the appropriate phrasal verb from the given options.

Marie asked me to <u>look into</u> for a while as she was caught up in a task.

A. hold on	**B.** light on

C. look up to	**D.** No improvement

Q.45 Direction: In the following question, some part of the sentence is underlined. Which of the options given below the sentence should replace the part underlined to make the sentence grammatically correct? If the sentence is correct as it is given then choose option (D) 'No Correction required' as the answer.

Considering the high demand for flights to Gulf countries airlines, <u>can risen</u> prices.

A. should rise

B. could raised

C. may raise

D. No correction required

Q.46 Direction: In the following question, some part of the sentence is underlined. Which of the options given below the sentence should replace the part underlined to make the sentence grammatically correct? If the sentence is correct as it is given then choose option (D) 'No Correction required' as the answer.

<u>Without both issue</u> is clarified the board will keep all other matters before it pending.

A. Unless both issues are

B. Until each issue were

C. Without the issue being

D. No correction required

Q.47 Direction: Fill in the blank with the suitable pronoun.

The teacher asked us to hurry up since ______ of the questions is compulsory and must be completed.

A. either	**B.** neither	**C.** each	**D.** both

Q.48 Direction: Fill in the blank with the suitable pronoun.

______ participant of the tournament was asked to submit a registration form.

A. Each	**B.** Either	**C.** Neither	**D.** Either of

Q.49 Direction: Fill in the blank with the most appropriate word.

______ Penguins live in the South Pole.

A. A	**B.** An

C. No article	**D.** The

Q.50 Direction: Insert appropriate articles where necessary.

Do you collect _____ stamps?

A. a	**B.** an

C. the	**D.** No article

Science

Q.51 Which of the following doesn't have kinetic energy?

A. Fired bullet	**B.** Running water

C. Working hammer	**D.** Stretched bow

Q.52 Calculate the work done by the force of gravity, when an object of 10 kg falls from a height of 10 m. (take g = 10 m/s^2)

A. 500 J	**B.** 1000 J	**C.** 100 J	**D.** 50 J

Q.53 The dimensions of intensity of wave are:

A. $[ML^2\,T^{-3}]$	**B.** $[ML^0\,T^{-3}]$

C. $[ML^{-2}\,T^{-3}]$	**D.** $[M^1\,L^2\,T^3]$

Q.54 The dimensional formula of a physical quantity is $[M^1L^1T^{-2}]$. What is its SI unit?

A. $kgs^{-2}\,m^{-1}$	**B.** $kg\,ms^{-2}$

C. $kg^2\,s^2\,m^2$	**D.** $kg\,ms^2$

Q.55 A rain drop of mass 0.1g is falling with uniform speed of 10cm/s. What is the net force the drop?

A. 10^{-2} N	**B.** 10^{-3} N

C. 2×10^{-3} N	**D.** Zero

Q.56 If the critical angle for total internal reflection from a medium to vacuum is $30°$, then the speed of light in the medium is:

A. $6 \times 10^8\, m/s$	**B.** $3 \times 10^8\, m/s$

C. $2 \times 10^8 \, m/s$ **D.** $1.5 \times 10^8 \, m/s$

Q.57 An endoscope is used by a physician to view the internal parts of a body organ. It is based on the principle of:
A. Refraction of light
B. Reflection of light
C. Total internal reflection of light
D. Dispersion of light

Q.58 Vector form of Biot-savart's law is:

A. $\vec{dB} = \frac{\mu_o}{4\pi} i \left(\frac{\vec{dl} \times \vec{r}}{r} \right)$ **B.** $\vec{dB} = \frac{\mu_o}{4\pi} i^2 \left(\frac{\vec{dl} \times \vec{r}}{r} \right)$

C. $\vec{dB} = \frac{\mu_o}{4\pi} i^2 \left(\frac{\vec{dl} \times \vec{r}}{r^2} \right)$ **D.** $\vec{dB} = \frac{\mu_o}{4\pi} i \left(\frac{\vec{dl} \times \vec{r}}{r^3} \right)$

Q.59 A circular coil of radius R having N number of turns carries a steady current I. The magnetic induction at the centre of the coil is 0.1 tesla. If the number of turns is doubled and the radius is halved, which one of the following will be the correct value for the magnetic induction at the centre of the coil?
A. 0.05 tesla   **B.** 0.2 tesla
C. 0.4 tesla   **D.** 0.8 tesla

Q.60 In an LCR circuit, the pd between the terminals of the inductance is $60V$, between the terminals of the capacitor is $30V$ and that between the terminals of resistance is $40V$. The supply voltage will be equal to:
A. $50V$ **B.** $70V$ **C.** $130V$ **D.** $10V$

Q.61 Two coils of self-inductance L_1 and L_2 are placed closer to each other so that total flux in one coil is completely linked with others. If M is mutual inductance between them, then:
A. $M = L_1 L_2$ **B.** $\frac{ML_1}{L_2}$
C. $M = \sqrt{L_1 L_2}$ **D.** $M = (L_1 L_2)^2$

Q.62 On what application does the speedometer works?
A. Lenz's law
B. Eddy current
C. Electromagnetic induction
D. Mutual inductance

Q.63 A spring block system having spring constant K and block has mass M. If we have to reduce the time period of SHM by 3 times then-new spring constant will be:
A. $3K$ **B.** $9K$ **C.** $27K$ **D.** K

Q.64 Which of the following statements are incorrect about ultrasonic waves?
A. The sound frequency of ultrasonic waves is above 20,000Hz.
B. Ultrasounds can be used to detect cracks and flaws in metal blocks.
C. The frequency range of ultrasonic waves is below 20Hz.
D. Ultrasound is generally used to clean parts located in hard-to-reach places.

Q.65 The heat exchanged between the system and the surrounding is + 60 J and the internal energy change is − 180 J. Find the work done by/on the system.
A. 150 J   **B.** 200 J   **C.** 220 J   **D.** 240 J

Q.66 The entropy of a closed system changes because:
A. There is a change in mass of the system.
B. There is no change in mass of the system.
C. There is an exchange of heat of system with the surrounding.
D. There is an increase in volume of the system.

Q.67 In an electromagnetic wave, the electric and magnetic fields are:
A. Always in phase
B. Always in antiphase
C. Always at 90 degree phase difference
D. Always at 45 degree phase difference

Q.68 Which one of the following statements is incorrect about electromagnetic waves?
A. Electromagnetic waves are deflected by an electric field and magnetic field.
B. They can also move in vacuum.
C. They have electric and magnetic components that are mutually perpendicular.
D. They move with a speed of 3 × 10⁸ m/s.

Q.69 What is Poisson's Ratio?
A. It is the ratio of lateral strain to longitudinal strain.
B. It is the ratio of force to the area.
C. It is the ratio of change in radius or diameter to the original radius or diameter.
D. It is the ratio of change in length to the original length.

Q.70 The reciprocal of the bulk modulus is called as:
A. Elasticity   **B.** Compressibility
C. Elastic limit   **D.** Modulus of rigidity

Q.71 Name the element that must be present in a compound to classify it as an organic compound.
A. Iron   **B.** Ammonia
C. Zinc   **D.** Carbon

Q.72 Gasohol is a mixture of–
A. Gasoline and Methanol
B. Gasoline and Ethanol
C. Gasoline and Propanol
D. Methanol and Ethanol

Q.73 Two copper wires A and B of length l and $2l$ respectively, have the same area of cross-section. The ratio of the resistance of wire A to the resistance of wire B is:
A. 4   **B.** 2   **C.** 1   **D.** $\frac{1}{2}$

Q.74 Three resistors $80\Omega, 120\Omega$ and 240Ω are connected in parallel. A $12V$ battery is connect across combination of resistors. Find the current drawn from the battery.
A. $0.3A$ **B.** $0.09A$ **C.** $0.9A$ **D.** $3A$

Q.75 Microsoft Office is an example of a:
A.   Closed source software
B.   Open-source software
C.   Horizontal market software
D.   Vertical market software

General Awareness

Q.76 The Union Government has authorised which bank for issue and encash Electoral Bonds through its 29 Authorized Branches from 1–10 th of July 2022?
A. State Bank of India
B. Axis Bank
C. ICICI Bank
D. HDFC Bank

Q.77 Direction: From the given alternatives, select the word which cannot be formed using the given word.
HALLUCINATION
A. LION
B. LOAN
C. NATION
D. LOTION

Q.78 Direction: In the following question, select the related word from the given alternatives.
Grammy : Music :: Pulitzer : ?
A. Film
B. Literature
C. Documentary
D. Journalism

Q.79 In a certain code, MISTAKEN is written as SRHLOFLB. How is GROUNDED written in that code?
A. CDCMTNQF
B. TNQFCDCM
C. EFEOTNQF
D. TNQFEFEO

Q.80 If FLOWER is coded as EMNXDS, then how can SHOWER be coded in that code?
A. RGNXDS
B. TINXDS
C. RINXDS
D. SINXDS

Q.81 Who among the following was the recipient of the first Gauri Lankesh Memorial Award for Journalism?
A. Ravish Kumar
B. Sagarika Ghose
C. Arnab Goswami
D. Rajat Sharma

Q.82 Where do you find the temple of Angkor Wat?
A. Thailand
B. Malaysia
C. Cambodia
D. Myanmar

Q.83 What is the capital of Chile?
A. Tehran
B. Santiago
C. Bishkek
D. Phnom penh

Q.84 With which of the following states is the harvest festival 'Nuakhai' traditionally associated?

[SSC Selection Post Phase IX, 2020]

A. Nagaland
B. Kerala
C. Odisha
D. Himachal Pradesh

Q.85 Which of the following is folk dance of Chandigarh?
A. Loor Dance
B. Giddha Dance
C. Lavani Dance
D. Monyo Asho Dance

Q.86 The name 'Aghanya' mentioned in many passages of the Rig veda refers to:
A. Priest
B. Women
C. Cows
D. Brahmanas

Q.87 Emperor Ashoka was the son of which of the following Mauryan rulers?
A. Samudragupta
B. Bindusara
C. Chandragupta
D. Kanishka

Q.88 Which city is known as Venice of the East?
A. Nagaur
B. Jaipur
C. Nagpur
D. Udaipur

Q.89 Where is Okhla Bird Sanctuary located?
A. Himachal Pradesh
B. NCR Region
C. Haryana
D. Punjab

Q.90 Pooja Rani is associated with which sports?
A. Hockey
B. Boxing
C. Weight lifting
D. Shooting

Q.91 Which line divides India and Pakistan?
A. McMahon Line
B. Durand Line
C. Radcliffe Line
D. Maginot Line

Q.92 River Ganga does not pass through which among the following states?
A. Jharkhand
B. Uttar Pradesh
C. Bihar
D. Andhra Pradesh

Q.93 H1N1 viruses are the cause of which of the following diseases?
A. Ebola
B. Swine Flu
C. Polio
D. Both (A) and (B)

Q.94 Who among the following wrote the book "How India Sees the World: Kautilya to the 21st Century"?
A. Saji Mathew
B. Aparna Pandel
C. Satya Nadela
D. Shyam Saran

Q.95 Who among is known for the discovered Catalysis?
A. Rayleigh
B. Berzelius
C. K Scheele
D. Rutherford

Q.96 Direction: A series is given with one missing term. Select the correct alternative from the given ones that will complete the series.
A4X, D9U, ?, J25O
A. F14R
B. F16S
C. G16R
D. E12T

Q.97 Who among the following is not the recipient of the prestigious 'Padma Vibhushan' award 2020?
A. Arun Jaitley
B. P V Sindhu
C. Sushma Swaraj
D. M.C. Mary Kom

Q.98 The Saddle Peak in Andaman and Nicobar is located in which of the following part of the territory?
A. Little Andaman
B. North Andaman
C. Great Nicobar
D. South Nicobar

Q.99 What is the full form of "IT"?

A. Intelligence Technology
B. Inter Technology
C. Interesting Technology
D. Information Technology

Q.100 Which of the following languages belongs to Nagaland?

(i) English

(ii) Nagamese

(iii) Angami Ao

A. Only (iii)

B. Both (i) and (ii)

C. Both (i) and (iii)

D. None of the above

// Smart Answer Sheet //

Correct — Percentage of students who answered correctly. **Skipped** — Percentage of students who skipped.

Q.	Ans.	Correct	Skipped	Q.	Ans.	Correct	Skipped	Q.	Ans.	Correct	Skipped	Q.	Ans.	Correct	Skipped	Q.	Ans.	Correct	Skipped	Q.	Ans.	Correct	Skipped
1	C	88.57 %	11.14 %	18	B	68.67 %	30.21 %	35	D	53.58 %	38.86 %	52	B	46.88 %	48.12 %	69	A	88.97 %	10.09 %	86	C	43.61 %	38.52 %
2	C	67.67 %	31.67 %	19	D	87.87 %	11.36 %	36	D	68.66 %	30.99 %	53	B	76.75 %	16.44 %	70	B	60.64 %	30.36 %	87	B	77.14 %	21.15 %
3	C	68.56 %	31.27 %	20	A	43.19 %	55.69 %	37	B	44.77 %	54.51 %	54	B	89.76 %	10.03 %	71	D	68.03 %	31.0 %	88	D	42.87 %	31.47 %
4	C	86.41 %	12.96 %	21	B	84.64 %	15.01 %	38	D	88.9 %	10.2 %	55	D	81.5 %	17.38 %	72	B	44.24 %	34.73 %	89	B	48.63 %	43.8 %
5	C	69.36 %	30.09 %	22	A	82.36 %	11.77 %	39	C	88.08 %	11.35 %	56	D	76.4 %	23.33 %	73	D	77.37 %	10.07 %	90	B	65.74 %	30.75 %
6	B	77.06 %	10.03 %	23	B	49.27 %	47.67 %	40	C	63.0 %	32.9 %	57	C	80.52 %	12.12 %	74	A	78.76 %	20.41 %	91	C	47.69 %	32.45 %
7	B	56.36 %	43.29 %	24	C	52.83 %	37.37 %	41	A	62.51 %	33.57 %	58	D	79.26 %	11.4 %	75	C	82.93 %	15.39 %	92	D	77.15 %	13.22 %
8	D	81.58 %	13.63 %	25	B	64.73 %	35.04 %	42	C	86.75 %	12.11 %	59	C	44.37 %	40.57 %	76	A	81.59 %	14.62 %	93	B	56.36 %	35.82 %
9	C	89.49 %	10.08 %	26	B	88.17 %	11.81 %	43	B	84.51 %	13.91 %	60	A	88.45 %	10.63 %	77	D	83.9 %	15.01 %	94	D	85.63 %	13.61 %
10	D	53.1 %	45.86 %	27	A	64.86 %	34.51 %	44	A	55.92 %	43.63 %	61	C	87.67 %	10.81 %	78	D	77.37 %	17.55 %	95	B	76.86 %	10.77 %
11	C	79.72 %	18.87 %	28	C	88.64 %	11.04 %	45	C	65.37 %	33.39 %	62	B	76.37 %	14.5 %	79	D	85.65 %	11.22 %	96	C	87.53 %	10.45 %
12	C	63.64 %	35.72 %	29	D	83.06 %	14.84 %	46	A	49.59 %	30.41 %	63	B	81.97 %	13.07 %	80	C	83.71 %	14.67 %	97	B	77.6 %	20.07 %
13	B	58.49 %	30.56 %	30	D	78.15 %	17.62 %	47	C	79.61 %	16.39 %	64	C	60.37 %	39.13 %	81	A	66.1 %	32.44 %	98	B	86.81 %	11.81 %
14	D	85.89 %	12.28 %	31	C	87.02 %	11.48 %	48	A	88.06 %	11.82 %	65	D	85.6 %	12.68 %	82	C	44.1 %	40.91 %	99	D	85.64 %	11.5 %
15	B	66.85 %	30.29 %	32	B	89.44 %	10.23 %	49	C	59.87 %	31.24 %	66	C	76.82 %	19.86 %	83	B	85.85 %	12.23 %	100	B	78.17 %	19.06 %
16	A	69.59 %	30.15 %	33	C	88.6 %	10.63 %	50	D	41.03 %	32.27 %	67	A	86.14 %	12.22 %	84	C	76.12 %	21.9 %				
17	C	89.81 %	10.16 %	34	C	88.59 %	11.21 %	51	D	89.27 %	10.23 %	68	A	87.47 %	10.3 %	85	B	42.87 %	31.27 %				

//Hints and Solutions//

1. Given,

$\sin \alpha + \cos \alpha = p$

By squaring both sides, we get

$\sin^2 \alpha + \cos^2 \alpha + 2 \sin \alpha \cos \alpha = p^2$

As we know that,

$\sin^2 x + \cos^2 x = 1$ and $\sin 2x = 2 \sin x \cos x$

$\Rightarrow 1 + \sin 2\alpha = p^2$

$\Rightarrow \sin 2\alpha = p^2 - 1$

$\therefore \cos^2 2\alpha = 1 - \sin^2 2\alpha = 1 - (p^2 - 1)^2$

$= p^2 (2 - p^2)$

Hence, the correct option is (C).

2. Given,

$\cos^{-1}\left(\frac{1-x^2}{1+x^2}\right)$

Put $x = \tan\theta$

$= \cos^{-1}\left(\frac{1-\tan^2\theta}{1+\tan^2\theta}\right)$

$= \cos^{-1}\left(\frac{1-\tan^2\theta}{\sec^2\theta}\right)$

$= \cos^{-1}(\cos^2\theta - \sin^2\theta)$

$= \cos^{-1}(\cos 2\theta) \; (\because \cos 2\theta = \cos^2\theta - \sin^2\theta)$

$= 2\theta \; (\because \cos^{-1}\cos x = x)$

$= 2\tan^{-1}x \; (\because x = \tan\theta)$

Hence, the correct option is (C).

3. Given,

$\left|\vec{a}\right| = 3, \left|\vec{b}\right| = 4$ and $\vec{a} \cdot \vec{b} = 6$

As we know,

$\vec{a} \cdot \vec{b} = \left|\vec{a}\right| \times \left|\vec{b}\right| \times \cos\theta$

$\Rightarrow 6 = 3 \times 4 \times \cos\theta$

$\Rightarrow \cos\theta = \frac{6}{12} = \frac{1}{2}$

$\therefore \theta = 60°$

As we know that,

If $\vec{a}$ and $\vec{b}$ are two vectors, then

$\vec{a} \times \vec{b} = \left|\vec{a}\right| \times \left|\vec{b}\right| \times \sin\theta \times \hat{n}$

$\left|\vec{a} \times \vec{b}\right| = \left|\vec{a}\right| \times \left|\vec{b}\right| \times |\sin\theta| \times |\hat{n}| = \left|\vec{a}\right| \times \left|\vec{b}\right| \times$

$\sin\theta \; (\because$ Magnitude of a unit vector is one)

$\left|\vec{a} \times \vec{b}\right| = 3 \times 4 \times \sin 60°$

$\therefore \left|\vec{a} \times \vec{b}\right| = 3 \times 4 \times \frac{\sqrt{3}}{2} = 6\sqrt{3}$

Hence, the correct option is (C).

4. As we know,

The sum of the roots of a quadratic equation is given by,

$\alpha + \beta = -\frac{b}{a} = -\frac{\text{coefficient of } x}{\text{coefficient of } x^2}$

The product of the roots is given by,

$\alpha\beta = \frac{c}{a} = \frac{\text{constant term}}{\text{coefficient of } x^2}$

Given,

Equation is $ax^2 + bx + c = 0$ with the roots α, β.

The roots of the equation $ax^2 + bx + c = 0$ are reciprocal to each other.

So, $\beta = \frac{1}{\alpha}$

If α, β are the roots of quadratic the equation $ax^2 + bx + c = 0$ then $\alpha\beta = \frac{c}{a}$

Product of roots $= \frac{c}{a}$

$\Rightarrow \alpha \cdot \frac{1}{\alpha} = \frac{c}{a}$

$\Rightarrow 1 = \frac{c}{a}$

$\Rightarrow a = c$

$\therefore a - c = 0$

Hence, the correct option is (C).

5. Let,

$P(A) =$ probability of getting a blue ball from the 2nd bag.

$P(E_1) =$ probability of getting a red ball from the 1st bag.

$P(E_2) =$ probability of getting a blue ball from the 1st bag.

$P(E_1) = \frac{6}{11}$

$P(E_2) = \frac{5}{11}$

$P\left(\frac{A}{E_1}\right) = \frac{8}{14}$

$P\left(\frac{A}{E_2}\right) = \frac{9}{14}$

$P(A) = P(A \cap E_1) + (A \cap E_2)$

$= P(E_1)P\left(\frac{A}{E_1}\right) + P(E_2)P\left(\frac{A}{E_2}\right)$

$= \frac{6}{11} \times \frac{8}{14} + \frac{5}{11} \times \frac{9}{14}$

$= \frac{93}{154}$

Hence, the correct option is (C).

6. Given,

$A = \begin{bmatrix} 3 & 1 & 2 \\ 4 & 2 & 1 \\ 2 & a & 1 \end{bmatrix}$

For A^{-1} does not exist, then $|A| = 0$

$|A| = \begin{vmatrix} 3 & 1 & 2 \\ 4 & 2 & 1 \\ 2 & a & 1 \end{vmatrix} = 0$

$\Rightarrow |A| = 3(2 - a) - 1(4 - 2) + 2(4a - 4)$

$\Rightarrow |A| = 6 - 3a - 2 + 8a - 8$

$\Rightarrow |A| = 5a - 4$

$\Rightarrow |A| = 0$

$\Rightarrow 5a - 4 = 0$

$\therefore a = \dfrac{4}{5}$

Hence, the correct option is (B).

7. As we know,

n^{th} term of the G.P. is an = ar^{n-1}

Given,

Series: 5, x, y, z, 80

We have 1st term, a = 5, and 5th term, a_5 = 80

$\therefore a_5 = 5 (r)^{5-1}$

$\Rightarrow 80 = 5r^4$

$\Rightarrow r^4 = 16$

$\Rightarrow r = 2$

$\therefore x = 5(2)^{2-1} = 10$

And, y = $5(2)^{3-1}$ = 5 × 4 = 20

Also, z = $5(2)^{4-1}$ = 5 × 8 = 40

Hence, the correct option is (B).

8. For any complex number $z = x + iy$ the conjugate $\bar z$ is given by,

$\bar z = x - iy$

$z = \dfrac{i+3}{2i+1}$

$z = \dfrac{i+3}{2i+1} \times \dfrac{-2i+1}{-2i+1}$

Multiply numerator and denominator with $-2i + 1$, we get

$\Rightarrow z = \dfrac{-2i^2 - 6i + i + 3}{1 - (2i)^2}$

$\Rightarrow z = \dfrac{5 - 5i}{1 + 4}$

$\Rightarrow z = \dfrac{5(1-i)}{5}$

$\Rightarrow z = 1 - i$

Conjugate of $z = \bar z = 1 + i$

Hence, the correct option is (D).

9. As we know,

A ∪ B = {x : x ∈ A or x ∈ B}

Set A = {1, 2, 7, 9, 12}

x² - 10x + 16 = 0

$\Rightarrow$ x² - 2x - 8x + 16 = 0

$\Rightarrow$ (x - 2)(x - 8) = 0

$\Rightarrow$ x = 2, 8

Set B = {2, 8}

$\therefore$ Set (A ∪ B) = {1, 2, 7, 8, 9, 12}

Hence, the correct option is (C).

10. Chain Rule (Differentiation by substitution): If y is a function of u and u is a function of x.

$\dfrac{dy}{dx} = \dfrac{dy}{du} \times \dfrac{du}{dx}$

Given,

$y^2 + x^2 + 3x + 5 = 0$

Differentiating with respect to x, we get

$2y\dfrac{dy}{dx} + 2x + 3(1) + 0 = 0$

$\Rightarrow 2y\dfrac{dy}{dx} + 2x + 3 = 0$

$\Rightarrow 2y\dfrac{dy}{dx} = -(2x + 3)$

$\Rightarrow \dfrac{dy}{dx} = -\dfrac{2x+3}{2y}$

Now at $(0, -3)$

$\Rightarrow \dfrac{dy}{dx} = -\dfrac{2(0)+3}{2(-3)}$

$\Rightarrow \dfrac{dy}{dx} = -\dfrac{3}{(-6)}$

$\therefore \dfrac{dy}{dx} = \dfrac{1}{2} = 0.5$

Hence, the correct option is (D).

11. $\cos^2 15° - \cos^2 75°$

$= \cos^2 15° - \cos^2(90° - 15°)$

$= \cos^2 15° - \sin^2 15°$

$= \cos(2 \times 15°) \ (\because \cos^2\theta - \sin^2\theta = \cos 2\theta)$

$= \cos 30°$

$= \dfrac{\sqrt 3}{2}$

Hence, the correct option is (C).

12. Let $\Delta = \begin{vmatrix} \sec^2 x & \tan^2 x & 1 \\ 2 & 1 & 1 \\ 10 & 8 & 2 \end{vmatrix}$

Apply $C_1 \to C_1 - C_2$

$\Delta = \begin{vmatrix} \sec^2 x - \tan^2 x & \tan^2 x & 1 \\ 2 - 1 & 1 & 1 \\ 10 - 8 & 8 & 2 \end{vmatrix}$

$\Delta = \begin{vmatrix} 1 & \tan^2 x & 1 \\ 1 & 1 & 1 \\ 2 & 8 & 2 \end{vmatrix} \ (\because \sec^2 x - \tan^2 x = 1)$

As we know,

If two rows or two columns of a determinant are identical the value of the determinant is zero.

Here C_1 and C_3 are identical.

So, $\Delta = 0$

Hence, the correct option is (B).

13. Given,

A = {x, y, z} and B = {1, 2}

$\Rightarrow$ n(A) = 3 and n(B) = 2

As we know that,

If A and B are two non-empty sets such that n(A) = p and n(B) = q then the number of relations that can be defined from A to B = 2^{pq}

Here, p = 3 and q = 2

So, the number of relations from A to B = 2^6

Hence, the correct option is (B).

14. As we know,

The slope of the tangent to a curve $y = f(x)$ is $m = \frac{dy}{dx}$.

Given,

Curve $= y^2 - 3x^3 + 2 = 0$

Differentiating the equation wrt x, we get

$2y\frac{dy}{dx} - 9x^2 + 0 = 0$

$\Rightarrow 2y\frac{dy}{dx} = 9x^2$

Slope at $(1, -1)$,

$2(-1)\frac{dy}{dx} = 9(1)$

$\Rightarrow -2\frac{dy}{dx} = 9$

$\Rightarrow \frac{dy}{dx} = -4.5$

The slope of the tangent $(m) = \frac{dy}{dx}$

$\therefore m = -4.5$

Hence, the correct option is (D).

15. As we know,

Mean of n elements $= \dfrac{\text{Sum of all n elements}}{\text{Total number of elements (n)}}$

Let the 8th observation be x.

Given,

Mean $= 25$,

Total elements $= 8$

$\therefore \dfrac{30+24+27+22+18+26+32+x}{8} = 25$

$\Rightarrow 179 + x = 200$

$\Rightarrow x = 21$

Hence, the correct option is (B).

16. As we know,

$\lim\limits_{x \to a}\frac{f(x)}{g(x)} = \lim\limits_{x \to a}\frac{f'(x)}{g'(x)}$

Given,

$\lim\limits_{x \to 1}\frac{1-\sqrt{x}}{\cos^{-1}x}$

Apply L-hospital rule

$= \lim\limits_{x \to 1}\dfrac{0 - \frac{1}{2\sqrt{x}}}{-\frac{1}{\sqrt{1-x^2}}}$

$= \lim\limits_{x \to 1}\dfrac{\sqrt{1-x^2}}{2\sqrt{x}} = 0$

Hence, the correct option is (A).

17. The relation between arithmetic mean (AM), geometric mean (GM) and harmonic mean (HM): $(GM)^2 = (AM) \times (HM)$

Given,

$AM = 27$ and $GM = 9$

$(GM)^2 = (AM) \times (HM)$

$\Rightarrow (9)^2 = 27 \times HM$

$\Rightarrow HM = \frac{81}{27} = 3$

Hence, the correct option is (C).

18. Given,

The third term in the binomial expansion of $(1 + x)^m$ is $\left(\frac{-1}{8}\right)x^2$.

$(1 + x)^m = 1 + mx + \frac{m(m-1)}{2!}x^2 + \frac{m(m-1)(m-2)}{3!}x^3 + \cdots$

So, the third term in the binomial expansion of $(1 + x)^m$ is $\frac{m(m-1)}{2!}x^2$.

$\frac{m(m-1)}{2!}x^2 = \left(\frac{-1}{8}\right)x^2$

$\Rightarrow \frac{m(m-1)}{2} = \frac{-1}{8}$

$\Rightarrow 4m^2 - 4m + 1 = 0$

$\Rightarrow (2m - 1)^2 = 0$

$\Rightarrow 2m - 1 = 0$

$\therefore m = \frac{1}{2}$

Hence, the correct option is (B).

19. Let $\vec{a} = a_1\hat{i} + b_1\hat{j} + c_1\hat{k}, \vec{b} = a_2\hat{i} + b_2\hat{j} + c_2\hat{k}$ and $\vec{c} = a_3\hat{i} + b_3\hat{j} + c_3\hat{k}$ be the three vectors.

Condition for coplanarity, $\vec{a} \cdot \left(\vec{b} \times \vec{c}\right) =$

$\begin{vmatrix} a_1 & b_1 & c_1 \\ a_2 & b_2 & c_2 \\ a_3 & b_3 & c_3 \end{vmatrix} = 0$

Given,

$\hat{i} - \hat{j} + \hat{k}, 2\hat{i} + \hat{j} - \hat{k}, \hat{i}\lambda - \hat{j} + \hat{k}\lambda$ are coplanar.

$\begin{vmatrix} 1 & -1 & 1 \\ 2 & 1 & -1 \\ \lambda & -1 & \lambda \end{vmatrix} = 0$

$\Rightarrow 1(\lambda - 1) + 1(2\lambda + \lambda) + 1(-2 - \lambda) = 0$

$\Rightarrow 3\lambda = 3$

$\Rightarrow \lambda = 1$

Hence, the correct option is (D).

20. Let $f(x) = x(1 - x)^9$

Now using property, $\int_a^b f(x)dx = \int_a^b f(a + b - x)dx$

$\int_0^1 x(1-x)^9 dx = \int_0^1 (1-x)\{1-(1-x)\}^9 dx$

$= \int_0^1 (1-x) x^9 dx$

$= \int_0^1 (x^9 - x^{10}) dx$

$= \left[\dfrac{x^{10}}{10} - \dfrac{x^{11}}{11}\right]_0^1$

$= \dfrac{1}{10} - \dfrac{1}{11}$

$= \dfrac{1}{110}$

Hence, the correct option is (A).

21. $I = \int \dfrac{x}{3x^2+4} dx$

Let $3x^2 + 4 = t$

Differentiating with respect to x, we get

$6xdx = dt$

$\Rightarrow xdx = \dfrac{dt}{6}$

Now,

$I = \dfrac{1}{6}\int \dfrac{1}{t} dt$

$= \dfrac{1}{6}\log t + c \ \left(\because \int \dfrac{1}{x} dx = \log x + c\right)$

$= \dfrac{1}{6}\log(3x^2 + 4) + c$

Hence, the correct option is (B).

22. Let $A_1 x + B_1 y + C_1 z + D_1 = 0$ and $A_2 x + B_2 y + C_2 z + D_2 = 0$ are the equations of two planes aligned at an angle θ where A_1, B_1, C_1 and A_2, B_2, C_2 are the direction ratios of the normal to the planes, then the cosine of the angle between the two planes is given by:

$\cos\theta = \left|\dfrac{A_1 A_2 + B_1 B_2 + C_1 C_2}{\sqrt{A_1^2 + B_1^2 + C_1^2}\sqrt{A_2^2 + B_2^2 + C_2^2}}\right|$

Given,

Planes are $x + 2y + z = 7$ and $2x - y + z = 13$.

$\cos\theta = \left|\dfrac{1\times2 - 2\times1 + 1\times1}{\sqrt{1^2+2^2+1^2}\sqrt{2^2+(-1)^2+1^2}}\right| = \dfrac{1}{6}$

$\therefore \theta = \cos^{-1}\left(\dfrac{1}{6}\right)$

Hence, the correct option is (A).

23. As we know that,

The properties of a rectangular hyperbola $\dfrac{x^2}{a^2} - \dfrac{y^2}{b^2} = 1$.

Length of latus rectum of a hyperbola is given by $\dfrac{2b^2}{a}$.

$\Rightarrow \dfrac{2b^2}{a} = 4$

$\Rightarrow b^2 = 2a$

As we know that,

The eccentricity of a hyperbola is given by $e = \dfrac{\sqrt{a^2+b^2}}{a}$.

$\Rightarrow a^2 e^2 = a^2 + b^2$

$\Rightarrow 9a^2 = a^2 + 2a$

$\Rightarrow a = \dfrac{1}{4}$

$\because b^2 = 2a$

$\Rightarrow b^2 = \dfrac{1}{2}$

$\therefore$ Required hyperbola is, $\dfrac{x^2}{\left(\frac{1}{4}\right)^2} - \dfrac{y^2}{\frac{1}{2}} = 1$

$\Rightarrow \dfrac{x^2}{\frac{1}{16}} - \dfrac{y^2}{\frac{1}{2}} = 1$

$\Rightarrow 16x^2 - 2y^2 = 1$

So, the equation of the required hyperbola is $16x^2 - 2y^2 = 1$.

Hence, the correct option is (B).

24. Given,

$\dfrac{x^2}{16} + \dfrac{y^2}{25} = 1$

Compare with the standard equation $\dfrac{x^2}{a^2} + \dfrac{y^2}{b^2} = 1$

So, $a^2 = 16$ and $b^2 = 25$

$\therefore a = 4$ and $b = 5 (b > a)$

So, eccentricity $= \sqrt{1 - \dfrac{a^2}{b^2}}$

$= \sqrt{1 - \dfrac{16}{25}}$

$= \dfrac{3}{5}$

Hence, the correct option is (C).

25. As we know,

Equation of a line with slope m and passing through (x_1, y_1) is (y - y_1) = m (x - x_1).

Given,

The line has the slope 3 and passes through (3, 2).

$\therefore$ Equation of the line is (y - y_1) = m (x - x_1).

$\Rightarrow$ y - 2 = 3 (x - 3)

$\Rightarrow$ y - 3x + 7 = 0

Hence, the correct option is (B).

26. According to the passage, we can infer that it is about 'The role of fire in primitive man's life'.

The first paragraph of the passage states that the firebrand was used to provide light (illumination).

This can be inferred from the lines of the passage 'His discovery that the firebrand, from which the torch may very well have developed, could be used for illumination'.

Hence, the correct option is (B).

27. According to the second paragraph of the passage, early lamps were made by just floating a lighted reed in a vessel containing fat. This can be inferred from the line of the passage 'All he had to do was to fashion a vessel to contain fat and float a lighted reed in it'.

'Floating a reed in the seashell' could be a potential answer but it is incorrect because just this won't help, we need to float a reed in the fat contained by a seashell, then, it would be an early lamp.

Hence, the correct option is (A).

28. According to the second paragraph of the passage, lamps were developed just by chance (by accident) as the primary purpose of primitive man was to preserve fire and not to develop lamps. This can be inferred from the line of the passage 'Lamps, too, probably developed by accident'.

'Fate' could be a potential answer but it is incorrect because 'fate' gives the context of something which was anyway destined to happen' and 'chance' gives the context of something that comes up unexpectedly.

Hence, the correct option is (C).

29. According to the first paragraph of the passage, the most important uses of fire for primitive man were to provide warmth and to cook food. This can be inferred from the lines of the passage 'Primitive man was probably more concerned with fire as a source of warmth and as a means of cooking food than as a source of light'.

'To provide light' could be a potential answer but it's not correct because it is clearly mentioned in the passage that primitive man was not much concerned with fire providing light.

Hence, the correct option is (D).

30. The word is taken from the line 'could be used for illumination was probably incidental to the primary purpose of preserving a flame.' in the above passage.

According to the passage, we can guess the meaning of 'primary' that it is something related to 'main/essential' because the context stated earlier is that the primitive man wanted to preserve fire, so, it was the essential reason behind the discovery of 'firebrand'.

'Fundamental' which means 'foundation/basic' could be a potential answer but it is not correct according to the context of the passage because the purpose here cannot be fundamental.

'Elemental' means 'the lowest level of something' which is not apt according to the context.

Hence, the correct option is (D).

31. The visitor was shown her drawing by the little girl.

In the given question the sentence 'The little girl showed the visitor her drawing' is in 'Active voice' which is in the past indefinite and we know that after converted this sentence into 'Passive voice' the tense will same which also should in the past indefinite i.e 'The visitor was shown her drawing by the little girl'.

Past indefinite structure:

Subject + V2 + object (Active)

Object + was/were + V3 + by + subject (Passive)

Hence, the correct option is (C).

32. The sentence has been given in active voice, it has to be converted into passive voice:

While Changing the voice, the subject and the object change their places:

'A new car' becomes the subject and 'Him' (objective case for the pronoun 'he') becomes the object.

'V2' in active voice changes to 'was/were + V3' in the passive voice.

The conjunction 'by' is used before the object.

Lining up the remaining part of the sentence: for the journey.

Hence, the correct option is (B).

33. The given sentence is a direct speech.

The basic rules for changing or converting direct speech into indirect speech:

The commas and inverted commas are removed, and "that" is added.

The first-person pronoun 'I' is converted into the third-person pronoun 'she'.

The present perfect tense format 'Subject + have + V3 (made) + Object' will be changed into the past simple tense format 'Subject + had + V3 (made) + Object'.

Hence, the correct option is (C).

34. The given sentence is in indirect form.

To change it to direct form, we need to do the following -

Change in pronoun - In direct speech, the pronoun changes to the first person. So, 'she' will become 'I'.

Change in statement sentence - In direct speech, the 'told' is converted either to 'said' or remains the same. So, it either remains 'told' or becomes 'said'.

Change in tense - The past continuous tense (was leaving) in the indirect speech changes to present continuous tense (am leaving) in direct speech.

Hence, the correct option is (C).

35. Erudite- having or showing great knowledge that is based on careful study.

Scholarly- spending a lot of time studying and having a lot of knowledge about an academic subject

Naive- without enough experience of life and too ready to believe or trust other people.

Equivocate- use ambiguous language so as to conceal the truth or avoid committing oneself.

Tireless- putting a lot of hard work and energy into something over a long period of time without stopping or losing interest.

We can see that 'Erudite' and 'Scholarly' has a similar meaning.

Hence, the correct option is (D).

36. Worsen: to make something inferior in quality or character, deteriorate

Improve: to make or become better or to enhance in value or quality

Disappear: to pass from view or to cease to be visible.

Leave: to go away from.

Command: to direct with authority, to order

Thus, the word 'improve' is the most appropriate antonym of 'worsen'.

Hence, the correct option is (D).

37. The word 'Placate' means to lessen the anger or agitation of someone.

The antonyms of the word 'Placate' are "enrage, anger, infuriate".

From the antonym of the given word, we can say that the word 'Enrage' is the opposite in meaning.

The word 'Enrage' means to make someone very angry.

Hence, the correct option is (B).

38. Gaudy- extravagantly bright or showy, typically so as to be tasteless

Flashy- ostentatiously attractive or impressive

Simple- easily understood or done; presenting no difficulty

Plain- not decorated or elaborate; simple or ordinary in character

Proper- truly what something is said or regarded to be, genuine

We can see that 'Gaudy' and 'Flashy' have a similar meaning.

Hence, the correct option is (D).

39. The given sentence is in the positive degree of comparison because they begin with the words 'No other'. As we have studied, sentences that begin with 'no other' are usually positive degree sentences, 'sentences with more than any other' are comparative, and 'those with the best/most of all' are superlative.

Option (C): 'As strong as' is in the positive degree. It agrees with the sentence, that 'no other team is as strong as our team'.

Hence, the correct option is (C).

40. Adjectives are words that modify nouns or pronouns to make them more specific. There are 3 degrees of adjectives: Positive, comparative and superlative. In the sentence given, the narrator says 'I like pop music" but 'not all'. This means that the narrator likes an unspecified number of songs in pop music and so the correct word to use is 'some'.

Option (A) little is used in cases when the noun is uncountable but singular.

Option (B) less is used in comparative cases where the noun is uncountable but plural.

Option (D) any is used in a negative sentence.

Hence, the correct option is (C).

41. A preposition is a word that comes before a noun or a pronoun and establishes a relationship between the elements of a clause or words. In is correct as it indicates a colour. The other

options are wrong as to, with, and at indicate a direction, inclusion, and a specific location respectively. These uses don't fit in the given question.

Complete sentence: We've got this jumper in red.

Hence, the correct option is (A).

42. A preposition is a word that comes before a noun or a pronoun and establishes a relationship between the elements of a clause or words. About is correct as it indicates a piece of information. The other options are wrong as with and of indicating inclusion and possession respectively. These uses don't fit in the given question.

Hence, the correct option is (C).

43. Take after - to resemble

Look for - to search for something

Bring up - to raise or rear

Back out - to choose not to do something

According to the context of the given sentence, the subject looks like his grandfather.

So, from the given meanings, we find that takes after is the correct choice here.

Hence, the correct option is (B).

44. Hold on- wait a short while

Look into- to investigate

Light on- to explain

Look up to- to respect

According to the context of the given sentence, Marie asked the subject to wait for a short while.

So, from the given meanings, we find that hold on is the correct choice here.

Hence, the correct option is (A).

45. As the context in the sentence suggests a possibility, use of the modal 'may' would be appropriate and as it is followed by the base form of a verb, 'rise' instead of of 'risen' will be used here.

The underlined part 'can risen', therefore, must be replaced with 'may rise' to make it a grammatically correct sentence.

Hence, the correct option is (C).

46. As the sentence is a type 1 conditional sentence, the use of 'Unless' which means 'Except on the condition that' instead of 'Without' will be more appropriate.

Second, as 'both' suggests 'two', the noun that is followed by it must be in plural form.

The correct formation will be- "Unless both issues are clarified, the board will keep all other matters before it pending."

Hence, the correct option is (A).

47. Option (C) is correct as the statement is about every question. Option (A) is wrong as 'either' means there are only two questions. Option (B) is wrong as 'neither' means none and Option (D) is wrong as the statement does not specify that there are two questions.

Hence, the correct option is (C).

48. Each, either, either of and neither are distributive pronouns. 'Each' is used to present the members of a group as individuals. Whereas 'either', 'either of' and 'neither' are used when there is a comparison or choice between two things. Since the given sentence is speaking about a number of participants in a tournament, 'either', 'either of' and 'neither' cannot be used. The focus is on the fact that each individual participant is asked to submit a form; not just two.

Hence, the correct option is (A).

49. There are two types of articles:

Definite article (The): Article 'the' is used to refer to a DEFINITE thing or person.

Indefinite article (A/An): Article 'a/an' is used to refer to a thing or person in general. For instance: man, door etc.

Article 'a' is used with consonant sounds whereas article 'an' is used with vowel sounds.

In the first blank, "no article" or "zero article" will be used. 'No article' is used to refer to general things. (the speaker is making a general statement)

Hence, the correct option is (C).

50. No article is used before countable plural nouns used in a general sense. Here 'stamps' is a countable plural noun used in a general sense.

Hence, the correct option is (D).

51. The stretched bow doesn't possess kinetic energy. It possesses potential energy as it is in a static position. Since fired bullet, running water and working hammer are in motion, they possess kinetic energy.

Hence, the correct option is (D).

52. Given,

Mass (m) = 10 kg

Height (h) = 10 m

The Work done in this case will be equal to the Potential Energy of the stone at that height.

Thus, work done (W) = m $\times$ g $\times$ h

$\Rightarrow$ W = 10 $\times$ 10 $\times$ 10

$\Rightarrow$ W = 1000 kgm²/s² = 1000 J

Hence, the correct option is (B).

53. Intensity of wave $I = \dfrac{Power}{area} = \dfrac{Energy}{area \times Time}$

Power $= [ML^2 T^{-3}]$

area $= [L^2]$

$I = \dfrac{[ML^2 T^{-3}]}{[L^2]}$

$I = [ML^0 T^{-3}]$

Hence, the correct option is (B).

54. The different dimensions represent the different physical quantity. M^1 represents kg, L^1 represents m and T^{-2} represents s^{-2}.

Thus SI unit of that physical quantity is $kg\ ms^{-2}$.

Hence, the correct option is (B).

55. Uniform speed means that a body is traveling at a constant speed along a straight line. So, it has no acceleration. Thus net force =ma=0.

Hence, the correct option is (D).

56. Given,

Critical angle $(C) = 30°$

The relation between refractive index and critical angle is $\mu = \dfrac{1}{\sin C}$.

$\Rightarrow \mu = \dfrac{1}{\sin 30°} = 2$

As we know,

The refractive index is written as $\mu = \dfrac{c}{v}$.

$\Rightarrow v = \dfrac{3 \times 10^8}{2} = 1.5 \times 10^8\ m/s$

Hence, the correct option is (D).

57. The transmission of light through a glass fiber of the endoscope depends on the phenomenon of total internal reflection. If a fiber of the endoscope is straight or curved, then light entering one end travels in a zigzag path and gets repeatedly reflected off by the internal surface of the fiber, until it emerges out from the other end.

Hence, the correct option is (C).

58.

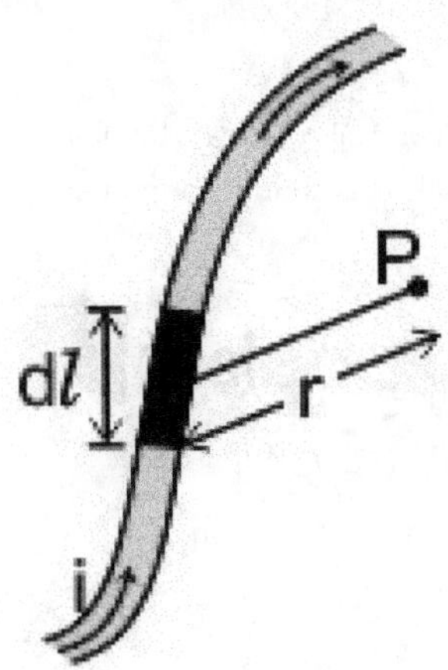

According to Biot-Savart Law,

The magnetic field at point ' P ' due to the current element $\overrightarrow{idl}$ is given by the expression,

$$d\vec{B} = \frac{\mu_0}{4\pi} i \left(\frac{\vec{dl} \times \vec{r}}{r^3} \right)$$

Where, $\mu_0 = $ Absolute permeability of air or vacuum, $\vec{idl} = $ Current element and $r = $ distance.
Hence, the correct option is (D).

59. Given,

$$B = 0.1 \text{ tesla}$$

The magnetic field at the centre of a circular coil is given by
$$B = \frac{\mu_0 NI}{2R} = 0.1 \text{ tesla}$$

If the number of turns is doubled and the radius is halved i.e.

Number of turns, $N' = 2N$ and radius $R' = \frac{R}{2}$

Then new magnetic induction is,

$$B' = \frac{\mu_0 N' I}{2R'}$$

$$= \frac{\mu_0 2NI}{2\left(\frac{R}{2}\right)}$$

$$= \frac{4\mu_0 NI}{2R}$$

$$\because B = \frac{\mu_0 NI}{2R} = 0.1$$

$$= 4 \times 0.1 = 0.4T$$

Hence, the correct option is (C).

60. Given,
$$V_R = 40\,V,\ V_L = 60\,V,\ V_C = 30\,V$$
For a series LCR circuit, the total potential difference of the circuit is given by,
$$V = \sqrt{V_R^2 + (V_L - V_C)^2}$$
$$\Rightarrow V = \sqrt{(40)^2 + (60 - 30)^2} = \sqrt{2500} = 50V$$
The supply voltage is $50\,V$.

Hence, the correct option is (A).

61. Mutual induction between the two coils of area A, number of turns N_1 and N_2 with the length of secondary or primary l is given by,
$$M = -\frac{e_2}{\frac{dI_1}{dt}} = -\frac{e_1}{\frac{dI_2}{dt}}$$

Emf induced in coil 1 is given by $e_1 = -L_1 \frac{dI_1}{dt}$

Emf induced in coil 2 is given by $e_2 = -L_2 \frac{dI_2}{dt}$

If all the flux of coil 2 links coil 1 and vice versa, then
$$M^2 = \frac{e_1 e_2}{\left(\frac{dI_1}{dt}\right)\left(\frac{dI_2}{dt}\right)}$$

$$\Rightarrow M^2 = L_1 L_2$$

$$\Rightarrow M = \sqrt{L_1 L_2}$$

Hence, the correct option is (C).

62. The speedometer works on eddy current.

In a speedometer, a magnet rotates with the speed of the vehicle. The magnet is placed inside an aluminium drum which is carefully pivoted and held in position by a hairspring. As the magnet rotates, eddy currents are set up in the drum which opposes the motion of the magnet. A torque is exerted on the drum in the opposite direction which deflects the drum through an angle depending on the speed of the vehicle.

Hence, the correct option is (B).

63. Given,

Time period (T_2) of the new system is $\frac{1^{rd}}{3}$ of the given time period (T)
$$T_2 = \frac{T}{3}$$
As we know, $T \alpha \frac{1}{\sqrt{k}}$

$$\Rightarrow \frac{T_2}{T} = \sqrt{\frac{k}{k_2}}$$

Where $k = $ spring constant for first spring and $k_2 = $ spring constant for second spring
$$\Rightarrow \sqrt{k_2} = \left(\frac{T}{T_2}\right)\sqrt{k}$$
By squaring both sides, we get
$$k_2 = \left(\frac{T}{T_2}\right)^2 k$$

$$\Rightarrow k_2 = \left(\frac{T}{\left(\frac{T}{3}\right)}\right)^2 k$$

$$\Rightarrow k_2 = (3)^2 K$$
$$\Rightarrow k_2 = 9K$$

Hence, the correct option is (B).

64.

- The types of sound waves whose frequencies are higher than the upper audible limit of human hearing are called ultrasound. The sound frequency of ultrasonic waves is above 20,000Hz.

- Ultrasounds can be used to detect cracks and flaws in metal blocks..

- The frequency range of infrared waves is below 20Hz.

- Ultrasound is generally used to clean parts located in hard-to-reach places.

Hence, the correct option is (C).

65. Given,

ΔQ = + 60 J and ΔU = - 180 Cal

According to the first law of Thermodynamics,

Heat exchanged (ΔQ) = ΔW + ΔU

ΔW = ΔQ - ΔU = + 60 - (- 180) = 240 J

Hence, the correct option is (D).

66.

- As in case of closed system there is no change in mass of the system.
- The no change in mass is not the sufficient reason of entropy change.
- According to the definition of the closed system there is may be the transfer of heat energy. So, entropy of the system will change.
- The volume of the system remains constant.

Hence, the correct option is (C).

67. Electromagnetic waves or EM waves are waves that are created as a result of vibrations between an electric field and a magnetic field. The electric field and magnetic field of an electromagnetic wave are perpendiculars (at right angles - 90°) to each other. They are also perpendicular to the direction of the EM wave. But they are in the same phase. Thus in an electromagnetic wave, the electric and magnetic fields are always at a 0-degree phase difference.

Hence, the correct option is (A).

68.

- As we know that EM waves do not have any charge, thus they are not deflected by an electric field and magnetic field.
- Electromagnetic waves do not require any matter to propagate from one place to another as it consists of photons. They can move in a vacuum.
- The electromagnetic wave moves with the speed of light.
- Electromagnetic waves or EM waves are waves that are formed as a result of vibrations between an electric field and a magnetic field and they are perpendicular to each other and to the direction of the wave.

Hence, the correct option is (A).

69. The ratio of lateral strain to longitudinal strain is called Poisson's ratio (σ).

$$\sigma = \frac{\text{Lateral strain}}{\text{Longitudinal strain}}$$

$$\sigma = \frac{\frac{dr}{r}}{\frac{dL}{L}} = -\frac{dr \times L}{dL \times r}$$

The negative sign indicates that the radius of the bar decreases when it is stretched. Poisson's ratio is a dimensionless and a unitless quantity.

Hence, the correct option is (A).

70. The reciprocal of bulk modulus is compressibility.

So, Compressibility $\propto \dfrac{1}{\text{Bulk modulus}}$

Hence, the correct option is (B).

71. Organic compound, any of a large class of chemical compounds in which one or more atoms of carbon are covalently linked to atoms of other elements, most commonly hydrogen, oxygen, or nitrogen. Life is based on carbon; organic chemistry studies compounds in which carbon is a central element. The properties of carbon make it the backbone of the organic molecules which form living matter. Carbon is a such a versatile element because it can form four covalent bonds.

Hence, the correct option is (D).

72. Gasohol is a mixture of gasoline and ethanol that consists of one part ethanol and nine parts of lead-free gasoline. A mixture of petrol (gasoline) and alcohol (i.e. typically ethanol at 10%, or methanol at 3%), used as an alternative fuel for cars and other vehicles in many countries. The ethanol is obtained as a biofuel by fermentation of agricultural crops or crop residues, for example, sugar cane waste.

Hence, the correct option is (B).

73. Length of wire $A(l_A) = l$

Length of wire $B(l_B) = 2l$

Resistance $(R) = \dfrac{\rho l}{A}$

Resistance of wire $A(R_A) = \dfrac{\rho l_A}{A} = \dfrac{\rho l}{A} = R$

Resistance of wire $B(R_B) = \dfrac{\rho l_B}{A} = \dfrac{\rho 2 \times l}{A} = 2 \times \dfrac{\rho l}{A} = 2R$

Ratio $= \dfrac{R_A}{R_B} = \dfrac{R}{2R} = \dfrac{1}{2}$

Hence, the correct option is (D).

74. Given,

Potential $(V) = 12\ V$

$R_1 = 80\Omega, R_2 = 120\Omega$ and $R_3 = 240\Omega$

As we know,

Equivalent resistance is given by (R).

$$\frac{1}{R} = \frac{1}{R_1} + \frac{1}{R_2} + \frac{1}{R_3}$$

$$= \frac{1}{80} + \frac{1}{120} + \frac{1}{240} = \frac{6}{240} = \frac{1}{40}$$

$$R = 40\Omega$$

According to Ohm's law

$$I = \frac{V}{R}$$

Electric current drawn $(I) = \dfrac{12}{40} = 0.3\ A$

Hence, the correct option is (A).

75. Microsoft Office is an example of a Horizontal market software.

In computers, the software is a collection of programs that performs a task. Horizontal market software is application software that is useful in a wide range of industries. Horizontal market software is also known as "productivity software."

Hence, the correct option is (C).

76. The Union Government has authorized the State Bank of India to issue and encashes Electoral Bonds through its 29 Authorized Branches from 1–10 th of July 2022.

The Electoral Bonds will be valid for fifteen calendar days from the date of issue and no payment will be made to any payee Political Party if the Electoral Bond is deposited after the expiry of the validity period.

Hence, the correct option is (A).

77.

Letters	H	A	L	U	C	I	N	T	O
No. of repetition	1	2	2	1	1	2	2	1	1

(A) LION - HALLUCINATION (Can be formed)

(B) LOAN - HALLUCINATION (Can be formed)
(C) NATION - HALLUCINATION (Can be formed)
(D) LOTION - HALLUCINATION (Cannot be formed as there is only one 'O' in HALLUCINATION)

Hence, the correct option is (D).

78. 'Grammy award' is awarded to Musicians;

Similarly,

'Pulitzer award' is awarded to Journalists.

Hence, the correct option is (D).

79. Notice the following pattern in MISTAKEN:

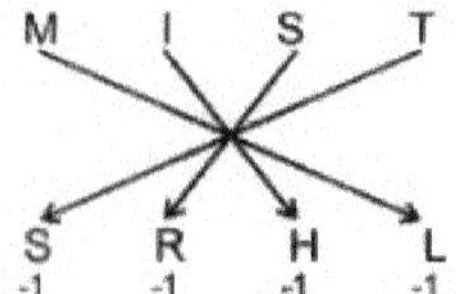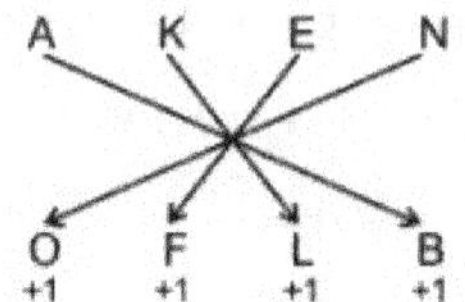

So, GROUNDED can be coded as:

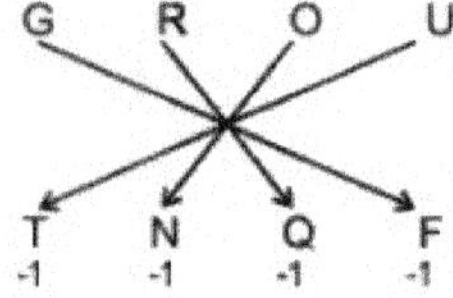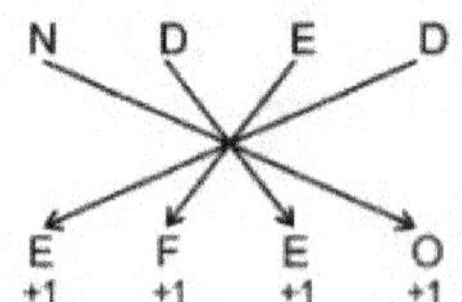

So, 'GROUNDED' is coded as 'TNQFEFEO'.

Hence, the correct option is (D).

80. The pattern followed for FLOWER is:

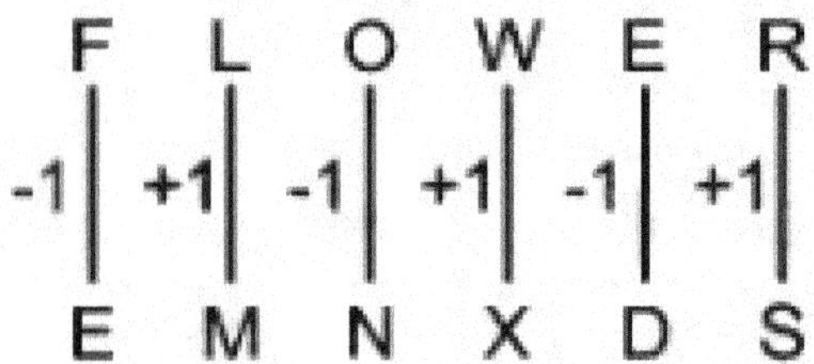

Similarly, for SHOWER,

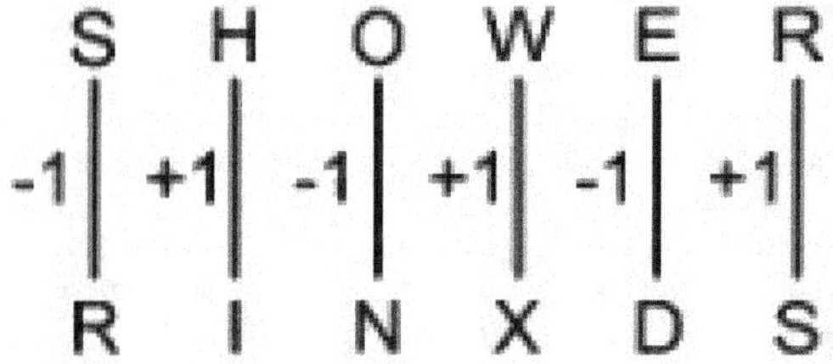

SHOWER can be coded as RINXDS.

Hence, the correct option is (C).

81. The first Gauri Lankesh Memorial award for journalism was given to Ravish Kumar. He received the award on 22 September 2019. For sharp news analysis, the Gauri Lankesh award was given to him. Gauri Lankesh Memorial Trust has set up this award. The newspaper named 'Nyaya Patha' was also launched in the event.

Hence, the correct option is (A).

82. Angkor Wat is a Buddhist temple complex located in Cambodia. It was built in the 12th century by King Suryavarman II of the Khmer empire in Angkor Wat style dedicated to Hindu God Vishnu. Later it was gradually transformed into a Buddhist temple towards the end of the 12th century. It is designated as a UNESCO World Heritage site.

Hence, the correct option is (C).

83. Santiago de Chile or simply Santiago is the capital and largest city of Chile. It is the center of Chile's largest and most densely populated conurbation. Chile is situated in the South American continent. This country shares its borders with Bolivia, Peru, and Argentina. The national language of Chile is Spanish.
Hence, the correct option is (B).

84. Nuakhai or Navakhai is an agricultural festival mainly observed by people of Western Odisha and Southern Chhattisgarh in India. Nuakhai is one of the unique social festivals which gets its name from the word nua meaning new and khai meaning food.

Hence, the correct option is (C).

85. Giddha is a popular folk dance of women in the Chandigarh region. The dance is often considered derived from the ancient dance known as the ring dance and is just as energetic as Bhangra, at the same time, it manages to creatively display feminine grace, elegance, and flexibility.

Hence, the correct option is (B).

86. "Aghanya" refers to Cows in Rig Veda. Rig Veda is one of the 4 Vedas. It consists of Sanskrit hymns. It is the oldest of the four sacred Vedas. It contains 10 mandalas (chapters) and 10,552 verses.

Hence, the correct option is (C).

87. Bindusara is known as "The Son of a Great Father and the Father of a Great Son" because he was the son of a great father Chandragupta Maurya and the father of a great son Ashoka, the Great. He ruled the Mauryan dynasty from 298 BC to 273 BC. Bindusara brought sixteen states under the Mauryan Empire and thus conquered almost the entire Indian peninsula.

Hence, the correct option is (B).

88. Udaipur is known as the city of lakes. The city was the historical capital of Mewar and falls in the southern region of Rajasthan in the western part of India. Udaipur is famous for its history, culture, and scenic beauty and is called the 'Venice of the East'.

Hence, the correct option is (D).

89. Okhla Bird Sanctuary is located in the NCR region. Okhla Bird Sanctuary is officially known as Shaheed Chander Shekhar Azad Sanctuary. It is one among 15 bird sanctuaries in the state. It was notified as a bird sanctuary in the year 1990. It is located on the banks of the river Yamuna. At present, it is one of the 466 IBAs (Important Bird Areas) in India. Okhla Bird Sanctuary is the home for around 300 different species of birds.

Hence, the correct option is (B).

90. Pooja Rani is associated with Boxing.

Pooja Rani Bohra was born on 17 February 1991. She won the bronze medal at the 2014 Asian Games in the 75 kg category. She won the gold medal in the South Asian Games 2016. She also won Silver (2012) and Bronze (2015) in Asian Championship 75 kg weight categories. She represented India at the Glasgow Commonwealth Games 2014 in the 75 kg category. In 2020, she becomes the first Indian to qualify for the 2020 Summer Olympics. Pooja Rani belongs to Bhiwani District, Haryana.

Hence, the correct option is (B).

91. The Radcliffe Line became the international border between India and Pakistan during the partition of India. Sir Cyril Radcliffe, drew the Radcliffe line which divides India and Pakistan.

Hence, the correct option is (C).

92. River Ganga does not pass through the state of Andhra Pradesh.

The River Ganga originates from the Gangotri glacier in Uttarakhand. Alaknanda River joins Bhagirathi at Devprayag and from there the river is called Ganga. Yamuna(Largest right bank tributary of Ganga), Damodar (Sorrow of Bengal), Ghagra, Gomti, Gandak, Ramganga, Kosi (Sorrow of Bihar), Son, Mahananda are major tributaries of River Ganga. It flows through the states of Uttarakhand, Uttar Pradesh, Bihar, Jharkhand, and West Bengal.

Hence, the correct option is (D).

93. H1N1 virus is a combination of viruses from pigs, birds and humans that causes disease in humans. During the 2009-10 flu season, H1N1 caused a respiratory infection in humans that was commonly referred to as swine flu.

Hence, the correct option is (B).

94. Shyam Saran wrote the book "How India Sees the World: Kautilya to the 21st Century" in 2017. The book shows part memoir and part thesis on India's International relations since Independence. Shyam Saran is a career diplomat born on September 4, 1946. He has been India's Ambassador to Myanmar, Indonesia and the Nepal and High Commissioner to Mauritius.

Hence, the correct option is (D).

95. Catalysis was discovered by Berzelius. It is a term used for the reactions which occur in the presence of certain substances that increases the rate of the reaction without being consumed.

Hence, the correct option is (B).

96. The pattern followed is:

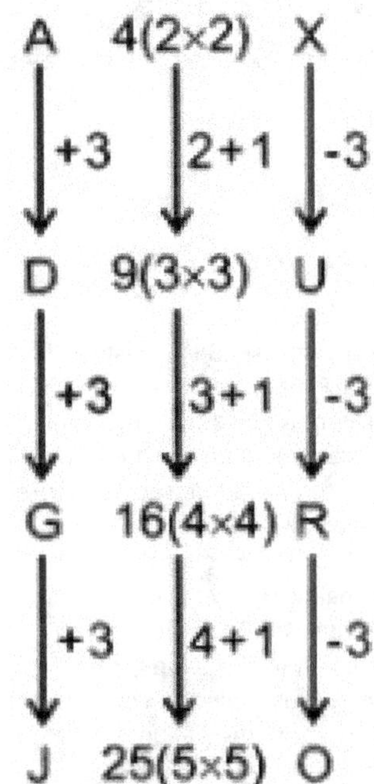

Hence, the correct option is (C).

97.

- P V Sindhu was not in the list of Padma Vibhushan Awardees. She was awarded the Padma Bhushan award.

- Arun Jaitley and Sushma Swaraj were posthumously awarded the prestigious Padma Vibhushan award for their contribution in the field of Public Affairs.

- M.C Mary Kom was given the Padma Vibhushan award for her excellent performance in the field of sports (boxing).

Hence, the correct option is (B).

98. Saddle Peak is located on the North Andaman. It is the highest peak on Andaman and Nicobar islands with an elevation of 731m. It is located near Diglipur, a town in North Andaman Island.

Hence, the correct option is (B).

99. The full form of IT is Information Technology. IT is used in the context of computers. The IT-sector uses software and computers to handle information. Computer software and electronic computers are used here to transform, secure, and store information and data.

Hence, the correct option is (D).

100. The Nagaland Assembly declared English as the official language of Nagaland in 1967. Every tribe has its own mother tongue but communicates with other tribes in Nagamese or English. English is the prevailing spoken and written language in Nagaland.

Hence, the correct option is (B).

English

Q.1 Direction: Read the given passage carefully and answer the question that follows.

Marie Curie was one of the most accomplished scientists in history. Together with her husband, Pierre, she discovered radium, an element widely used for treating cancer and studied uranium and other radioactive substances. Pierre and Marie's amicable collaboration later helped to unlock the secrets of the atom. Marie was born in 1867 in Warsaw, Poland, where her father was a professor of physics. At an early age, she displayed a brilliant mind and a casual personality. Her great exuberance for learning prompted her to continue with her studies after high school. She became disgruntled, however, when she learned that the university in Warsaw was closed to women. Determined to receive a higher education, she defiantly left Poland in 1891 entered the Sorbonne, a French university, where she earned her master's degree and a doctorate in physics.

What kind of collaboration helped Curie's to unlock the secrets of the atom?

A. Friendly   **B.** Competitive

C. Courteous   **D.** Industrious

Ques (2-5):Direction: Read the given passage carefully and answer the question that follows.

Marie Curie was one of the most accomplished scientists in history. Together with her husband, Pierre, she discovered radium, an element widely used for treating cancer, and studied uranium and other radioactive substances. Pierre and Marie's amicable collaboration later helped to unlock the secrets of the atom.

Marie was born in 1867 in Warsaw, Poland, where her father was a professor of physics. At an early age, she displayed a brilliant mind and a casual personality. Her great exuberance for learning prompted her to continue with her studies after high school. She became disgruntled, however, when she learned that the university in Warsaw was closed to women. Determined to receive a higher education, she defiantly left Poland in 1891 entered the Sorbonne, a French university, where she earned her master's degree and doctorate in physics.

Q.2 What will best describe Marie Curie's personality?

A. Determined   **B.** Lighthearted

C. Humorous   **D.** Envious

Q.3 When she learned that she could not attend the university in Warsaw, Marie felt ______.

A. hopeless   **B.** annoyed

C. happy   **D.** perversely excited

Q.4 Marie ______ left Poland and travelled to France to enter the Sorbonne.

A. boldly   **B.** intelligently

C. curiously   **D.** strangely

Q.5 Marie Curie's doctorate was in which academic discipline?

A. Medicine

B. Cancer studies

C. Radiation Chemistry

D. Physics

Q.6 Direction: Choose the antonym of the given word:

Meandering

A. Sliding   **B.** Sloping   **C.** Strained   **D.** Straight

Q.7 Direction: Choose the synonym of the given word:

Venial

A. Corrupt   **B.** Superficial

C. Respected   **D.** Pardonable

Q.8 Direction: Choose the correct sentence from the following:

A. When I was young, I used to visit my grandparents every winter.

B. When I were young, I used to visit my grandparents every winter.

C. When I was young, I used visit my grandparents every winter.

D. When I was young, I shall visit my grandparents every winter.

Q.9 Direction: Choose the correct spelling :

A. Preposesing   **B.** Prepossessing

C. Prepossesing   **D.** Preposesing

Q.10 Direction: Choose the correctly punctuated sentence:

A. He always enjoyed sweets? chocolates and cakes:

B. He always enjoyed sweets; chocolates and cakes!

C. He always enjoyed sweets, chocolates and cakes.

D. He always enjoyed sweets, chocolates and cakes?

Q.11 Direction: Pick out the meaning of the given word:

Edify

A. Speech   **B.** Oration

C. Sermonize   **D.** Elocution

Q.12 Direction: Change active to passive or vice versa as the case may be:

I wrote the letter and posted it.

A. The letter was written and posted by me.

B. The letter was wrote and posted by me.

C. The letter had been written and posted by me.

D. The letter was written and had been posted by me.

Q.13 Direction: Change active to passive or vice versa as the case may be:

A massive search operation has been launched to nab the suspects.

A. The police had launched a massive search operation to

nab the suspects.

B. The police have launched a massive search operation to nab the suspects.

C. The police launched a massive search operation to nab the suspects.

D. The police had been launched a massive search operation to nab the suspects.

Q.14 Direction: Change Direct to Indirect speech or vice versa as the case may be:

I said, "Water is essential for life."

A. Water is essential for life was said by me.

B. I exclaimed that water was essential for life.

C. I said that water is essential for life.

D. I told that water was essential for life.

Q.15 Direction: Change Direct to Indirect speech or vice versa as the case may be:

The lady asked me how my uncle was.

A. The lady said to me, "How is your uncle?"

B. The lady asked me, "How is your uncle doing?"

C. The lady asked me, "How has your uncle been?"

D. The lady said to me, "How was your uncle?"

Q.16 Direction: Choose the most appropriate alternative to complete the sentence:

The manager was _____ an explanation of his conduct.

A. called for   **B.** called off

C. called to   **D.** called up

Q.17 Direction: Choose the most appropriate to complete the sentence:

All of us are devoted _________ one another.

A. of   **B.** at   **C.** for   **D.** to

Q.18 Direction: Choose the most appropriate to complete the sentence:

Raj _________ English before he moved to England.

A. has been studying   **B.** has studied

C. is studying   **D.** had studied

Q.19 Direction: Choose the most appropriate to complete the sentence:

All civilized nations now believe in _________ treatment of prisoners.

A. human   **B.** humane

C. humanitarian   **D.** humiliating

Q.20 Direction: Choose the most appropriate to complete the sentence:

All she wanted was _______ moments on her own.

A. few   **B.** little   **C.** the few   **D.** a few

Q.21 Direction: Choose the most appropriate to complete the sentence:

Tarun would you have abandoned you at the station if you _______ the train.

A. have missed   **B.** had missed

C. missed   **D.** missing

Q.22 Direction: Choose the most appropriate to complete the sentence:

Even though Rishi had made a fortune, he _____ working as a assistant.

A. went on   **B.** was going on

C. will go on   **D.** had gone

Q.23 The teacher set some homework _______the end of the lesson.

A. about   **B.** in   **C.** at   **D.** of

Q.24 Direction: Choose the most appropriate to complete the sentence:

The train is expected to arrive between 11 pm to 12 pm.

A. The train is expecting to between by 11pm to 12pm.

B. The train is expected to arrive between 11pm and 12pm.

C. The train is expected to arrive between 11pm or 12pm.

D. The train is expected for arrival between 11pm to 12pm.

Q.25 He came along_________his sister to meet us.

A. with   **B.** by   **C.** at   **D.** of

Science

Q.26 A metal block is experiencing an atmospheric pressure of 10^5 Nm^{-2}, when the same block is placed in a vacuum chamber, the fractional change in its volume : (the bulk modulus of metal is 1.25 $\times 10^{11}$ Nm^{-2})

A. 4×10^{-7} **B.** 2×10^{-7} **C.** 8×10^{-7} **D.** 1×10^{-7}

Q.27 Modulus rigidity of ideal liquids is :

A. Infinity

B. Zero

C. Unity

D. Some finite small non-zero constant value

Q.28 What would be the value of acceleration due to gravity at a point 5 km below the earth's surface? $(R_E = 6400 km, g_E = 9.8 ms^{-2})$

A. $9.6\ ms^{-2}$ **B.** $9.79\ ms^{-2}$

C. $9.89\ ms^{-2}$ **D.** $10\ ms^{-2}$

Q.29 Two blocks of masses 10 kg and 4 kg are connected by a spring of negotiable mass and placed on a frictionless horizontal surface. An impulse gives a velocity of 14ms^{-1} in the direction of the lighter block to heavier block. The velocity of the Centre of mass is:

A. 30 ms^{-1} **B.** 20 ms^{-1} **C.** 10 ms^{-1} **D.** 5 ms^{-1}

Q.30 A stone of mass 2 kg projected upwards with KE of 98 J. the height at which the KE of the body becomes half its original value, is given by : (take g = 9.8 ms^{-2})

A. 5 m   **B.** 2.5 m   **C.** 1.5 m   **D.** 0.5 m

Q.31 If the critical angle for total internal reflection from a medium to vacuum is 30°, the velocity of light in the medium is:

A. 3 X 10^8 m/s   **B.** 1.5 X 10^8 m/s

C. 0.5 X 10^8 m/s   **D.** 0.2 X 10^8 m/s

Q.32 Two weights w_1 and w_2 are suspended from the ends of a light string passing over a smooth fixed pulley. If the pulley is pulled up with the acceleration of g. the tension in the string will be

A. $\frac{4w_1w_2}{w_1+w_2}$ **B.** $\frac{2w_1w_2}{w_1+w_2}$ **C.** $\frac{w_1-w_2}{w_1+w_2}$ **D.** $\frac{4w_1w_2}{2(w_1+w_2)}$

Q.33 A ball dropped from the top of a building having the height of 100m. At the same time, another ball is thrown in upwards direction with a velocity of 40 ms^{-1} from the bottom position of the building. The two balls will meet after the time of :

A. 5 s   **B.** 2.5 s   **C.** 2 s   **D.** 3 s

Q.34 Which among the following forces is the strongest?

A. Gravitational force   **B.** Nuclear force
C. Magnetic force   **D.** Electrical force

Q.35 What is atomic number of Flourine?

A. 15   **B.** 9   **C.** 10   **D.** 14

Q.36 Which of the following statement is true about Esters?

A. Esters are sweet- smelling substances
B. Esters are derived from a carboxylic acid and an alcohol
C. They are used in making perfumes
D. All of the above

Q.37 S- block elements belongs to which group?

A. 13-18 group   **B.** 3-12 group
C. 1-2 group   **D.** None of these

Q.38 A body of mass $10kg$ is moved with a uniform speed on a rough horizontal surface, for a distance of $2\ m$. The work done is $150\ J$. The surface is inclined to the horizontal at $30°$. The same body is moved over the inclined plane for a distance of $2\ m$. The work done against friction will be : ($g = 10\ ms^{-2}$)

A. $250\ J$ **B.** $50\ J$ **C.** $150\ J$ **D.** $75\sqrt{3}\ J$

Q.39 Which of the following is best natural conductor of heat?

A. Graphite   **B.** Asbestos
C. Glass   **D.** Diamond

Q.40 A particle executes a simple harmonic motion of time period T. Find the time taken by the particle to go directly from its mean position to half the amplitude :

A. $\frac{T}{2}$ **B.** $\frac{T}{4}$ **C.** $\frac{T}{8}$ **D.** $\frac{T}{12}$

Q.41 What does the internal resistance of a cell mean?

A. The resistance of the material used in the cell
B. The vessel of the cell
C. The electrodes of the cell
D. The electrolyte used in the cell

Q.42 Structure of solids is investigated by using ________ :

A. γ -rays   **B.** X-rays
C. cosmic rays   **D.** infrared radiation

Q.43 Choose the incorrect statements from the following regarding magnetic lines of field.

A. The direction of magnetic field at a point is taken to be the direction in which the north pole of a magnetic compass needle points.
B. Magnetic field lines are closed curves.
C. If magnetic field lines are parallel and equidistant, they represent zero field strength.
D. Relative strength of magnetic field is shown by the degree of closeness of the field lines.

Q.44 Induction type single phase energy meters measure electric energy in:

A. kW   **B.** Wh   **C.** kWh   **D.** VAR

Q.45 A charge $Q\ \mu C$ is placed at the centre of a cube. The flux coming out from any surface will be :

A. $\frac{Q}{6\varepsilon_0} \times 10^{-6}$ **B.** $\frac{Q}{6\varepsilon_0} \times 10^{-3}$
C. $\frac{Q}{4\varepsilon_0}$ **D.** $\frac{Q}{8\varepsilon_0}$

Q.46 A p-type semiconductor is:

A. Positively charged
B. Negatively charged
C. Neutral
D. Uncharged at 0 °K but charged at higher temperatures

Q.47 Through which mode of propagation, the radio waves can be sent from one place to another?

A. Space wave propagation
B. Sky wave propagation
C. Ground wave propagation
D. All of the above

Q.48 In C++ every statement end with:

A. Colon(:)   **B.** Comma (,)
C. Dot (.)   **D.** Semicolon (;)

Q.49 Define quality factor of resonance in series LCR circuit. What is its SI unit?

A. $\frac{1}{R}\sqrt{\frac{L}{C}}$ **B.** $\frac{3}{R}\sqrt{\frac{L}{C}}$ **C.** $\frac{4}{R}\sqrt{\frac{L}{C}}$ **D.** $\frac{2}{R}\sqrt{\frac{L}{C}}$

Q.50 When a body falls from an aeroplane, there is increase in its:

A. Kinetic energy   **B.** Mass
C. Acceleration   **D.** Potential energy

Mathematics

Q.51 If $\cos^{-1}x - \sin^{-1}x = 0,$ then x is equal to:

A. $\pm\frac{1}{\sqrt{2}}$ **B.** 1   **C.** $\pm\frac{1}{\sqrt{3}}$ **D.** $\frac{1}{\sqrt{2}}$

Q.52 If $\log 2 = 0.3010,$ the value of $\log_5 512$ is:

A. 2.870   **B.** 2.967   **C.** 3.876   **D.** 3.912

Q.53 Find the sum of 12 terms of an A.P. whose nth term is given by $a_n = 3n + 4$:

A. 262   **B.** 272   **C.** 282   **D.** 292

Q.54 The median of the data is :
155 160 145 149 150 147 152 144 148 :

A. 149   **B.** 150   **C.** 147   **D.** 144

Q.55 Which of the following are quadratic equation in x :

A. $x^2 - 3x - \sqrt{x} + 4$

B. $\frac{x-6}{x} = 3$

C. $x^2 - \frac{1}{x^2} = 5$

D. $(2x + 3)(3x + 2) = 6(x - 1)(x - 2)$

Q.56 Which of the following equation has y = c₁eˣ + c₂e⁻ˣ as the general solution ?

A. $\frac{d^2y}{dx^2} + y = 0$ **B.** $\frac{d^2y}{dx^2} - y = 0$

C. $\frac{d^2y}{dx^2} + 1 = 0$ **D.** $\frac{d^2y}{dx^2} - 1 = 0$

Q.57 If $f : R \to R$ be a function defined by $f(x) = 4x^3 - 7$. Then:

A. f is one-one -into   **B.** f is many-one -into

C. f is many-one onto   **D.** f is bijective

Q.58 Find the value of x for which $y = [x(x - 2)]^2$ is an increasing function :

A. 0 < x < 1   **B.** x > 2

C. Both A and B   **D.** Neither A nor B

Q.59 AD and AC are two diameters of a circle of radius r and they are mutually perpendicular. What is the ratio of the area of the circle to the area of the triangle ACD.?

A. $\frac{\pi}{2}$ **B.** π **C.** $\frac{\pi}{4}$ **D.** 2π

Q.60 Four points $A(6,3), B(-3,5), C(4,-2)$ and $D(x, 3x)$ are given in such a way that $\frac{\Delta DBC}{\Delta ABC} = \frac{1}{2}$, find x:

A. 1.374   **B.** 1.378   **C.** 1.375   **D.** 1.376

Q.61 If x is a solution of the equation $\sqrt{2x + 1} - \sqrt{2x - 1} = 1, \left(x \geq \frac{1}{2}\right)$, then $\sqrt{4x^2 - 1}$ is equal to:

A. 2   **B.** $\frac{3}{4}$ **C.** $2\sqrt{2}$ **D.** $\frac{4}{7}$

Q.62 What is $\int_0^1 \frac{e^{tan^{-1}} dx}{1+x^2}$ equal to?

A. $e^{\frac{\pi}{4}} - 1$ **B.** $e^{\frac{\pi}{4}} + 1$ **C.** $e - 1$ **D.** e

Q.63 Let $\left|\vec{a}\right| = 7, \left|\vec{b}\right| = 11, \left|\vec{a} + \vec{b}\right| = 10\sqrt{3}$ What is the angle between $(\overline{a} + \overline{b})$ and $(\overline{a} - \overline{b})$?

A. $\frac{\pi}{2}$ **B.** $\frac{\pi}{3}$

C. $\frac{\pi}{6}$ **D.** None of the above

Q.64 A straight line passes through (1, -2, 3) and perpendicular to the plane 2x + 3y- z = 7.
What is the image of the point (1, -2, 3) in the plane?

A. (2, -1, 5)   **B.** (-1, 2, -3)

C. (5, 4, 1)   **D.** None of the above

Q.65 If $f(x) = \frac{\sin(e^{x-2} - 1)}{\log(x-1)}, x \neq 2$ and $f(x) = k$ For $x = 2$, then value of k for which f is continuous is:

A. -2   **B.** -1   **C.** 0   **D.** 1

Q.66 What is the sum of the major and minor axes of the ellipse whose eccentricity is $\frac{4}{5}$ and length of latus rectum is 14.4 unit?

A. 32 unit   **B.** 48 unit

C. 64 unit   **D.** None of the above

Q.67 What is the equation of the midway between the lines 3x – 4y + 12 = 0 and 3x – 4y = 6?

A. $3x - 4y - 9 = 0$ **B.** $3x - 4y + 9 = 0$

C. $3x - 4y - 3 = 0$ **D.** $3x - 4y + 3 = 0$

Q.68 Find $\int_0^2 (x^2 + 1)\, dx$ as the limit of a sum :

A. $\frac{4}{3}$ **B.** $\frac{14}{3}$

C. $\frac{14}{5}$ **D.** None of these

Q.69 If any two adjacent rows or columns of a determinant are interchanged in position, the value of the determinant:

A. Becomes zero   **B.** Remains the same

C. Changes its sign   **D.** Is doubled

Q.70 One of the roots of $\begin{vmatrix} x+a & b & c \\ a & x+b & c \\ a & b & x+c \end{vmatrix} = 0$ is:

A. abc   **B.** a + b + c

C. -(a + b + c)   **D.** -abc

Q.71 It has been found that if A and B play a game 12 times, A wins 6 times, B wins 4 times and they draw twice. A and B take part in a series of 3 games. The probability that they win alternately is:

A. $\frac{5}{12}$ **B.** $\frac{5}{36}$ **C.** $\frac{19}{27}$ **D.** $\frac{5}{27}$

Q.72 A box contains 3 white and 2 black balls. Two balls are drawn at random one after the other. If the balls are not replaced, what is the probability that both the balls are black?

A. $\frac{2}{5}$ **B.** $\frac{1}{5}$

C. $\frac{1}{10}$ **D.** None of the above

Q.73 Consider the following relations from A to B where A = {u, v, w, x, y, z} and B = {p, q, r, s}:

1) {(u, p), (v, p), (w, p), (x, q), (y, q), (z,q)}

2) {(u, p), (v, q), (w, r), (z, s)}

3) {(u, s), (v, r),(w, q),(u, p),(v, q),(z, q)}

4) {(u, q),(v, p),(w, s),(x, r),(y, q),(z, s)}

Which of the above relations are not functions?

A. 1 and 2   **B.** 1 and 4   **C.** 2 and 3   **D.** 3 and 4

Q.74 Let X be the set of all citizens of India. Elements x, y in X are said to be related if the difference of their age is 5 years. Which one of the following is correct?

A. The relation is an equivalence relation on X.

B. The relation is symmetric but neither reflexive nor transitive.

C. The relation is reflexive but neither symmetric nor

transitive.

D. None of the above

Q.75 Prove that the term independent of x in the expansion of $\left(x + \frac{1}{x}\right)^{2n}$ is:

A. $\frac{1\cdot 3\cdot 5...(2n-1)}{\lfloor n}2^n$

B. $\frac{1\cdot 3\cdot 5...(2n-2)}{\lfloor n}2^n$

C. $\frac{1\cdot 4\cdot 5...(2n-3)}{\lfloor n}2^n$

D. $\frac{1\cdot 2\cdot 5...(2n-4)}{\lfloor n}2^n$

General Knowledge

Q.76 Who is the author of the book 'The Struggle for Police Reforms in India', released in May 2022?

A. Rakesh Asthana

B. Kinjal Singh

C. Satya Narayan Pradhan

D. Prakash Singh

Q.77 If RIVER = 72 then LAND=?

A. 30　　**B.** 29　　**C.** 31　　**D.** 28

Q.78 In a certain code 37 means 'which class' and 583 means 'caste and class', What is the code for 'caste'?

A. 3

B. 7

C. 8

D. Either 5 or 8

Q.79 In how many ways the letter 'SOLVING' can be rearranged to make 7 letter words such that none of the letters repeat?

A. 1060　　**B.** 7020　　**C.** 5040　　**D.** 3080

Q.80 Find correct spelling :

A. Abbreviate

B. Abreviate

C. Abrrviate

D. Abbreviat

Q.81 Look at this series: $36, 34, 30, 28, 24, ...$ What number should come next?

A. 20　　**B.** 22　　**C.** 23　　**D.** 26

Q.82

Look at this series: $5.2, 4.8, 4.4, 4, ...$ What number should come next?

A. 3　　**B.** 3.3　　**C.** 3.5　　**D.** 3.6

Q.83 What was invented or measured by Robert Andrews Millikan in Physics?

A. Electronic Charge

B. Neutrino

C. Both A & B

D. All of the above

Q.84 The deficiency diseases can be prevented by __________:

A. Prolonged cooking

B. Eating only fruits

C. Eating only vegetables

D. Eating food with good nutritional value

Q.85 Who takes care of Ellora caves?

A. Government of Maharashtra

B. Archaeological Survey of India

C. Ministry of Culture

D. Ministry of Tourism

Q.86 'Yakshagana' is the dance, related to __________ state.

A. Himachal Pradesh

B. Madhya Pradesh

C. Andhra Pradesh

D. Karnataka

Q.87 What is the national currency of South Africa?

A. Rand　　**B.** Pound　　**C.** Franc　　**D.** Dinar

Q.88 What is the National Reptile of India.

A. Crocodile

B. Earthwarm

C. Lizard

D. King Cobra

Q.89 How many Minor ports in India?

A. 189　　**B.** 200　　**C.** 178　　**D.** 169

Q.90 What is the full form of D.V.D?

A. Dynamic Video Disc

B. Dynamic Versatile Disc

C. Digital Versatile Disc

D. None of these

Q.91 Arrange languages in Ascending order of Highest Speaking Language :

A. Arabic, Spanish, Chinese, English

B. Arabic, English, Spanish, Chinese

C. Bengali, French, English, Chinese

D. Spanish, English, Russian, Chinese

Q.92 If in the English alphabet, every alternate letter from B onwards is written in small letters while others are written in capitals, then how will the 3rd day from Tuesday will be coded?

A. W e D N e S d A Y

B. W E d n E S d A Y

C. T H U R S d A Y

D. f r I d A Y

Q.93 Which of the following is not fit in the match?

A. French Open

B. US Open

C. Australian Open

D. Cincinnati Masters

Q.94 Which of the following region has won the Ranji Trophy tournament 2019?

A. Saurashtra

B. Mumbai

C. Vidarbha

D. Rajasthan

Q.95 Which of the following trophy is not related to Cricket in India?

A. Syed Mushtaq Ali Trophy

B. Deodhar Trophy

C. Santosh Trophy

D. Duleep Trophy

Q.96 Under which article did the Supreme Court declared the right to hoist the National Flag as the Fundamental Right?

A. Article 19 (i)

B. Article 14

C. Article 18

D. Article 21

Q.97 What is the full form of 'WEF' :

A. World bank

B. IMF

C. World Trade Organisation

D. World Economic Forum

Q.98 Who is the author of One Night @ the Call Centre?

A. Anurag Mathur　　　**B.** Chetan Bhagat
C. Robin Sharma　　　**D.** Vikram Seth

Q.99 Which among the following apparently impressed Jahangir to issue a farman in 1613 A.D. to the English to establish a factory at Surat?

A. Reconciliation between the English and Portuguese
B. A secret offer of naval help to the Mughal emperor to oust the Portuguese
C. A heavy dose of bribe to Nur Jahan
D. The defeat of Portuguese naval squadrons by the English

Q.100 Nalgonda Technique is used for:

A. Chlorination of water
B. Defluoridation of water
C. Iodisation of salt
D. Detoxification of contaminated mustard oil

// Smart Answer Sheet //

Correct — Percentage of students who answered correctly. **Skipped** — Percentage of students who skipped.

Q.	Ans.	Correct	Skipped	Q.	Ans.	Correct	Skipped	Q.	Ans.	Correct	Skipped	Q.	Ans.	Correct	Skipped	Q.	Ans.	Correct	Skipped	Q.	Ans.	Correct	Skipped
1	A	59.33 %	33.9 %	18	D	40.86 %	49.86 %	35	B	83.93 %	15.86 %	52	C	63.7 %	31.83 %	69	C	47.49 %	42.79 %	86	D	67.16 %	32.56 %
2	A	61.83 %	33.07 %	19	B	42.38 %	52.65 %	36	D	62.39 %	30.17 %	53	C	88.18 %	10.83 %	70	C	24.69 %	68.84 %	87	A	57.87 %	31.51 %
3	B	67.95 %	32.02 %	20	D	45.39 %	34.19 %	37	C	85.18 %	10.51 %	54	A	52.64 %	31.85 %	71	B	42.81 %	50.37 %	88	D	47.27 %	42.39 %
4	A	66.76 %	32.99 %	21	B	63.89 %	35.36 %	38	D	31.26 %	67.33 %	55	B	81.33 %	15.01 %	72	B	43.7 %	47.65 %	89	B	25.36 %	68.74 %
5	D	47.04 %	31.53 %	22	A	47.31 %	32.19 %	39	D	84.37 %	15.43 %	56	B	63.18 %	34.44 %	73	C	56.38 %	31.49 %	90	C	79.84 %	16.43 %
6	D	29.04 %	69.31 %	23	C	64.34 %	34.7 %	40	D	63.17 %	36.21 %	57	D	15.75 %	79.12 %	74	B	59.51 %	35.27 %	91	A	60.05 %	33.59 %
7	D	54.6 %	39.05 %	24	B	58.9 %	40.85 %	41	D	81.42 %	14.54 %	58	C	27.78 %	70.01 %	75	A	49.58 %	45.32 %	92	D	52.48 %	32.07 %
8	A	82.27 %	14.85 %	25	A	69.63 %	30.26 %	42	B	42.74 %	35.54 %	59	B	59.86 %	30.45 %	76	D	44.41 %	45.04 %	93	D	55.88 %	42.96 %
9	B	63.25 %	31.28 %	26	C	42.61 %	53.9 %	43	C	60.9 %	35.44 %	60	C	27.07 %	69.57 %	77	C	81.52 %	12.52 %	94	C	67.58 %	30.4 %
10	C	41.1 %	40.48 %	27	B	69.03 %	30.5 %	44	C	78.3 %	20.44 %	61	B	20.01 %	79.03 %	78	D	54.35 %	35.81 %	95	C	43.21 %	33.16 %
11	C	42.69 %	30.95 %	28	B	55.94 %	43.93 %	45	A	16.43 %	80.82 %	62	A	63.46 %	35.58 %	79	C	44.09 %	46.8 %	96	A	23.46 %	75.57 %
12	A	76.52 %	21.82 %	29	C	43.88 %	52.89 %	46	C	84.1 %	13.82 %	63	D	62.32 %	33.8 %	80	A	54.71 %	38.17 %	97	D	61.51 %	34.53 %
13	B	54.34 %	35.47 %	30	B	67.4 %	31.3 %	47	D	49.44 %	31.64 %	64	C	79.56 %	14.53 %	81	B	55.94 %	33.78 %	98	B	65.26 %	33.03 %
14	C	55.67 %	42.96 %	31	B	64.25 %	31.28 %	48	D	86.0 %	11.22 %	65	D	58.79 %	34.56 %	82	D	63.3 %	30.45 %	99	D	28.62 %	70.83 %
15	A	59.54 %	34.52 %	32	A	69.65 %	30.07 %	49	A	55.24 %	33.52 %	66	C	63.55 %	35.29 %	83	A	11.61 %	81.23 %	100	B	55.35 %	32.2 %
16	A	40.25 %	59.37 %	33	B	76.28 %	20.82 %	50	C	52.31 %	47.24 %	67	D	66.2 %	31.79 %	84	D	41.43 %	45.61 %				
17	D	62.57 %	31.54 %	34	B	58.33 %	36.09 %	51	D	82.34 %	16.73 %	68	C	12.97 %	86.57 %	85	B	68.21 %	31.04 %				

//Hints and Solutions//

1. It is mentioned in the passage 'Pierre and Marie's amicable collaboration later helped to unlock the secrets of the atom.' The word 'amicable' means 'friendly'.

Hence, the correct option is (A).

2. Marie Curie was determined in her actions. When she learned that the university in Warsaw was closed for women, she decided to receive higher education and left Poland in 1891 to enter the Sorbonne, a French university.
Hence, the correct option is (A).

3. The word 'disgruntled' means 'annoyed or displeased.' It is mentioned in the passage that she became disgruntled.
Hence, the correct option is (B).

4. The word 'boldly' fits here as Marie showed courage and determination in pursuing her higher studies.
Hence, the correct option is (A).

5. It is mentioned in the passage that she earned her master's degree and doctorate in physics.
Hence, the correct option is (D).

6. Let's first learn the meanings of the words:
Meandering = following a route which is not straight or direct
Sliding = move smoothly along a surface
Sloping = inclined from a horizontal or vertical line
Strained = showing signs of nervousness, tension or tiredness
So, the antonym of "meandering" is "straight".

Hence, the correct option is (D).

7. Venial = an evil act which can be forgiven;
pardonableSuperficial = lacking in depth or solidity, not seriousPardonable = able to be forgivenCorrupt = having or showing a willingness to act dishonestly in return for money or personal gain.
Hence, the correct option is (D).

8. We use 'used to' to talk about past events which we no longer do. We only use it to talk about the past. The only option with the correct sentence structure is option A.
Hence, the correct option is (A).

9. The correct spelling is 'Prepossessing'.
Prepossession is defined as the state or condition of being prepossessed by someone.
Ex- (1)- He wasn't a very prepossessing sort of person.
(2)- The box didn't look very prepossessing, but the necklace inside was beautiful.
Hence, the correct option is (B).

10. Out of the given alternatives, option C is the correctly punctuated sentence.

Hence, the correct option is (C).

11. Edify = to enlighten, to educate.Sermonize = to deliver an opinionated and dogmatic talk to someone.Oration = a formal speech, especially one given on a ceremonial occasion.Elocution = a particular style of speaking.
Hence, the correct option is (C).

12. The given sentence is in active form of simple past tense. The structures for active/passive voices are: Active: Subject + verb (IInd form) + object... Passive: Object + was/were + verb (IIIrd form) + by + subject... So, with the help of the above structures, we can convert the given sentence into passive voice: The letter was written and posted by me.
Hence, the correct option is (A).

13. The given sentence is of present perfect tense and it is in passive form. The structures for active/passive voices are: Active: Subject + has/have + verb (IIIrd form) + object...Passive: Object + has/have + been + verb (IIIrd form) + by + subject...So, the active voice of the given sentence would be: The police have launched a massive search operation to nab the suspects.
Hence, the correct option is (B).

14. The given sentence is of direct narration. To convert it into an indirect narration, remove inverted commas and add conjunction "that" to join the reporting verb with the reported speech. If there is any universal truth or habitual fact in the reporting speech, no changes are made to the reported verb's tense. So, the direct speech of the given sentence would be: I said that water is essential for life.
Hence, the correct option is (C).

15. The given sentence is of indirect narration. Since "asked" is followed by an object, so it'll change to "said to" in the direct speech. It is an interrogative sentence and is in simple past, so, it will change into simple present in the interrogative sentence format. The question mark will be used in place of full stop and inverted commas will be placed before and after the reported speech.
Hence, the correct option is (A).

16. Let's understand the meaning of each phrasal verb in order to find out which one fits best in the sentence:
Call for means to summon.
Call off means to cancel something.
Call to means to speak loudly, as to attract attention.
Call up means to bring forward for consideration.
The manager is being summoned for an explanation.
Hence, the correct option is (A).

17. The verb "devote" is followed by the preposition "to".

He was entirely **devoted** to the affairs of his regimen.
Hence, the correct option is (D).

18. When we use past perfect and simple past in a sentence, it shows that an action happened before something else in the past. The phrase in the past perfect tense is used to show that something happened before another action in the past (for the action that happened first). And the phrase in the simple past is used for the action that happened later.
Hence, the correct option is (D).

19. The word humane (Adjective) means to show kindness towards people and animals by making them sure that they do not suffer. A civilized nation believes in the proper treatment of all its people and animals.
Hence, the correct option is (B).

20. We use little with singular uncountable nouns. We use "few" for countable nouns.

We use "few, a few, and the few" in the following contexts:

Few: means a small amount, but the amount is almost nothing.

A few: mean a small amount, but it's enough.

The few: mean a small specific amount.

Here, a few fit the blank perfectly as the woman in the sentence wants some quality time for herself.

So, the complete sentence is: All she wanted was <u>a few</u> moments on her own.

Hence, the correct option is (D).

21. The third conditional sentence is used to explain that present circumstances would be different if something different had happened in the past. We use the past perfect (had + past participle) in the if-clause. The modal auxiliary (would, could, shoud, etc.) + have + past participle in the main clause expresses the theoretical situation that could have happened.

Hence, the correct option is (B).

22. When we use past perfect and simple past in a sentence, it shows that an action happened before something else in the past. The phrase in the past perfect tense is used to show that something happened before another action in the past (for the action that happened first). And the phrase in the simple past is used for the action that happened later.
Hence, the correct option is (A).

23. The teacher set some homework 'at' the end of the lesson.
Hence, the correct option is (C).

24. The train is expected to arrive between 11pm and 12pm.
Hence, the correct option is (B).

25. He came along 'with' his sister to meet us.
Hence, the correct option is (A).

26. Given:
$p = 0$ (for vaccume)
$\Delta p = 1 \times 10^{-5} Nm^{-2}$ and $B = 1.25 \times 10^{11} Nm^{-2}$
As the bulk modulus (B) $\frac{\Delta v}{v} = \frac{\Delta p}{B}$
$\therefore \frac{\Delta v}{v} = \frac{\Delta p}{B} = \frac{10^5}{1.25 \times 10^{11}}$
$= 8 \times 10^{-7}$
Hence, the correct option is (C).

27. The ratio between tangential stress and shearing strain is called modulus rigidity of the material. In this, shape of a body changes but volume remains unchanged.

With ideal liquid Modulus rigidity is zero because frictional force cannot exist in this case. So, shear stress and tangential force are zero.
Hence, the correct option is (B).

28. Given:
$R_E = 6400km, \ g_E = 9.8ms^{-2} \ d = 5km$
The value of g at a depth h from the earth's surface
$g = g_E \left(1 - \frac{d}{R}\right)$.........(i)

where, g_E acceleration due to gravity at the earth's surface
put value in (i),
$g = 9.8 \left(1 - \frac{5}{6400}\right)$
$= 9.8 \left(\frac{6395}{6400}\right)$
$= 9.79 ms^{-2}$
Hence, the value of acceleration due to gravity at a point $5km$ below the earth's surface is $9.79 ms^{-2}$
Hence, the correct option is (B).

29. Given:
$V_1 = 14ms^{-1}, \ V_2 = 0, \ M_1 = 10kg, \ M_2 = 4kg$
The velocity of the centre of mass,
$V_{CM} = \frac{V_1 M_1 + V_2 M_2}{M_1 + M_2}$.........(i)
put value in (i),
$V_{CM} = \frac{10(14) + 4(0)}{10 + 4}$
$= 10 ms^{-1}$
Hence, the correct option is (C).

30. Applying Energy conservation formula,
Total energy = $K.E + P.E.$
At this height, P.E. will be half of its $K.E.$
Then,
mgh =982
2 × 9.8 × h = 49
h = 2.5 m
Hence, at the height of 2.5 m $K.E.$ become half.
Hence, the correct option is (B).

31. Given:

critical angle $= C = 30°$
Refractive index of a medium $= \mu$
$= \frac{1}{(\sin C)}$
$= \frac{1}{(\sin 30°)}$
$= 2.$
Refracctive index $= \frac{\text{speed of light in vacuum}}{\text{speed of light in medium}}$
$= \frac{3 \times 10^8}{v}$
$\Rightarrow 2 = \frac{3 \times 10^8}{v}$
$\Rightarrow v = \frac{3 \times 10^8}{2}$
$= 1.5 \times 10^8 \ m/s$

Hence, the correct option is (B).

32. If pulley goes upward, then one weight goes down, and the other one will go upward.

Let the w_1 goes upward and w_2 goes down.

Then,

Acceleration relative to the pulley $w_1 - T = \frac{w_1}{g}(a_r - g)$ ...... (i)

Acceleration relative to the ground, $T - w_2 = \frac{w_2}{q}(a_r + g)$ ...... (ii)

Solving eqn (i) and (ii), we get,

$$T = \frac{4w_1w_2}{w_1+w_2}$$

Hence, the correct option is (A).

33. Relative acceleration $= 0$ between those balls because both have a free fall under the gravity, and the relative velocity is $40\ ms^{-1}$, and relative separation is $100\ m$.
Then,

$$\therefore \text{time} = \frac{100}{40} = 2.5s$$

Hence, the correct option is (B).

34. Nuclear force is among the 4 fundamental forces of nature.

The Strong Nuclear Force is the strongest force and its range is very short. Also, at a distance of 0.7 Fermi and less, this force becomes repulsive.

It is present inside the atom responsible for binding the Protons and Neutrons and also inside the Proton and Neutron in binding up the Quarks.

Hence, the correct option is (B).

35. Fluorine is a chemical element with the symbol F and atomic number 9.

It is the lightest halogen and exists as a highly toxic pale yellow diatomic gas at standard conditions.

It is the most electronegative element

Hence, the correct option is (B).

36.

- Esters are most commonly formed by reaction of an acid and an alcohol.
- Esters are sweet-smelling substances.
- These are used in making perfumes and as flavouring agents.
- Esters react in the presence of an acid or base to give back the alcohol and carboxylic acid and this reaction is known as saponification because it is used in the preparation of soap.

Hence, the correct option is (D).

37.

- S-block elements are the elements found in Group 1 and Group 2 on the periodic table.
- Group 1 are the alkali metals that have one valence electron. They have low ionization energies which makes them very reactive.
- Group 2 is the alkali earth metals that have two valence electrons, filling their s sublevel.

Hence, the correct option is (C).

38. Given,
Mass $M = 10\ kg$
Displcement on horizontal = displacement on incline $= d = 2\ m$
Friction force on horizontal plane, $F_r = \mu mg$
Friction force on incline plane, $F_r' = \mu mg cos\theta$
Speed is uniform means net acting force is equal to friction force
Work done, $W = F_r \cdot d = \mu mg. d$

$$\Rightarrow \mu = \frac{W}{mg \cdot d}$$
$$= \frac{150}{10 \times 10 \times 2}$$
$$= 0.75$$

Work done on incline plane, $W = F_r'd = \mu mg cos\theta. d$
$$\Rightarrow W = 0.75 \times 10 \times 10 \times cos30° \times 2$$
$$\Rightarrow W = 75\sqrt{3}\ J$$

Work done against friction is $75\sqrt{3}\ J$
Hence, the correct option is (D).

39.

- The natural conductor of heat is material that allow heat to pass through them easily are called good conductors of heat.
- Diamond is a bad conductor of electricity but good conductor of heat.
- Diamond is a good conductor of heat because in diamond each carbon atom is arranged in tetrahedral arrangement. All the electrons are close together due to a strong bond between the atoms causing vibrations.
- But it is poor conductor of electricity because it has no free electrons available.

Hence, the correct option is (D).

40. The displacement equation $x = A \sin wt$ where A is the amplitude of oscillation.

The particle is at mean position initially i.e at $t = 0, x = 0$
At the instant t, the particle is at a position of half amplitude i.e

$$X = \frac{A}{2}$$
$$\therefore \quad \frac{A}{2} = A sinwt$$
$$0.5 = sinwt$$
$$\Rightarrow wt = \frac{\pi}{6}$$
$$\frac{2\pi}{T} \times t = \frac{\pi}{6}$$
$$\Rightarrow t = \frac{T}{12}$$

Hence, the correct option is (D).

41. Internal resistance refers to the opposition to the flow of current offered by the cells and batteries themselves resulting in the generation of heat. Internal resistance is measured in Ohms.

The relationship between internal resistance (r) and emf (e) of cell s given by e = I (r + R).

Hence, the correct option is (D).

42. X-rays have wavelength of order of inter-atomic spacing of atoms of solid crystals. So X-rays are most suited for investigating solid structure.

Hence, the correct option is (B).

43. This statement is false about the magnetic field lines that if magnetic field lines are parallel and equidistant then they represent zero-field strength because if they are parallel and are at an equal distance then they have a uniform magnetic field and don't have zero magnetic field strength.

Hence, the correct option is (C).

44.

- Induction type of energy meter are universally used for measurement of energy in domestic and industrial A.C circuit.
- The unit of electrical energy is kilowatt hour (kWh).
- Induction type of energy meter used is based on "electromagnetic induction" principle.
- They are known as induction type instruments.
- An induction meter can handle current up to 100 A.

Hence, the correct option is (C).

45. Total flux coming out $= \dfrac{Q_{enclosed}}{E_0}$

$$\int E.ds = \dfrac{Q \times 10^{-6}}{\epsilon_0} \, (\text{guass law})$$

As Q is placed at center, flux coming out of all 6 sides will be equal.

$\therefore$ flux from one of the side

$$= \dfrac{Q \times 10^{-6}}{6\epsilon_0}$$

$$= \dfrac{Q}{6\varepsilon_0} \times 10^{-6}$$

Hence, the correct option is (A).

46. A p-type semiconductor is created by doping an intrinsic semiconductor with acceptor impurities. In a p-type semiconductor, holes are the majority carriers and the electrons are the minority carriers but it is electrically neutral.

Hence, the correct option is (C).

47. Radio waves can be sent from one place to another via space wave propagation, sky wave propagation as well as ground wave propagation.

Hence, the correct option is (D).

48. A simple C++ statement is each of the individual instructions of a program, like the variable declarations and expressions. They always end with a semicolon (;), and are executed in the same order in which they appear in a program.

Hence, the correct option is (D).

49. Quality factor of resonance is a dimensionless parameter that describes how underdamped an oscillator or resonator is, and characterizes a resonator bandwidth relative to its center frequency.

At resonance, $\qquad X_C = X_L$

$$\Rightarrow w_o = \sqrt{\dfrac{1}{LC}}$$

$\therefore$ Quality factor in series LCR circuit,

$$Q = \dfrac{w_0 L}{R}$$

$$= \dfrac{1}{R}\sqrt{\dfrac{L}{C}}$$

As quality factor is dimensionless, thus it has no SI unit.

Hence, the correct option is (A).

50. The energy possessed by a body by virtue of its motion is called kinetic energy. Potential Energy is the energy possessed by virtue of its position or configuration. When a body falls from an aeroplane, there is increase in its acceleration.

Hence, the correct option is (C).

51. Given:

$$\cos^{-1}x - \sin^{-1}x = 0$$

$$\because \cos^{-1}\theta + \sin^{-1}\theta = \dfrac{\pi}{2} \text{........(i)}$$

$$\Rightarrow \cos^{-1}x - \dfrac{\pi}{2} + \cos^{-1}x = 0 \text{........(ii) (put value of}$$

$\sin^{-1}\theta$ from (i) into (ii))

$$\Rightarrow 2\cos^{-1}x = \dfrac{\pi}{2}$$

$$\Rightarrow \cos^{-1}x = \dfrac{\pi}{4}$$

$$\Rightarrow x = \dfrac{1}{\sqrt{2}}$$

Hence, the correct option is (D).

52. Given:

$$\log2 = 0.3010 \text{........(i)}$$

We have to find the value of,

$$\log_5 512 = \dfrac{\log 512}{\log 5}$$

$$\Rightarrow \dfrac{\log 2^9}{\log\left(\dfrac{10}{2}\right)}$$

put value from (i),

$$\Rightarrow \dfrac{9\log 2}{\log 10 - \log 2}$$

$$\Rightarrow \dfrac{9 \times 0.3010}{1 - 0.3010}$$

$$\Rightarrow \dfrac{2.709}{0.699}$$

$$\Rightarrow \dfrac{2709}{699}$$

$$\Rightarrow 3.876$$

Hence, the correct option is (C).

53. Given:

$$n = 12 \text{ and } a_n = 3n + 4 \text{........(i)}$$

put $n = 1,2,3$ in (i)
$$a_1 = 7, a_2 = 10, a_3 = 13$$
$$a = 7, \; d = 10 - 7 = 3$$
$$S_n = \frac{n}{2}[2a + (n-1) \times d] \quad \text{......(ii)}$$

put the value of a, n, d in (ii)
$$S_{12} = \frac{12}{2}[2 \times 7 + (12 - 1) \times 3]$$
$$= 6[14 + 33]$$
$$= 6 \times 47$$
$$= 282$$
Hence, the correct option is (C).

54. Given:

The median of the data:

155 160 145 149 150 147 152 144 148 is:

First arrange the data in ascending order.

144 145 147 148 149 150 152 155 160

Since, the number of observations here is odd, therefore,

$$\text{Median,} = \frac{(n+1)^{th}}{2}$$
$$= \frac{(9+1)}{2}$$
$$= \frac{10}{2}$$
$$= 5^{th} \text{ number}$$
$$= 149$$

Hence, the correct option is (A).

55. (A) $\dfrac{x-6}{x} = 3$
$$x^2 - 6 = 3x$$
$x^2 - 3x - 6 = 0$ is quadratic polynomial; therefore, the given equation is quadratic.

(B) $x^2 - 3x - \sqrt{x} + 4$ contains a term with x, i.e., $x^{\frac{1}{2}}$, where $\frac{1}{2}$ is not a ineger Therefore, it is not a quadratic polynomial. $x^2 - 3x - \sqrt{x} + 4$ is not a quadratic equation.

(C) $x^2 - \dfrac{1}{x^2} = 5$
$$x^4 - 1 = 5x^2$$
$x^4 - 5x^2 - 1 = 0$ is a polynomial with degree 4 so it is not a quadratic equation.

(D) $(2x + 3)(3x + 2) = 6(x - 1)(x - 2)$
$$6x^2 + 4x + 9x + 6 = 6(x^2 - 2x - x + 2)$$
$$6x^2 + 4x + 9x + 6 = 6x^2 - 18x + 12$$
$$31x - 6 = 0$$
So, the given equation is not a quadratic equation.
Hence, the correct option is (B).

56. Given:

$$y = c_1 e^x + c_2 e^{-x}$$
Differentiating with respect to x,
$$\frac{dy}{dx} = c_1 e^x - c_2 e^{-x}$$

Again, Differentiating with respect to x, we get
$$\frac{d^2y}{dx^2} = c_1 e^x + c_2 e^{-x}$$
$$\frac{d^2y}{dx^2} = y$$
$$\frac{d^2y}{dx^2} - y = 0$$
This is the required differential equation of the given equation of curve.
Hence, the correct option is (B).

57. Given,
$$f(x) = 4x^3 - 7, x \in R.$$
Let, $x_1, x_2 \in R$ and $f(x_1) = f(x_2)$
$$\Rightarrow 4x_1^3 - 7 = 4x_2^3 - 7$$
$$\Rightarrow 4x_1^3 = 4x_2^3$$
$$\Rightarrow x_1^3 = x_2^3$$
$$\Rightarrow x_1^3 - x_2^3 = 0$$
$$\Rightarrow (x_1 - x_2)(x_1^2 + x_1 x_2 + x_2^2) = 0$$
$$\Rightarrow (x_1 - x_2)\left[\left(x_1 + \frac{x_2}{2}\right)^2 + \frac{3x_2^2}{4}\right] = 0$$
$\Rightarrow x_1 - x_2 = 0$, because the other factor is non-zero.
$$\Rightarrow x_1 = x_2$$
$\therefore f$ is one-one f is onto.
Let, $k \; \varepsilon \; R$ any real number
$$f(x) = k$$
$$\Rightarrow 4x^3 - 7 = k$$
$$\Rightarrow x = \left[\frac{k+7}{3}\right]^{\frac{1}{3}}$$
Now,
$$\left[\frac{k+7}{4}\right]^{\frac{1}{3}} \varepsilon R, \text{ because } k \varepsilon R \text{ and } f\left[\left(\frac{k+7}{4}\right)^{\frac{1}{3}}\right]$$
$$= 4\left[\left(\frac{k+7}{4}\right)^{\frac{1}{3}}\right]^3 - 7$$
$$= 4\left[\frac{k+7}{4}\right] - 7 = k$$
$\therefore k$ is the image of $\left[\frac{k+7}{4}\right]^{\frac{1}{3}}$
$\therefore f$ is onto.
$\therefore f$ is a bijective function.
Hence, the correct option is (D).

58. Given:
$$y = [x(x - 2)]^2 = [x^2 - 2x]^2$$
Diff. w.r.t. to x,
$$\frac{dy}{dx} = y = 2(x^2 - 2x)(2x - 2) = 4x(x - 2)(x - 1)$$
$$\frac{dy}{dx} = 0$$
$x = 0, x = 2$ and $x = 1$
The points $x = 0, x = 1$ and $x = 2$ divide the real line into four disjoint intervals i.e., $(-\infty, 0), (0,1), (1,2)(2, \infty)$

In intervals $(-\infty, 0)$ and $(1,2) \frac{dy}{dx} < 0 : y$ is strictly decreasing in intervals $(-\infty, 0)$ and $(1,2)$ However, in intervals (0,1) and $(2,\infty), \frac{dy}{dx} > 0$

$\therefore y$ is strictly Increasing in intervals $(0,1)$ and $(2,\infty)$

$\therefore y$ is the strictly increasing intervals $0,2$

Hence, the correct option is (C).

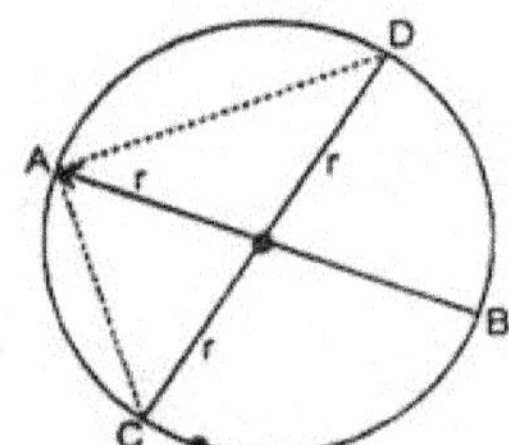

59.

Area of circle $= \pi r^2$

Area of $\triangle ACD = \frac{1}{2} \times (2r) \times r$

$= r^2$

Ratio of the area of the circle to the triangle $\triangle ACD$,

$= \frac{\pi r^2}{r^2}$

$= \pi$

Hence, the correct option is (B).

60.

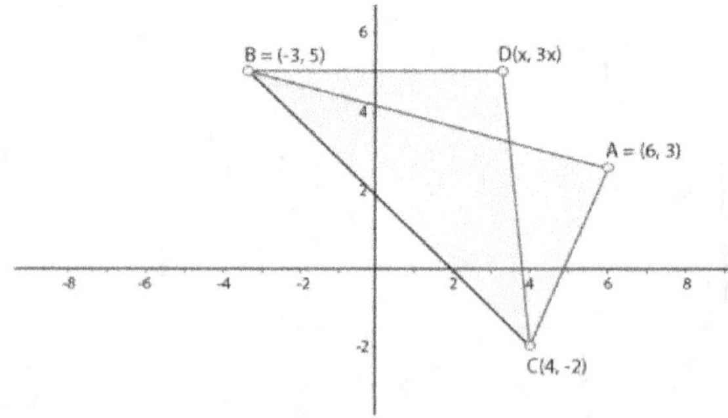

Given:

The coordinates of triangle are shown in the above figure.

Also, $\frac{\Delta DBC}{\triangle ABC} = \frac{1}{2}$

Now, let us consider Area of a ΔPQR

Where, $P(x_1, y_1), Q(x_2, y_2)$ and $R(x_3, y_3)$ be the 3 vertices of ΔPQR So, Area of ΔPQR,

$= \frac{1}{2}[x_1(y_2 - y_3) + x_2(y_3 - y_1) + x_3(y_1 - y_2)]$

Area of ΔDBC,

$= \frac{1}{2}[x(5 - (-2)) + (-3)(-2 - 3x) + 4(3x - 5)]$

$= \frac{1}{2}[7x + 6 + 9x + 12x - 20]$

$= 14x - 7$

Similarly, area of ΔABC,

$= \frac{1}{2}[6(5 - (-2)) + (-3)(-2 - 3) + 4(3 - 5)]$

$= \frac{1}{2}[42 + 15 - 8]$

$= \frac{49}{2}$

$= 24.5$

$\therefore \frac{\Delta DBC}{\triangle ABC}$

$= \frac{1}{2} = \frac{14x - 7}{24.5}$

$24.5 = 28x - 14$

$28x = 38.5$

$x = \frac{38.5}{28}$

$= 1.375$

Hence, the correct option is (C).

61. Given:

$\sqrt{2x + 1} - \sqrt{2x - 1} = 1$

$\Rightarrow \sqrt{2x + 1} = 1 + \sqrt{2x - 1}$

squaring both sides, we get,

$\Rightarrow 2x + 1 = 1 + 2x - 1 + 2\sqrt{2x - 1}$

$\Rightarrow 0 = -1 + 2\sqrt{2x - 1}$

$\Rightarrow 2\sqrt{2x - 1} = 1$

squaring both sides, we get.

$4\left(\sqrt{2x - 1}\right)^2 = 1$

$\Rightarrow 2x - 1 = \frac{1}{4}$

$\Rightarrow 2x = \frac{1}{4} + 1$

$\Rightarrow 2x = \frac{5}{4}$

$\Rightarrow x = \frac{5}{8}$

$\therefore \sqrt{x^2 - 1}$

$\Rightarrow \sqrt{4 \times \left(\frac{5}{8}\right)^2 - 1}$

$\Rightarrow \sqrt{4 \times \frac{25}{64} - 1}$

$\Rightarrow \sqrt{\frac{100 - 64}{64}}$

$\Rightarrow \sqrt{\frac{36}{64}}$

$\Rightarrow \frac{6}{8}$

$\Rightarrow \dfrac{3}{4}$

Hence, the correct option is (B).

62. $I = \int_0^1 \dfrac{e^{\tan^{-1}x}dx}{1+x^2}$

Let $\tan^{-1}x = t$

$\dfrac{1}{1+x^2}dx = dt$

Lower limit $\rightarrow t = \tan^{-1}0 = 0$

Upper limit $\rightarrow t = \tan^{-1}1 = \dfrac{\pi}{4}$

$\therefore \int_0^{\frac{\pi}{4}} e^t\, dt = [e^t]_0^{\frac{\pi}{4}}$

$e^{\frac{\pi}{4}} - e^0 = e^{\frac{\pi}{4}} - 1$

Hence, the correct option is (A).

63. Let angle between $\left(a + \overline{b}\right)$ and $\left(a - \overline{b}\right)$ be α,

$\cos\alpha = \dfrac{\left(\vec{a}+\vec{b}\right)\left(\vec{a}-\vec{b}\right)}{\left|\vec{a}+\vec{b}\right\|\left|\vec{a}-\vec{b}\right|}$

$= \dfrac{(7)^2-(11)^2}{10\sqrt{3}\times 2\sqrt{10}}$

$= \dfrac{(7+11)(7-11)}{20\sqrt{3}\times\sqrt{10}}$

$= -\dfrac{18}{5\sqrt{30}}$

$= \dfrac{-6\times 3}{5\sqrt{30}} \times \dfrac{\sqrt{30}}{\sqrt{30}}$

$= -\dfrac{3\sqrt{30}}{25}$

$\alpha = \cos^{-1}\left(-\dfrac{3}{5}\sqrt{\dfrac{6}{5}}\right)$

Hence, the correct option is (D).

64. Let $Q(x,y,z)$ is the image of $(1,-2,3)$ in the plane

$\dfrac{x+1}{2} = 3 = x = 5$

$\dfrac{y-2}{2} = 1 = y = 4$

$\dfrac{z+3}{2} = 2 = z = 1$

$\therefore$ image of $(1,-2,3)$ are $(5,4,1)$

Hence, the correct option is (C).

65. $\lim\limits_{x\to 2} \dfrac{\sin(e^{x-2}-1)}{\log(x-1)}$

$= \lim\limits_{h\to 0} \dfrac{\sin(e^h-1)}{\log(1+h)}$

On substituting $h = x - 2$

$= \lim\limits_{h\to 0} \dfrac{\sin(e^h-1)}{e^h-1}\cdot\dfrac{e^h-1}{h}\cdot\dfrac{h}{\log(1+h)}$

$= 1\cdot 1\cdot 1$

$= 1$

Hence, the correct option is (D).

66. Let, $2a$ and $2b$ be the length of major and minor axis respectively.

$\sqrt{1 - \dfrac{b^2}{a^2}} = \dfrac{4}{5}$

$\dfrac{b^2}{a^2} = \dfrac{9}{25}$ .... (i)

$\dfrac{2b^2}{a} = 14.4$

$\dfrac{b^2}{a} = 7.2, b^2 = 7.2a$

Putting the value of $\dfrac{b^2}{a}$ in equation (i),

$\dfrac{7.2}{a} = \dfrac{9}{25} = a = 20$

$b^2 = 7.2 \times 20 = 144$

$b = 12$

The sum of major and minor axis

$= 2a + 2b$

$= 2(a+b) = 2(20+12)$

$= 64$ units

Hence, the correct option is (C).

67. $3x - 4y + 12 = 0$ or $y = \dfrac{3}{4}x + 3$

$3x - 4y = 6$ or $y = \dfrac{3}{4}x - \dfrac{3}{2}$

Equation of line mid-way between these two lines,

$y = mx + c$........(i), $\left(m = \dfrac{3}{4}\right)$ $C = \dfrac{C_1-C_2}{2}$

put values in (i),

$y = \dfrac{3}{4}x + \left(\dfrac{3-\frac{3}{2}}{2}\right)$

$y = \dfrac{3}{4}x + \dfrac{3}{4}$

$4y = 3x + 3$

$3x - 4y + 3 = 0$

Hence, the correct option is (D).

68. We know that:

$\int_a^b f(x)dx = (b-a)\lim\limits_{n\to\infty}\dfrac{1}{n}(f(a) + f(a+h) + \ldots + f(a+(n-1)h))$

Putting $a = 0$, $b = 2$, $h = \dfrac{b-a}{n} = \dfrac{2-0}{n} = \dfrac{2}{n}$

in $\int_0^2 x^2 + 1\,dx$

$I = (2-0)\lim\limits_{n\to\infty}\dfrac{1}{n}(f(0) + f(n) + f(2n) + \ldots + fn - 1)h$

$f(0) = 1$

$f(h) = h^2 + 1$

$= \left(\dfrac{4}{n^2}\right) + 1$

$f((n-1)h) = (n-1)^2 \times \dfrac{4}{n^2} + 1$

$\therefore I = 2\lim\limits_{n\to\infty}\dfrac{1}{n}$

$\left((1 + 1 + \ldots n \text{ times}) + \left(0 + \dfrac{4}{n^2} + \dfrac{16}{n^2} + \ldots + \dfrac{(n-1)^2}{n^2}\right)\right)$

$= 2\lim\limits_{n\to\infty}\dfrac{1}{n}\left(n + \dfrac{4}{n}\dfrac{(n-1)n(2n-1)}{6}\right)$

$= 2\lim\limits_{n\to\infty}\left(1 + \dfrac{2}{3}\left(1 - \dfrac{1}{n}\right)\left(2 - \dfrac{1}{n}\right)\right)$

$$= 2 \times \left(1 + \frac{4}{3}\right)$$
$$= \frac{14}{3}$$

Hence, the correct option is (C).

69. If any two adjacent rows or columns of a determinant are interchanged in position, the value of the determinant changes its sign.

For example,

$$A = \begin{vmatrix} 1 & 2 & 3 \\ 4 & 5 & 6 \\ 2 & 1 & 2 \end{vmatrix}$$

The value of determinant is:

$A = 1[5 \times 2 - 6 \times 1] - 2[4 \times 2 - 6 \times 2] + 3[4 \times 1 - 5 \times 2]$

$A = 1[10 - 6] - 2[8 - 12] + 3[4 - 10]$

$A = 4 + 8 - 18 = -6$

Now changing the row R_1 with R_2,

$$A = \begin{vmatrix} 4 & 5 & 6 \\ 1 & 2 & 3 \\ 2 & 1 & 2 \end{vmatrix}$$

The value of determinant is:

$A = 4[2 \times 2 - 3 \times 1] - 5[1 \times 2 - 3 \times 2] + 6[1 \times 1 - 2 \times 2]$

$A = 4[4 - 3] - 5[2 - 6] + 6[1 - 4]$

$A = 4 + 20 - 18 = 6$

Now changing the column C_1 with C_2,

$$A = \begin{vmatrix} 2 & 1 & 3 \\ 5 & 4 & 6 \\ 1 & 2 & 2 \end{vmatrix}$$

The value of determinant is:

$A = 2[4 \times 2 - 6 \times 2] - 1[5 \times 2 - 6 \times 1] + 3[5 \times 2 - 4 \times 1]$

$A = 2[8 - 12] - 1[10 - 6] + 3[10 - 4]$

$A = -8 - 4 + 18 = 6$

Hence, the correct option is (C).

70.
$$\begin{vmatrix} x+a & b & c \\ a & x+b & c \\ a & b & x+c \end{vmatrix} = 0$$

Applying, $C_1 \rightarrow C_1 + C_2 + C_3$

$$\begin{vmatrix} a+b+c+x & b & c \\ a+b+c+x & x+b & c \\ a+b+c+x & b & c+x \end{vmatrix} = 0$$

$$(a+b+c+x)\begin{vmatrix} 1 & b & c \\ 1 & x+b & c \\ 1 & b & c+x \end{vmatrix} = 0$$

$C_2 \rightarrow C_2 - C_1, C_3 \rightarrow C_3 - C_1$

$$(a+b+c+x)\begin{vmatrix} 1 & b & c \\ 0 & x & 0 \\ 0 & 0 & x \end{vmatrix} = 0$$

$(a+b+c+x)1.x^2 = 0$

$x = 0, -(a+b+c)(since, x \neq 0)$

Hence, the correct option is (C).

71. Probability of A wining games $P(A)$,

$$= \frac{6}{12}$$
$$= \frac{1}{2}$$

Probability of B wining games $P(B)$,

$$= \frac{4}{12}$$
$$= \frac{1}{3}$$

$$P(A \text{ and } B) = \frac{1}{3}$$

Required probability $= \frac{1}{2} P(A \text{ and } B) \times P(A) + \frac{1}{2} P(A$ and $B) \times P(B)$

$$= \frac{1}{2} \times \frac{1}{3} \times \frac{1}{2} + \frac{1}{2} \times \frac{1}{3} \times \frac{1}{3}$$
$$= \frac{1}{12} + \frac{1}{18}$$
$$= \frac{5}{36}$$

Hence, the correct option is (B).

72. Total number of balls $= 5$

Number of black balls $= 2$

Required probability $= \frac{1}{2} \frac{n(E)}{n(s)}$

$$= \frac{2}{5} \times \frac{1}{2}$$
$$= \frac{1}{5}$$

Hence, the correct option is (B).

73. Given:

A = {u, v, w, x, y, z}; B = {p, q, r, s}

As we know mapping $f : x \rightarrow y$ is said to be a function, if each element in the set x has its image in set y.

It is also possible that there are few elements in set y which are not the image of any element in set x. but Every element in set x should have one or more than one image in set y.

Then that will show the relational function between those two sets.

Hence, the correct option is (C).

74. $X = $set of all citizens of India

$$R = \{(x, y): x, y \in X, |x - y| = 5\}$$
$$|x - x| = 0 \neq 5 (R \text{ is not reflective })$$

$xRy \Rightarrow |y - x| = 5$
$xRy \Rightarrow |x - y| = 5 (R$ is symmetric $)$
$xRy \Rightarrow |y - x| = 5$
$yRz \Rightarrow |y - z| = 5 \mid$ but $x - z \mid \neq 5 so (R$ is not transitive $)$
Hence, the correct option is (B).

75. There are $(2n + 1)$ terms in expansion.

$\therefore t_{n+1}$ is the middle term.

$t_{n+1} = 2_nC_n(x)^{2n-n}\left(\frac{1}{x}\right)^n$

$t_{n+1} = 2_nC_n(x)^{2n-n}\left(\frac{1}{x}\right)^n$

$t_{n+1} = 2_nC_n x^n \frac{1}{x^n} = 2nC_n = \frac{\lfloor 2n}{\lfloor n \lfloor n}$

$= \frac{(2n)(2n-1)(2n-2)...4\cdot3\cdot2\cdot1}{n(n-1)...2\cdot1\lfloor n}$

$= \frac{(2n-1)(2n-3)...3\cdot1 n(n-1)(n-2)...3\cdot2\cdot1 2^n}{n(n-1)(n-2)...3\cdot2\cdot1\lfloor n}$

$= \frac{(2n-1)...3\cdot1}{\lfloor n} 2^n = \frac{1\cdot3\cdot5...(2n-1)}{\lfloor n} 2^n$

Hence, the correct option is (A).

76. Vice President M Venkaiah Naidu released a book, 'The Struggle for Police Reforms in India', in May 2022. It has been authored by former IPS officer Prakash Singh. He also flagged certain issues that need to be addressed on a war footing, including filling up vacancies in police departments and strengthening the police infrastructure in tune with the requirements of modern age policing.

Hence, the correct option is (D).

77. Given:

RIVER = 72

LAND = ?

by alphabetically

L = 12

A = 1

N = 14

D = 4

The sum of all alphabets number is 31.

so,

LAND = 31

Hence, the correct option is (C).

78. Given,

'which class' $= 37$

'caste and class' $= 583$

The common word 'class' is coded as '3'.

'caste' is coded as '5' or '8'.

Hence, the correct option is (D).

79. Given:

S , O, L, V , I , N , G - No letter repeats itself twice.

We use either of 7 letters to fill the first place and remain with the rest 6 letters and 6 positions.

We use either of 6 remaining letters to put in the second position and remain with the rest 5 letters and 5 positions.

And so on, by Multiplication Principle, we get the n.o of such words as:

$7 \times 6 \times 5 \times 4 \times 3 \times 2 \times 1 \Rightarrow 7! \Rightarrow 5040$

Just to make sure no word repeats itself, note that the position occupation took place in a unique order.

Hence, the correct option is (C).

80. Abbreviate 'means to make something smaller.

Hence, the correct option is (A).

81. $36 - 34 = 2$

$34 - 30 = 4$

$30 - 28 = 2$

$28 - 24 = 4$

so,

$24 - x = 2$

$x = 24 - 2 = 22$

Hence, the correct option is (B).

82. $5.2 - 0.4 = 4.8$

$4.8 - 0.4 = 4.4$

$4.4 - 0.4 = 4$

So,

$4 - 0.4 = 3.6$

Hence, the correct option is (D).

83. Robert Andrews Millikan (March 22, 1868 – December 19, 1953) was an American experimental physicist who was awarded the Nobel Prize in Physics in 1923 for his work on the measurement of the primary electric charge and the photoelectric effect.

Hence, the correct option is (A).

84. A balanced diet is extremely important for the good health of a person. Any imbalance in the diet might lead to excess or insufficient intake of certain nutrients. Insufficient intake of a particular nutrient can lead to a deficiency disease.

Hence, the correct option is (D).

85. Government of India, Archaeological Survey of India, UNESCO(United Nations Educational, Scientific and Cultural Organisation) takes care of Ellora caves.

Hence, the correct option is (B).

86. Yakshagana, dance-drama of South India, associated most strongly with the state of Karnataka. Elaborate and colourful costumes, makeup, and masks constitute some of the most-striking features of the art form.

Hence, the correct option is (D).

87. The rand is the official currency of South Africa. It is subdivided into 100 cents. The rand is legal tender in the Common Monetary Area between South Africa, Eswatini, Lesotho, and Namibia, although the last three countries do have their own currencies pegged at par with the rand. Before 1976, the rand as legal tender in Botswana.

Hence, the correct option is (A).

88. The king cobra (Ophiophagus hannah) is a large elapid endemic to forests from India through Southeast Asia. It is the world's longest venomous snake. Adult king cobras are 3.18 to 4 m (10.4 to 13.1 ft) long on average. The longest known individual measured 5.85 m (19.2 ft). It is the sole member of the genus Ophiophagus. It preys chiefly on other snakes and occasionally on some other vertebrates, such as lizards and rodents. It is a highly venomous and dangerous snake when agitated or provoked that has a fearsome reputation in its range, although it is typically shy and avoids confrontation with humans when possible.
Hence, the correct option is (D).

89. India has about 200 minor ports dotting its 4,600 miles of coastline. For example, Adani Group-owned Mundra Port, Jawaharlal Nehru Port Trust (JNPT).
Hence, the correct option is (B).

90. DVD stands for Digital Versatile Disc. The DVD is a digital optical disc data storage format invented and developed in 1995 and released in late 1996.

Hence, the correct option is (C).

91. Standard Arabic- 274 million total speakers.

Spanish- 534 million total speakers.

Chinese- 1.117 billion total speakers.

English. 1.132 billion total speakers.

Hence, the correct option is (A).

92. The small letters are b, d, f, h, j, l, n, p, r, t, v, x, z. The third day from tuesday will be friday and code will be frIdAY.

Hence, the correct option is (D).

93. Cincinnati Masters is not the Grand Slam Tournament while other tournaments are Grand Slams. The Cincinnati Masters is an annual hardcourt tennis event held in Ohio, USA.

Hence, the correct option is (D).

94. Ranji Trophy is a premier first-class cricket tournament held in India. It is Administered by the BCCI and 38 teams participated in the 2019–20 edition of this tournament.

Vidarbha clinched 2nd successive Ranji Trophy title, beat Saurashtra in the final.

Hence, the correct option is (C).

95. Santosh Trophy is not related to cricket because it is a football tournament held in India. It was founded in 1941 and 31 teams participates in this tournament.

Hence, the correct option is (C).

96. In 2002, the Supreme Court had declared the right to hoist the National Flag under Article 19 (i) (a) of the Constitution as the Fundamental Right.

Hence, the correct option is (A).

97. The full form of 'WEF' is 'World Economic Forum'. The WEF's mission is stated as "committed to improving the state of the world by engaging business, political, academic, and other leaders of society to shape global, regional, and industry agendas". Global Competitive Report is released by the World Economic Forum. Human capital, enabling environment, innovation, and Ecosystem are the key parameters of this report.

Hence, the correct option is (D).

98. Chetan Bhagat is the author of One Night @ The Call Center.

Other important novels of Chetan Bhagat:

- Five Point Someone (2004)
- Life's 3 Mistakes (2008)
- 2 States (2009)

Hence, the correct option is (B).

99. On March 12, 1612, Jahangir granted a firman permitting the British establishing factories at Surat, Gogha, Ahmedabad, and Cambay. Thus, Surat became the first established settlement of British in India and a factory was established there in 1612-13. The newly formed company had sent four ships under Captain Thomas Best to trade with India. These were mercantile ships but were capable of defending themselves. They defeated the Portuguese, who were already there in Surat for at least 100 years. This defeat apparently so impressed Emperor Jahangir that he granted the British squadron a firman to trade.

Hence, the correct option is (D).

100. Defluoridation of water by the Nalgonda technique is a commonly used household process in areas of endemic fluorosis in villages around Nalgonda (Andhra Pradesh, India).

Hence, the correct option is (B).

English

Ques (1-5):Direction: Read the passage given below and answer the question that follows by selecting the most appropriate option.

Gravitation is not a first principle. In this spirit, Verlinde frames gravity as an emergent phenomenon. Emergent phenomena appear when interactions on a small scale give rise to new laws, principles and structures on a larger scale. Consider the beautiful ice crystals we call snowflakes. The formation of snowflakes is driven by thermodynamics, the laws that govern the transfer of heat energy between molecules. And yet, crystals do not exist on the scale of individual molecules. They appear only on a larger scale, when many molecules exchange energy in a particular manner. Much as we can obtain snowflakes from thermodynamics, Verlinde argues that we can obtain gravitation from thermodynamics. If the Universe were a computer program, there would be no line for gravitation in the code. In this view, gravitation is less like a constitutional article and more like a side effect.

Q.1 In the above passage, gravitation is compared to:

A. Thermodynamics

B. Snowflakes

C. Transfer of heat

D. Constitutional article

Q.2 Verlinde believes that gravitation to us is:

A. Side effect

B. Thermodynamics

C. Snowflakes

D. Exchanged energy

Q.3 Why did Verlinde portray gravity as an emergent?

A. Because gravity is not the first principle.

B. It has no line of code in the universe and is more like a side-effect.

C. Gravity can be obtained through thermodynamics and appear on large scale

D. Gravity can be obtained through small interactions.

Q.4 What is the author trying to convey in the passage?

A. Gravitation is just another principle and can be obtained from thermodynamics

B. Snowflakes can be formed through the principle of thermodynamics

C. Crystals forming snowflakes go through the process of heat transfer between the molecules

D. Gravitation is a side effect and much less than a constitutional article

Q.5 What is the essential factor in the law of thermodynamics?

A. Interactions on small scale make way for new laws

B. Crystals appear on the large scale of individual molecules

C. In reference to computer code, it is nonetheless than line in the code

D. Transfer of heat energy among the molecules

Q.6 Direction: Select the word which is closest to the opposite in the meaning of the given word.

Vacillation

A. Steeliness

B. Intransigence

C. Steadfastness

D. Occupation

Q.7 Direction: In the following question, out of the four alternatives, select the one which best expresses the meaning of the given word.

Protrude

A. Lengthen

B. Uphold

C. Bulge

D. Refute

Q.8 Direction: Choose the correct sentence from the following:

I and my parents were watching television when the power go off.

A. My parents and I were watching television when the power gone.

B. My parents and I was watching television when the power gone.

C. My parents and I were watching television when the power went off.

D. I and my parents was watching television when the power go off.

Q.9 Direction: In the following question, a sentence has been given in Direct/Indirect. Out of the four alternatives suggested, select the one which best expresses the same sentence in Indirect/Direct.

Suraj said, "I am going to visit my old friend tomorrow."

A. Suraj said that he was going to visit his old friend the next day.

B. Suraj said that he would visit his old friend tomorrow.

C. Suraj said he wanted to visit his old friend tomorrow.

D. Suraj said that he might visit his old friend the next day.

Q.10 Direction: Choose the most appropriate option to change the narration (direct/indirect) of the given sentence.

David said to Anna, "Mona will leave for her native place tomorrow."

A. David told Anna that Mona will leave for her native place tomorrow.

B. David told Anna that Mona left for her native place the next day.

C. David told to Anna that Mona would be leaving for her native place tomorrow.

D. David told Anna that Mona would leave for her native place the next day.

Q.11 Direction: In the following sentence three parts labelled (a), (b), and (c). Read the sentence to find out whether there is an error in any part and indicate your response by marking the correct option. If you find no error, your response should be indicated as (d).

The Surat Municipal Corporation (SMC) has added yet another (a)/ feather in its cap by winning the first prize at the annual water (b)/ awards by the Federation of Indian Chamber of Commerce and Industry. (c)/ No Error (d)

A. (a)   **B.** (b)   **C.** (c)   **D.** (d)

Q.12 Direction: Change active to passive or vice versa as the case may be:

They didn't give me the money.

A. I am not given the money.
B. I was not given the money.
C. I have not been given the money.
D. I will not be given the money.

Q.13 Direction: Change active to passive or vice versa as the case may be:

You will be well looked after.

A. They will look after you well.
B. They can look after you well.
C. They may look after you well.
D. They shall look after you well.

Q.14 Direction: Change Direct to Indirect speech or vice versa as the case may be:

He said to me, "Hurry up or you will miss the train."

A. He said to me that hurry up or I will miss the train.
B. He told me that hurry up or I will miss the train.
C. He told me to hurry up or I would miss the train.
D. He said to me to hurry up or he would miss the train.

Q.15 Direction: Change Direct to Indirect speech or vice versa as the case may be:

He said that he would have to go the following week.

A. He said, "I will have to go the following week".
B. He said, "I would go the next week".
C. He said, "I must have to go the next week."
D. He said, "I will have to go the next week."

Q.16 Direction: In the following sentence three parts labelled (a), (b), and (c). Read the sentence to find out whether there is an error in any part and indicate your response by marking the correct option. If you find no error, your response should be indicated as (d).

A time slot of fifteen minutes (a)/ are allowed (b)/ to each speaker. (c)/ No error (d)

A. (a)   **B.** (b)   **C.** (c)   **D.** (d)

Q.17 Which of the following is correct among the given sentences?

A. He prides upon his patriotism.
B. He prides himself upon his patriotism.
C. He prides upon himself his patriotism.
D. No Error

Q.18 Direction: Choose the most appropriate alternative to complete the sentence:

My cousin will arrive __________ Sunday.

A. in   **B.** at   **C.** the   **D.** on

Q.19 Direction: Choose the most appropriate alternative to complete the sentence:

Students of St. Xavier's _____ all the prizes.

A. bear of   **B.** bore away
C. bore on   **D.** bear on

Q.20 Direction: Choose the most appropriate alternative to complete the sentence:

My sister and _________ are pleased to accept your invitation.

A. I   **B.** me   **C.** mine   **D.** myself

Q.21 Direction: Choose the most appropriate alternative to complete the sentence:

He was _________ angry to speak to me.

A. so   **B.** too   **C.** that   **D.** such

Q.22 Direction: Choose the most appropriate alternative to complete the sentence:

It is due to lack of careful advance planning that your scheme has come _____ a grief.

A. to   **B.** for   **C.** in   **D.** at

Q.23 Which of these is used to separate a series of loosely related clauses?

A. Comma   **B.** Full stop
C. Semicolon   **D.** Colon

Q.24 Direction: In the following sentence three parts labelled (a), (b), and (c). Read the sentence to find out whether there is an error in any part and indicate your response by marking the correct option. If you find no error, your response should be indicated as (d).

Two new French wells of a 55 million liters per day (MLD) capacity are under construction (a)/ and that tenders have been issued for the construction of six new French wells identified under (b)/ the aquifer mapping survey conducted by the National Geophysical Research Institute (NGRI). (c)/ No Error (d)

A. (a)   **B.** (b)   **C.** (c)   **D.** (d)

Q.25 Which of these is used between sentences which are grammatically independent?

A. Colon   **B.** Semicolon
C. Comma   **D.** Hyphen

Science

Q.26 What are the essential properties a medium must possess for the propagation of mechanical waves?

A. Stable pressure
B. Maximum friction
C. Constant temperature
D. Minimum friction

Q.27 Cyclotron is used for:

A. An instrument to change or remove the direction of an electric current
B. Studying the properties of atoms by smashing them
C. An instrument for measuring the emission of radiant energy
D. Measuring the strength of winds

Q.28 A 100Ω resistance and a capacitor of 100Ω reactance are connected in series across a $220V$ source. When the capacitor is 50% charged, the peak value of the displacement current is:

A. $2.2\ A$ **B.** $11\ A$ **C.** $4.4\ A$ **D.** $11\sqrt{2}\ A$

Q.29 Which of the following statements given below is correct?
A. Candela is base unit for luminous density.
B. Base unit for temperature is Fahrenheit.
C. Heat is measured in Joule/kg.
D. Amount of substance is measure in Kg.

Q.30 A body of mass m is accelerated uniformly from rest to a speed v in a time T. The instantaneous power delivered to the body as a function of time is given by:

A. $\frac{mv^2}{T^2}\cdot t$ **B.** $\frac{mv^2}{T^2}\cdot t^2$
C. $\frac{1}{2}\frac{mv^2}{T^2}\cdot t$ **D.** $\frac{1}{2}\frac{mv^2}{T^2}\cdot t^2$

Q.31 For tracking a plant's uptake of fertiliser from the roots to the leaves, isotope of phosphorus which is added to fertilizers, is
A. Phosphorus-31   **B.** Phosphorus-32
C. Phosphorus-33   **D.** Phosphorus-34

Q.32 Which of the following statements are correct in the context of transistor action:
A) The size and doping concentrations should have similar Base, emitter and collector regions.
B) The base region should be doped lightly and thin.
C) The collector junction is reverse biased and the emitter junction is biased forward.
D) Emitter and collector junction are forward biased.
Which statement is/are correct?
A. A and B   **B.** B and C
C. A and C   **D.** A, B and C

Q.33 The absorption of radio waves by the atmosphere depends on:
A. Their frequency
B. The polarisation of the wave
C. Their distance from the transmitter
D. The polarisation of the atmosphere

Q.34 Domestic electrical wiring basically a:
A. Series connection
B. Parallel connection
C. Combination of series and parallel connection
D. Parallel connection in room and series connection as well

Q.35 The same force acts on two bodies of different masses 2kg and 4kg initially at rest. The ratio of times required to acquire the same final velocity is:
A. $2:1$ **B.** $1:2$ **C.** $1:1$ **D.** $4:16$

Q.36 When a ball is thrown in a vertically upward direction than which of the following remains constant?
A. Velocity   **B.** Speed

C. Acceleration   **D.** Momentum

Q.37 According to Hooke's law of elasticity, if stress is increased, then the ratio of stress to strain:
A. Becomes zero   **B.** Remains constant
C. Decreases   **D.** Increases

Q.38 Night blindness is caused due to the deficiencies of______.
A. Vitamin A   **B.** Vitamin B
C. Vitamin C   **D.** Vitamin E

Q.39 The non-metal which is liquid at room temperature is:
A. Chlorine   **B.** Fluorine   **C.** Bromine   **D.** Iodine

Q.40 Which of the following food components give energy to our body?
A. Proteins   **B.** Vitamins
C. Minerals   **D.** Carbohydrates

Q.41 Name the site where the digestion of proteins occurs:
A. Pancreas   **B.** Rectum   **C.** Liver   **D.** Ileum

Q.42 An aluminum ring B faces an electromagnet A. If a current I through A is altered then which of the following case is possible:

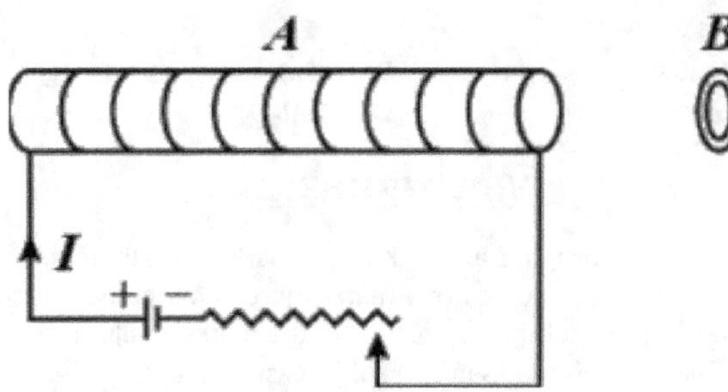

A. If I increase, A will repel B.
B. If I increase, A will attract B.
C. Whether I increase or decrease, B will not experience any force.
D. None of these

Q.43 An ideal gas is taken through a cyclic thermodynamics process through four steps. The amount of heat involved in the steps are $Q_1 = 5960\ J, Q_2 = -5600\ J, Q_3 = -3000\ J, Q_4 = -3600\ J$ respectively. The corresponding quantities of Internal energy changes are $\Delta U_1 = 3.760\ J, \Delta U_2 = -4800\ J, \Delta U_3 = -1800\ J, \Delta U_4 =?$
Find the value ΔU_4 and net work done:
A. $2930\ J, 960\ J$ **B.** $2830\ J, 900\ J$
C. $2930\ J, -960\ J$ **D.** $-2930\ J, 960\ J$

Q.44 If there is a positive error of 50% in the measurement of velocity of a body, then the error in the measurement of kinetic energy is:
A. 25%   **B.** 50%   **C.** 100%   **D.** 125%

Q.45 A convex mirror of radius of curvature 20 cm forms an image which is half the size of the object. How far is the object from the mirror?

A. 5 cm   **B.** 7.5 cm   **C.** −30 cm   **D.** 12.5 cm

Q.46 If a satellite is revolving very close to the surface of the earth, then its orbital velocity does not depend upon it:

A. Mass of satellite   **B.** Mass of earth
C. Radius of earth   **D.** Orbital radius

Q.47 The device used for producing electric current is called a __________.

A. Motor   **B.** Generator
C. Galvanometer   **D.** Ammeter

Q.48 Bauxite is an ore of:

A. Iron   **B.** Aluminum
C. Mercury   **D.** Copper

Q.49 During adiabatic compression of a gas, its temperature __________.

A. Falls   **B.** Remains constant
C. Rises   **D.** Becomes zero

Q.50 In the given reaction, $Al_2O_3 + NaOH \rightarrow \cdots \ldots X \ldots \ldots + H_2O$
What is element X?

A. $NaAlO_2$ **B.** Na_3Al
C. Na_2O_3 **D.** $NaAl_2O_3$

Mathematics

Q.51 In a class test, the sum of Kamal's marks in mathematics and English is 40. Had he got 3 marks more in mathematics and 4 marks less in English, the product of the marks would have been 360. Find his marks in two subjects separately.

A. 12, 28   **B.** 21, 19
C. 22, 18   **D.** Both A and B

Q.52 The value of $\dfrac{1}{\log_3 e} + \dfrac{1}{\log_3 e^2} + \dfrac{1}{\log_3 e^4} + \cdots$ up to infinite terms is:

A. $\log_e 9$ **B.** 0   **C.** 1   **D.** $\log_e 3$

Q.53 A tea party is arranged for 16 people along two sides of a long table with eight chairs on each side. Four particular men wish to sit on one particular side and two particular men on the other side. The number of ways they can be seated is

A. $\dfrac{6!8!10!}{4!6!}$ **B.** $\dfrac{8!8!10!}{4!6!}$
C. $\dfrac{8!8!6!}{6!4!}$ **D.** None of these

Q.54 Two parallel lines AB and CD are intersected by a transversal line EF at M and N respectively. The lines MP and NP are the bisectors of the interior $\angle BMN$ and $\angle DNM$ on the same side of the transversal. Then, $\angle MPN$ is equal to:

A. 75°   **B.** 60°   **C.** 45°   **D.** 90°

Q.55 If $m[-3 \quad 4] + n[4 \quad -3] = [10 \quad -11]$, then find m and n.

A. $m = -2, n = 1$ **B.** $m = 2, n = -1$
C. $m = -2, n = -1$ **D.** $m = 2, n = 1$

Q.56 If $A = \begin{bmatrix} 1 & 2 \\ 3 & 4 \end{bmatrix}$, such that $AX = I$, then find X.

A. $\begin{bmatrix} 1 & -2 \\ 3/2 & -1/2 \end{bmatrix}$ **B.** $\begin{bmatrix} -1 & 1 \\ 3/2 & -1/2 \end{bmatrix}$
C. $\begin{bmatrix} 1 & 1 \\ 3/2 & -1/2 \end{bmatrix}$ **D.** $\begin{bmatrix} -2 & 1 \\ 3/2 & -1/2 \end{bmatrix}$

Q.57 If $A = \{x \in Z: x^3 - 1 = 0\}$ and $B = \{x \in Z: x^2 + x + 1 = 0\}$, where Z is set of complex numbers, then what is $A \cap B$ equal to?

A. Null set
B. $\left\{\dfrac{-1+\sqrt{3}i}{2}, \dfrac{-1-\sqrt{3}i}{2}\right\}$
C. $\left\{\dfrac{-1+\sqrt{3}i}{4}, \dfrac{-1-\sqrt{3}i}{4}\right\}$
D. $\left\{\dfrac{1+\sqrt{3}i}{2}, \dfrac{1-\sqrt{3}i}{2}\right\}$

Q.58 Evaluate $\tan^{-1}\left(\dfrac{1}{2}\right) + \tan^{-1}\left(\dfrac{1}{3}\right)$

A. $\dfrac{\pi}{6}$ **B.** $\dfrac{\pi}{2}$ **C.** $\dfrac{\pi}{8}$ **D.** $\dfrac{\pi}{4}$

Q.59 If the range for $y = (\cot^{-1}x)(\cot^{-1}(-x))$ is $0 < y \leq \dfrac{\pi^a}{b}$. Find the value of $a + b$

A. 2   **B.** 4   **C.** 5   **D.** 6

Q.60 What is the value of expression after solving limits: $\lim_{x \to \infty} \left(\dfrac{x^2+5x+3}{x^2+x+3}\right)^x$

A. e^4 **B.** e^2 **C.** e^3 **D.** 1

Q.61 If $A = \begin{bmatrix} a & b \\ b & a \end{bmatrix}$, then $|A + A^T|$ equals

A. $4(a^2 - b^2)$ **B.** $2(a^2 - b^2)$
C. $(a^2 - b^2)$ **D.** $4ab$

Q.62 If E is the universal set and $A = B \cup C, B$ then the set $E - \left(E - \left(E - \left(E(E - A)\right)\right)\right)$ is same as the set

A. $B' \cup C'$ **B.** $B \cup C$ **C.** $B' \cap C'$ **D.** $B \cap C$

Q.63 The set of points where the function $f(x) = x|x|$ is differentiable is:

A. $(-\infty, \infty)$ **B.** $(-\infty, 0) \cup (0, \infty)$
C. $(0, \infty)$ **D.** $(0, \infty)$

Q.64 The integral of $\int e^x(\sin x + \cos x)dx$ is

A. $e^x \cos x + c$ **B.** $e^x \sin x + c$
C. $e^x \sec x + c$ **D.** None of these

Q.65 Let S be a set of all distinct numbers of the form $\dfrac{p}{q}$, where $p, q \in [1,2,3,4,5,6]$. What is the cardinality of the set S?

A. 21   **B.** 23   **C.** 32   **D.** 36

Q.66 What is the curve which passes through the point $(1,1)$ and whose slope is $\frac{2y}{x}$?

A. Circle
B. Parabola
C. Ellipse
D. Hyperbola

Q.67 If $xdy = ydx + y^2dy, y > 0$ and $y(1) = 1$, then what is $y(-3)$ equal to?

A. 3 only
B. -1 only
C. Both -1 and 3
D. Neither -1 nor 3

Q.68 If $A = \{x : x$ is a multiple of 2 $\}, B = \{x : x$ is a multiple of 5 $\}$ and $C = \{x : x$ is a multiple of 10 $\}$, then $A \cap (B \cap C)$ is equal to

A. A
B. B
C. C
D. {x : x is a multiple of 100}

Q.69 If C is an arbitrary constant then solution of differential equation $x^2dy - y^2dx - xy^2(x - y)dy = 0$ can be

A. $\ln\left|\frac{xy}{x-y}\right| + \frac{y^2}{2} = c$
B. $\ln\left|\frac{x-y}{xy}\right| + \frac{y^2}{2} = c$
C. $(x - y)e^{\frac{y^2}{2}} = cxy$
D. Both B and C

Q.70 Write the vector equation of the line $\frac{x-5}{3} = \frac{y+4}{7} = \frac{z-6}{2}$.

A. $5\hat{\imath} + (-4)\hat{\jmath} + 6\hat{k} + \alpha(3\hat{\imath} + 7\hat{\jmath} + 2\hat{k})$
B. $5\hat{\imath} + (-4)\hat{\jmath} + 7\hat{k} + \alpha(3\hat{\imath} + 2\hat{\jmath} + 2\hat{k})$
C. $5\hat{\imath} + (-4)\hat{\jmath} + 8\hat{k} + \alpha(3\hat{\imath} + 4\hat{\jmath} + 2\hat{k})$
D. $5\hat{\imath} + (-4)\hat{\jmath} + 7\hat{k} + \alpha(3\hat{\imath} + 6\hat{\jmath} + 2\hat{k})$

Q.71 Find the eccentricity and the coordinates of foci of the hyperbola $25x^2 + 9y^2 = 225$:

A. $\frac{\sqrt{34}}{3}, \left(\pm\frac{\sqrt{34}}{0}\right)$
B. $\frac{\sqrt{32}}{3}, \left(\pm\frac{\sqrt{30}}{0}\right)$
C. $\frac{\sqrt{34}}{3}, \left(\pm\frac{\sqrt{36}}{0}\right)$
D. $\frac{\sqrt{34}}{2}, \left(\pm\frac{\sqrt{34}}{0}\right)$

Q.72 What is the least value of $\tan^2\theta + \cot^2\theta + \sin^2\theta + \cos^2\theta + \sec^2\theta + cosec^2\theta$

A. 1
B. 3
C. 5
D. 7

Q.73 X and Y are centres of circles of radius 9 cm and 2 cm respectively $XY = 17$ cm. Z is the centre of a circle of radius r cm which touches the above two circles externally. Given that $-\angle XZY = 90^0$ the value of r is-

A. 9 cm
B. 8 cm
C. 13 cm
D. 6 cm

Q.74 If $\tan\theta + \cot\theta = x$, then what is the value of $\tan^4\theta + \cot^4\theta$?

A. $(x^3 - 3)^2 + 2$
B. $(x^4 - 2x) + 4$
C. $x(x - 4) + 2$
D. $x^2(x^2 - 4) + 2$

Q.75 The perpendicular distance between the straight lines $6x + 8y + 15 = 0$ and $3x + 4y + 9 = 0$ is

A. $\frac{3}{2}$ units
B. $\frac{3}{10}$ unit
C. $\frac{3}{4}$ unit
D. $\frac{2}{7}$ unit

General Knowledge

Q.76 Vinesh Phogat is recently honouredwith which National Award ?

[HTET PGT - Computer Science, 2020]

A. Dronacharya Award
B. Arjuna Award
C. Rajiv Gandhi Khel Ratna Award
D. Dhyanchand Award

Q.77 Iconic French filmmaker ____________ passed away in September 2022.

A. Humbert Balsan
B. Jacques Bar
C. Christophe Barratier
D. Jean-Luc Godard

Q.78 The Centre and__________ government have signed a tripartite peace accord with 8 tribal outfits of the state on 15 September 2022?

A. Tripura
B. Assam
C. Manipur
D. Nagaland

Q.79 Who launched a grand challenge programme called "जनCARE" on September 28, 2021?

[Haryana Police Constable Commando Wing, 2021]

A. Dr. Jitendra Singh
B. Jyotiraditya Scindia
C. Nirmala Sitharaman
D. Smriti Irani

Q.80 Direction: What should come in the place of question mark (?) in the following letter series based on the English alphabetical order?

YCL, MQZ, AEN,?

A. OTC
B. OSB
C. PUE
D. MPX

Q.81 Which of the following is not an All India Service:

A. Indian Administration Service
B. Indian Police Service
C. Indian Foreign Service
D. Indian Forest Service

Q.82 The salary of the President is taken from:

A. Prime Minister's fund
B. Consolidated fund
C. Contingency fund
D. None of these

Q.83 Which of the following temple is dedicated to lord sun?

A. Konark
B. Modhera
C. Martand
D. All of these

Q.84 If GLUED is coded as 142442108, then how will START be coded as?

A. 384023640
B. 046320483
C. 192011820
D. 028110291

Q.85 Akbaranama was written by:

A. Akbar   **B.** Birbal
C. Abul Fazal   **D.** Bhagawan Das

Q.86 Consider the following statements:

1- The centre of Madhubani painting is Jitwarpur village.

2- The selection of colours is natural, so the pictures look attractive.

3- The centre of this art is based on a religious plot.

Select the correct answer using the code given below.

A. Both 1,2   **B.** Only 2
C. 1 and 3   **D.** 1,2 and 3

Q.87 Bidhan Chandra Roy Award is given in the field of:

A. Environment   **B.** Journalism
C. Music   **D.** Medicine

Q.88 If a mirror is placed on the line PQ, then which of the answer figure would be the right image of the given figure?

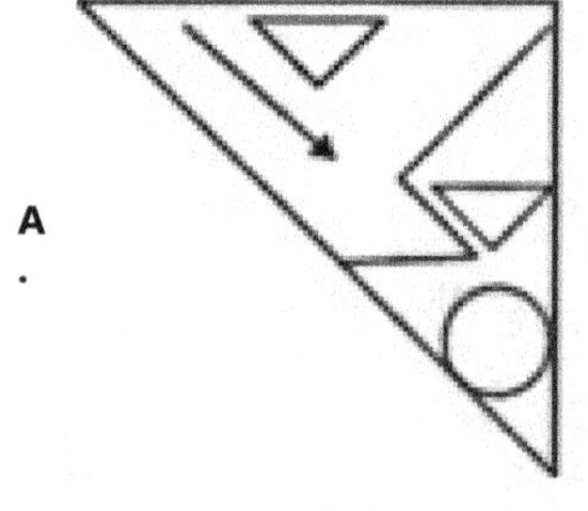
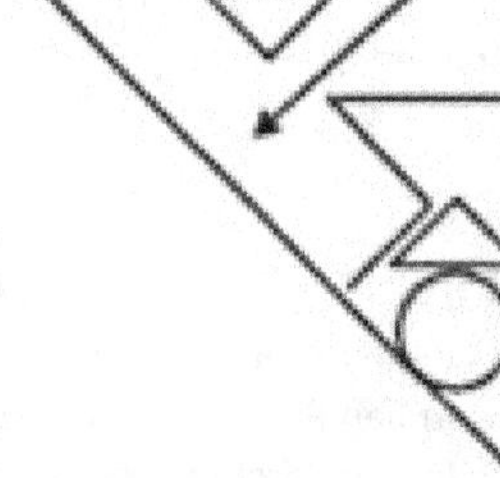

A.
B.

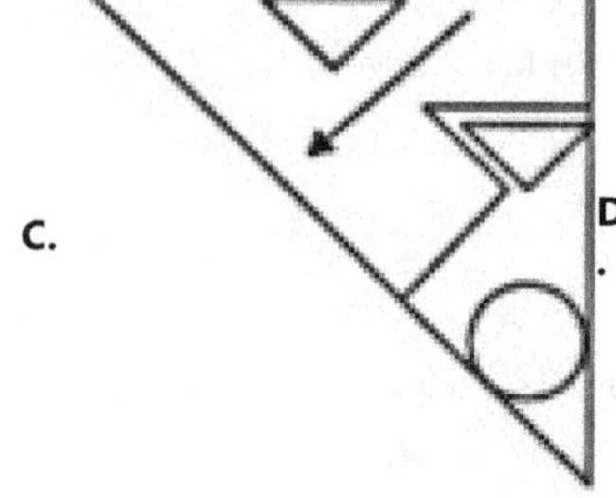
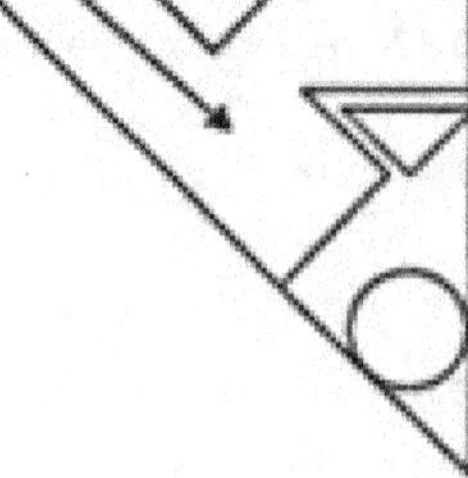

C.
D.

Q.89 Most extensive soil found in India is:

A. Desert soil   **B.** Laterite soil
C. Alluvial soil   **D.** Black soil

Q.90 The most abundant gas in Erath's atmosphere is:

A. Nitrogen   **B.** Oxygen
C. Carbon dioxide   **D.** Hydrogen

Q.91 Which is the largest peninsular river of India:

A. Krishna   **B.** Godavari
C. Cauvery   **D.** Mahanadi

Q.92 Which one of the following is a type of tropical grassland?

A. Savanna   **B.** Pampas   **C.** Steppe   **D.** Down

Q.93 Which of the following is the capital of china ?

A. Wuhan   **B.** Beijing
C. Shanghai   **D.** Shenzhen

Q.94 Peter Ebdon has announced his retirement from which sports recently?

A. Snooker   **B.** Football
C. Volleyball   **D.** Golf

Q.95 Who among the following veteran actors has been chosen for the Raj Kapoor Lifetime Achievement Award?

A. Rishi Kapoor   **B.** Dharmendra
C. Jeetendra   **D.** Shatrughan Sinha

Q.96 Polio is caused by _________ .

A. Bacteria   **B.** Virus   **C.** Fungus   **D.** Protozoa

Q.97 Which of the following part of India receives the first monsoon in summer?

A. Eastern Ghats   **B.** Western Ghats
C. Himalayas   **D.** Meghalaya Plateau

Q.98 Who is known as "The Iron Man of India"?

A. Vivekanand   **B.** Sardar Patel
C. Dr. Rajendra Prased   **D.** Aurobindo Ghosh

Q.99 What is the full form of "BRIC"?

A. Bangladesh, Romania, Indonesia and Cambodia
B. Botswana, Rwanda, Ivory Coast and Croatia
C. Bangladesh, Romania, India and Cambodia
D. Brazil, Russia, India and China

Q.100 An autobiography titled "Mind Master" is written by:

A. Viswanathan Anand   **B.** Gukesh
C. Surya Shekhar   **D.** Harikrishna

// Smart Answer Sheet //

Correct — Percentage of students who answered correctly. **Skipped** — Percentage of students who skipped.

Q.	Ans.	Correct	Skipped	Q.	Ans.	Correct	Skipped	Q.	Ans.	Correct	Skipped	Q.	Ans.	Correct	Skipped	Q.	Ans.	Correct	Skipped	Q.	Ans.	Correct	Skipped
1	B	79.22 %	18.02 %	18	D	86.92 %	10.2 %	35	B	79.82 %	14.77 %	52	A	64.7 %	32.43 %	69	D	69.87 %	30.01 %	86	C	56.53 %	43.28 %
2	A	84.64 %	12.91 %	19	B	83.84 %	14.66 %	36	C	81.98 %	16.92 %	53	B	87.46 %	11.92 %	70	A	53.8 %	42.45 %	87	D	26.2 %	73.26 %
3	C	23.93 %	75.15 %	20	A	76.58 %	16.92 %	37	B	80.31 %	12.49 %	54	D	55.26 %	30.32 %	71	A	79.75 %	10.39 %	88	C	86.31 %	10.44 %
4	A	80.12 %	18.03 %	21	B	49.21 %	44.93 %	38	A	47.11 %	50.4 %	55	A	57.29 %	31.95 %	72	D	83.85 %	10.68 %	89	C	89.01 %	10.75 %
5	D	76.98 %	19.07 %	22	A	78.18 %	20.18 %	39	C	86.77 %	10.47 %	56	D	78.96 %	11.42 %	73	D	21.1 %	76.98 %	90	A	89.19 %	10.58 %
6	C	52.52 %	45.91 %	23	C	76.78 %	17.63 %	40	D	81.65 %	17.07 %	57	B	40.61 %	46.21 %	74	D	78.18 %	13.15 %	91	B	87.82 %	10.69 %
7	C	85.35 %	10.08 %	24	A	46.97 %	41.58 %	41	A	63.31 %	32.25 %	58	D	79.46 %	15.97 %	75	B	54.53 %	33.59 %	92	A	56.85 %	35.94 %
8	C	87.85 %	10.65 %	25	A	81.29 %	10.34 %	42	A	52.87 %	40.4 %	59	D	41.15 %	41.86 %	76	C	83.07 %	10.57 %	93	B	83.49 %	14.7 %
9	A	64.56 %	31.05 %	26	D	89.86 %	10.01 %	43	A	15.93 %	69.42 %	60	A	43.15 %	39.47 %	77	D	57.96 %	32.62 %	94	A	63.31 %	30.25 %
10	D	26.07 %	70.86 %	27	B	54.19 %	44.42 %	44	C	58.69 %	32.78 %	61	A	83.48 %	15.84 %	78	B	20.29 %	76.08 %	95	B	77.75 %	14.17 %
11	B	64.65 %	32.68 %	28	A	89.89 %	10.09 %	45	C	19.33 %	69.48 %	62	C	77.27 %	12.68 %	79	A	55.24 %	34.49 %	96	B	44.48 %	48.45 %
12	B	41.87 %	43.66 %	29	A	86.83 %	10.74 %	46	A	83.24 %	15.33 %	63	A	63.63 %	34.17 %	80	B	48.04 %	35.82 %	97	B	44.9 %	30.4 %
13	A	40.99 %	32.18 %	30	A	46.85 %	47.25 %	47	B	83.9 %	13.47 %	64	B	86.35 %	11.32 %	81	C	59.95 %	39.85 %	98	B	85.72 %	10.69 %
14	C	41.64 %	54.94 %	31	B	57.44 %	38.81 %	48	B	81.42 %	11.49 %	65	B	63.15 %	36.56 %	82	B	49.89 %	41.36 %	99	D	79.79 %	10.67 %
15	D	40.07 %	34.45 %	32	B	86.88 %	13.01 %	49	C	80.46 %	17.62 %	66	B	86.85 %	10.25 %	83	D	89.5 %	10.36 %	100	A	83.87 %	13.99 %
16	B	65.85 %	31.92 %	33	A	47.9 %	36.64 %	50	A	60.11 %	37.91 %	67	A	16.61 %	81.95 %	84	A	54.38 %	35.85 %				
17	B	85.21 %	13.85 %	34	B	80.61 %	15.86 %	51	D	67.63 %	30.44 %	68	C	87.39 %	12.26 %	85	C	81.86 %	13.04 %				

//Hints and Solutions//

1. According to the passage, gravitation can be obtained from thermodynamics, just like snowflakes can be formed through the law of transfer of heat energy between the molecules.
Hence, the correct option is (B).

2. According to the passage it is mentioned that Verlinde believes gravitation is less like a constitutional article and more of a side effect to us.

Hence, the correct option is (A).

3. According to the passage it is mentioned that emergent phenomena appear when interactions on small scale give rise to new laws, structures, and principles on a larger scale. This is just how snowflakes can be formed through the transfer of heat energy through molecules that are driven by thermodynamics.

Hence, the correct option is (C).

4. According to the passage, the whole passage gives an idea that gravitation can be obtained from the law of thermodynamics, which doesn't make it any unique.
Hence, the correct option is (A).

5. According to the passage, it is clearly mentioned in the passage that thermodynamics is the law that governs the transfer of heat energy between the molecules.

Hence, the correct option is (D).

6. Steadfastness : sure, dependable, reliable, constant, unwavering.

Vacillation : the inability to decide between different opinions or actions; indecision.

Steeliness : toughness, hardness or durability resembling (likened to) that of steel.

Intransigence : inflexibility; refusal to change one's views or to agree about something.

Occupation : a job or profession.

Thus, we can see that the word steadfastness is completely opposite in meaning to the word vacillation.
Hence, the correct option is (C).

7. Bulge : a rounded swelling which distorts an otherwise flat surface, swell or protrude to an incongruous extent.

Lengthen : make or become longer.

Protrude : to stick out from a place or surface; bulge, extend beyond or above a surface.

Uphold : confirm or support (something which has been questioned), maintain a custom or practice.

Refute : prove (a statement or theory) to be wrong or false; disprove.

Thus, we can see that the word bulge is completely the same in meaning as the word protrude.
Hence, the correct option is (C).

8. When we use Simple past and Past continuous tense together in a sentence, it shows us that the simple past action happened in the middle of the past continuous action, while it was in progress. Also, the order of subjects is - My parents and I.
Hence, the correct option is (C).

9. Suraj said, "I am going to visit my old friend tomorrow." (Direct)

Suraj said that he was going to visit his old friend the next day. (Indirect)

Present Continuous → Past Continuous(Is/are/am → was/were)

Tomorrow → the next day.

'I' will change as per as subject of the reported verb. (I→He)
Hence, the correct option is (A).

10. Rules for changing direct speech into indirect speech are given below:

- The inverted commas (" ") used in Direct Narration is removed in Indirect Narration and "that" conjunction is used.

- Says to/said to changes to tells/told in indirect speech if they are followed by an object. If not, they would remain the same in indirect speech.

How to changes the tense in indirect speech

- If the reporting verb is in the present or future tense, no changes are made to the verb/tense of the reported speech.

- If the reporting verb is in past tense, we make changes to the reported verb as per the below rule:

- Simple present tense changes to simple past tense.

- Present continuous tense changes to past continuous tense.

- Present perfect tense changes to past perfect tense.

- Present Perfect continuous tense changes to past perfect continuous tense.

- Simple past tense changes to past perfect tense.

- Past continuous tense changes to past perfect continuous tense.

- No changes are made to past perfect and past perfect continuous tense.

- Can, shall, will, may, must change to could, should, would, might and must respectively.

- If there is any universal truth, habitual fact in the reporting speech, no changes are made to the reported verb's tense.

How some words change in indirect speech

- Words like "this, these, tomorrow, yesterday change to that, those, the next day, the previous day" respectively.

Below are the rules for changing the pronouns correctly:

- First-person pronoun changes according to the subject of reporting speech.

- Second person pronoun changes according to the object of reporting speech.
- Third-person pronoun does not change in indirect speech.

Hence, the correct option is (D).

11. The first prize would indicate the order in which the prizes were given. The first prize (no definite article) denotes the top prize. Here, the context is denoted by 'added another feather' meaning 'achieving something' such as the top prize in a competition. So, remove the definite article 'the' from part (b) of the sentence.

Hence, the correct option is (B).

12. The given sentence is in active voice, as the subject 'they' performs an action 'didn't give' against the object 'the money'.

To change to passive voice, the object takes the place of the subject and vice versa and the word 'by' is introduced as now the subject receives the action by the object. The verb form of the sentence is also changed from active form to passive.

'Subject (They) + verb (didn't give) + indirect object (me) + direct object (the money)' changes to:

'New subject (I) + verb (was not given) + direct object (the money)'

The new object 'by them' is implied.

This can be seen in option D, hence it's the right answer.

The pronoun 'they' is non specific, it does not refer to a particular person. Hence in passive voice it can be implied.

Option A: The verb form 'am not given' expresses the simple present tense whereas the sentence is in simple past tense.

Option C: The verb phrase 'have not been given' is in the present perfect tense whereas the sentence is in simple tense.

Option D: 'Will not be given' refers to the future; the sentence is in past.

Hence, the correct option is (B).

13. The given sentence is in the passive voice of simple future tense. Let us understand the structures for active/passive voices for such sentences.

Active: Subject + will/shall + verb (Ist form) + object...

Passive: Object+ will/shall + be + verb (IIIrd form) + by + subject...

So, with the help of the above structures, we can convert the sentence into an active voice: They will look after you well.
Hence, the correct option is (A).

14. The given sentence is of direct speech. So, "said to" will be changed into, "told". The inverted commas will be removed and the reporting and reported speech will be connected by the conjunction "that". Since the reporting verb is of past tense, the tense of the reported speech will be changed too. So, "will" gets changed into "would".
Hence, the correct option is (C).

15. The given sentence is in indirect speech. "Said" will remain the same as it is not followed by any object. "Would have" is the past of "will have" which will be used in direct speech. "The following week" will convert to "the next week" indirect speech. The conjunction "that" will be replaced by inverted commas (" ").
Hence, the correct option is (D).

16. Option B: The error lies in part (b): 'are allowed', which is in plural form. The correct form of the verb is 'is allowed', i.e., singular verb form.

'Each' in 'each speaker' is a singular determiner, which refers to every single speaker in particular. So, the verb too will be in singular form 'is allowed'. When the subject is singular, the verb must also be singular. The same goes for plural subjects and their plural verbs.

Therefore, the corrected sentence is: A time slot of fifteen minutes is allowed to each speaker.

So, the option with the error is option B.

Options A and C do not have errors.

Option D is incorrect as the sentence has an error.

Hence, the correct option is (B).

17. The correct answer is "He prides himself upon his patriotism". Here as "pride" means a feeling of deep pleasure or satisfaction derived from one's own achievements. Therefore, it is considered to be used with a reflexive pronoun of the same noun used. Hence, the correct option is (B).

18. The preposition "on" will be used in the above sentence. It is because "on" is used to specify days and dates. See below examples:

I was born on 14th June 1988.

The movie will be released on Friday.
Hence, the correct option is (D).

19. Here, bore away is the right usage.

bear away (Phr. V.) : bear off; carry away; take away; carry off

bear on (Phr. V.) : to be relevant to or burdensome to

Hence, the correct option is (B).

20. The sentence needs a subjective pronoun whereas "me", "myself" and "mine" are objective or possessive pronouns. Therefore, they cannot be used in the sentence. The pronoun "I" is in subjective case, so, it is the correct response.
Hence, the correct option is (A).

21. The correct adverb to be used in the sentence is "too" as it fits in the context of the sentence. We can get the hint from the use of the preposition "to" in the end of the sentence. The grammatical construction too + adjective/adverb + to infinitive has a negative meaning. So, the sentence means to say that he was so angry with me that he did not want to speak to me.

The complete sentence is: He was _too_ angry to speak to me.

Hence, the correct option is (B).

22. The correct preposition to be used in the sentence is "to". "To come to something" means to reach a particular point or situation.

Hence, the correct option is (A).

23. The semicolon is used to separate a series of loosely related clauses. For example: Today we love what tomorrow we hate; today we seek what tomorrow we shun.
Hence, the correct option is (C).

24. The error is in the inappropriate usage of indefinite article 'a' in part (a) of the sentence. Here the mention of the capacity of the wells indicates an attempt to emphasize some particular well and thus, must be preceded by a definite article 'the'. Thus, replace 'a' with 'the' in part (a) of the sentence.

Hence, the correct option is (A).

25. The colon is used between sentences which are grammatically independent but closely connected in sense. For example, "Truth is the greatest inspiration of all: nothing is of greater value."

Hence, the correct option is (A).

26. To oscillate continuously for a long time and long distance the friction force among the particles should be minimum, so a wave can travels a long distance through a medium.

Constant temperature and pressure is already stable so no effect on it. If the friction will be maximum then it affects the particle movement.

Hence, the correct option is (D).

27. Commutator is an instrument to change or remove the direction of an electric current, in dynamo used to convert alternating current into direct current.

Cyclotron: Study of properties of matter by the process of smashing them.

Radiometer: An instrument for measuring the emission of radiant energy.

Anemometer is the instrument which is used for measuring the strength of winds

Hence, the correct option is (B).

28. Given:
$$R = 100\Omega, X_c = 100\Omega$$
Net impedance,
$$Z = \sqrt{R^2 + X_L^2}$$
$$= 100\sqrt{2}\,\Omega$$
Peak value of displacement current=Maximum conduction current in the circuit
$$= \frac{\varepsilon_0}{Z} = \frac{220\sqrt{2}}{100\sqrt{2}} = 2.2\ A$$
Hence, the correct option is (A).

29. Candela is the base unit for luminous density. Kelvin is the base unit for temperature. Heat is measured in Joules and Joule/kg is a unit of latent heat. The amount of substance is measured in mole and Kg is the unit of mass.

Hence, the correct option is (A).

30. $P_{\text{inst}} = F_{\text{inst}} \times v_{\text{inst}}$
As it was given constant acceleration, force is also constant.
$$F_{\text{inst}} = F_{\text{const}} = ma$$
$$a = \frac{v}{T}$$
$$v_{\text{inst}} = (a \times t) = \frac{v}{T} \times t$$
$$P_{\text{inst}} = \left(m \times \frac{v}{T}\right) \times \left(\frac{v}{T} \times t\right)$$
$$P_{\text{inst}} = m\frac{v^2}{T^2}t$$
Hence, the correct option is (A).

31. Phosphorus-32 is a radioactive isotope of phosphorus. 15 protons and 17 neutrons are there in nucleus of phosphorus-32. It only exists in small quantity on earth as it is having short half-life, 14.29 days and decays rapidly.

Phosphorus-32 is used for tracking a plant's uptake of fertiliser from the roots to the leaves. This is given to plants and by emitting beta radiation we can trace the usage of phosphorus.
Hence, the correct option is (B).

32. The base region is made very thin and lightly doped, as its the main function is to control the flow of electrons through the transistor. It's lightly doped hence, less number of majority carriers will be there resulting in a lesser percentage of emitter current flow through the base than the collector. That's why the base current is negligibly small.

After this transistor will be inactive region. Otherwise, no current flows through the transistor. (Cut-off or saturation region)

Hence, the correct option is (B).

33. The absorption of radio waves by the atmosphere depends on their frequency. When radio waves enter the earth's atmosphere from space, the electrons present in the ionosphere absorb the sum of waves while others pass through and are detectable to ground-based absorbers.

The frequency of each of these waves will determine whether or not each of them is absorbed are able to pass through the atmosphere.

Hence, the correct option is (A).

34. In order to operate the load independently parallel circuits are used in homes. It means you can turn on one electrical item without turning on other loads. A parallel circuit allows all the other loads to continue when one of the load fails.

Hence, the correct option is (B).

35. Now acceleration will be different in the two masses.
They will be $\frac{F}{2}$ and $\frac{F}{4}$.
Let v be the same velocity attained by them starting from rest.
So using $v = u + a.t$ $\quad V_1 = \frac{F}{2} \times T_1$
$$V_2 = \frac{F}{4} \times T_2$$
Given $v_1 = v_2$
$$\frac{F}{2} \times T_1 = \frac{F}{4} \times T_2$$

$= 1:2$

Hence, the correct option is (B).

36. Acceleration due to gravity: The earth always attracts the body towards its centre and the acceleration due to this force is called acceleration due to gravity.

It is denoted by g.

g = 10 m/s^2 which is constant.

When a ball is thrown in the air then this acceleration acts on it. Thus the acceleration of the ball remains constant which is equal to g in a downward direction. So option 3 is correct.

Due to this acceleration, the speed, velocity and momentum of the ball changes with time as the velocity reduce because of retardation due to gravity.

Hence, the correct option is (C).

37. According to Hook's law-
We know,

$$\frac{\text{Stress}}{\text{Strain}} = \text{Constant}$$

So, the ratio between stress and strain is always constant. So, if stress is increased, then strain changes in that way so that this ratio always remains constant.
Hence, the correct option is (B).

38. Night blindness is caused due to deficiency of Vitamin A in our food.

Vitamin A is a fat-soluble vitamin that is also a powerful antioxidant. Vitamin A plays a critical role in maintaining healthy vision, neurological function, healthy skin, healthy immune system, and cell growth. Night blindness is caused by a deficiency of vitamin A in blood and tissues.

Hence, the correct option is (A).

39. Bromine is the only non-metal which is liquid and diatomic molecule at room temperature.

It is a dense, reddish-brown liquid evaporating at standard temperature and pressure to give an orange vapour. It is one of the only two elements on the periodic table that are liquids at room temperature other than mercury.
Hence, the correct option is (C).

40. The major nutrients in our food are carbohydrates, proteins, fats, vitamins and minerals. In addition, food also contains dietary fibres and water. Carbohydrates and fats mainly provide energy to our body. Proteins and minerals are needed for the growth and maintenance of our body.

Hence, the correct option is (D).

41. The pancreas secretes a number of proteases as zymogens into the duodenum where they must be activated before they can cleave peptide bonds. This activation occurs through an activation cascade. Protein digestion occurs in the stomach and duodenum in which 3 main enzymes, pepsin secreted by the stomach and trypsin and chymotrypsin secreted by the pancreas, break down food proteins into polypeptides that are then broken down by various exopeptidases and dipeptidases into amino acids.

Hence, the correct option is (A).

42. A current is passed through solenoid A as shown. Current, entering at end A is clockwise. When seen from the side of A, so it develops south polarity at A and north polarity at B. When current I through A increases, it is like north of the magnet approaching the ring B and due to Lenz's law face of ring B facing B develops north polarity and hence there is repulsion between the two.

Hence, the correct option is (A).

43. Since in cycle process total internal change is zero.
$$\Delta U_1 + \Delta U_2 + \Delta U_3 + \Delta U_4 = 0$$
$$3670 - 4800 - 1800 + \Delta U_4 = 0$$
$$\Delta U_4 = 2930\ J$$
Now in Cycle $\Delta W = \Delta Q$
$$= 5960 - 5600 - 3000 + 3600 = 960\ J.$$
Hence, the correct option is (A).

44. Given that,

$\frac{\Delta v}{v} \times 100$ is the % error in velocity $= 50\%$

Kinetic energy $K.E = \frac{1}{2}mv^2$

Error in the kinetic energy
$$\frac{\Delta K \cdot E}{K \cdot E} \times 100 = m \times 2\frac{\Delta v}{v} \times 100$$

m is as a constant

Now, percentage error
$$\frac{\Delta K.E}{K.E} \times 100 = 2\frac{\Delta v}{v} \times 100$$
$$\frac{\Delta K \cdot E}{K.E} \times 100 = 2 \times 50\%$$
$$\frac{\Delta K.E}{K.E} \times 100 = 100\%$$
Therefore, the error in the measurement of kinetic energy is 100%

Hence, the correct option is (C).

45. Radius of curvature $= 20$ cm

So, focal length $= 10$ cm

We are given, $\frac{h_o}{2} = h_i$

$$\Rightarrow h_o = 2h_i$$
$$\Rightarrow m = h_i = h_o$$
$$\Rightarrow m = \frac{h_o}{2h_o}$$
$$\Rightarrow m = -\frac{v}{u}$$
$$\Rightarrow \frac{1}{2} = -\frac{v}{u}$$
$$\Rightarrow u = -2v$$

By mirror formula,
$$\frac{1}{f} = \frac{1}{v} + \frac{1}{u}$$
$$\frac{1}{10} = \frac{1}{v} - \left(-\frac{1}{2v}\right)$$
$$\frac{1}{10} = \frac{1}{v} + \frac{1}{2v}$$
$$\Rightarrow \frac{1}{10} = \frac{3}{2v}$$
$$\Rightarrow 2v = 30$$

$\Rightarrow v = 15$ cm

$u = -2(v) = -30$

Hence, the correct option is (C).

46. Orbital velocity, $v = \sqrt{\dfrac{GM}{r}}$ where r is the orbital radius and M is the mass of earth.

Thus, v is independent of the mass of the satellite(m).
Hence, the correct option is (A).

47. The device used for producing electric current is called an electric generator, whereas an electric motor uses electric current to do mechanical work.

A galvanometer detects the presence of current in the circuit and an ammeter is used to measure the current in the circuit.
Hence, the correct option is (B).

48. Bauxite ore is the world's primary source of aluminum. The ore must first be chemically processed to produce alumina (aluminum oxide). Alumina is then smelted using an electrolysis process to produce pure aluminum metal. Bauxite is typically found in topsoil located in various tropical and subtropical regions.

Hence, the correct option is (B).

49. During adiabatic compression of a gas, its temperature rises. The work done on the gas during the adiabatic process increases its internal energy.
Using $\Delta Q = \Delta W + \Delta U$
For adiabatic process $\Delta Q = 0$
$\Rightarrow \Delta U = -\Delta W$
Since work is done in compressing a gas is negative, thus $\Delta U > 0$
No heat goes out, the work done on the system increases the internal energy, so the temperature of the gas increases.
Hence, the correct option is (C).

50. Aluminum oxide is amphoteric in nature, i.e., it reacts with acids as well as bases to form salt and water.
Here, aluminum oxide behaves as acid as it reacts with $NaOH$, a base and forms sodium aluminate $(NaAlO_2)$ and water:
$Al_2O_3 + NaOH \rightarrow 2NaAlO_2 + H_2O$
Hence, the correct option is (A).

51. Let the marks of Kamal in mathematics and English be x and y, respectively.
According to the question:
$x + y = 40$.....(i)
Also, $(x + 3)(y - 4) = 360$
$\Rightarrow (x + 3)(40 - x - 4) = 360$ [From (i)]
$\Rightarrow (x + 3)(36 - x) = 360$
$\Rightarrow 36x - x^2 + 108 - 3x = 360$
$\Rightarrow 33x - x^2 - 252 = 0$
$\Rightarrow -x^2 + 33x - 252 = 0$
$\Rightarrow x^2 - 33x - 252 = 0$
$\Rightarrow x^2 - (21 + 12)x + 252 = 0$

$\Rightarrow x^2 - 21x - 12x + 252 = 0$
$\Rightarrow x(x - 21) - 12(x - 21) = 0$
$\Rightarrow (x - 21)(x - 12) = 0$
$\Rightarrow x = 21$ or $x = 12$
If $x = 21$
$y = 40 - 21 = 119$
Thus, Kamal scored 21 and 19 marks in mathematics and English, respectively.
If $x = 12$
$y = 40 - 12 = 28$
Thus, Kamal scored 12 and 28 marks in mathematics and English, respectively.
Hence, the correct option is (D).

52. $\left(\dfrac{1}{\log_3 e}\right) + \left(\dfrac{1}{\log_3 e^2}\right) + \left(\dfrac{1}{\log_3 e^4}\right) + \cdots \ldots \ldots$

$= \left(\dfrac{1}{\log_3 e}\right) + \left(\dfrac{1}{2\log_3 e}\right) + \left(\dfrac{1}{4\log_3 e}\right) + \cdots \ldots \ldots$

$= (\log_e 3) + \left(\log_e \dfrac{3}{2}\right) + \left(\log_e \dfrac{3}{4}\right) + \cdots \ldots \ldots$

$= \log_e 3 \left(1 + \dfrac{1}{2} + \dfrac{1}{4} + \cdots \ldots\right)$

$= \log_e 3 \left(\dfrac{1}{1} - \dfrac{1}{2}\right)$

$= 2\log_e 3$

$= \log_e 3^2$

$= \log_e 9$

Hence, the correct option is (A).

53. There are 8 chair on each side of the table.
Let the sides be represented by A and B.
Let four persons sit on side A, then number of ways of arranging 4 persons on 8 chairs on side $A = {}^8P_4$
And two persons sit on side B.
The number of ways of arranging 2 persons on 8 chairs on side $B = {}^8P_2$
The remaining 10 persons can be arranged in remaining 10 chairs in $10!$ ways.
Hence, the total number of ways in which the persons can be arranged is ${}^8P_4 \times {}^8P_2 \times 10! = \dfrac{8!8!10!}{4!6!}$
Hence, the correct option is (B).

54. As, $\angle BMN + \angle DNM = 180°$
$\angle PMN + \angle PNM = 90°$

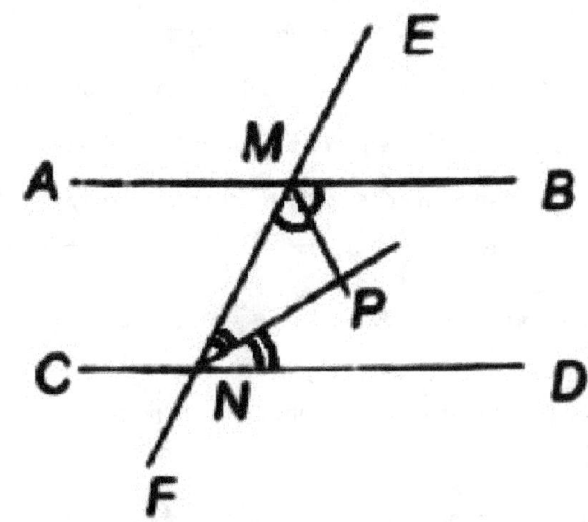

$$\angle MPN = 180° - (\angle PMN + \angle PNM)$$
$$= 180° - 90° = 90°$$

Hence, the correct option is (D).

55. Given,

$$m\begin{bmatrix}-3 & 4\end{bmatrix} + n\begin{bmatrix}4 & -3\end{bmatrix} = \begin{bmatrix}10 & -11\end{bmatrix}$$
$$\Rightarrow \begin{bmatrix}-3m + 4n & 4m - 3n\end{bmatrix} = \begin{bmatrix}10 & -11\end{bmatrix}$$

By equating above matrices, we get

$$-3m + 4n = 10 \Rightarrow 12m - 16n = -40 ......(i)$$
$$4m - 3n = -11 \Rightarrow 12m - 9n = -33 ....(ii)$$

Solving equation (i) and (ii), we get,

$$-7n = -7$$
$$\therefore n = 1 \text{ and } m = -2$$

Hence, the correct option is (A).

56. Given,

$$A = \begin{bmatrix}1 & 2\\3 & 4\end{bmatrix} \text{ and } AX = I$$

We have to find the value of X.

$$AX = I$$
$$\Rightarrow X = A^{-1}$$
$$= \frac{1}{|A|} adjA = \frac{1}{(4-6)}\begin{bmatrix}4 & -2\\-3 & 1\end{bmatrix}$$
$$X = -\frac{1}{2}\begin{bmatrix}4 & -2\\-3 & 1\end{bmatrix}$$
$$= \begin{bmatrix}-2 & 1\\3/2 & -1/2\end{bmatrix}$$

Hence, the correct option is (D).

57. $A = \{x \in Z : x^3 - 1 = 0\}$ and $B = \{x \in Z : x^2 + x + 1 = 0\}$, where Z is set of complex numbers, then $A \cap B$

$$A = \{x \in Z : x^3 - 1 = 0\}$$
$$x^3 - 1 = (x - 1)(x^2 + x + 1)$$

Therefore roots are $1, \dfrac{-1+\sqrt{3}i}{2}, \dfrac{-1-\sqrt{3}i}{2}$

i.e, $A = \left\{1, \dfrac{-1+\sqrt{3}i}{2}, \dfrac{-1-\sqrt{3}i}{2}\right\}$

$$B = \{x \in Z : x^2 + x + 1 = 0\}$$

The roots are $\dfrac{-1+\sqrt{3}i}{2}, \dfrac{-1-\sqrt{3}i}{2}$

$$B = \left\{\dfrac{-1+\sqrt{3}i}{2}, \dfrac{-1-\sqrt{3}i}{2}\right\}$$
$$(A \cap B) = \left\{1, \tfrac{-1+\sqrt{3}i}{2}, \tfrac{-1-\sqrt{3}i}{2}\right\} \cap$$
$$\left\{\tfrac{-1+\sqrt{3}i}{2}, \tfrac{-1-\sqrt{3}i}{2}\right\} = \left\{\tfrac{-1+\sqrt{3}i}{2}, \tfrac{-1-\sqrt{3}i}{2}\right\}$$

Hence, the correct option is (B).

58. We have,

$$\tan^{-1}\frac{1}{2} + \tan^{-1}\frac{1}{3}$$

We know that,

$$\tan^{-1}x + \tan^{-1}y = \tan^{-1}\left(\frac{x+y}{1-xy}\right)$$

So, $\tan^{-1}\frac{1}{2} + \tan^{-1}\frac{1}{3} = \tan^{-1}\left(\dfrac{\frac{1}{2}+\frac{1}{3}}{1-\frac{1}{2}\times\frac{1}{3}}\right)$

$$= \tan^{-1}\left(\dfrac{\frac{3+2}{6}}{1-\frac{1}{6}}\right)$$
$$= \tan^{-1}\left(\frac{5}{5}\right)$$
$$= \tan^{-1}1$$
$$= \tan^{-1}\tan\frac{\pi}{4}$$
$$= \frac{\pi}{4}$$

Hence, the correct option is (D).

59. Given,

$$y = (\cot^{-1}x)(\cot^{-1}(-x))$$
$$= \cot^{-1}(x)(\pi - \cot^{-1}(x))$$

Now $\cot^{-1}(x)$ and $(\pi - \cot^{-1}(x)) > 0$

Using A.M. $\geq$ G.M., we get $\dfrac{\cot^{-1}x + (\pi - \cot^{-1}(x))}{2} \geq$

$$\sqrt{(\cot^{-1}x)(\pi - \cot^{-1}(x))}$$

$$\Rightarrow 0 < \sqrt{\cot^{-1}(x)(\pi - \cot^{-1}(x))} \leq$$
$$\frac{\cot^{-1}x + (\pi - \cot^{-1}(x))}{2} = \frac{\pi}{2}$$
$$\Rightarrow 0 < y \leq \frac{\pi^2}{4}$$

Hence, the correct option is (D).

60. $\displaystyle\lim_{x\to\infty}\left(\frac{x^2+5x+3}{x^2+x+2}\right)^x = \lim_{x\to\infty}\left(1 + \frac{4x+1}{x^2+x+2}\right)^x$

$$= \lim_{x\to\infty}\left[\left(1 + \frac{4x+1}{x^2+x+2}\right)^{\frac{x^2+x+2}{4x+1}}\right]^{\frac{(4x+1)x}{x^2+x+2}}$$

$$= e^{\lim\limits_{x\to\infty}\frac{4x^2+x}{x^2+x+2}}\left[\because \lim_{x\to\infty}(1+\lambda x)^{\frac{1}{x}} = e^{\lambda}\right]$$

$$= e^{\lim\limits_{x\to\infty}\frac{4+\frac{1}{x}}{1+\frac{1}{x}+\frac{2}{x^2}}} = e^4$$

Hence, the correct option is (A).

61. $A + A^T = \begin{bmatrix} a & b \\ b & a \end{bmatrix}\begin{bmatrix} a & b \\ b & a \end{bmatrix} = \begin{bmatrix} 2a & 2b \\ 2b & 2a \end{bmatrix}$

$|A + A^T| = 4a^2 - 4b^2$

Hence, the correct option is (A).

62. Since E is a universal set $E - A = A'$

$E - \left(E - \left(E - (E - (E - A))\right)\right)$

$E - \left(E - \left(E - (E - A')\right)\right)$

$E - \left(E - (E - A)\right)$

$E - (E - A')$

$E - A$

A'

$(B \cup C)'$

$B' \cap C'$

Hence, the correct option is (C).

63. We have, $f(x) = \begin{cases} x^2, & x \geq 0 \\ -x^2 & x < 0 \end{cases}$

Clearly, $f(x)$ is differentiable for all $x > 0$ and for all $x < 0$. So, we check the differentiability at $x = 0$.

Now, (RHD at $x = a$)

$= \left(\dfrac{d}{dx}(x^2)\right)_{x=0} = (2x)_{x=0} = 0$

$\therefore$ (LHD at $x = 0$) $= \left(\dfrac{d}{dx}(-x^2)\right)_{x=0} =$

$(-2x)_{x=0} = 0$

(LHD at $x = 0$) $=$ (RHD at $x = 0$)

So, $f(x)$ is differentiable for all x i.e., the set of all points where $f(x)$ is differentiable is $(-\infty, \infty)$ i.e., R.

Hence, the correct option is (A).

64. Given:

$\int e^x(\sin x + \cos x)\,dx$

It is of form

$\int e^x\left(f(x) + f'(x)\right)dx = e^x f(x) + c$

Now, $\int e^x(\sin x + \cos x)\,dx$

$= \int e^x \sin x\,dx + \int e^x \cos x\,dx$

$= e^x(\sin x) - \int (\cos x) \cdot e^x\,dx + \int e^x \cos x\,dx$

$= e^x(\sin x) + c\,[$ Where c is integrating constant $]$

Hence, the correct option is (B).

65. Total possible numbers of form $\dfrac{p}{q}$ when $p \neq q$ is $=$

$^6C_2 = 30$

Numbers when $p = q$ is $= {}^6C_1 = 6$

Therefore total numbers $30 + 6 = 36$

$\dfrac{1}{1} = \dfrac{2}{2} = \dfrac{3}{3} = \dfrac{4}{4} = \dfrac{5}{5} = \dfrac{6}{6}$ (five numbers deducted from cardinality of set)

$\dfrac{1}{2} = \dfrac{2}{4} = \dfrac{3}{6}$ (two numbers deducted from cardinality of set)

$\dfrac{2}{1} = \dfrac{4}{2} = \dfrac{6}{3}$ (two more numbers deducted from cardinality of set)

$\dfrac{1}{3} = \dfrac{2}{6}$ (one number deducted from cardinality of set)

$\dfrac{3}{1} = \dfrac{6}{2}$ (one more number deducted from cardinality of set)

$\dfrac{2}{3} = \dfrac{4}{6}$ (one number deducted from cardinality of set)

$\dfrac{3}{2} = \dfrac{6}{4}$ (one more number deducted from cardinality of set)

So, the cardinality of set $= 36 - 5 - 2 - 2 - 1 - 1 - 1 - 1 = 23$.

Hence, the correct option is (B).

66. Let the curve be $y = f(x)$

$\therefore$ Slope of the tangent drawn at any point on the curve is

$\dfrac{df(x)}{dx} = f'(x)$

Given that slope at any point on the curve is $\dfrac{2y}{x}$,

$\Rightarrow \dfrac{dy}{dx} = \dfrac{2y}{x}$

$\Rightarrow \int \dfrac{1}{y}\,dy = \int \dfrac{2}{x}\,dx$

$\Rightarrow \ln y = 2\ln x + c$

Where c is the integration constant,

Given that the curve passes through the point $(1,1)$,

$\Rightarrow c = 0$

$\therefore y = x^2$ is the equation of the curve which is a parabola.

Hence, the correct option is (B).

67. Given,

$xdy = ydx + y^2dy$

$1 = \dfrac{4}{x} \cdot \dfrac{dx}{dy} + \dfrac{y^2}{x}$

$\dfrac{dx}{dy} + x = \dfrac{x}{y}$

$\dfrac{dx}{dy} - \dfrac{x}{y} = -y$

$P = -\dfrac{1}{y}, Q = -y$

Integrating factor $= e^{\int P dy} = e^{-\log y} = \dfrac{1}{y}$

$\dfrac{1}{y}\dfrac{dx}{dy} - \dfrac{x}{y^2} = -1$

Multiply the equation with Integrating factor

$\dfrac{x}{y} = \int \dfrac{1}{y}(-y)\,dy + c$

$\dfrac{x}{y} = \int -1\,dy + C$

$\dfrac{x}{y} = -y + c$

$y(1) = 1$

$\dfrac{1}{1} = -1 + c; c = 2$

$\dfrac{1}{x}{y} = -y + 2; x = -y^2 + 2y$

$y(-3); -3 = -y^2 + 2y$

$y^2 - 2y - 3 = 0$

$y = \dfrac{+2 \pm \sqrt{4+12}}{2} = \dfrac{2 \pm 4}{2}$

$y = 3, -1$

$y = 3$, since $y > 0$
Hence, the correct option is (A).

68. $A = \{x : x \text{ is a multiple of 2 }\} = \{2,4,6,8,10,12,14, \dots\}$
$B = \{x : x \text{ is a multiple of 5 }\} = \{5,10,15,20,25, \dots\}$ and
$C = \{x : x \text{ is a multiple of 10 }\} = \{10,20,30,40, \dots\}$
Here, $C \subset A$ and $C \subset B$
$C = A \cap B = A \cap (B \cap C)$
$= A \cap C = C$
Hence, the correct option is (C).

69. $x^2 dy - y^2 dy - xy^2(x - y)dy = 0$
$\dfrac{dy}{y^2} - \dfrac{dx}{x^2} - y\left[\dfrac{1}{y} - \dfrac{1}{x}\right] dy = 0$
$\Rightarrow \dfrac{dy}{y^2} - \dfrac{dx}{x^2}$
$\dfrac{1}{y} - \dfrac{1}{x} - ydy = 0$
$\Rightarrow -\ln\left|\dfrac{1}{y} - \dfrac{1}{x}\right| - \dfrac{y^2}{2} = c$
$\Rightarrow \ln\left|\dfrac{x-y}{xy}\right| + \dfrac{y^2}{2} = c$
$\left|\dfrac{x-y}{xy}\right| = e^{c - \frac{y^2}{2}}$
$\left|\dfrac{x-y}{xy}\right| = C. e^{\frac{-y^2}{2}}$
$(x - y)e^{\frac{y^2}{2}} = cxy$
Hence, the correct option is (D).

70. Cartesian equation $= \dfrac{x-5}{3} = \dfrac{y+4}{7} = \dfrac{z-6}{2}$
Let $\dfrac{x-5}{3} = \dfrac{y+4}{7} = \dfrac{z-6}{2} = a$
$x = 3\alpha + 5, y = 7a - 4, z = 2\alpha + 6$
Let (x, y, z) be position vectors.
$\therefore x\hat{i} + y\hat{j} + z\hat{k} = 5\hat{i} + (-4)\hat{j} + 6\hat{k} + \alpha(3\hat{i} + 7\hat{j} + 2\hat{k})$
Vector form $: 5\hat{i} + (-4)\hat{j} + 6\hat{k} + \alpha(3\hat{i} + 7\hat{j} + 2\hat{k})$
Hence, the correct option is (A).

71. Given:
$25x^2 + 9y^2 = 225$

The given equation can be written as $\dfrac{x^2}{9} - \dfrac{y^2}{25} = 1$

Here, $a^2 = 9 \Rightarrow a = 3$ and $b^2 = 25 \Rightarrow b = 5$

Eccentricity, $e = \sqrt{1 + \dfrac{b^2}{a^2}} = \sqrt{1 + \dfrac{25}{9}}$
$= \sqrt{\dfrac{34}{9}} = \dfrac{\sqrt{34}}{3}$
Foci $= (\pm ae, 0)$
$= \left(\pm 3 \times \dfrac{\sqrt{34}}{3}, 0\right)$
$= (\pm\sqrt{34}, 0)$

So, the eccentricity and foci of the given hyperbola are $\dfrac{\sqrt{32}}{3}$ and $\left(\pm\dfrac{\sqrt{30}}{0}\right)$ respectively.
Hence, the correct option is (A).

72. $\sin^2\theta + \cos^2\theta + \sec^2\theta + \tan^2\theta + \cot^2\theta + cosec^2\theta$
$1 + \sec^2\theta + \tan^2\theta + cosec^2\theta + \cot^2\theta$
$1 + \sec^2\theta - \tan^2\theta + cosec^2\theta - \cot^2\theta + 2$
$(\tan^2\theta + \cot^2\theta)$
$1 + 1 + 1 + 2(\tan^2\theta + \cot^2\theta)$
$3 + 2[\tan^2\theta + \cot^2\theta]$ (minimum value of $a\tan^2\theta + b\cot^2\theta = 2\sqrt{ab}$)
So the minimum value $= 3 + 2 \times 2 = 7$
Hence, the correct option is (D).

73.

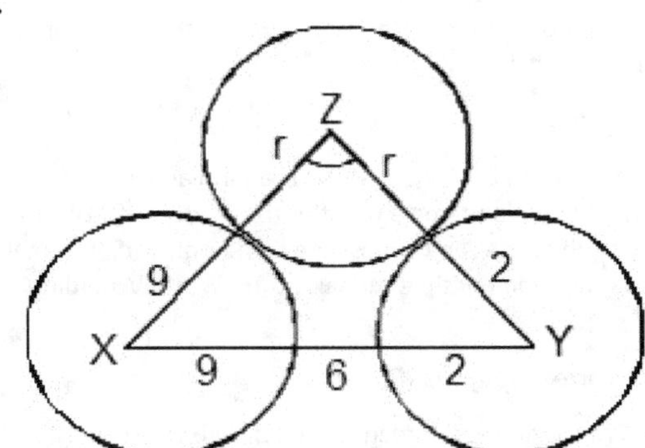

In right angle triangle XYZ $XZ^2 + YZ^2 = XY^2$
$(r + 9)^2 + (r + 2)^2 = 17^2$
$r^2 + 18r + 81 + r^2 + 4r + 4 = 289$
$2r^2 + 22r - 204 = 0$
$r^2 + 11r - 102 = 0$
$r^2 + 17r - 6r - 102 = 0$
$r(r + 17) - 6(r + 17) = 0$
$(r + 17) = 0$ or $r - 6 = 0$
$\Rightarrow r = 6 \ cm.$ (r cannot be negative)
Hence, the correct option is (D).

74. $\tan\theta + \cot\theta = x$
On doing square
$\tan^2\theta + \cot^2\theta + 2\tan\theta\cot\theta = x^2$
$\tan^2\theta + \cot^2\theta + 2 = x^2$
$\therefore \tan^2\theta + \cot^2\theta = x^2 - 2$
On doing square
$\tan^4\theta + \cot^4\theta = x^4 + 4 - 4x^2 - 2$
$\tan^4\theta + \cot^4\theta = x^2(x^2 - 4) + 2$
Hence, the correct option is (D).

75. Given lines are $6x + 8y + 15 = 0$ and $3x + 4y + 9 = 0$

$\Rightarrow 6x + 8y + 15 = 0$

Take 2 common from above equation, we get

$$\Rightarrow 3x + 4y + \frac{15}{2} = 0 ....(i)$$

And $3x + 4y + 9 = 0 .....(ii)$

Equation (i) and (ii) are parallel to each other.

$\therefore$ The distance between the parallel lines are given by, $\frac{|c_2 - c_1|}{\sqrt{a^2 + b^2}}$

$$= \frac{\left|\frac{15}{2} - 9\right|}{\sqrt{3^2 + 4^2}} = \frac{\left(\frac{3}{2}\right)}{5} = \frac{3}{10}$$

Hence, the correct option is (B).

76. Major Dhyan Chand Khel Ratna:

Major Dhyan Chand Khel Ratna Award (formerly Rajiv Gandhi Khel Ratna) is the highest sports award given in India. The award has been named after the best player of India and world hockey, who was a member of the Indian hockey team that won three Olympic gold medals.

Vinesh Phogat:

Vinesh Phogat (born 25 August 1994) is an Indian wrestler. She became the first Indian female wrestler to win gold in both the Commonwealth and Asian Games. She is the only Indian female wrestler to have won multiple medals at the World Wrestling Championships.

Hence, the correct option is (C).

77. Iconic French filmmaker Jean-Luc Godard passed away at the age of 91 in Switzerland.

- He revolutionized popular cinema in 1960 with his debut feature 'Breathless' & stood for years as one of the world's most vital and provocative directors.
- He started his career as a film critic in the 1950s.
- In December 2007, he was honoured by the European Film Academy with a lifetime achievement award.

Hence, the correct option is (D).

78. The Centre and Assam govt on 15 Sept 2022 signed a tripartite peace accord with 8 tribal outfits of Assam in the presence of Union home minister Amit Shah.

Around 1100 people have shunned the path of violence with the signing of this agreement. In January 2020, the Centre also signed a historic agreement with the Assam govt and Bodo representatives to end the over 50-year-old Bodo crisis.

Hence, the correct option is (B).

79. Dr. Jitendra Singh launched a grand challenge programme called "जनCARE" on September 28, 2021.

Celebrating the Azadi Ka Amrit Mahotsav, Union Minister of State (Independent Charge) Science and Technology, Dr Jitendra Singh, launched the 'Amrit Grand Challenge Program' titled 'जनCARE' on 28 September 2021. The 'Amrit Grand Challenge Program' was launched under the umbrella of the Azadi Ka Amrit Mahotsav. It has become most important for new growing start-up ventures and entrepreneurs to come out with innovative Ideas

and solutions for healthcare challenges faced by India. Biotechnology Industry Research Assistance Council (BIRAC), NASSCOM and NASSCOM Foundation jointly launched the 'Amrit Grand Challenge Program'. It is a nationwide 'Discover - Design - Scale' program and the challenge will end on 31 December 2021.

Hence, the correct option is (A).

80. The first letter of the series is the 12th letter to the left of the preceding series, i.e.,

Y – 12 = M.

M – 12 = A.

A – 12 = O.

Similarly,

C – 12 = Q.

Q – 12 = E.

E – 12 = S.

Similarly,

L – 12 = Z.

Z – 12 = N.

N – 12 = B.

Therefore the letter OSB.

Hence, the correct option is (B).

81. Indian Foreign Service is not part of All India Services. All India Services are mentioned in Article 312 of the Indian Constitution.

The modern Indian Administrative Service and Indian Police Service were created under Article 312(2) in part XIV of the Constitution of India, and the All India Services Act, 1951. Hence, the correct option is (C).

82. In India, the President is not elected directly by the public. The President's salary is given from the Consolidated Fund of India, which is exempt from income tax. According to Article 54 of the Constitution of India, the President will be elected by such an electoral college, which consists of elected members of Parliament (Lok Sabha and Rajya Sabha) and State Legislative Assemblies. Provided by the President's Salary, Allowance and Pension (Amendment) Act 2008.

Hence, the correct option is (B).

83. Konark temple is located in Orissa and is also called black pagoda, Modhera temple is located in Gujarat and Martand Temple is located in J&K and all of these are dedicated to Lord's sun as the entrances east face.

Hence, the correct option is (D).

84. The given code follow this pattern:

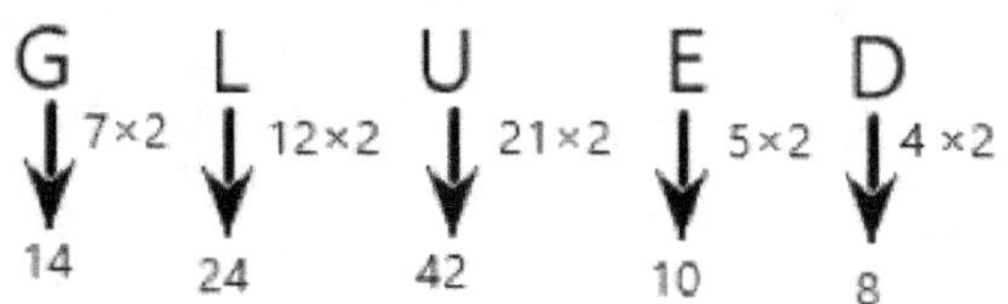

Similarly,

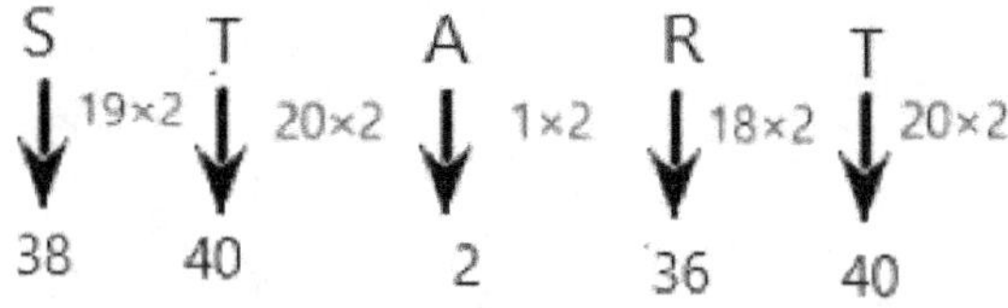

Thus, the word START can be written as "384023640".

Hence, the correct option is (A).

85. Abul Fazl was the author of Akbarnama, the official history of Akbar's reign in 3 volumes. Akbar reigned from 1556 to 1605 and extended Mughal power over most of the Indian subcontinent. Hence, the correct option is (C).

86. The famous art of Madhubani painting is a distinct place for people in India. this art center is located in Jitwarpur village of Madhubani district. The subject of paintings of this style is related to the stories of religious and public life. In it, the selection of colors is natural. even then the pictures look to impact the paintings of this genre.

Hence, the correct option is (C).

87. Bidhan Chandra Roy Award is given in the field of medicine. Bidhan Chandra Roy Award was instituted in 1962 in memory of B. C. Roy by the Medical Council of India. The Award is given annually in each of the following categories: Statesmanship of the Highest Order in India, Medical man-cum-Statesman, Eminent Medical Person, Eminent person in Philosophy, Eminent person in Science and Eminent person in Arts.

Hence, the correct option is (D).

88.

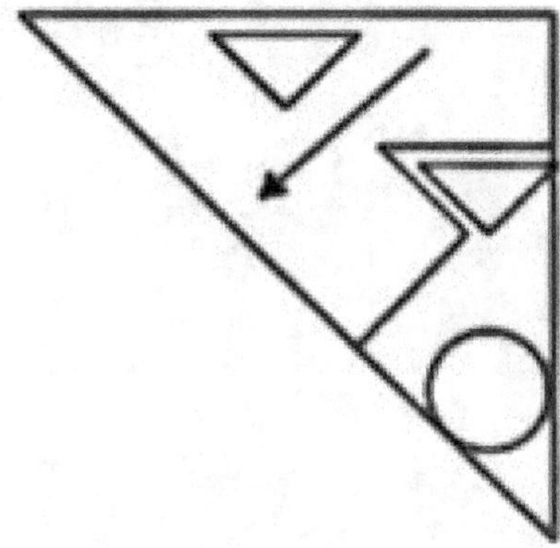

Hence, the correct option is (C).

89. The most extensive soil in India is Alluvial soil. Alluvial soil in India is mainly found in northern plains. It is deposited by three important Himalayan river systems - the Indus, the Ganga and the Brahmaputra.

Hence, the correct option is (C).

90. The most abundant gas in the atmosphere is Nitrogen and Oxygen is the second abundant gas in the atmosphere. Argon, an inert gas is the third most abundant gas in the atmosphere.

The atmosphere contains many gases, most in small amounts, including some pollutants and greenhouse gases.

Hence, the correct option is (A).

91. The Godavari is the largest Peninsular River of India. It is also called the Dakshin Ganga. It rises in the Nasik district of Maharashtra and discharges its water into the Bay of Bengal. Its tributaries run through the states of Maharashtra, Madhya Pradesh, Chhattisgarh, Orissa and Andhra Pradesh.

Hence, the correct option is (B).

92. Tropical grassland, also called savanna, is a terrestrial grassland that features vast open spaces consisting of scattered small shrubs and trees. Savanna support some of the world's most recognizable species such as lions, cheetahs, hyenas, zebras, gazelles, elephants, giraffes, wildebeests and warthogs.

Hence, the correct option is (A).

93. Beijing is the capital of the People's Republic of China. It is the world's most populous capital city.

Hence, the correct option is (B).

94. Former English World Snooker Champion Peter Ebdon has announced his retirement from the sport due to an ongoing neck injury. The 49-year-old played in the professional game for 29 years.

Hence, the correct option is (A).

95. Veteran actor Dharmendra and filmmaker Rajkumar Hirani will be conferred with the prestigious Raj Kapoor Lifetime Achievement and Raj Kapoor Special Contribution awards, respectively. Both the lifetime achievement awards carry a citation and cash reward of Rs 5,00,000, while the special contribution awards carry a citation and Rs 3,00,000 cash prize each.

Hence, the correct option is (B).

96. Polio virus is an enterovirus and a member of the Picornaviridae family; types 1, 2 and 3 cause disease, although type 2 has been eradicated as a wild-type virus.

Hence, the correct option is (B).

97. India receives rainfall from two monsoons. South-West Monsoon and North-East Monsoon. South-West Monsoon is a major one which occurs from July -September. The majority of Indian states receive rainfall from this Monsoon. Rain hits first the state of Kerala and along with the coastal areas of Karnataka / Maharastra (Konken coastal area). After it gains momentum it crosses the Western ghats downpours in all other states of India.

Hence, the correct option is (B).

98. Sardar Patel persuaded almost every princely state to accede to India. His commitment to national integration in the newly independent country was total and uncompromising, earning him the sobriquet "Iron Man of India".

Hence, the correct option is (B).

99. BRICS is an acronym for Brazil, Russia, India, China, and South Africa. Goldman Sachs economist Jim O'Neill coined the term BRIC (without South Africa) in 2001, claiming that by 2050 the four BRIC economies would come to dominate the global economy by 2050.

Hence, the correct option is (D).

100. India's first Grandmaster Viswanathan Anand released his autobiography titled Mind Master. It was co-written by Susan Ninan. The book offers an insight into Anand's greatest wins and worst losses. He has also shared his experience of facing the best minds in the world.

Hence, the correct option is (A).

English

Ques (1-5):Direction: Read the given passage carefully and answer the questions that follow.

The crowd surged forward through the narrow, streets of Paris, there was a clatter of shutters being closed hastily by trembling hands – the citizens of Paris knew that once the fury of the people was excited there was no telling what they might do. They came to an old house which had a workshop on the ground floor. A head popped out of the door to see what it was all about. Get him! Get Thimonier! Smash his devilish machines!', yelled the crowd.

They found the workshop without its owner. M, Thimonier had escaped by the back door. Now that fury of the demonstrators turned against the machines that were standing in the shop, ready to be delivered to buyers. They were systematically broken, up and destroyed dozens of them. Only when the last wheel and spindle had been trampled underfoot did the infuriated crowd recover their senses.

'That is the end of M' sieur Thimonier and his sewing machines', they said to one another and went home satisfied. Perhaps now they would find work, for they were all unemployed tailors and seamstresses who believed that their livelihood was threatened by that new invention.

Q.1 The passage throws light on

A. Why inventions should be avoided altogether?

B. How a well-meant invention can be misunderstood?

C. What mischief an inventor can do to ordinary people?

D. How dangerous an invention can prove to be?

Q.2 The crowd was protesting against

A. the closing of workshops.

B. the misdoings of Thimonier.

C. the newly invented sewing machine.

D. Thimonier keeping the invention a secret.

Q.3 The aim of the crowd was to

A. kill Thimonier

B. drive Thimonier away

C. bring discredit to Thimonier

D. destroy the sewing machines

Q.4 The people thought that

A. their lives were in danger

B. Thimonier was mad

C. the sewing machine was dangerous

D. Thimonier was depriving them of their livelihood

Q.5 Shutters were being closed hastily because the shopkeepers

A. wanted to attack the crowd

B. wanted to protect Thimonier

C. feared their shops would be invaded

D. wanted to show their solidarity with the crowd

Q.6 Direction: Choose the antonym of the given word.

Eternal

A. Usual

B. Active

C. Realistic

D. Temporary

Q.7 Direction: Choose the synonym of the given word.

Spurious

A. Modest

B. Spontaneous

C. Fake

D. Sincere

Q.8 Direction: Choose the correct sentence from the following.

A. They were discussing the matter among themselves.

B. They was discussing the matter among themselves.

C. They were discussing the matter among themself.

D. They were discussing the matter between themselves.

Q.9 Direction: Choose the correct meaning of the phrase.

Takes after

A. constitutes

B. follows

C. resembles

D. accepts

Q.10 Direction: Choose the correctly punctuated sentence.

A. These are Peters books.

B. These are Peter's books?

C. These are Peter books.

D. These are Peter's books.

Q.11 Direction: Choose the correct sentence from the following.

20 km <u>are not a great distance</u> in these days of fast-moving vehicles.

A. is not a great distance

B. is no distance

C. aren't a great distance

D. No improvement

Q.12 Direction: Change active to passive or vice versa as the case may be.

I have flown this plane for seven years.

A. This plane is flying me for seven years.

B. I am flying this plane for seven years.

C. Seven years have happened since I have been flying this plane.

D. This plane has been flown by me for seven years.

Q.13 Direction: Change active to passive or vice versa as the case may be.

A lion may be helped even by a little mouse.

[Territorial Army Officer, 2017]

A. A little mouse may be even help a lion.

B. Even a little mouse may help a lion.

C. A little mouse can even help a lion.

D. Even a little mouse ought to help a lion.

Q.14 Direction: Change direct to indirect speech or vice versa as the case may be.

Adavik said, "What a mesmerising performance it is!"

A. Adavik expressed sorrowfuly that it was a mesmerising performance.

B. Adavik exclaimed that it is a mesmerising performance.

C. Adavik exclaimed with joy that it was a very mesmerising performance.

D. Adavik said that it had been a mesmerising performance.

Q.15 Direction: Choose the correct sentence from the following.

It became clear that the strangers were heading into a serious disaster.

A. along

B. towards

C. for

D. No improvement

Q.16 Direction: Change direct to indirect speech or vice versa as the case may be.

Kiran asked me, "Did you see the Cricket match on television last night?"

A. Kiran asked me whether I saw the Cricket match on television the earlier night.

B. Kiran asked me whether I had seen the Cricket match on television the earlier night.

C. Kiran asked me did I see the Cricket match on television the last night.

D. Kiran asked me whether I had seen the Cricket match on television the last night.

Q.17 Direction: Change direct to indirect speech or vice versa as the case may be.

David said to Anna, "Mona will leave for her native place tomorrow."

A. David told Anna that Mona will leave for her native place tomorrow.

B. David told Anna that Mona left for her native place the next day.

C. David told Anna that Mona would be leaving for her native place tomorrow.

D. David told Anna that Mona would leave for her native place the next day.

Q.18 Direction: Choose the most appropriate pronoun to complete the sentence.

Have you put the chicken on ___ grill yet?

A. a

B. an

C. the

D. None of these

Q.19 Direction: Choose the most appropriate alternative to complete the sentence.

There were _______ participants at the conference that we had trouble seating them.

A. much more

B. many more

C. so many

D. too many

Q.20 Direction: Choose the most appropriate preposition to complete the sentence.

I have distaste ____ publicity.

A. at

B. for

C. about

D. against

Q.21 Direction: Choose the most appropriate preposition to complete the sentence.

I have been waiting here for him ___ three weeks.

A. on

B. for

C. from

D. since

Q.22 Direction: Choose the most appropriate alternative to complete the sentence.

Every year millions of tourists _____ the Anna Centenary Library in Chennai.

A. visiting

B. visit

C. are visiting

D. visited

Q.23 Direction: Choose the most appropriate alternative to complete the sentence.

Look after your health _______ you should repent later on.

A. as

B. because

C. till

D. lest

Q.24 Direction: Choose the adjective in the given sentence. Ram and Shyam live in a beautiful house.

A. house

B. beautiful

C. live

D. and

Q.25 Direction: Choose the pronoun in the given sentence. Who will come to the party?

A. will

B. come

C. who

D. party

Science

Q.26 The oil layer on the surface of water appears coloured, due to interference. For this effect to be visible the thickness of oil layers will be:

A. $1\ mm$

B. $1\ cm$

C. 100 Å

D. 1000 Å

Q.27 High quality camera lenses are often coated to prevent reflection. A lens has an optical index of refraction of 1.72 and a coating with an optical index of refraction of 1.31. For near normal incidence the minimum thickness of the coating to prevent reflection for wavelength of $5.3 \times 10^{-7} m$ is:

A. $0.75 \mu m$

B. $0.2 \mu m$

C. $0.1 \mu m$

D. $1.75 \mu m$

Q.28 For a body moving in a circular path, the work done by the centripetal force is_________.

A. Negative

B. Positive

C. Constant

D. Zero

Q.29 A machine gun fires 60 bullets per minute, with a velocity of $700\ m/s$. If each bullet has a mass of $50\ g$, find the power developed by the gun.

A. 1225 W

B. 12250 W

C. 122.5 W

D. 122 W

Q.30 A particle is executing simple harmonic motion at midpoint of mean position and extremely. What is the potential energy in terms of total energy (E)?

A. $\frac{E}{4}$ **B.** $\frac{E}{16}$ **C.** $\frac{E}{2}$ **D.** $\frac{E}{8}$

Q.31 A mass m is suspended from a spring. Its frequency of oscillation is f. The spring is cut into two halves and the same mass is suspended from one of the two pieces of the spring. The frequency of oscillation of mass will be __________.

A. $\sqrt{2}f$ **B.** $\frac{f}{2}$ **C.** f **D.** $2f$

Q.32 A spherical ball of mass $20\ kg$ is stationary at the top of a hill of height $100\ m$. It rolls down a smooth surface to the ground, then climbs up another hill of height $30\ m$, and finally rolls done to a horizontal base at a height of $20\ m$ above the ground. The velocity attained by the ball is __________.

A. $10\ m/s$ **B.** $10\sqrt{30}\ m/s$
C. $40\ m/s$ **D.** $20\ m/s$

Q.33 If mass-energy equivalence is taken into account when water is cooled to form ice, the mass of water should __________.

A. Increase
B. Remain unchanged
C. Decrease
D. First increase and then decrease

Q.34 Which of the following stays in equilibrium even after being slightly displaced?
A. Stable equilibrium
B. Unstable equilibrium
C. Neutral equilibrium
D. Rigid body

Q.35 The flying wheel attached to the shaft of steam engine works on the principle of __________.
A. Centripetal action
B. Moment of inertia
C. Newton's third law of motion
D. Conservation of momentum

Q.36 A cylinder rolls up an inclined plane, reaches some height and then rolls down (without slipping throughout these motions). The direction of the frictionless force acting on the cylinders is __________.
A. Up the incline, while ascending and down the incline, while descending.
B. Up the incline, while ascending as well as descending.
C. Down the incline, while ascending and up the incline, while descending.
D. Down the incline, while ascending as well as descending.

Q.37 A solid sphere is rotating in free space. If the radius of the sphere is increased keeping mass same, which one of the following will not be affected?
A. Moment of inertia
B. Angular momentum
C. Angular velocity
D. Rotational kinetic energy

Q.38 Which of the following is a crystalline solid?

A. Anisotropic substances
B. Isotropic substances
C. Supercooled liquids
D. Amorphous solids

Q.39 Why are the glasses of building appears milky?
A. Because of unwanted deposits
B. Because it becomes old
C. Because it is brittle
D. Because it changes in properties

Q.40 Which, among the following qualities, is not affected by the magnetic field?
A. Moving charge
B. Change in magnetic flux
C. Current flowing in a conductor
D. Stationary charge

Q.41 When a charged particle moves at right angles to the magnetic field, the variable quantity is?
A. Momentum   **B.** Speed
C. Energy   **D.** Moment of inertia

Q.42 A piston-cylinder contains air at $600\ kPa, 290\ K$, and a volume of $0.01 m^3$. A constant pressure process gives $54\ kJ$ of work out. Find the final volume of the air.
A. $0.05 m^3$ **B.** $0.01 m^3$ **C.** $0.10 m^3$ **D.** $0.15 m^3$

Q.43 A piston-cylinder device initially contains air at $150\ kPa$ and $27°C$. At this state, the volume is 400 litre. The mass of the piston is such that a $350\ kPa$ pressure is required to move it. The air is now heated until its volume has doubled. Determine the total heat transferred to the air.
A. $747 kj$ **B.** $757 kj$ **C.** $767 kj$ **D.** $777 kj$

Q.44 Which among the following is not an example of hydrogen bond?
A. H_2O **B.** Liquid HCl
C. NH_3 **D.** $CHCl_3$

Q.45 Atoms undergo bonding in order to __________.
A. Attain stability   **B.** Lose stability
C. Move freely   **D.** Increase energy

Q.46 A mixture of a metal(s) and a non-metal(s) is called?
A. Composite   **B.** Alloy
C. Dislocation   **D.** Cermet

Q.47 If the pouring basin has a much larger cross-sectional area than the sprue bottom, then the velocity of the molten metal is?
A. low   **B.** high
C. normal   **D.** either high or low

Q.48 What is the effective value of current?
A. RMS current
B. Average current
C. Instantaneous current
D. Total current

Q.49 In a sinusoidal wave, average current is always _______ RMS current.

A. greater than
B. less than
C. equal to
D. not related

Q.50 Which of the following is not a hereditary disease-

A. Haemophilia
B. Cretinism
C. Cystic fibrosis
D. Thalassemia

Mathematics

Q.51 If $\vec{a}, \vec{b}$ and $\vec{c}$ are three non coplanar vectors, then $\left(\vec{a} + \vec{b} + \vec{c}\right) \cdot [\left(\vec{a} + \vec{b}\right) \times \left(\vec{a} + \vec{c}\right)]$ equals:

A. 0
B. $[\vec{a}\vec{b}\vec{c}]$
C. $2[\vec{a}\vec{b}\vec{c}]$
D. $-[\vec{a}\vec{b}\vec{c}]$

Q.52 Two finite sets have N and M elements. The number of elements in the power set of the first set is 48 more than the total number of elements in the power set of the second test. Then the value of M and N are:

A. 7,6
B. 6,4
C. 7,4
D. 6,3

Q.53 One of the two points of trisection of the line segment joining the points $A(7, -2)$ and $B(1, -5)$ which divides the line in the ratio $1:2$ are:

A. $(5, -3)$
B. $(5, 3)$
C. $(-5, -3)$
D. $(13, 0)$

Q.54 The area of a triangle with vertices $A(3,0), B(7,0)$ and $C(8,4)$ is:

A. 14
B. 28
C. 8
D. 6

Q.55 The value of $\lim\limits_{x \to a} \dfrac{x^2 - (1+a)x + a}{x^2 + (1-a)x - a}$

A. 1
B. a
C. $\dfrac{(a+1)}{(a-1)}$
D. $\dfrac{(a-1)}{(a+1)}$

Q.56 The range of the function $f(x) = 3x - 2$, is:

A. $(-\infty, \infty)$
B. $R - \{3\}$
C. $(-\infty, 0)$
D. $(0, -\infty)$

Q.57 Which one of the following factors does the expansion of the determinant $\begin{vmatrix} x & y & 3 \\ x^2 & 5y^3 & 9 \\ x^3 & 10y^5 & 27 \end{vmatrix}$ contain?

A. $x - 3$
B. $x - y$
C. $y - 3$
D. $x - 3y$

Q.58 If A, B and C are the angles of a triangle and $\begin{vmatrix} 1 & 1 & 1 \\ 1 + \sin A & 1 + \sin B & 1 + \sin C \\ \sin A + \sin^2 A & \sin B + \sin^2 B & \sin C + \sin^2 C \end{vmatrix} = 0$ then which one of the following is correct?

A. The triangle ABC is isosceles
B. The triangle ABC is equilateral
C. The triangle ABC is scalene
D. No conclusion can be drawn with regard to the nature of the triangle

Q.59 If $B = \begin{bmatrix} 3 & 2 & 0 \\ 2 & 4 & 0 \\ 1 & 1 & 0 \end{bmatrix}$, then what is adjoint of B equal to?

[UPSC NDA, 2019]

A. $\begin{bmatrix} 0 & 0 & 0 \\ 0 & 0 & 0 \\ -2 & -1 & 8 \end{bmatrix}$
B. $\begin{bmatrix} 0 & 0 & -2 \\ 0 & 0 & -1 \\ 0 & 0 & 8 \end{bmatrix}$

C. $\begin{bmatrix} 0 & 0 & 2 \\ 0 & 0 & 1 \\ 0 & 0 & 0 \end{bmatrix}$
D. It does not exist

Q.60 A, B, C are three mutually exclusive and exhaustive events associated with a random experiment. If $P(B) = \left(\dfrac{3}{2}\right) P(A)$ and $P(C) = \left(\dfrac{1}{2}\right) P(B)$, find $P(A)$.

A. $\dfrac{2}{5}$
B. $\dfrac{3}{13}$
C. $\dfrac{2}{13}$
D. $\dfrac{4}{13}$

Q.61 If $\sin\beta$ is the harmonic mean of $\sin\alpha$ and $\cos\alpha$, and $\sin\theta$ is the arithmetic mean of $\sin\alpha$ and $\cos\alpha$, then which of the following is/are correct?

1) $\sqrt{2}\sin\left(\alpha + \dfrac{\pi}{4}\right)\sin\beta = \sin 2\alpha$

2) $\sqrt{2}\sin\theta = \cos\left(\alpha - \dfrac{\pi}{4}\right)$

Select the correct answer using the code given below:

A. 1 only
B. 2 only
C. Both 1 and 2
D. Neither 1 nor 2

Q.62 What is the sum of all two-digit numbers which when divided by 3 leave 2 as the remainder?

A. 1565
B. 1585
C. 1635
D. 1655

Q.63 Find the coefficients X^7 and X^8 in the expansion of $\left(2 + \dfrac{X}{3}\right)^n$

A. $X^7 = \binom{n}{7}\dfrac{2^{n-7}}{3^7}; X^8 = \binom{n}{8}\dfrac{2^{n-8}}{3^8}$
B. $X^7 = \binom{n}{7}\dfrac{2^{7n-7}}{3^7}; X^8 = \binom{n}{8}\dfrac{2^{n-8}}{3^8}$
C. $X^7 = \binom{n}{7}\dfrac{2^{n-7}}{3^7}; X^8 = \binom{n}{8}\dfrac{2^{8n-8}}{3^8}$
D. $X^7 = \binom{n}{7}\dfrac{2^{n+7}}{3^7}; X^8 = \binom{n}{8}\dfrac{2^{n+8}}{3^8}$

Q.64 In a blindfolded game, a boy can hit the target 8 times out of 12. If he fired 8 shots, find out the probability of more than 4 hits?

A. 2.530
B. 0.1369
C. 0.5938
D. 3.998

Q.65 Evaluate the expression $(y + 1)^4 - (y - 1)^4$.

A. $3y^2 + 2y^5$
B. $7(y^4 + y^2 + y)$
C. $8(y^3 + y^1)$
D. $y + y^2 + y^3$

Q.66 What is the value of the sum $\sum_{n=2}^{11}(i^n + i^{n+1})$ where $i = \sqrt{-1}$?

A. i
B. $2i$
C. $-2i$
D. $1 + i$

Q.67 Find the value of $\cos 75°$

A. $\dfrac{\sqrt{3}-1}{2\sqrt{2}}$
B. $\dfrac{\sqrt{3}+1}{2\sqrt{2}}$
C. $\dfrac{\sqrt{3}-1}{\sqrt{2}}$
D. $\dfrac{\sqrt{3}+1}{\sqrt{2}}$

Q.68 The value of $\int_0^{\frac{\pi}{4}} \sqrt{\tan x}\, dx + \int_0^{\frac{\pi}{4}} \sqrt{\cot x}\, dx$ is equal to

A. $\frac{\pi}{4}$　　**B.** $\frac{\pi}{2}$　　**C.** $\frac{\pi}{2\sqrt{2}}$　　**D.** $\frac{\pi}{\sqrt{2}}$

Q.69 $\cos^4 x - \sin^4 x$ is equal to ?

A. $\sin 2x$　　**B.** $\cos 2x$　　**C.** $\cos^2 x$　　**D.** $\sin^2 x$

Q.70 What is $i^{1000} + i^{1001} + i^{1002} + i^{1003}$ equal to (where $i = \sqrt{-1}$)?

A. 0　　**B.** i　　**C.** $-i$　　**D.** 1

Q.71 Which one of the following graph represents the function $f(x) = \frac{x}{x}, x \neq 0$?

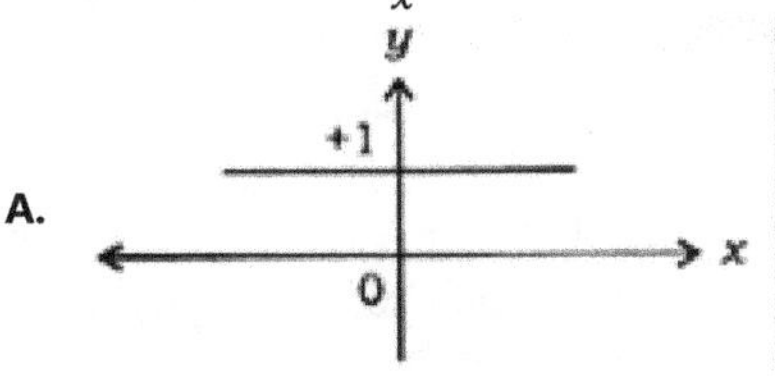

A.

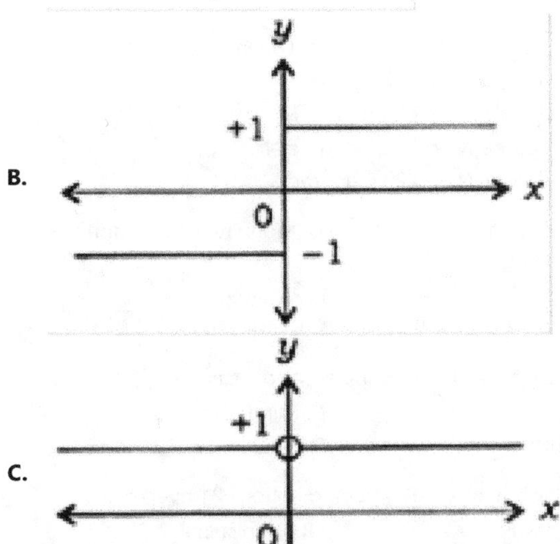

B.

C.

D. None of the above

Q.72 Let $f(n) = \left[\frac{1}{4} + \frac{n}{1000}\right]$ where $[x]$ denote the integral part of x. Then the value of $\sum_{n=1}^{1000} f(n)$ is-

A. 251　　**B.** 250　　**C.** 1　　**D.** 0

Q.73 Consider the following in respect of the function $f(x) = \begin{cases} 2 + x, & x \geq 0 \\ 2 - x, & x < 0 \end{cases}$

1) $\lim\limits_{x \to 1} f(x)$ does not exist.

2) f(x) is differentiable at x = 0.

3) f(x) is continuous at x = 0.

Which of the above statements is/are correct?

A. 1 only　　**B.** 3 only

C. 2 and 3 only　　**D.** 1 and 3 only

Q.74 If the ellipse $9x^2 + 16y^2 = 144$ intercepts the line $3x + 4y = 12$ then what is the length of the chord so formed?

A. 5 units　　**B.** 6 units　　**C.** 8 units　　**D.** 10 units

Q.75 Which of the following statement is true.

A. The line $x + 3y = 0$ is a diameter of the circle $x^2 + y^2 + 6x + 2y = 0$

B. The shortest distance from the point $(2, -7)$ to the circle $x + y^2 - 14jc - 10y - 151 = 0$ is equal to s.

C. If the line $x + my = 1$ is a tangent to the circle $x^2 + y^2 = a^2$, then the point $(1, m)$ lies on a circle.

D. The point $(1,2)$ lies inside the circle $x^2 + y^2 - 2x + 6y + 1 = 0$

General Knowledge

Q.76 In which of the following states/union territories was an election NOT held during MarchApril 2021?

[SSC CGL, 2022]

A. West Bengal　　**B.** Bihar

C. Tamil Nadu　　**D.** Puducherry

Q.77 Who among the following introduced the Preventive Detention Bill in 1950 in the Indian parliament?

A. Baldev Singh

B. Narahar Vishnu Gadgil

C. Sardar Patel

D. Jawahar Lal Nehru

Q.78 Which of the following country has granted a patent to an 'artificial intelligence system' relating to a "food container based on fractal geometry" innovation?

A. Canada　　**B.** South Africa

C. Australia　　**D.** Russia

Q.79 "Shooting Stars" are formally known as?

A. Meteor　　**B.** Meteoroids

C. Meteorite　　**D.** Neutron Stars

Q.80 The 63rd National Shooting championship has been held in ______

A. Guwahati　　**B.** Kolkata

C. Pune　　**D.** Bhopal

Q.81 Famous sportsperson and Arjuna Awardee Sunita Chandra passed away recently, she is associated with which sports?

A. Cricket　　**B.** Badminton

C. Hockey　　**D.** Football

Q.82 With regard to Cripps Mission, which of the following statements is not correct:

A. The Cripps Mission came to India in 1942

B. The Cripps Mission proposed a Dominion Status for India

C. The Cripps Mission agreed to the demand for a Constituent Assembly

D. The Cripps Mission was successful in soliciting the support of Congress

Q.83 Which of the following crop is Kharif crop as well as Rabi crop?

A. Paddy **B.** Cotton
C. Castor seed **D.** Groundnut

Q.84 Which of the following sites of Indus Valley Civilization is **incorrectly** matched?

A. Harappa: Western Punjab
B. Rakhigarhi: Haryana
C. Mohenjo-Daro: Sindh
D. Kalibangan: Gujarat

Q.85 The 73rd amendment act of 1992 does not provide for:

A. a three-tier system of Panchayati Raj in states of India
B. direct elections of the members of Panchayats at the village, intermediate and district levels
C. a five-year term of office to the Panchayat at every level
D. the reservation of seats for women in every Panchayat in the proportion of their population to the total population in the panchayat area

Q.86 Who was involved in the Second Battle of Panipat:

A. Ahmad Shah Abdali
B. Babur
C. Humayun
D. Hem Chandra Vikramaditya

Q.87 Which of the following articles of the Constitution makes special provisions for the state of Nagaland:

A. Article 371-A **B.** Article 371-B
C. Article 371-C **D.** Article 371-D

Q.88 Which of the following was a journal brought out by Abdul Kalam Azad-

A. Al-Hilal
B. Navbharat
C. The Indian Sociologist
D. Amrita Bajar Patrika

Q.89 Under which of the following articles, the Directive Principles provide for the promotion of the educational and economic interests of SCs, STs, and other weaker sections of the society:

A. Article 45 **B.** Article 46
C. Article 47 **D.** Article 48

Q.90 The country's first Super Fab Lab was launched in which state of India?

A. Karnataka **B.** Tamil Nadu
C. Andhra Pradesh **D.** Kerala

Q.91 Choose the correct match of the following mountains and their locations:

A. Rockies: South America
B. Andes: North America
C. Atlas: Africa
D. Drakensburg; Australia

Q.92 In India, coral reefs are not found in:

A. Lakshadweep **B.** Sunderbans
C. Andamans **D.** Gulf of Kutch

Q.93 Which of the following rivers does not originate in Himachal Pradesh:

A. Chenab **B.** Ravi **C.** Beas **D.** Satluj

Q.94 Who among the following were figured in Forbes' 20 people list to watch in the 2020s?

A. Narendra Damodardas Modi and Amit Shah
B. Kanhaiya Kumar and Prashant Kishor
C. Ravish Kumar and Barkha Dutt
D. Rahul Gandhi and Sonia Gandhi

Q.95 Prarthana Samaj, 1867 was founded by:

A. Atmaram Pandurang
B. Mahadev Govind Ranade
C. Jyotirao Govindrao Phule
D. Kesab Chandra Sen

Q.96 The metamorphic rock of 'Slate' has been formed from:

A. Limestone **B.** Dolomite
C. Granite **D.** Shale

Q.97 The belt of 'Doldrums' lies between latitudes of:

A. 10 degree N and 10 degree S
B. 10 degree N and 23.5 degree N
C. 23.5 degree N and 66.5 degree N
D. 23.5 degree N and 23.5 degree S

Q.98 What is the popular name of Monolithis rock shrines at Mahabalipuram

A. Rathas **B.** Prasadas
C. Mathika **D.** Gandhakuti

Q.99 Hinayana and mahayana are two sects of?

A. Sikhism **B.** Hinduism
C. Buddhisn **D.** Jainism

Q.100 Which hymn of Rig Veda mentions 21 rivers?

A. Purushasukta **B.** Nadisukta
C. Himvant **D.** Sindhu

// Smart Answer Sheet //

Correct — Percentage of students who answered correctly. **Skipped** — Percentage of students who skipped.

Q.	Ans.	Correct / Skipped	Q.	Ans.	Correct / Skipped	Q.	Ans.	Correct / Skipped	Q.	Ans.	Correct / Skipped	Q.	Ans.	Correct / Skipped	Q.	Ans.	Correct / Skipped
1	B	44.87 % / 40.07 %	18	C	43.36 % / 31.89 %	35	B	45.76 % / 31.39 %	52	B	79.72 % / 10.24 %	69	B	66.99 % / 31.86 %	86	D	57.48 % / 30.81 %
2	C	80.94 % / 18.75 %	19	C	62.93 % / 35.98 %	36	B	15.57 % / 82.75 %	53	A	25.98 % / 72.32 %	70	A	55.01 % / 35.71 %	87	A	44.93 % / 31.63 %
3	A	43.65 % / 51.52 %	20	B	44.26 % / 30.29 %	37	B	84.29 % / 15.57 %	54	C	83.3 % / 16.36 %	71	C	85.45 % / 10.06 %	88	A	15.14 % / 83.59 %
4	D	80.34 % / 15.45 %	21	B	86.49 % / 10.24 %	38	A	66.68 % / 32.31 %	55	D	81.6 % / 11.04 %	72	A	29.73 % / 70.18 %	89	B	12.26 % / 86.22 %
5	C	47.48 % / 30.23 %	22	B	65.1 % / 30.89 %	39	D	77.94 % / 16.31 %	56	A	44.91 % / 52.87 %	73	D	56.99 % / 31.42 %	90	D	59.58 % / 30.35 %
6	D	43.18 % / 51.73 %	23	D	12.22 % / 73.39 %	40	D	83.89 % / 10.32 %	57	A	69.64 % / 30.34 %	74	A	64.21 % / 30.34 %	91	C	31.04 % / 68.95 %
7	C	27.39 % / 72.28 %	24	B	62.64 % / 30.27 %	41	A	25.85 % / 73.18 %	58	A	54.89 % / 32.9 %	75	C	27.43 % / 72.52 %	92	B	58.17 % / 35.02 %
8	A	41.57 % / 34.88 %	25	C	51.55 % / 35.8 %	42	C	49.05 % / 38.75 %	59	A	18.79 % / 68.16 %	76	B	84.08 % / 11.64 %	93	D	69.07 % / 30.21 %
9	C	79.76 % / 13.12 %	26	D	87.03 % / 12.86 %	43	C	26.41 % / 72.02 %	60	D	15.06 % / 74.71 %	77	C	47.93 % / 45.91 %	94	B	27.66 % / 70.63 %
10	D	86.58 % / 10.78 %	27	C	54.34 % / 38.44 %	44	B	45.19 % / 53.98 %	61	C	48.05 % / 48.02 %	78	B	65.27 % / 33.23 %	95	A	23.56 % / 71.1 %
11	A	43.14 % / 45.73 %	28	D	65.69 % / 34.05 %	45	A	26.59 % / 72.22 %	62	C	51.13 % / 34.87 %	79	A	46.78 % / 46.19 %	96	D	59.58 % / 38.62 %
12	D	40.24 % / 45.38 %	29	B	17.93 % / 80.48 %	46	B	89.44 % / 10.24 %	63	A	48.88 % / 35.6 %	80	D	22.04 % / 67.95 %	97	A	64.09 % / 32.77 %
13	B	80.35 % / 12.65 %	30	A	50.77 % / 43.38 %	47	A	53.93 % / 33.63 %	64	C	76.33 % / 17.26 %	81	C	51.72 % / 40.9 %	98	A	61.13 % / 34.46 %
14	C	10.99 % / 67.81 %	31	A	77.9 % / 17.47 %	48	A	88.31 % / 10.18 %	65	C	17.24 % / 73.08 %	82	D	22.57 % / 77.03 %	99	C	54.58 % / 32.7 %
15	B	44.85 % / 47.49 %	32	C	10.41 % / 82.84 %	49	B	25.48 % / 73.97 %	66	C	43.44 % / 49.15 %	83	D	61.96 % / 33.18 %	100	B	64.05 % / 33.44 %
16	B	69.19 % / 30.22 %	33	A	89.25 % / 10.35 %	50	B	67.73 % / 30.27 %	67	A	30.5 % / 67.19 %	84	D	54.76 % / 36.0 %			
17	D	51.45 % / 31.86 %	34	C	84.97 % / 10.25 %	51	D	56.05 % / 41.64 %	68	D	22.61 % / 74.28 %	85	D	57.4 % / 37.95 %			

//Hints and Solutions//

1. It is understood from the passage that people were angry because they were unemployed and they thought that the new invention would be a threat to their employment. Although the sewing machine was a great invention, it was misunderstood by the people.

Hence, the correct option is (B).

2. It can be inferred from the passage that the crowd was protesting against the invention of the sewing machine.

Hence, the correct option is (C).

3. The main aim of the crowd was to kill Thimonier. However, when they found that he had already escaped, their fury turned against the machines that were standing in his shop.

Hence, the correct option is (A).

4. The crowd was furious over the invention of sewing machines as the people took it to be a threat to their livelihood. Thimonier was the owner of the workshop where the machines were kept. So, people thought that he was responsible for any loss to their employment. Hence, the correct option is (D).

5. The shopkeepers were afraid that the crowd might do anything in anger and even their shops might be invaded.

Hence, the correct option is (C).

6. Eternal means lasting or existing forever; without end.

Temporary means lasting for only a limited period of time; not permanent.

Hence, the correct option is (D).

7. Spurious = not being what it purports to be; false or fake.

Modest = not large in size or amount, or not expensive; not usually talking about or making obvious your own abilities and achievements

Spontaneous = happening or done in a natural, often sudden way, without any planning or without being forced.

Sincere = free from pretence or deceit; proceeding from genuine feelings.

Hence, the correct option is (C).

8. Option (A) is the correct sentence because:

1. The helping verb were is used for pronoun according to subject-verb agreement.

2. Among is used when we are talking about more than two people. Between is used for two people.

3. Reflexive pronoun themselves will be used according to the main subject that is they.

Hence, the correct option is (A).

9. The phrasal verb "take after" means to resemble in appearance or habit.

Hence, the correct option is (C).

10. Out of the given alternatives, the correct statement is: These are Peter's books.

Hence, the correct option is (D).

11. The correct sentence will be:

20 km is not a great distance in these days of fast-moving vehicles.

Hence, the correct option is (A).

12. The given sentence is of present perfect tense and it is in active form. The structures for active/passive voices are:

Active: Subject + has/have + verb (IIIrd form) + object...

Passive: Object + has/have + been + verb (IIIrd form) + by + subject...

So, the passive voice of the given sentence would be: This plane has been flown by me for seven years.

Hence, the correct option is (D).

13. The given sentence is of passive voice and it uses a modal verb. The structures for active/passive voices for modal verbs are:

Active: Subject + modal verb + verb (Ist form) + object...

Passive: Object + modal verb + be + verb (IIIrd form) + by + subject...

So, with the help of the above structures, we can convert the given sentence into active voice:

Even a little mouse may help a lion.

Hence, the correct option is (B).

14. The given sentence is the direct speech of an Exclamatory sentence, which is a kind of happiness or joy. The inverted comma ("") will be replaced by the conjunction "that". The tense of the reporting speech will change from simple present to simple. In exclamatory sentences, the word 'very' is used to emphasis the noun. Here, 'mesmerising' should be changed into 'very mesmerising'.

Hence, the correct option is (C).

15. It became clear that the strangers were heading towards a serious disaster.

Hence, the correct option is (B).

16. The indirect form of the sentence will be:

Kiran asked me whether I had seen the Cricket match on television the earlier night.

Hence, the correct option is (B).

17. The indirect form of the sentence will be:

David told Anna that Mona would leave for her native place the next day.

Hence, the correct option is (D).

18. Here, we are talking about a specific location, i.e. grill. So, it is necessary to use "the" in order to make the noun specific.

Hence, the correct option is (C).

19. The correct pronoun is "so many.....that". Since the sentence uses "that" which gives us a hint that "so that" will also be used in the sentence.

Hence, the correct option is (C).

20. I have distaste for publicity.

Hence, the correct option is (B).

21. I have been waiting here for him for three weeks.

Hence, the correct option is (B).

22. The sentence describes a usual activity which happens every year. Therefore, it must be kept in simple present tense. Now, "millions of tourists" is a plural noun; therefore, it must be followed by a plural verb which is given in option B only.

Hence, the correct option is (B).

23. The correct filler for the sentence is "lest". This word has a negative meaning. Therefore, it should not be used with not. The only auxiliary verb that can follow lest is "should".

Look after your health lest you should repent later on.

Hence, the correct option is (D).

24. Option (B) has the adjective here. Beautiful means delighting the senses or exciting intellectual or emotional admiration.

Hence, the correct option is (B).

25. Words such as "who, whom, which, that" are known as relative pronouns.

Hence, the correct option is (C).

26. A phase difference of π occurs after reflection from the oil surface. But for the second beam, this does not happen when reflected from water surface, This gives the condition for constructive interference as $2\mu_{oil}d = \dfrac{\lambda_{air}}{2}$

Hence, $\lambda = 4\mu_{\text{oil}}\,d$

For $400nm < \lambda < 700nm$

$400nm < 4\mu_{oil}d < 700nm$

$\mu_{oil} = 1.45$

Therefore 689.65Å $< d < 1206.8$Å

Hence, the correct option is (D).

27. Using the destructive interference equation so that no light is reflected, $2t = \dfrac{\lambda_{\text{film}}}{2}$

where t is the thickness of coating.

and, $\lambda_{\text{film}} = \dfrac{\lambda}{refractive\ index}$

$= \dfrac{5.3\times10^{-7}}{1.31} = 4.04 \times 10^{-7}$

So, thickness $t = \dfrac{4.04\times10^{-7}}{4} \approx 0.1 \times 10^{-6} = 0.1\mu m$

Hence, the correct option is (C).

28. For a body moving in a circular path, the centripetal force and the displacement are perpendicular to each other. So the work done by the centripetal force is zero.

Hence, the correct option is (D).

29. Given,

Power $= \dfrac{kinetic\ energy}{time\ (t)}$

KE $= \left(\dfrac{1}{2}mv^2\right) \times v$

t $= 60$ sec

P $= \dfrac{1}{2} \times \dfrac{5\times10^{-2}\times(700)}{60} \times 60$

$= \dfrac{5}{120} \times 49 \times 100 \times 60$

$= 12250\ W$

Hence, the correct option is (B).

30. At $y = \dfrac{A}{2}$,

Potential energy $= \dfrac{1}{2} \times kx^2$

Potential energy $= \dfrac{1}{2} \times k \times \dfrac{A^2}{2^2}$

$\Rightarrow \dfrac{1}{4} \times \dfrac{1}{2} \times k \times A^2$

$\Rightarrow \dfrac{1}{4} \times E$

$\Rightarrow \dfrac{E}{4}$

Hence, the correct option is (A).

31. When spring is cut into two halves, spring constant of each half is $2k$.

$f' = \dfrac{1}{2\pi} \times \sqrt{\left(\dfrac{2k}{m}\right)} = \sqrt{2}f$.

Hence, the correct option is (A).

32. Total energy at $100m$ height = Total energy at $20m$ height

$mgh_1 = mgh_2 + \dfrac{1}{2}mv^2$

$v = \sqrt{(2g(h_1 - h_2))} = \sqrt{(2 \times 10 \times (100 - 20))} = 40m/s$

Hence, the correct option is (C).

33. The heat energy possessed by water gets converted into mass when ice is formed. This increases the mass. Therefore, when water is cooled to form ice, then mass of the water should increase.

Hence, the correct option is (A).

34. If a body stays in equilibrium position even after being slightly displaced and released, it is said to be in neutral equilibrium. When a body is slightly displaced, its centre of mass is neither raised nor lowered and its potential energy remains constant.

Hence, the correct option is (C).

35. A flywheel is attached to the shaft of an engine. Because of its large moment of inertia, the flywheel opposes the sudden increase or decrease in the speed of the vehicle. It allows a gradual change in the speed and prevents jerky motions and hence ensures a smooth ride for the passengers.

Hence, the correct option is (B).

36. Whether the cylinder rolled up or down, the centre of mass and the point of contact of the cylinder has an acceleration g sinθ in the downward direction. So, in both cases, the force of friction acts up the inclined plane.

Hence, the correct option is (B).

37. As the radius increases, the moment of inertia of the sphere increases. As no external torque acts in free space, the speed of rotation decreases but the angular momentum remains constant.

Hence, the correct option is (B).

38. Crystalline solids are those in which atoms are arranged in an orderly fashion. They have directional properties and therefore are called anisotropic substances.

Hence, the correct option is (A).

39. Glasses of the building appear milky because it undergoes heating during the day and cooling during the night. Therefore it acquires some crystalline properties.

Hence, the correct option is (D).

40. A stationary charge is not affected by a magnetic field because stationary charges do not have any velocity. Magnetic field cannot occur in a particle having zero velocity.

Hence, the correct option is (D).

41. When a charged particle moves perpendicular to the field, its speed remains the same whereas its velocity keeps on changing. Momentum is the product of the mass of the particle and the velocity if the particle, hence since velocity varies, momentum also varies.

Hence, the correct option is (A).

42. $W = \int P dV = P\Delta V$

$$\Delta V = \frac{W}{P} = \frac{54}{600} = 0.09 m^3$$

$$V2 = V1 + \Delta V$$

$$\Rightarrow 0.01 + 0.09 = 0.10 m^3$$

Hence, the correct option is (C).

43. Qin - Wout $= \Delta U = m(u3 - u1)$

$$m = \frac{P1V1}{RT1} = 0.697\ kg$$

$$u1 = u@300\ K = 214.36\ kj/kg$$

$$u3 = u@1400\ K = 1113.43\ kj/kg$$

Therefore, $Qin = 767\ kj$

Hence, the correct option is (C).

44. There is no hydrogen bond in liquid HCl since the bond breaks up when dissolved in water.

Hence, the correct option is (B).

45. Atoms undergo bonding to attain stable electronic configuration and to gain energy. NaCl is a compound because it has an ionic bond between Na and Cl. The other three options have both covalent bonds as well as ionic bonds, hence they can be termed as both molecules and compounds.

Hence, the correct option is (A).

46. A mixture of metal and non-metal is termed as an alloy, whereas a combination of two different materials (may not have metal in it) is called as composite.

Hence, the correct option is (B).

47. The molten metal flows through a sprue to a runner and a gate and fills the mold cavity. If the pouring basin has a much larger cross-sectional area than the sprue bottom, then the velocity of the molten metal at the top of the pouring basin is very low and can be taken to be zero.

Hence, the correct option is (A).

48. RMS current is also known as the effective current. RMS stands for Root Mean Square. This value of current is obtained by squaring all the current values, finding the average and then finding the square root.

Hence, the correct option is (A).

49. The average value of current is the sum of all the currents divided by the number of currents whereas RMS current is obtained by squaring all the current values, finding the average and then finding the square root. Hence RMS current is greater than average current.

Hence, the correct option is (B).

50.

- Haemophilia is an inherited bleeding disorder where the blood doesn't clot properly as the blood does not have enough clotting factors. It is C-linked recessive disorder related to a deficiency of antihaemophilic globulin protein.

- Cretinism is a condition characterised by physical deformity and learning difficulties that are caused by congenital thyroid deficiency. So it is a disease of the endocrine system which is non-inheritable.

- Cystic fibrosis is an autosomal recessive disorder in which fibrous cyst formation takes place in lungs and pancreas. The gene for the disease is present on Chromosome 7.

- Thalassemia is a quantitative disease. It is a hereditary hemolytic disease caused by faulty hemoglobin synthesis, widespread in African and Asian countries.

Hence, the correct option is (B).

51. We have,

$$\left(\vec{a} + \vec{b} + \vec{c}\right) \cdot \left[\left(\vec{a} + \vec{b}\right) \times \left(\vec{a} + \vec{c}\right)\right]$$

$$\Rightarrow \left(\vec{a} + \vec{b} + \vec{c}\right) \cdot \left[\vec{a} \times \vec{a} + \vec{a} \times \vec{c} + \vec{b} \times \vec{a} + \vec{b} \times \vec{c}\right]$$

$$\Rightarrow \left(\vec{a} + \vec{b} + \vec{c}\right) \cdot \left[\vec{a} \times \vec{c} + \vec{b} \times \vec{a} + \vec{b} \times \vec{c}\right] \quad [\because \vec{a} \times \vec{a} = 0]$$

$$\Rightarrow \vec{a} \cdot \vec{a} \times \vec{c} + \vec{a} \cdot \vec{b} \times \vec{a} + \vec{a} \cdot \vec{b} \times \vec{c} + \vec{b} \cdot \vec{a} \times \vec{c} + \vec{b} \cdot \vec{b} \times \vec{a} + \vec{b} \cdot \vec{b} \times \vec{c} + \vec{c} \cdot \vec{a} \times \vec{c} + \vec{c} \cdot \vec{b} \times \vec{a} + \vec{c} \cdot \vec{b} \times \vec{c}$$

$$\Rightarrow [\vec{a}\,\vec{b}\,\vec{c}] - [\vec{a}\,\vec{b}\,\vec{c}] - [\vec{a}\,\vec{b}\,\vec{c}] = -[\vec{a}\,\vec{b}\,\vec{c}]$$

Hence, the correct option is (D).

52. Let, A and B be two sets having m and n numbers of elements respectively,

Number of subsets of $A = 2m$

Number of subsets of $B = 2n$

Now, according to question

$$2m - 2n = 48$$

$$\Rightarrow 2n(2m - n - 1) = 24(22 - 1)$$

So, $n = 4$ and $m - n = 2$

$$\Rightarrow m - 4 = 2$$

$$\Rightarrow m = 2 + 4$$

$$\Rightarrow m = 6$$

Hence, the correct option is (B).

53. Given,

$A(7, -2)$ and $B(1, -5)$

Required point of trisection that divides the given line in the ratio $1 : 2$ is,

By using formula of trisection,

$$P(x, y) = \left(\frac{c \cdot m + a \cdot n}{m + n}, \frac{d \cdot m + b \cdot n}{m + n}\right)$$

[where line joining two points (a, b) and (c, d) in the ratio $m : n$]

$$\Rightarrow \left(\frac{1(1) + 2(7)}{1 + 2}, \frac{1(-5) + 2(-2)}{1 + 2}\right)$$

$$\Rightarrow \left(\frac{15}{3}, \frac{-9}{3}\right)$$

$$\Rightarrow (5, -3)$$

Hence, the correct option is (A).

54. Let us assume the triangle is:

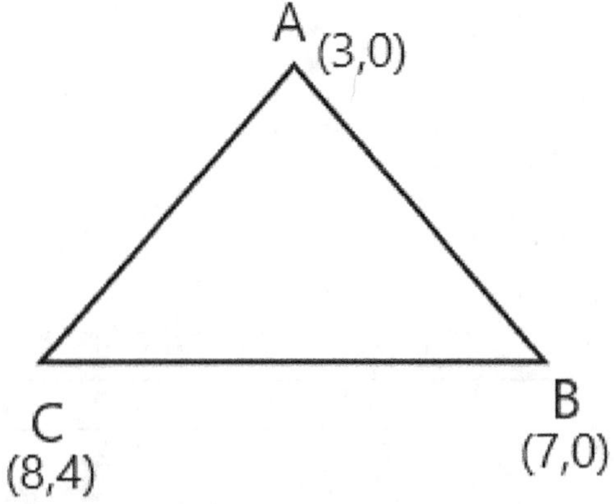

Area of the triangle is calculated as,

$$\text{Area} = \frac{1}{2}\left(x_1(y_2 - y_3) + x_2(y_3 - y_1) + x_3(y_1 - y_2)\right)$$

$$\Rightarrow \text{Area} = \frac{1}{2}\left(3(0 - 4) + 7(4 - 0) + 8(0 - 0)\right)$$

$$\Rightarrow \text{Area} = \frac{1}{2}|-12 + 28|$$

$$\Rightarrow \text{Area} = \frac{1}{2}|16|$$

$$\Rightarrow \text{Area} = 8$$

Hence, the correct option is (C).

55. $\lim_{x \to a} \dfrac{x^2 - (1+a)x + a}{x^2 + (1-a)x - a}$, This is $\dfrac{0}{0}$ form.

Here we use factorization method.

$$\lim_{x \to a} \frac{(x-a)(x-1)}{(x-a)(x+1)}$$

$$\lim_{x \to a} \frac{(x-1)}{(x+1)} = \frac{(a-1)}{(a+1)}$$

Hence, the correct option is (D).

56. Let, the given function is:

$$y = 3x - 2$$

$$\Rightarrow y + 2 = 3x$$

$$\Rightarrow x = \frac{(y+2)}{3}$$

Now x is saisfied by all values.

So, Range $\{f(x)\} = R = (-\infty, \infty)$

Hence, the correct option is (A).

57.

x	y	3
x^2	$5y^3$	9
x^3	$10y^5$	27

$$C_1 \rightarrow C_1 - C_3$$

$x-3$	y	3
x^2-9	$5y^3$	9
x^3-27	$10y^5$	27

$(x-3)$

1	y	3
$x+3$	$5y^3$	9
x^2- $3x+9$	$10y^5$	27

Common term is: $x-3$

Hence, the correct option is (A).

58.

1	1	1
$1+\sin A$	$1+\sin B$	$1+\sin C$
$\sin A+\sin^2 A$	$\sin B+\sin^2 B$	$\sin C+\sin^2 C$

$$C_2 \rightarrow C_1 - C_2 \text{ and } C_3 \rightarrow C_1 - C_3$$

1	0	0
$1+\sin A$	$\sin A-\sin B$	$\sin A-\sin C$
$\sin A+\sin^2 A$	$\sin^2 A+\sin^2 B$	$\sin^2 A +\sin^2 C$
1	0	0
$1+\sin A$	1	$\sin A-\sin C$
$\sin A+\sin^2 A$	$\sin A+\sin B$	$\sin A +\sin C$

$$(\sin A - \sin B)(\sin A - \sin C) = 0$$

$$(\sin A - \sin B)(\sin A - \sin C)(\sin C - \sin B) = 0$$

$(\sin A - \sin B) = 0$ or $(\sin A - \sin C) = 0$ or $(\sin C - \sin B) = 0$

$$\sin A = \sin B \text{ or } \sin A = \sin C \text{ or } \sin C = \sin B$$

Hence, the correct option is (A).

59. Given:

$$B = \begin{bmatrix} 3 & 2 & 0 \\ 2 & 4 & 0 \\ 1 & 1 & 0 \end{bmatrix}$$

Adjoint of $B = [\text{Cofactor of } B]^T$

Adjoint of $B = A_{11} =$

$$(-1)^{1+1} \begin{vmatrix} 4 & 0 \\ 1 & 0 \end{vmatrix} = (-1)^2(0) = 0$$

$A_{12} =$

$$(-1)^{1+2} \begin{vmatrix} 2 & 0 \\ 1 & 0 \end{vmatrix} = (-1)^3(0) = 0$$

$A_{13} =$

$$(-1)^{1+3} \begin{vmatrix} 2 & 4 \\ 1 & 1 \end{vmatrix} = (-1)^4(-2) = -2$$

Similarly,

$$A_{21} = (-1)^3(0) = 0$$
$$A_{22} = (-1)^4(0) = 0$$
$$A_{23} = (-1)^5(1) = -1$$
$$A_{31} = (-1)^4(0) = 0$$
$$A_{32} = (-1)^5(0) = 0$$
$$A_{33} = (-1)^6(8) = 8$$

$$\text{Adjoint of } B = \begin{bmatrix} 0 & 0 & -2 \\ 0 & 0 & -1 \\ 0 & 0 & 8 \end{bmatrix}$$

$$= \begin{bmatrix} 0 & 0 & 0 \\ 0 & 0 & 0 \\ -2 & -1 & 8 \end{bmatrix}$$

Hence, the correct option is (A).

60. A,B,C are mutually exclusive events and exhaustive events

$$P(B) = \left(\frac{3}{2}\right) P(A) \text{ and } P(C) = \left(\frac{1}{2}\right) P(B)$$

Formula used:

$$P(A) + P(B) + P(C) = 1$$

For mutually exclusive events A,B and C, $P(A \text{ and } B) = P(B \text{ and } C) = P(A \text{ and } C) = 0$

Let $P(A) = x$

$$P(B) = \left(\frac{3}{2}\right)x \text{ and } P(C) = \left(\frac{1}{2}\right) = \left(\frac{3}{2}\right)x = \left(\frac{3}{2}\right)x(x)$$

$$x + \frac{3}{2}x + \frac{3}{4}x = 1$$

$$x = \frac{4}{13}$$

$$P(A) = \frac{4}{13}$$

Hence, the correct option is (D).

61. According to the data:

$$\sin\beta = \frac{(2\sin\alpha\cos\alpha)}{(\sin\alpha+\cos\alpha)}$$

$$= \frac{\sin2\alpha}{\sqrt{2}\left(\frac{1}{\sqrt{2}}\sin\alpha+\frac{1}{\sqrt{2}}\cos\alpha\right)}$$

$$\sqrt{2}\sin\left(\alpha+\frac{\pi}{4}\right)\sin\beta = \sin2\alpha$$

$$= \sin\theta = \frac{\sin\alpha+\cos\alpha}{2}$$

$$= \sin\theta = \frac{\sqrt{2}}{2}\times\left(\frac{1}{\sqrt{2}}\sin\alpha+\frac{1}{\sqrt{2}}\cos\alpha\right)$$

$$\sqrt{2}\sin\theta = \cos\left(\alpha-\frac{\pi}{4}\right)$$

Hence, the correct option is (C).

62. The first and the last 2-digit number which leaves 2 as the remainder when divided by 3 are 11 and 98. Let there are n number between 11 and 98 which leaves 2 as the remainder when divided by 3.

Then $11 + (n-1)3 = 98$

or, $(n-1)3 = 87$

or, $n = 30$

$\therefore$ the sum of all these numbers $= \frac{30}{2}(11 + 98) =$

$15 \times 109 = 1635$

Hence, the correct option is (C).

63. Coefficients X^7 and X^8

Formula: $t_r + 1 = \binom{n}{r}a^{n-r}b^r$

Here, $a = 2, b = \frac{X}{3}$

We have, $t_{r+1} = \binom{n}{r}a^{n-r}b^r$

Therefore, $t_{r+1} = \binom{n}{r}(2)^{n-r}\left(\frac{X}{3}\right)^r$

$$= \binom{n}{r}\frac{2^{n-r}}{3^r}X^r$$

To get a coefficient of X^7, we must have,

$X^7 = X^r$

$r = 7$

Therefore, the coefficients $X^7 = \binom{n}{7}\frac{2^{n-7}}{3^7}$

And To get a coefficient of X^8, we must have,

$X^8 = X^r$

$r = 8$

Therefore, the coefficients $X^8 = \binom{n}{8}\frac{2^{n-8}}{3^8}$

Conclusion:

The coefficients $X^7 = \binom{n}{7}\frac{2^{n-7}}{3^7}$

The coefficients $X^8 = \binom{n}{8}\frac{2^{n-8}}{3^8}$

Hence, the correct option is (A).

64. Here, $n = 8, p = 0.6, q = 0.4$.

Suppose $X =$ number of hits, $x_0 = 0$ number of hits, $x_1 = 1$ hit, $x_2 = 2$ hits, and so on.

So, $(X) = P(x_5) + P(x_6) + P(x_7) + P(x_8) = {}^8C_5(0.6)^5(0.4)^3 +$

$${}^8C_5(0.6)^6(0.4)^2 + {}^8C_7(0.6)^7(0.4)^1 + {}^8C_8(0.6)^8(0.4)^0$$

$$= 0.5938$$

Hence, the correct option is (C).

65. By using Binomial theorem,

The expression $(y+1)^4 - (y-1)^4$ can be expanded as

$$= (y+1)^4 = {}^4C_0y^4 +$$

$${}^4C_1y^3 + {}^4C_2y^2 + {}^4C_3y^1 + {}^4C_4y^0$$

and,

$$(y-1)^4 = {}^4C_0y^4 - {}^4C_1y^3 +$$

$${}^4C_2y^2 - {}^4C_3y^1 + {}^4C_4y^0$$

Now,

$$(y+1)^4 - (y-1)^4$$

$$= \left({}^4C_0y^4 + {}^4C_1y^3 + {}^4C_2y^2 + {}^4C_3y^1 + {}^4C_4y^0\right) - \left({}^4C_0y^4 - {}^4C_1y^3 + {}^4C_2y^2 - {}^4C_3y^1 + {}^4C_4y^0\right)$$

$$= 2({}^4C_1y^3 + {}^4C_3y^1)$$

$$= 8(y^3 + y^1)$$

Hence, the correct option is (C).

66. Given,

$$\Sigma(n = 2 \text{ to } 11)(i^n + i^{n+1})$$
$$\Sigma(n = 2 to 11)i^n(i+1)$$
$$\Rightarrow i + 1(i^2 + i^3 + \cdots \ldots \ldots .. + i^{11})$$
$$\Rightarrow (i+1)(-1-i)$$
$$\Rightarrow -2i$$

Hence, the correct option is (C).

67. According to the formula:

$$\cos(x+y) = \cos x\cos y - \sin x\sin y$$

$$\cos(x-y) = \cos x\cos y + \sin x\sin y$$

We get,

$\cos 75°$

$= \cos(45° + 30°)$

$= \cos 45° \cos 30° - \sin 45° \sin 30°$

$= \frac{1}{\sqrt{2}} \times \frac{\sqrt{3}}{2} - \frac{1}{\sqrt{2}} \times \frac{1}{2}$

$= \frac{\sqrt{3}-1}{2\sqrt{2}}$

Hence, the correct option is (A).

68. Given,

$= \int_0^{\frac{\pi}{4}} \sqrt{\tan x}\, dx + \int_0^{\frac{\pi}{4}} \sqrt{\cot x}\, dx$

$= \int_0^{\frac{\pi}{4}} (\sqrt{\tan x} + \sqrt{\cot x})\, dx$

$= \int_0^{\frac{\pi}{4}} \frac{(\sin x + \cos x)}{\sqrt{\sin x} + \sqrt{\cos x}}\, dx$

$= \sqrt{2} \int_0^{\frac{\pi}{4}} \frac{(\sin x + \cos x)}{\sqrt{1-(\sin^2 x + \cos^2 x - 2\sin x \cos x)}}\, dx$

$=$ Put $\sin x - \cos x = t;\ (\cos x + \sin x)dx = dt$

$=$ When $x = 0, t = -1$ and $x = \frac{\pi}{4}, t = 0$

$= \sqrt{2}[\sin^{-1}(0) - \sin^{-1}(-1)]$

$= \sqrt{2}\left[0 - \left(-\frac{\pi}{2}\right)\right] = \frac{\pi}{\sqrt{2}}$

Hence, the correct option is (D).

69. According to the formula:

$a^2 - b^2 = (a-b)(a+b)$

$\cos^2 x + \sin^2 x = 1$

$\cos 2x = \cos^2 x - \sin^2 x = 2\cos^2 x - 1 = 1 - 2\sin^2 x$

We get,

$\cos^4 x - \sin^4 x$

$\Rightarrow (\cos^2 x - \sin^2 x)(\cos^2 x + \sin^2 x)$
$(\because a^2 - b^2 = (a-b)(a+b))$

$\Rightarrow \cos 2x \times 1 \quad (\because \cos^2 x + \sin^2 x = 1)$

$\Rightarrow \cos 2x$

Hence, the correct option is (B).

70. Given,

$i^{1000} + i^{1001} + i^{1002} + i^{1003}$

$i^2 = -1$

$\Rightarrow i^{1000} = (i^2)^{500} = (-1)^{500} = 1$

$\Rightarrow i^{1001} = i^{1000} \times i = i$

$\Rightarrow i^{1002} = i^{1000} \times i^2 = -1$

$\Rightarrow i^{1003} = i^{1002} \times i = -i$

So adding them all $-1 + 1 + i - i = 0$

Hence, the correct option is (A).

71. $= f(x) = \frac{x}{x}, x \neq 0$

$\therefore$ The graph is discontinous at $x = 0$, and correctly shown in option.

Hence, the correct option is (C).

72. Given,

$f(n) = \left[\frac{1}{4} + \frac{n}{1000}\right]$

$= \sum_{n=1}^{1000} f(n) = \left[\frac{1}{4} + \frac{1}{1000}\right] + \left[\frac{1}{4} + \frac{2}{1000}\right] + \cdots\cdots$
$\cdots\cdots + \left[\frac{1}{4} + \frac{1000}{1000}\right]$

We get $'0'$ for all values of n from 1 to 750.

From $n = 750$, we get all the values as 1

$$\sum_{n=1}^{1000} f(n) = 0 + 0 + \left[\frac{1}{4} + \frac{750}{1000}\right] + \left[\frac{1}{4} + \frac{751}{1000}\right]$$
$$0 + 0 + 0 + \cdots + \cdots\cdots\cdots\cdots + \left[\frac{1}{4} + 1\right]$$

$= 1 + 1 + 1 + 1 + \cdots\cdots(251 \text{ times})$

$= 251$

Hence, the correct option is (A).

73. For $x = 0^+$
$= \lim_{x\to 1} f(x) = \lim_{x\to 1} 2 + x = 2 + 1 = 3$
For $x = 0^-$
$= \lim_{x\to 1} f(x) = \lim_{x\to 1} 2 - x = 2 - 1 = 1$
So, Limit does not exist at $x = 1$
At $x = 0$
For $x = 0^+$
$= \lim_{x\to 0} f(x) = \lim_{x\to 1} 2 + 0 = 2$
For $x = 0^-$
$= \lim_{x\to 0} f(x) = \lim_{x\to 1} 2 - 0 = 2$
$F(x)$ is continuous at $x = 0$
Differentiability:
$= \lim_{h\to 0^-} \frac{f(0-h)-f(0)}{-h} = \lim_{h\to 0^-} \frac{2+h-2}{-h} = -\frac{h}{h} = -1$
$= \lim_{h\to 0^+} \frac{f(0+h)-f(0)}{h} = \lim_{h\to 0^+} \frac{2+h-2}{h} = 1$
$LHD \neq RHD$
So, $f(x)$ is not differentiable at $x = 0$

Hence, the correct option is (C).

74. Substitute the line equation into ellipse equation:

$$3x + 4y = 12; \quad x = \frac{12-4y}{3}$$

So, $9\left(\frac{12-4y}{3}\right)^2 + 16y^2 = 144$

On solving we get, $y = 0, 3$

For $y = 0; x = 4$

For $y = 3; x = 0$

Length of the chord $= \sqrt{(0-3)^2 + (4-0)^2} = \sqrt{9+16} = 5$ units

Hence, the correct option is (A).

75. Given circle is $x^2 + y^2 = a^2$

Therefore Radius $= a$ and centre $= (0,0)$

Now given that line $lx + my - 1 = 0$ is equal to radius a

Therefore, $\left|\frac{0+0-1}{\sqrt{l^2+m}}\right| = a$

$\Rightarrow l^2 + m^2 = \frac{1}{a^2}$

Thus, locus of (l, m, n) is $x^2 + y^2 = \frac{1}{a^2}$, which is a circle.

Hence, the correct option is (C).

76. The election was not held in Bihar during March-April 2021.

- Members of the Seventeenth Bihar Legislative Assembly were elected in three parts from October to November.
- The previous Bihar Sixteenth Legislative Assembly's tenure concluded on November 29, 2020.
- Following the elections, incumbent Chief Minister Nitish Kumar was re-sworn in as Chief Minister after being chosen as the leader of the National Democratic Alliance in Bihar, and two new deputy Chief Ministers, Tarkishore Prasad, and Renu Devi were recruited into the new administration.

Hence, the correct option is (B).

77. The first preventive detention bill of Independent India was moved in 1950 by Sardar Patel. Patel had said that he had several sleepless nights before deciding if it was necessary to introduce the bill. Consequently, the Preventive Detention Act, 1950 was enacted by the Parliament on 26th February 1950.

Hence, the correct option is (C).

78. South Africa, first time in the world, has granted a patent to an 'artificial intelligence system' relating to a "food container based on fractal geometry" innovation.

The innovation involves interlocking food containers that are easy for robots to grasp and stack.

Hence, the correct option is (B).

79. Meteor – also known as "shooting stars" are the light phenomena which results when a small meteoroid enters the Earth's atmosphere burns up as it passes through our atmosphere and vaporizes.

Meteoroid - are fragments of a comet or asteroid orbiting the Sun or interplanetary debris.

Meteorite – is a meteoroid that survives its fall through the atmosphere and lands on the Earth's surface.

Neutron Stars - are star that have mass between 1.35 and 2.1 times the mass of the Sun.

Hence, the correct option is (A).

80. The 63rd National Shooting Championship Competitions (NSCC) 2019 in Small Bore Rifle & Pistol events (including Para events) was held at Shooting Academy Shooting Ranges, **Bhopal**, Madhya Pradesh (MP) from 7th December 2019 – 4th January 2020.

Hence, the correct option is (D).

81.

- Former Indian women's hockey team captain and Arjuna awardee Sunita Chandra passed away.
- She had played for the Indian women's hockey team between 1956 to 1966 and served as skipper from 1963 to 1966.

Hence, the correct option is (C).

82.

- The Cripps Mission was sent to India in March 1942 by the British government to secure Indian cooperation and support for their efforts in World War II.
- The mission proposed for an Indian Union with 'Dominion Status'. The mission had also proposed that after the end of World War II, a Constituent Assembly would be convened to frame a new Constitution of India.
- The mission was rejected by Congress as the mission provided for no real transfer of power. Muslim League rejected the mission as it did not meet the demand for Pakistan sufficiently and preferred a scheme of United India.

Hence, the correct option is (D).

83. The Kharif crops include rice, maize, sorghum, pearl millet/bajra, finger millet/ragi (cereals), arhar (pulses), soyabean, groundnut (oilseeds), cotton etc. The rabi crops include wheat, barley, oats (cereals), chickpea/gram (pulses), linseed, mustard (oilseeds) etc.

Hence, the correct option is (D).

84. Indus Valley Civilisation was discovered when archaeologists began excavating the sites connected with it in the 1920s. The first sites to be excavated were Harappa and Mohenjo-Daro. That is why it is also called Harappa Civilisation.

At present, hundreds of sites of this culture are known. The most important cities:

- Harappa (Western Punjab),
- Mohenjo-Daro (Sindh),
- Lothal (Gujarat),

- Kalibangan (Rajasthan),
- Ropar (Punjab),
- Banawali and Rakhigarhi (Haryana), and
- Dholavira (Gujarat).

Hence, the correct option is (D).

85. The 73rd amendment act of 1992 provides for the reservation of seats for Scheduled Castes and Scheduled Tribes in every Panchayat in proportion of their population to the total population in the panchayat area.

The act also provides for the reservation of not less than one-third of the total number of seats for women (including the number of seats reserved for women belonging the SCs and STs).

Hence, the correct option is (D).

86. The Second Battle of Panipat was fought between the forces of Samrat Hem Chandra Vikramaditya, popularly called Hemu, the Hindu king who was ruling North India from Delhi, and the army of Akbar, on November 5, 1556. It was a decisive victory for Akbar's generals Khan Zaman I and Bairam Khan.

Hence, the correct option is (D).

87.

- Article 371-A makes the special provisions for Nagaland. Article 371-B makes the special provisions for Assam. Article 371-C makes the special provisions for Manipur. Article 371-D makes the special provisions for Andhra Pradesh and Telangana.

- Articles 371 to 371-J in Part XXI of the Constitution contain special provisions for twelve states1 viz., Maharashtra, Gujarat, Nagaland, Assam, Manipur, Andhra Pradesh, Telangana, Sikkim, Mizoram, Arunachal Pradesh, Goa and Karnataka.

Hence, the correct option is (A).

88. Al- Hilal was a journal that was brought out by Maulana Abdul Kalam Azad.

Sisir Ghosh and Moti Lal Ghosh started Amrita Bazar Patrika as a weekly first.

The Indian Sociologist journal was edited by Shyamji Krishnavarma from 1905 to 1914, and then between 1920 and 1922.

Hence, the correct option is (A).

89. Article 46 provides for the Gandhian Directive Principles, which provides for the promotion of the educational and economic interests of SCs, STs, and other weaker sections of the society.

Hence, the correct option is (B).

90.

- The country's first Super Fab Lab was launched at the Integrated Startup Complex of the Kerala Startup Mission (KSUM).

- The lab will give a major push to the hardware industry in the country and the only such facility outside the U.S.

- The Super Fab Lab will function in collaboration with the Massachusetts Institute of Technology (MIT).

Hence, the correct option is (D).

91. The Rockies are in North America; the Andes are in South America and Drakensburg is in South Africa, as shown in the figure below:

Hence, the correct option is (C).

92.

- Coral reefs are one of the most productive and complex coastal ecosystems with high biological diversity; hence they are referred to as 'the Tropical Rainforests of the Oceans'.

- Coral reefs in India are found in A&N islands, Gulf of Kutch, Gulf of Mannar, and Lakshadweep

- Coral reefs don't form in areas where there is a significant intrusion of freshwater and cold water. Most of the mighty Indian Rivers flow into the Bay of Bengal and hence coral reefs are absent on the east coast of India.

Hence, the correct option is (B).

93.

- The Chenab is the largest tributary of the Indus. It is formed by two streams, the Chandra and the Bhaga, which join at Tandi near Keylong in Himachal Pradesh. Hence, it is also known as Chandrabhaga.

- The Ravi rises west of the Rohtang pass in the Kullu hills of Himachal Pradesh and flows through the Chamba valley of the state. Before entering Pakistan and joining the Chenab near Sarai Sidhu, it drains the area lying between the southeastern part of the Pir Panjal and the Dhauladhar ranges.

- The Beas originates from the Beas Kund near the Rohtang Pass at an elevation of 4,000 m above the mean sea level. The river flows through the Kullu valley and forms gorges at Kati and Largi in the Dhaoladhar range. It enters the Punjab plains where it meets the Satluj near Harike.

- The Satluj originates in the Rakas lake near Mansarovar at an altitude of 4,555 m in Tibet where it is known as Langchen Khambab. It flows almost parallel to the Indus for about 400 km before entering India and comes out of a gorge at Rupar. It passes through the Shipki La on the Himalayan ranges and enters the Punjab plains.

Hence, the correct option is (D).

94.

- Two youth leaders from Bihar Kanhaiya Kumar and Prashant Kishor included in the Forbes India list of 20 people to watch in the 2020s.

- Poll strategist Prashant Kishor is Janata Dal (United) National Vice President while Kanhaiya Kumar is former President of Jawaharlal Nehru University Students Union.

Hence, the correct option is (B).

95.

- Prarthana Samaj was founded by Atmaram Pandurang in 1867 when Keshab Chandra Sen visited Maharashtra. Prarthana Samaj became popular after Mahadev Govind Ranade joined it.

- It sought to remove caste restrictions, abolish child marriage, the shaving of widows' heads, the heavy cost of marriages and other social functions, encourage the education of women and promote widow remarriage.

- Like Brahmo Samaj, it advocated the worship of one God. It condemned idolatry and the domination of the priestly castes in religious matters.

Hence, the correct option is (A).

96. Metamorphic rocks are formed when igneous or sedimentary rocks undergo high temperature and pressure. Some of the important metamorphic rocks are their parent rocks are given below in the table:

Parent Rock and its Metamorphic changed form:

NAME OF THE ROCK	TYPE OF ROCK	NAME OF THE METAMORPHIC ROCK
Limestone	Sedimentary Rock	Marble
Dolomite	Sedimentary Rock	Marble
Shale	Sedimentary Rock	Slate
Granite	Igneous Rock	Gneiss

Hence, the correct option is (D).

97. This belt of Doldrums extends from the equator to $10°$ N and $10°$ S latitudes. Due to excessive heating, the horizontal movement of air is absent here, and only conventional currents are there. Therefore this belt is called doldrums (the zone of calm) due to the virtual absence of surface winds. These are the regions of convergence because the winds flowing from subtropical high-pressure belts converge here. This belt is also known as as-Inter Tropical Convergence Zone (ITCZ).

Hence, the correct option is (A).

98. The Five Rathas or Panch Rathas are five monolithic temple structures built by the Pallavas in early 7th century AD. Situated in a common complex to west of the Shore temple in Mahabalipuram, the Panch Rathas display exquisite carvings carved out from a single large boulder.

Hence, the correct option is (A).

99. Only 100 years after Lord Buddha's nirvana, differences among the Buddhists started to emerge. In the second Buddhist musical of Vaishali, Ther monks expelled the monks, who kept the differences out of the Union. Divided these monks, at the same time, they formed their own separate union and called themselves 'Mahasanghika' and those who had taken them the name 'inferior', which, in the end, took the form of Mahayana and Hinayana.

Hence, the correct option is (C).

100. The Rig Veda mentions 40 rivers in early Vedic period The Nadisukta hymn consists of 21 rivers mentioning Ganges in East and Kubha in West. According to Rig Veda Saraswati is the most pious river and the most mentioned river is Sindhu. Also, Ganga was mentioned 1 time and Yamuna 3 times in Rig Veda.

Hence, the correct option is (B).

Sectional Test 01

Q.1 Choose the correct sentence from the following.

A. Her picture was seen by all of us.

B. Her picture seen by all of us.

C. Her picture was seen all of us.

D. Her picture seen was by all of us.

Q.2 Choose the option that best punctuates the given sentence:

Could I have a five-kilo pack of rice said the customer

A. "Could I have a five kilo, pack of rice ?"said the customer.

B. "Could I have a five kilo pack of rice, said the customer."

C. "Could I have a five kilo pack of rice said the customer."

D. "Could I have a five kilo pack of rice?" said the customer.

Q.3 Choose the correct form of tense for the given sentence:

He _____ to a well-to-do family and has an expensive motorbike.

A. belongs

B. is belonging

C. was belonging

D. has been belonging

Q.4 Choose the appropriate prepositional phrase to complete the given sentence.

India won the match _______.

A. at ease

B. with ease

C. of ease

D. by ease

Q.5 Choose the correct form of modal auxiliary verb for the given sentence:

I wonder why she ignored me when we met in the hallway. Do you think she _____ have not recognized me?

A. should   **B.** might   **C.** can   **D.** will

Q.6 A sentence has been given in Active/Passive Voice. Out of the four alternatives suggested, select the one which best expresses the same sentence in Passive/Active Voice.

Let the apples be brought for me from the market.

A. I should be brought apples from the market.

B. You should bring for me apples from the market.

C. Bring apples for me from the market.

D. Let us bring me apples from the market.

Q.7 Choose the correct option:

If it _______, the dance recital will be cancelled.

A. rains

B. raining

C. will rain

D. was raining

Q.8 In the following question, a sentence is given in Direct/Indirect speech. Out of the four alternatives choose the one which best expresses the sentence in Indirect/Direct Speech.

The teacher asked Jamal if he had finished writing.

A. The teacher said to Jamal, "Had he finished writing?"

B. The teacher said to Jamal, "Had you finished writing?"

C. The teacher said to Jamal, "Have you finished writing?"

D. The teacher said to Jamal, "Did you finish writing?"

Q.9 In the following question, a sentence is given in Direct/Indirect speech. Out of the four alternatives choose the one which best expresses the sentence in Indirect/Direct Speech.

"Call the second witness." said the judge.

A. The judge ordered them to call the second witness.

B. The judge orders them to call the second witness.

C. The judge requested them to call the second witness.

D. None of the above

Q.10 Choose which part of speech is the underlined word.

I came across him at the shopping mall.

A. Pronoun

B. Noun

C. Preposition

D. Verb

Q.11 A sentence has been given in Active/Passive voice. Out of the four alternatives suggested, select the one which best expresses the same sentence in Passive/Active voice.

They have painted the door.

A. The door was painted.

B. The door has been painted.

C. The door is painted.

D. The door be painted.

Q.12 A sentence has been given in Active/Passive voice. Out of the four alternatives suggested, select the one which best expresses the same sentence in Passive/Active voice.

I keep the butter in the fridge.

A. The fridge was kept with butter by me.

B. The butter was in the fridge.

C. The butter is kept in the fridge.

D. I kept the butter.

Q.13 In the following question, out of the given four alternatives, select the one which is opposite in meaning of the given word.

Unfair

A. Prejudice

B. Dishonest

C. Crooked

D. Just

Q.14 In the following question, out of the given four alternatives, select the one which best expresses the meaning of the given word.

Creep

A. Tiptoe   **B.** Public   **C.** Frank   **D.** Open

Q.15 In the following question, out of the given four alternatives, select the one which best expresses the meaning of the given word.

Convict

A. Casualty   **B.** Victim   **C.** Innocent   **D.** Culprit

Q.16 A sentence has been given in Active/Passive voice. Out of the four given alternatives, select the one which best expresses the same sentence in Passive/Active voice.

Was Daksh writing the homework?

A. Is the homework written by Daksh?

B. Had Daksh written the homework?

C. Was the homework being written by Daksh?

D. Has Daksh written the homework?

Q.17 In the following question, out of the four alternatives, select the word similar in meaning to the given word.

Mighty

A. Gigantic   **B.** Respectable

C. Fearful   **D.** Puny

Q.18 Choose the synonym for the given word:

ELEMENT

A. Prime   **B.** Component

C. Particle   **D.** Persons

Q.19 Select the most appropriate ANTONYM of the given word

IMPRISON

A. Occupy   **B.** Compensate

C. Enslave   **D.** Release

Q.20 In each of the following items, choose the opposite in meaning to the given word.

Enough

A. Less   **B.** Inadequate

C. Scarce   **D.** Deficit

Ques (21-24):Direction: Read the following passage carefully and choose the most appropriate answer to the question out of the four alternatives.

The Mahabodhi Temple is a Buddhist temple in Bodh Gaya, Bihar. Lord Buddha is said to have attained enlightenment at Bodh Gaya. About 200 years after Lord Buddha attained enlightenment, Emperor Ashoka visited Bodh Gaya with the intention of establishing a monastery and shrine. As part of the temple, he built the diamond throne (called the Vajrasana), attempting to mark the exact spot of the Buddha's enlightenment. Ashoka is considered the founder of the Mahabodhi Temple.

Q.21 What material is used in building the Vajrasana?

A. Diamonds   **B.** Bronze

C. Gold   **D.** Silver

Q.22 Where is Mahabodhi temple located?

A. Bodh Gaya   **B.** Jaipur

C. Delhi   **D.** Raipur

Q.23 Who was considered to be the founder of Mahabodhi temple?

A. Ashoka

B. Jhansi Rani

C. King Pratap Varma

D. Sri Krishna Devarayala

Q.24 After how many years of the enlightenment of Lord Buddha did Ashok visit Bodh Gaya?

A. 200 years   **B.** 400 years

C. 500 years   **D.** 300 years

Q.25 Choose the correctly punctuated sentence.

A. Reba; please come here.

B. Reba, please come here.

C. Reba. please come here.

D. Reba! please come here.

// Smart Answer Sheet //

Correct — Percentage of students who answered correctly. **Skipped** — Percentage of students who skipped.

Q.	Ans.	Correct / Skipped	Q.	Ans.	Correct / Skipped	Q.	Ans.	Correct / Skipped	Q.	Ans.	Correct / Skipped	Q.	Ans.	Correct / Skipped	Q.	Ans.	Correct / Skipped
1	A	34.2 % / 9.28 %	6	C	23.03 % / 13.28 %	11	B	13.75 % / 46.53 %	16	C	38.66 % / 19.86 %	21	A	49.0 % / 23.97 %			
2	D	24.44 % / 22.33 %	7	A	24.68 % / 14.22 %	12	C	18.8 % / 47.36 %	17	A	16.1 % / 35.84 %	22	A	45.59 % / 26.21 %			
3	A	10.46 % / 10.22 %	8	C	37.25 % / 15.86 %	13	D	24.32 % / 48.54 %	18	B	20.21 % / 28.32 %	23	A	29.38 % / 34.19 %			
4	B	43.13 % / 15.27 %	9	A	43.36 % / 18.1 %	14	A	19.51 % / 49.7 %	19	D	16.69 % / 45.12 %	24	D	17.39 % / 19.39 %			
5	B	45.83 % / 12.1 %	10	C	15.39 % / 45.48 %	15	D	31.61 % / 18.33 %	20	A	39.72 % / 22.09 %	25	B	24.32 % / 29.38 %			

//Hints and Solutions//

1. Her picture was seen by all of us.

Option (B) is incorrect. An auxiliary verb should be written before the verb 'seen'. Therefore, 'was' should be written here because the sentence is in the simple past tense.

Option (C) is incorrect. The preposition 'by' should be added before 'all'.

Option (D) is incorrect. The auxiliary verb 'was' should be written before the verb3 (seen).

Hence, the correct option is (A).

2. "Could I have a five kilo pack of rice?" said the customer.

Let's have a look at the given formations of sentences:

- Since the given sentence is in indirect speech, the sentence will commence with inverted commas.
- An inverted form of the verb will now be used as the sentence is an interrogative one.
- Now the rest of the sentence will follow, ending with a question mark.
- As soon as the additional information ends, we need to close it with another set of inverted commas.
- Now the rest of the sentence will follow ending with a full stop.

Hence, the correct option is (D).

3. He **belongs** to a well-to-do family and has an expensive motorbike.

The simple present tense is used when an action is happening right now, or when it happens regularly or unceasingly.

- For example:
  - He plays badminton daily.
- In the given blank part of the sentence, we need a present participle of the given verb as the verb used for showing possession or belongingness, is always used in present participle form.

Hence, the correct option is (A).

4. India won the match **with ease**.

- The phrase 'with ease' refers to something without difficulty or done easily.
- In this case, using with ease refers to India winning the match easily.

Hence, the correct option is (B).

5. I wonder why she ignored me when we met in the hallway. Do you think she **might** have not recognized me?

- Might is a modal verb most commonly used to express possibility.
- Should is used to indicate obligation, duty, or correctness, typically when criticizing someone's actions.

- The phrase 'can have not' is incorrect.
- Will is used to talk about future.

Hence, the correct option is (B).

6. Bring apples for me from the market.

The sentence is in the passive voice. Whenever 'let' is used in the sentence, we can be certain that the active voice must be an imperative sentence.

Now, look closely at the sentence. The sentence does not use 'requested', which means it is not a request but an order. So, the sentence becomes,

Simple present tense verb (imperative) 'bring'+ the object 'apples'+ the phrase 'for me from the market'.

Hence, the correct option is (C).

7. If it **rains**, the dance recital will be cancelled.

The given is a type 1 conditional sentence. Therefore, in the if clause 'simple present tense' must be used.

A conditional sentence expresses an imaginary or hypothetical situation and its consequence. Example: If you give your best you will be successful.

Hence, the correct option is (A).

8. The teacher said to Jamal, "Have you finished writing?"

The given sentence is in Indirect Speech and needs to be converted to Direct Speech.

There are several rules for doing the same:

1. It is important to use the correct tense of the reporting verb (asked).

2. The conjunctions 'that, to, if, whether' must be removed.

3. Quotation marks, question marks, exclamation marks and full stop must be inserted wherever necessary.

4. A comma must be inserted before the statement.

5. The order of words must be carefully looked at.

6. Pay attention to the correct conjugation of the verbs in the given statement.

7. The perspective must be changed from 'he' to 'you'.

Hence, the correct option is (C).

9. The judge ordered them to call the second witness.

Direct speech describes when something is being repeated exactly as it was, usually in between a pair of inverted commas. Indirect speech is a report on what someone else said or wrote without using that person's exact words.

The sentence here is in direct speech, we have to convert it into indirect speech.

Hence, the correct option is (A).

10. The underlined word 'across' which is used to express position or orientation. So, it is a preposition.

Hence, the correct option is (C).

11. The door has been painted.

- The given is a declarative sentence and written in present perfect tense.

The construction of the given sentence:

They	have	painted	the door.
Subject	has/have	verb3	object

- The object of the given sentence becomes the subject(subject1) of the passive voice.

The construction of the sentence in passive voice should be:

The door	has	been	painted.
Subject1	has/have	been	verb3

Hence, the correct option is (B).

12. The butter is kept in the fridge.

When changing from active to passive voice, the object of the active sentence becomes the subject of the passive sentence and the subject of the active sentence becomes the object of the passive sentence (or is dropped).

We follow the order "Subject + helping verb+ past participle+ by+ agent.

Here the verb is 'keep' whose past participle is 'kept'.

Hence, the correct option is (C).

13. The opposite of unfair is just.

- Unfair: Unjust; not based on the principles of equality and justice.

- Just: Based on or behaving according to what is morally right and fair.

- Prejudice: Preconceived opinion that is not based on reason or actual experience.

- Dishonest: Behaving or prone to behave in an untrustworthy, deceitful or insincere way.

- Crooked: Bent or twisted out of shape; dishonest or illegal.

Hence, the correct option is (D).

14. The meaning of creep is tiptoe.

- Creep: Move slowly and carefully in order to avoid being heard or noticed.

- Tiptoe: Walk quietly and carefully with one's heels raised and one's weight on the balls of the feet.

- Public: Of or concerning the people as a whole.

- Frank: Open, honest or direct in speech or writing.

- Open: Allow access, not closed or blocked.

Hence, the correct option is (A).

15. The meaning of convict is culprit.

- Convict: A person found guilty of a criminal offence.

- Culprit: A person who is responsible for a crime or misdeed.

- Casualty: A person killed or injured in a war or an accident.

- Victim: A person harmed, injured or killed as a result of a crime, accident or any other action.

- Innocent: Not guilty of a crime or an offence.

Hence, the correct option is (D).

16. Was the homework being written by Daksh?

The given sentence is in the Active voice, therefore, it has to be changed to the Passive voice, where something was done by the subject, and it was 'passive'.

Example: Was Daksh writing the homework? (Active Voice) (Here 'Daksh' is subject, 'written' is a verb and 'the homework' is an object.)

While changing the sentence into passive, this structure becomes.

Was/were + subject + being + V3 + by + agent ? (Passive Voice).

Hence, the correct option is (C).

17. The meaning of mighty is gigantic.

Mighty means possessing great and impressive power or strength, especially because of size.

- Gigantic means of very great size or extent; huge or enormous.

- Respectable means regarded by society to be good, proper, or correct.

- Fearful means feeling or showing fear or anxiety.

- Puny means small and weak.

Hence, the correct option is (A).

18. The synonym of element is component.

Element means an essential or characteristic part of something abstract.

- Component means a part or element of a larger whole, especially a part of a machine or vehicle.

- Prime means of first importance; main.

- Particle means a minute portion of matter.

- Person means a human being regarded as an individual.

Hence, the correct option is (B).

19. The antonym of imprison is release.

- The word 'Imprison' means to put or keep someone or something in prison or a place like a prison.

- The word 'Release' means to allow or enable someone or something to escape from confinement; set free.

Hence, the correct option is (D).

20. The opposite of enough is less.

- Enough: As much as required.

- Less: A smaller amount; not as much.
- Inadequate: Lacking the quality or the quantity required.
- Scarce: Insufficient for the demand.
- Deficit: The amount by which something, especially a sum of money, is too small.

Hence, the correct option is (A).

21. Diamonds are used in building the Vajrasana.

The following is mentioned in the passage:

"As part of the temple, he built the diamond throne (called the Vajrasana), attempting to mark the exact spot of the Buddha's enlightenment."

Hence, the correct option is (A).

22. The Mahabodhi temple is located in Bodh Gaya.

The following is mentioned in the passage:

"The Mahabodhi Temple is a Buddhist temple in Bodh Gaya, Bihar."

Hence, the correct option is (A).

23. Ashoka was considered to be the founder of Mahabodhi temple.

The following is mentioned in the passage:

"Ashoka is considered the founder of the Mahabodhi Temple."

Hence, the correct option is (A).

24. Ashok visited Bodh Gaya 200 years after the enlightenment of Lord Buddha.

The following is mentioned in the passage:

"About 200 years after Lord Buddha attained enlightenment, Emperor Ashoka visited Bodh Gaya with the intention of establishing a monastery and shrine."

Hence, the correct option is (D).

25. Reba, please come here.

- Option (A) is incorrect. The semicolon is used to join two complete sentences or independent clauses. Example: Your mother looks worried; she has checked your report card.
- Option (C) is incorrect. The full stop is used at the end of a sentence. Example: It is a paper.
- Option (D) is incorrect. The exclamation mark is used to express wonder, surprise or to emphasize. Example: I have found the lost photo album!

Hence, the correct option is (B).

Ques (1-5):Direction: Read the following passage and answer the question that follows.

At this stage of civilization, when many nations are brought in to close and vital contact for good and evil, it is essential, as never before, that their gross ignorance of one another should be diminished, that they should begin to understand a little of one another's historical experience and resulting mentality. It is the fault of the English to expect the people of other countries to react as they do, to political and international situations. Our genuine goodwill and good intentions are often brought to nothing because we expect other people to be like us. This would be corrected if we knew the history, not necessarily in detail but in broad outlines, of the social and political conditions which have given to each nation its present character.

Q.1 According to the author 'Mentality' of a nation is mainly product of its:

A. Present character

B. International position

C. Politics

D. History

Q.2 The character of a nation is the result of its:

A. Gross ignorance

B. Cultural heritage

C. Socio-political conditons

D. Mentality

Q.3 The need for a greater understanding between nations:

A. Is more today than ever before

B. Was always there

C. Is no longer there

D. Will always be there

Q.4 Englishmen like others to react to political situations like:

A. Others   **B.** Us

C. Themselves   **D.** Each others

Q.5 According to the author his countrymen should:

A. Read the story of other nations

B. Have a better understanding of other nations

C. Not react to other actions

D. Have vital contact with other nations

Q.6 Direction: Choose the antonym for the given word.

Rapport

A. Unfriendliness   **B.** Unrapport

C. Disrapport   **D.** Unbehaviour

Q.7 Direction: Choose the synonym for the given word.

Scorn

A. Disallow   **B.** Disdain

C. Highlight   **D.** Willful

Q.8 Choose the correct sentence from the following.

A. There going to help us?

B. The're going to help us.

C. Is they go to help us?

D. Are they going to help us?

Q.9 Direction: Choose the most appropriate preposition to complete the sentence.

The man is an important element _________ the environment.

A. to   **B.** in   **C.** over   **D.** of

Q.10 Choose the correctly punctuated sentence.

A. Sir. I would like you to grant me leave.

B. Sir; I would like you to grant me leave.

C. Sir! I would like you to grant me leave.

D. Sir, I would like you to grant me leave.

Q.11 Direction: Change Active to Passive Voice or vice - versa as the case may be.

The boy expected the ball.

A. The ball is expected by the boy.

B. The ball had been expected by the boy.

C. The ball has been expected by the boy.

D. The ball was expected by the boy.

Q.12 Direction: Change Active to Passive Voice or vice - versa as the case may be.

Peter was opening the window.

A. The window was opened by Peter.

B. The window was being opened by Peter.

C. The window is being opened by Peter.

D. The window has been opened by Peter.

Q.13 Direction: Change Direct to Indirect Speech or vice-versa as the case may be.

The man said, "No, I refuse to confess guilt."

A. The man was stubborn enough to confess guilt.

B. The man refused to confess his guilt.

C. The man emphatically refused to confess guilt.

D. The man told that he confesses guilt.

Q.14 Direction: Change Direct to Indirect Speech or vice - versa as the case may be.

The Prime Minister said that no one would be allowed to disturb the peace.

A. The Prime Minister said, "We will not allow anyone to disturb the peace."

B. The Prime Minister said, "No one can disturb the peace."

C. The Prime Minister said, "We would not allow no one to disturb the peace."

D. The Prime Minister said, "No one will disturb the peace."

Q.15 Direction: Choose the most appropriate preposition to complete the sentence.

Susan watched a movie at the theatre _________ a friend.

A. of   **B.** on   **C.** in   **D.** with

Q.16 Direction: Choose the most appropriate preposition to complete the sentence.

He had been in prison _______ 2 years at the time when he was still interested in cards.

A. at   **B.** in   **C.** since   **D.** for

Q.17 Direction: Choose the most appropriate form of verb/tense to complete the sentence.

After he _________ painting, he had a shower.

A. finished   **B.** had finished
C. has finished   **D.** finish

Q.18 Direction: Choose the most appropriate form of verb/tense to complete the sentence.

Anil was stopped by the police because he ________ fast.

A. was driving   **B.** has drive
C. drive   **D.** has driven

Q.19 Direction: Choose the adjective in the given sentence.

Kolkata is one of the liveliest cities in the world.

A. world   **B.** one   **C.** liveliest   **D.** city

Q.20 Direction: Choose the pronoun in the given sentence.

Pray, do not inconvenience yourself.

A. do   **B.** yourself   **C.** not   **D.** pray

Q.21 Direction: Choose the pronoun in the given sentence.

Only you are allowed to attend the party.

A. Only   **B.** You   **C.** To   **D.** Attend

Q.22 Choose the correctly punctuated sentence.

A.   Apples, Mangoes, and Bananas are my favourites.
B.   Apples, Mangoes and Bananas are my favourites.
C.   Apples, Mangoes, and Bananas, are my favourites.
D.   Apples, Mangoes and Bananas, are my favourites.

Q.23 Choose the correct sentence from the following.

A.   If the world ended tomorrow, I will be very sad.
B.   If the world ended tomorrow, I am very sad.
C.   If the world ended tomorrow, I was very sad.
D.   If the world ended tomorrow, I would be very sad.

Q.24 Direction: Fill in the blank with the correct pronoun.

Ram, ____ is a postman, is my friend.

A. which   **B.** who   **C.** whose   **D.** whom

Q.25 Direction: Select the correct adjective from the given options.

It is important that you select the team in a/an _______ way.

A. convenient   **B.** absolute
C. challenging   **D.** fair

// Smart Answer Sheet //

Correct Percentage of students who answered correctly.   **Skipped** Percentage of students who skipped.

Q.	Ans.	Correct / Skipped	Q.	Ans.	Correct / Skipped	Q.	Ans.	Correct / Skipped	Q.	Ans.	Correct / Skipped	Q.	Ans.	Correct / Skipped	Q.	Ans.	Correct / Skipped
1	D	22.86 % / 54.28 %	6	A	17.14 % / 62.86 %	11	D	14.29 % / 60.0 %	16	D	5.71 % / 91.43 %	21	B	8.57 % / 91.43 %			
2	C	31.43 % / 54.28 %	7	B	17.14 % / 60.0 %	12	B	17.14 % / 37.15 %	17	B	2.86 % / 91.43 %	22	B	5.71 % / 91.43 %			
3	A	8.57 % / 60.0 %	8	D	20.0 % / 34.29 %	13	B	31.43 % / 51.43 %	18	A	8.57 % / 91.43 %	23	D	8.57 % / 91.43 %			
4	C	11.43 % / 62.86 %	9	D	37.14 % / 31.43 %	14	A	17.14 % / 42.86 %	19	C	8.57 % / 91.43 %	24	B	8.57 % / 91.43 %			
5	B	14.29 % / 65.71 %	10	D	20.0 % / 65.71 %	15	D	17.14 % / 54.29 %	20	B	8.57 % / 91.43 %	25	D	2.86 % / 91.43 %			

//Hints and Solutions//

1. According to the passage, 'they should begin to understand a little of one another's historical experience and resulting mentality' which means that the **countries should start understanding one another's history** which results in the mentality of a country.

Hence, the correct option is (D).

2. According to the passage, "This would be corrected if we knew the history, not necessarily in detail but in broad outlines, of the social and political conditions which have given to each nation its present character" which clearly indicates that **the character of a nation is the result of its social and political conditions.**

Hence, the correct option is (C).

3. According to the passage, "At this stage of civilization, when many nations are brought in to close and vital contact for good and evil', it is essential, as never before, that their gross ignorance of one another should be diminished, that they should begin to understand a little of one another's historical experience and resulting mentality" which means that **at this stage of civilization, there is a need for a great understanding between the nations and it is more today than ever before.**

Hence, the correct option is (A).

4. According to the passage, 'It is the fault of the English to expect the people of other countries to react as they do, to political and international situations' which indicates that **Englishmen like others to react to political and international situations like themselves.**

Hence, the correct option is (C).

5. According to the passage, at this stage of civilization when nations are getting close, the author wants his countrymen to get a better understanding of other nations. The **ignorance between them should decline and they should gain an understanding of each other's historic experiences.**

Hence, the correct option is (B).

6. Rapport means a close and harmonious relationship in which the people or groups concerned understand each other's feelings or ideas and communicate well.

For example, He had a good rapport with his students.

Unfriendliness means the quality or state of not being friendly.

For example, His unfriendliness with us grew with time.

The words unrapport, disrapport, and unbehaviour are incorrect.

It is clear from the example that unfriendliness is the antonym for rapport.

So, options (B), (C), and (D) are incorrect.

Hence, the correct option is (A).

7. Scorn means a feeling and expression of contempt or disdain for someone or something.

For example, Do not become an object of scorn.

Disdain means the feeling that someone or something is unworthy of one's consideration or respect.

For example, His lips curled in disdain.

Disallow means refuse to declare valid.

Highlight means an outstanding part of an event or period of time.

Willful means intentional; deliberate.

It is clear from the examples that scorn and disdain are similar or synonymous in meaning.

So, options (A), (C), and (D) are incorrect.

Hence, the correct option is (B).

8. The correct sentence is:

Are they going to help us?

There is used to denote a location. It is often used to denote a location in an abstract way too.

For example, Stay there.

Option (A) is incorrect.

The're is an incorrect word. The correct contraction for they are is they're.

Option (B) is incorrect.

Is is used when we talk about a singular thing like he/she/it whereas are is used when we talk about other people or things in plural form like we/they.

For example, He is studying.

Option (C) is incorrect as it uses is. Also, the present continuous form of go i.e going should be used in order to denote the action that is going to place in the near future.

So, options (A), (B) and (C) are incorrect.

Hence, the correct option is (D).

9. The man is an important element of the environment.

Of is used when a thing belongs to, is related, or connected to another.

For example, I always dreamed of getting this role.

In the given sentence, of will be used to indicate the relationship or belonging i.e man belongs to the environment.

To is used for the purpose to mean in order to, for time expressions or for movement.

For example, I spent money to buy a house.

In is used when a thing is enclosed within an area.

For example, The dog was lying in his bed.

Over is used when one thing is touching or covering another.

For example, She put a blanket over her.

So, options (A), (B), and (C) are incorrect.

Hence, the correct option is (D).

10. Sir, I would like you to grant me leave.

A full stop (.) is used to mark the end of a statement and start a new sentence,

For example, I live in India. My house is big.

A semicolon (;) is used when we need to connect independent clauses and to show a close relationship between them.

For example, She was hurt; she knew he had said that to upset him.

An exclamation mark (!) is used to denote a sudden outcry or emphasis.

For example, His behaviour made me furious!

The comma (,) is used to separate ideas or elements. Also, it is used after salutation or ending.

For example, Thanks for your help, Tom.

Clearly, option (D) is correct.

So, options (A), (B) and (C) are incorrect.

Hence, the correct option is (D).

11. The ball was expected by the boy.

When we change the active voice to passive voice, the subject i.e. boy becomes the object and the object i.e. ball becomes the subject.

Option (D) follows all these rules.

So, options (A), (B) and (C) are incorrect.

Hence, the correct option is (D).

12. The window was being opened by Peter.

The sentence in active voice is in past continuous tense so, we use the past tense - was to denote the action being performed in the past and we use being opened to show continuous tense.

Option (A) uses the simple past tense (was opened).

Option (C) uses the present continuous tense (was being opened).

Option (D) uses the present perfect tense (had been opened).

So, options (A), (C) and (D) are incorrect.

Hence, the correct option is (B).

13. The man refused to confess his guilt.

While converting from direct to indirect speech, we narrate the words that were said in the past while changing the form of pronouns and tenses. We do not convey any additional information or feeling.

Options (A) and (C) conveys additional feelings which are not mentioned in the direct speech. So, they are incorrect.

In option (D), the sentence structure is incorrect.

So, options (A), (C) and (D) are incorrect.

Hence, the correct option is (B).

14. The indirect speech of the given sentence is correctly changed to direct speech in option (A).

The Prime Minister said, "We will not allow anyone to disturb the peace."

Option (A) is correct because it correctly changes the tense and the auxiliary verb to present tense from the past tense of the given sentence.

Option (B) is incorrect because if can is used in direct speech, it will be replaced by could in indirect speech. But, could is not present in the question.

Option (C) is incorrect because we would not allow no one is a double negative.

Option (D) is incorrect as it changes the meaning of the given sentence, which says no one would be allowed to disturb, but option (D) does away with the allow or permission part.

So, options (B), (C) and (D) are incorrect.

Hence, the correct option is (A).

15. Susan watched a movie at the theatre with a friend.

With is used to indicate in the company or in the presence of something or in the company of someone, using something or having something.

For example; She lives with her parents.

In the given sentence, Susan was accompanied to the theatre by a friend, so with will be used.

Of is used for belonging, relating, or in reference to something.

For example; This is the picture of my mother.

On is used to denote something above another thing or when something is attached to another thing.

For example; The books are lying on the table.

In is used to denote something within an area.

For example; She lives in India.

So, options (A), (B) and (C) are incorrect.

Hence, the correct option is (D).

16. He had been in prison for 2 years at the time when he was still interested in cards.

For is used to denote a period of time- how long something has happened.

For example; I have known her for 3 years.

In the given sentence, for will be used to denote the time period i.e 2 years during which he was in prison.

At is used to denote a specific time, position, or place when an event has occurred or will occur.

For example; She met him at the restaurant.

In is used to denote something within an area.

For example; The dog is in his bed.

Since is used to denote the beginning of a time period until the present. It is used with the starting point of an event.

For example; She has been missing since June.

Clearly, options (A), (B) and (C) are incorrect.

Hence, the correct option is (D).

17. This sentence is in the past perfect tense where two actions happened one after another.

In such cases, we translate the previous action in the past perfect tense and the later one in the past indefinite tense.

So, we will use past perfect tense i.e. had finished

Hence, the correct option is (B).

18. Anil was stopped by the police because he was driving fast.

In the given sentence, was indicates that the action has been performed in the past. But, we do not know whether the action has been completed or not. The only option which gives a past tense of the verb is an option (A).

was driving denotes the past continuous tense which means that the action was going on at some point in the past i.e Anil was driving fast (past continuous tense).

Has drive is incorrect because with has we use the third form of the verb drive i.e driven. Also, it is the present perfect tense that cannot be used in the given sentence.

Drive is the first form of the verb which is used mostly in the simple present tense.

Has driven is the present perfect tense which can not be used in the sentence.

So, options (B), (C) and (D) are incorrect.

Hence, the correct option is (A).

19. Adjectives are used to describe a noun.

For example; She is smart.

Here, smart is used to describe her.

In the given sentence, liveliest is used to describe the noun Kolkata, so liveliest is an adjective.

World is a noun.

One is used as a pronoun in the given sentence.

City is a noun.

So, options (A), (B) and (D) are incorrect.

Hence, the correct option is (C).

20. Pronouns are used to replace nouns in a sentence.

For example; Tom ran so fast, you'd think his life was on the line.

Here, his is used to replace Tom.

In the given sentence, yourself is a reflexive pronoun or the reflexive form of you that is used when the person being spoken

to is the same as the subject, it is used to emphasize the subject of the sentence.

Do is a verb that denotes an action.

Not is an adverb that is used with an auxiliary verb to form the negative.

Pray is a verb. It is also used like in the above sentence-- as a preface to polite requests or instructions. ex: Pray, continue

So, options (A), (C) and (D) are incorrect.

Hence, the correct option is (B).

21. In the given sentence Only you are allowed to attend the party. 'You' is the pronoun in the sentence.

Hence, the correct option is (B).

22. The correct sentence is- 'Apples, Mangoes and Bananas are my favourites.'

In the given sentence 'apple' 'mangoes' and 'bananas' are the three different fruits and we are writing them in one sentence so need to separate them by the using comma ",".

Hence, the correct option is (B).

23. "If the world ended tomorrow, I would be very sad".

This is the second conditional. It is for a future unreal condition. There is a very low chance the world will end tomorrow. The speaker does not believe that it will happen. Therefore, to show that it's not a real possibility, we use the second conditional. The second conditional is used in two ways, but the grammatical form is the same for both.

Rule: [If + subject + past tense] , (then) [subject + would/could/might + verb].

Hence, the correct option is (D).

24. A subject of a sentence is the person, place, or thing we are talking about. Generally, if we can replace the subject with a subject pronoun (I, you, he, she, it, we, they), the correct choice to refer back to it is by using the relative pronoun who.

Which is used for things without life and for animals.

Whose (the possessive form of who) is used in speaking of persons, animals and also things without life.

An object in a sentence is the person, thing, or place who is on the receiving end of the action. If we can replace the object with an object pronoun (me, you, him, her, it, us, them), the correct choice to refer back to it is by using the relative pronoun whom.

Here, Option (B) is correct. We use 'who' as we are referring to the subject of the sentence.

Hence, the correct option is (B).

25. It is important that you select the team in a fair way.

All the given options are adjectives.

Option (D) - 'Fair' means 'justified or equitable' and this adjective is appropriate for the given sentence because the context is about the selection of a team that should be just in all means, ie 'fair'.

Option (A) - 'Convenient' means 'suitable'.

Option (B) - 'Absolute' means 'complete or entire'.

Option (C) - 'Challenging' means 'demanding or testing'. None of which suits the given context.

Therefore, the appropriate option to complete the given sentence is Fair.

Hence, the correct option is (D).

Ques (1-5):Directions: Read the following passage and answer the questions given below it in the context of the passage.

Our voyage was very prosperous, but I shall not trouble the reader with a journal of it. The captain called in at one or two ports and sent in his long-boat for provisions and freshwater, but I never went out of the ship still we came into the Downs, which was on the 3rd day of June 1706, about nine months after my escape. I offered to leave my goods in security for payment of my freight, but the captain protested he would not receive one farthing. We took kind leave of each other, and I made him promise that he would come to see me at my house in Redriff. I hired a house and a guide for five shillings which I borrowed from the captain.

Q.1 When the writer uses the word 'prosperous' to describe the voyage, he means that:

A. it made him rich

B. it made him healthy

C. it was very pleasant

D. it was uneventful

Q.2 On the voyage, the author:

A. left the ship at intervals

B. was not able to leave the ship because it did not stop

C. never left the ship at all

D. never left the ship till they came into the Downs

Q.3 In the context of the passage, the word 'provisions' means:

A. mainly food

B. mainly security

C. money

D. mainly ammunition

Q.4 For the payment of the author's freight, the captain:

A. kept his goods as security

B. refused to accept any money

C. protested against being paid only a farthing

D. accepted a sum of money

Q.5 From the passage, it is clear that the captain's attitude to the author was:

A. one of hostility

B. one of indifference

C. one of extreme friendliness and kindness

D. one of disgust and irritation

Q.6 Choose the correct meaning of the phrase:

To go overboard:

A. To tell people about someone's secrets

B. To encourage someone in his bad times

C. To do too much of something

D. Once in a life-time

Q.7 Choose the correct meaning of the phrase:

On the rocks:

A. likely to fail

B. To feel very sad

C. To act confident in a difficult situation

D. To commit a fraud

Q.8 Choose the best alternative to correct the sentence:

<u>Being as I am a realist</u>, I could not accept his statement that supernatural beings have caused the disturbance.

A. That I am a realist

B. Being a realist

C. Being that I am a realist

D. Realist that I am

Q.9 Choose the best alternative to correct the sentence:

Although he is <u>able to</u> make political enemies with this decision, the Prime Minister does not mind doing it for the sake of public welfare.

A. liable form

B. of a mind to

C. acknowledging his liability to

D. liable to

Q.10 Choose the most appropriate word from the options given below to complete the following sentence.

She will __________ you a new pair of jeans on your birthday.

A. got   **B.** gotten   **C.** get   **D.** getting

Q.11 Choose the most appropriate word from the options given below to complete the following sentence.

I have been ______ to bake a perfect cake since morning.

A. tries   **B.** try   **C.** trying   **D.** tried

Q.12 Direction: Choose the appropriate noun form of the underlined adjective to fill the blank.

The athlete ran twice a week around the park.

A. rune   **B.** run   **C.** runnance   **D.** runnary

Q.13 Choose the most appropriate alternative to complete the sentence:

Indians love to conform to the traditional values. Their ______ sometimes stops them from evolving further.

A. Conformism   **B.** Conformation

C. Conformability   **D.** Conforming

Q.14 Change direct to indirect speech or vice versa as the case may be:

The teacher said, 'Suresh, you are wasting your time.'

A. The teacher told Suresh that he was wasting his time.

B. The teacher told that he was wasting my time.

C. The teacher told Suresh was wasting his time.

D. The teacher told Suresh that he is wasting his time.

Q.15 Change direct to indirect speech or vice versa as the case may be:

He said to him, 'Do not go there.'

A. He forbade him not to go there.

B. He told him not to go there.
C. He told him to not go there.
D. He told him to go there.

Q.16 Choose the correctly punctuated sentence.
A. Alas! We could not save the dog.
B. Alas? We could not save the dog.
C. Alas. We could not save the dog.
D. Alas, We could not save the dog.

Q.17 Choose the most appropriate alternative to complete the sentence:

Sherry's mother asked _____not to open the door for strangers.
A. Him   **B.** Her
C. Someone   **D.** Anyone

Q.18 Choose the pronoun to fill in the blank:

_____is a demonstrative pronoun?
A. Each other   **B.** Myself
C. It   **D.** This

Q.19 Fill in the blank with the most suitable verb and verb form:

The earth _______ around the sun.
A. Revolve   **B.** Revolves
C. Both A and B   **D.** None of these

Q.20 Fill in the blank with the most suitable verb and verb form:

Rajesh ________ his mother tongue very fluently.
A. Speak   **B.** Speaking
C. Speaks   **D.** None of these

Q.21 In which of these cases, the preposition is always placed at the end?
A. Relative pronoun   **B.** Reciprocal pronoun
C. Possessive pronoun   **D.** Reflexive pronoun

Q.22 Which of these is not a simple preposition?
A. From   **B.** Through   **C.** Above   **D.** With

Q.23 Which words are sound adjectives?
A. Large, small, gigantic
B. Loud, quiet, soothing
C. Red, green, yellow
D. Rough, smooth, cold

Q.24 Fill in the blanks with the adjective from the following alternatives:

He is _______ than his neighbors.
A. rich   **B.** richer   **C.** richest   **D.** None

Q.25 Find the correctly spelt word.
A. Affedevit   **B.** Afidevit
C. Affidevit   **D.** Affidavit

// Smart Answer Sheet //

Correct — Percentage of students who answered correctly. **Skipped** — Percentage of students who skipped.

Q.	Ans.	Correct / Skipped	Q.	Ans.	Correct / Skipped	Q.	Ans.	Correct / Skipped	Q.	Ans.	Correct / Skipped	Q.	Ans.	Correct / Skipped	Q.	Ans.	Correct / Skipped
1	C	49.15 % / 30.46 %	6	C	50.4 % / 45.32 %	11	C	46.86 % / 52.23 %	16	A	49.5 % / 43.35 %	21	A	65.97 % / 31.86 %			
2	D	84.65 % / 13.71 %	7	A	53.39 % / 43.63 %	12	B	50.01 % / 44.91 %	17	B	68.92 % / 30.72 %	22	C	12.68 % / 69.58 %			
3	A	65.98 % / 32.58 %	8	B	59.53 % / 33.72 %	13	A	13.41 % / 73.77 %	18	D	28.16 % / 71.7 %	23	A	41.23 % / 35.23 %			
4	B	85.63 % / 10.68 %	9	D	15.06 % / 71.04 %	14	A	52.47 % / 38.54 %	19	B	54.03 % / 33.91 %	24	B	50.67 % / 45.02 %			
5	C	13.82 % / 82.29 %	10	C	86.35 % / 10.35 %	15	B	44.82 % / 45.06 %	20	C	87.98 % / 11.69 %	25	D	66.3 % / 31.4 %			

//Hints and Solutions//

1. With regard to 'journey' it can be said that pleasant journey is being referred here. How can a journey be healthy for someone ? In passage as well there is no linkage of journey with the health of writer. So, option B can be rejected. Option D is also wrong as passage has no direct or indirect mention of eventless in the journey. Option A is incorrect for the same reason.
Hence, the correct option is (C).

2. Author has mentioned in third line of passage 'I never went out of the ship till we came into the Downs' So, statement of option D is clearly written and hence the obvious choice.
Hence, the correct option is (D).

3. In a long ship journey which continues for months there is a need of fresh water and food. It can be inferred from the passage that Captain sent in his lifeboat for fresh water and foods. For food and related items word 'provisions' is used which means Cookery, the act of supplying or providing food, etc.
Hence, the correct option is (A).

4. 'Farthing' is a unit of money and in the passage captain was not willing to receive any money from the author as a friendly gesture. Farthing means – A coin formerly used in Great Britain worth one-fourth of a penny.
Hence, the correct option is (B).

5. Passage shows relationship of author and captain in a positive light. As captain refused to take 'single penny for the services', 'author's invitation to captain' and 'borrowing of money from captain for home' are some examples that show that captain's attitude for the author was friendly and kind.
Hence, the correct option is (C).

6. To go overboard means to do too much; to be extravagant.

Ex. When it comes to having chicken, I go overboard.

Hence, the correct option is (C).

7. On the rocks means If something, like a relationship, is on the rocks, it is in trouble and may come to an end.

Ex. Their marriage is on the rocks.

Hence, the correct option is (A).

8. The underlined part must be replaced with 'Being a realist' to make it a grammatically correct sentence.
Hence, the correct option is (B).

9. The adjective 'liable' means 'at risk of or subject to experiencing or suffering something unpleasant.' and the word is used with 'to'.

Ex. liable to criminal charges; liable to diabetes.

The underlined part, must be replaced with 'liable to' in place of 'able to', the use of which is quite absurd in the context.
Hence, the correct option is (D).

10. She will **get** you a new pair of jeans on your birthday.
Hence, the correct option is (C).

11. I have been trying to bake a perfect cake since morning.
Hence, the correct option is (C).

12. The noun form of the verb, 'ran' is 'run'.

So, the sentence correct will be: The athlete <u>runs</u> twice a week around the park.

Option A: The word, 'rune' is a noun that refers to the letters of a particular alphabet used in Northern Europe in the past, which were believed to have magical powers. This has no relation to the word - 'run'. Hence, option A is incorrect.

Options C and D and incorrect as there is no word such as 'runnance' or 'runner' in the English language. These words have no meaning.

Hence, the correct option is (B).

13. We are to choose the correct nominalisation of the verb 'conform' from the given options.

Nominalisation refers to the noun form of a verb or an adjective.

Options B, C and D are incorrect because:

Option B: CONFORMATION: means a shape of something. This not comply with context of the sentence.

Option C: CONFIRMABILITY means the quality of confirming. This does not comply with the context of the sentence.

Option D: CONFORMING means to comply with rules. It is in the verb form.

So, these 3 options are incorrect.

Option A: CONFORMISM means the tendency to adopt attitudes. It is in the noun form and also complies with the meaning of the sentence.
Hence, the correct option is (A).

14. The indirect form of the sentence will be:

The teacher told Suresh that he was wasting his time.
Hence, the correct option is (A).

15. The indirect form of the sentence will be:

He told him not to go there.
Hence, the correct option is (B).

16. Option (A): is the correctly punctuated sentence.

Option (B): is incorrect. The question mark is used after asking a question. Example: What is her name?

Option (C): is incorrect. The full stop is used at the end of a sentence. Example: She is my sister.

Option (D): is incorrect. The comma is used when someone is directly addressed/to separate two clauses/to separate ideas, objects, names in a sentence. Example: I will go to Goa, Mumbai and Pune.
Hence, the correct option is (A).

17. Sherry's mother asked her not to open the door for strangers.
Hence, the correct option is (B).

18. "This" is a demonstrative pronoun.

Demonstratives are words, such as this and that, used to indicate which entities are being referred to and to distinguish those entities from others.

Hence, the correct option is (D).

19. A word used to describe an action, state, or occurrence, and forming the main part of the predicate of a sentence is a verb. Verbs with a third-person singular noun or pronoun (he, she, boat, courage) as a subject ever have an "-s" added on the end. Similarly, in this sentence, the earth is a third person. Thus, the answer would be "revolves" and not "revolve".
Hence, the correct option is (B).

20. A word used to describe an action, state, or occurrence, and forming the main part of the predicate of a sentence is a Verb. Verbs with a third-person singular noun or pronoun (he, she, boat, courage) as a subject have an "-s" added on the end. Rajesh (noun) is in third person which means we need to use an "s" at the end of the verb. "Speaking" is a verb that is used in present continuous tense which is not the case here. The answer here is "speaks".
Hence, the correct option is (C).

21. The preposition is always placed at the end when the object is an interrogative or a relative pronoun. For example: Here is the money that you asked for. What are you thinking of?
Hence, the correct option is (A).

22. At, by, for, from, in, of, off, as, out, through, till, to, up, with are simple prepositions. Compound prepositions are generally formed by prefixing a preposition to a noun, adjective or an adverb.

Example, above.
Hence, the correct option is (C).

23. Large, small, gigantic are sound adjectives.

The sound adjective refers to an adjective that you can rely on and that will probably give good results
Hence, the correct option is (A).

24. He is richer than his neighbors.
Hence, the correct option is (B).

25. "Affidavit" is the correctly spelt word.
Hence, the correct option is (D).

Q.1 What is the cause of diffraction?

A.   Interference of primary wavelets

B.   Interference of secondary wavelets

C.   Reflection of primary wavelets

D.   Reflection of secondary wavelets

Q.2 Choose the correct one which will react faster in the SN2 nucleophilic substitution reaction?

A. $CH_2 - CH = CH_2 = Br$

B. $CH_2 = CH - CH_2 - Br$

C. $CH_2 = CH - CH_2 = Br$

D. $CH = CH_2 - CH_2 - Br$

Q.3 A potentiometer using cell C of emf $5V$ and internal resistance 0.2 ohms is connected to a wire AB in the figure below. A standard cell C_0 of a constant emf of $1.10V$ gives a balance point at $55\ cm$ of the wire. When C_0 is replaced by a cell of emf E, the balance point is obtained at $85\ cm$. What is the value of E?

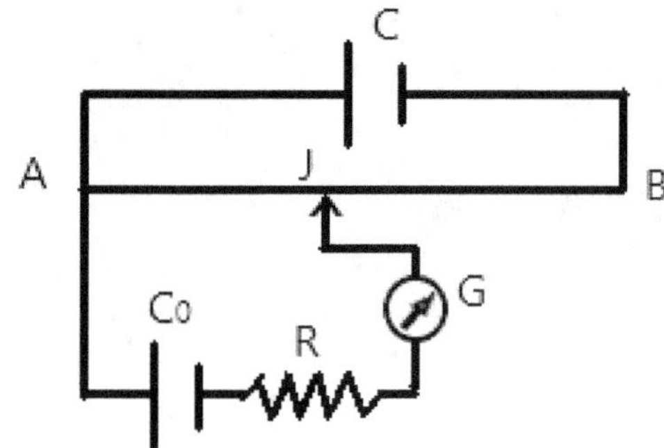

A. $1.4V$ **B.** $1.5V$ **C.** $1.7V$ **D.** $1.9V$

Q.4 Which of the following are conductors?

A. Ceramics   **B.** Plastics

C. Mercury   **D.** Rubber

Q.5 A rocket takes off from the earth and continues to move in a circular orbit with the thrusters on. What can be said about the angular velocity of the rocket?

A. It increases   **B.** It decreases

C. It remains constant   **D.** It changes abruptly

Q.6 The value of universal gravitational constant changes is which of the following medium?

A.   Air

B.   Water

C.   Plasma

D.   The gravitational constant is independent of the medium

Q.7 Mud thrown on a wall and sticking to it is an example for __________.

A.   Inelastic collision

B.   Elastic collision

C.   Super elastic collision

D.   Perfectly inelastic collision

Q.8 Force in a conductor is _________ to the square of the distance between the charges.

A.   Directly proportional

B.   Inversely proportional

C.   Not related

D.   Cannot be determined

Q.9 When food is given in the stomach or intestines directly then it is _______ nutrition.

A. Intravenous   **B.** Saline

C. Enteral   **D.** Parenteral

Q.10 Science of precise and accurate measurement of various physical quantities is termed as _________.

A. Metrology   **B.** Meteorology

C. Pedology   **D.** Mineralogy

Q.11 The energy possessed by a body, for doing work by virtue of its position, is called:

A. Potential energy   **B.** Kinetic energy

C. Electrical energy   **D.** Chemical energy

Q.12 In which type of matter, one won't find a free surface?

A. Solid   **B.** Liquid   **C.** Gas   **D.** Fluid

Q.13 Internal energy of a system is defined as?

A.   The sum of kinetic energies of all molecules of the system

B.   The sum of kinetic and potential energies of all molecules of the system

C.   The sum of potential energies of the system

D.   The average kinetic energy of all molecules

Q.14 If the intensity of incident radiation in a photo-cell is increased, how does the stopping potential vary?

A. Increases   **B.** Remains the same

C. Decreases   **D.** Infinite

Q.15 When a radioactive substance emits an α-particle, its position in the periodic table is lowered by which of the following?

A. One place   **B.** Two places

C. Three places   **D.** Four places

Q.16 Which of the following is an alloy of lead?

A. Vitallium   **B.** Brass

C. Invar   **D.** Solder

Q.17 Which of the following statements is true with respect to food processing?

A.   Sodium is lost during cooking and selenium is volatile and is lost by cooking or processing

B.   Vitamins can be removed from food via leaching

C. Mineral losses in food processing are more compared to Vitamins

D. Boiling has less mineral losses as compared to steaming

Q.18 Monoclonal antibodies are produced by __________ type of cells.

A. Uninucleate   B. Multinucleate

C. Hybridoma   D. Prokaryotes

Q.19 Calculate the frequency if the number of revolutions is 300 and the paired poles are 50.

A. $15kHz$ B. $150kHz$

C. $1500kHz$ D. $150Hz$

Q.20 The length of a simple pendulum executing simple harmonic motion is increased by 21%. The percentage increase in the time period of the pendulum of increases length is?

A. 50%   B. 21%   C. 30%   D. 10.5%

Q.21 A child swinging on a swing stands up. Then the time period of the swing will __________.

A. Increase

B. Decrease

C. Remain the same

D. Increase, if the child is long and decreases if the child is short

Q.22 If the earth stops rotating, the value of g at the equator __________.

A. Increases

B. Decreases

C. No effect

D. First increases and then decreases

Q.23 Isomerism that arises out of the difference in spatial arrangement of atoms or groups about the doubly bonded carbon atoms are called? (In specific)

A. Structural Isomerism

B. Stereo Isomerism

C. Geometrical Isomerism

D. Optical Isomerism

Q.24 Sterling silver is used for?

A. Used for casting of firearms

B. Used for making musical instruments

C. Used for making springs

D. Used for joining two metals

Q.25 Which of the following is a factor that affects the storage stability of food?

A. Type of raw material used

B. Quality of raw material used

C. Method/effectiveness of packaging

D. All of the mentioned

// Smart Answer Sheet //

Correct — Percentage of students who answered correctly. **Skipped** — Percentage of students who skipped.

Q.	Ans.	Correct / Skipped	Q.	Ans.	Correct / Skipped	Q.	Ans.	Correct / Skipped	Q.	Ans.	Correct / Skipped	Q.	Ans.	Correct / Skipped	Q.	Ans.	Correct / Skipped
1	B	0 % / 100 %	6	D	1.23 % / 96.3 %	11	A	2.47 % / 96.3 %	16	D	0 % / 100 %	21	B	1.23 % / 96.3 %			
2	B	1.23 % / 96.3 %	7	D	0 % / 100 %	12	C	0 % / 100 %	17	A	0 % / 100 %	22	A	0 % / 100 %			
3	C	0 % / 100 %	8	B	2.47 % / 96.3 %	13	B	0 % / 100 %	18	C	0 % / 100 %	23	C	0 % / 100 %			
4	C	2.47 % / 96.3 %	9	C	0 % / 100 %	14	B	2.47 % / 96.3 %	19	A	0 % / 100 %	24	B	1.23 % / 96.3 %			
5	A	1.23 % / 96.3 %	10	A	0 % / 100 %	15	B	2.47 % / 96.3 %	20	D	1.23 % / 96.3 %	25	D	1.23 % / 96.3 %			

//Hints and Solutions//

1. Diffraction occurs due to interference of secondary wavelets between different portions of a wavefront allowed to pass across a small aperture or obstacle. Interference can be either constructive or destructive. When interference is constructive, the intensity of the wave will increase.

Hence, the correct option is (B).

2. The carbocation character in the transition state causes stabilization of the resonance and hence $CH_2 = CH - CH_2 - Br$ (2-bromobutane) is the one which will react faster compared to the others.

Hence, the correct option is (B).

3. Given,

$$l_1 = 55cm$$

$$l_2 = 85cm$$

$$\frac{E}{C_0} = \frac{l_1}{l_2} \rightarrow E = C_0 \times \frac{l_2}{l_1}$$

$$E = 1.10 \times \frac{85}{55} = 1.7V$$

Hence, the correct option is (C).

4. Normally, metals are said to be good conductors. Here mercury is the only metal (which is in liquid form). The other options are insulators.

Hence, the correct option is (C).

5. When the rocket is in the orbit with the thrusters on, there is a tangential force that the rocket experiences. This force will result in increasing the tangential velocity. Since the angular velocity is directly proportional to the tangential velocity, the angular velocity will also increase.

Hence, the correct option is (A).

6. Since the gravitational constant is an empirical constant, it does not vary with the medium. Hence, the value of the gravitational constant is the same in any part of the known universe.

Hence, the correct option is (D).

7. If two bodies stick together after the collision and move as a single body with a common velocity, then the collision is said to be perfectly inelastic collision. A mud thrown on a wall sticks to the wall, therefore it is an example for perfectly inelastic collision.

Hence, the correct option is (D).

8. The force in a current carrying conductor is directly proportional to the product of the two charges and inversely proportional to the square of the distance between them.

Hence, the correct option is (B).

9. Enteral nutrition is a type of nutrition is given to those who have been unconscious or comatose for a longer period of time. The food is normal food but churned into a paste and diluted sufficiently. This food is given directly in the stomach with the help of tubes.

Hence, the correct option is (C).

10. Metrology is the science of measurement. Metrology includes all theoretical aspects of measurement. Meteorology is the branch of study about the atmosphere. Pedology is the branch of study about soil and Mineralogy is a branch of geology specializing in chemistry, chemical structure and physical properties of minerals.

Hence, the correct option is (A).

11.

- Potential energy is the energy possessed by a body for doing work, by virtue of its position.
- Kinetic energy is the energy possessed by a body, for doing work, by virtue of its mass and velocity of motion.
- Chemical energy is the energy possessed due to internal arrangement of atom in a compound.
- Electric energy is due to the flow of charge.

Hence, the correct option is (A).

12. Solid molecules have a definite shape due to large inter-molecular force. In liquids, molecules are free to move inside the whole mass but rarely escape from itself. Thus, liquids can form free surfaces under the effect of gravity. But, in case of gases, molecules tend to escape due to low forces of attraction. Thus, gases won't form any free surface.

Hence, the correct option is (C).

13. The internal energy of a system corresponds to the energy possessed by all molecules. Thus, it is the sum of kinetic and potential energies of all molecules in the system considered. Also, note that potential energy is frame-dependent, so we choose a frame in which the center of mass is at rest.

Hence, the correct option is (B).

14. There is no effect on stopping potential. The intensity of incident radiation is independent of stopping potential. Therefore, even if the incident radiation in a photo-cell is increased, the stopping potential remains unchanged.

Hence, the correct option is (B).

15. When a radioactive substance emits an α-particle, its atomic number decreases by a factor of 2. Therefore, its position in the periodic table is also lowered by two places.

Hence, the correct option is (B).

16. Solder is an alloy of lead. The alloying element is tin mainly, it is used for electrical connection by melting and fusing to form a permanent bond between two metal pieces.

Hence, the correct option is (D).

17. Sodium is lost during cooking and selenium is volatile and is lost by cooking or processing. Minerals can be removed from food via leaching. Vitamin losses in food processing are more compared to minerals. Boiling has more mineral losses as compared to steaming.

Hence, the correct option is (A).

18. Monoclonal antibodies are antibodies that are made by identical immune cells that are all clones of a unique parent cell. They bind to the same epitope. Monoclonal antibodies are produced by the Hybridoma type of cells.

Hence, the correct option is (C).

19. We know that, $f = p \times n$ where, p= 50 and n(number of revolutions) = 300

$$f = 50 \times 300$$

$$= 15000 Hz$$

$$= 15 kHz$$

Hence, the correct option is (A).

20. Time period, $T = 2\pi \sqrt{\left(\frac{l}{g}\right)}$

The percentage increase in a time period is given by,

$$\frac{\Delta T}{T} \times 100$$

$$\Rightarrow \frac{1}{2} \times \frac{\Delta l}{l} \times 100$$

$$\Rightarrow \frac{\Delta T}{T} \times 100$$

$$\Rightarrow \frac{1}{2} \times 21\% = 10.5\%$$

Hence, the correct option is (D).

21. The child and the swing together constitute a pendulum of a time period,

$$T \propto 2\pi \sqrt{\left(\frac{l}{g}\right)}$$

As the child stands up, her centre of gravity is raised. The distance between the point of suspension and the centre of gravity decreases, that is the length l decreases. Therefore the time period T decreases.

Hence, the correct option is (B).

22. At the equator, $g_e = g - R\omega^2$

When $\omega = 0, g_e = g$

The value of g increases if the earth stops rotating.

Hence, the correct option is (A).

23. Isomerism that arises out of the difference in spatial arrangement of atoms or groups about the doubly bonded carbon atoms are called Geometrical Isomerism. These geometrical isomers are not mirror images of each other and they differ in spatial arrangement from one another.

Hence, the correct option is (C).

24. Sterling silver is an alloy which is used for making musical instruments such as flute and saxophone. It is also used for making cutlery.

Hence, the correct option is (B).

25. All of the above mentioned factors are true. They all affect the storage stability of food.

Hence, the correct option is (D)

Q.1 What should be the order of the size of an obstacle or aperture for diffraction light?

A. Order of wavelength of light

B. Order of wavelength of obstacle

C. Order in ranges of micrometer

D. Order in ranges of nanometer

Q.2 What will be the reactivity of chlorobenzene in an electrophilic substitution reaction with benzene?

A. Reacts very slowly than benzene

B. Reacts in the same way as benzene

C. Reacts faster than benzene

D. Does not react with benzene

Q.3 A potentiometer wire of length 20 m has a resistance of 50 ohms. It is connected in series with a resistance box and a 5 V storage cell. If the potential gradient along the wire is 0.5 mV/cm, what is the resistance unplugged in the box?

A. 450 ohms   **B.** 400 ohms

C. 405 ohms   **D.** 500 ohms

Q.4 Alternating current measured in a transmission line will be:

A. Peak value   **B.** Average value

C. RMS value   **D.** Zero

Q.5 Which one of the following is not an example of the third law of motion?

A. Walking   **B.** Skiing

C. Walking on a boat   **D.** Cycling

Q.6 The value of gravitational constant was first determined by ____.

A. Albert Einstein   **B.** Isaac Newton

C. Henry Cavendish   **D.** Stephen Hawking

Q.7 Collision between two carom coins is an example for __________.

A. Oblique collision

B. Perfectly inelastic collision

C. Inelastic collision

D. Elastic collision

Q.8 The relation between the direction of force and the direction of magnetic field is _________.

A. Same direction   **B.** Opposite direction

C. Perpendicular   **D.** Unrelated

Q.9 In cases of renal insufficiency, what should take in place of proteins?

A. Triglycerides

B. Essential Amino Acids

C. Glucose

D. Vitamin K

Q.10 In a measurement, what is the term used to specify the closeness of two or more measurements?

A. Precision   **B.** Accuracy

C. Fidelity   **D.** Threshold

Q.11 The wheels of a moving car possess:

A. Potential energy only

B. Kinetic energy of translation only

C. Kinetic energy of rotation only

D. Kinetic energy of translation and rotation both.

Q.12 If a person studies about a fluid which is at rest, what will you call his domain of study?

A. Fluid Mechanics   **B.** Fluid Statics

C. Fluid Kinematics   **D.** Fluid Dynamics

Q.13 Select the correct statement.

A. Internal energy is a path variable

B. Heat is a path variable

C. Work done is a state variable

D. Internal energy is a microscopic variable

Q.14 How does retarding potential vary with the frequency of light causing photoelectric effect?

A. Infinite   **B.** Zero

C. Decreases   **D.** Increases

Q.15 If alpha, beta, and gamma rays carry the same momentum, which has the longest wavelength?

A. Alpha rays

B. Beta rays

C. Gamma rays

D. All have the same wavelength

Q.16 What are alloys with two components called?

A. Binary alloy   **B.** Ternary alloy

C. Quaternary alloy   **D.** None of these

Q.17 Which of the following do you think is a valid reason for decline of export of marine products to USA?

A. Emerging markets in USA

B. Anti- dumping procedure by US government on many marine products

C. Both (A) and (B)

D. None of these

Q.18 Which among the following is true regarding leucocytes?

A. They are enucleated

B. Produced in thymus

C. Sudden fall in number indicate cancer

D. They can squeeze through capillary walls

Q.19 When an electric current flows into the page, what is the direction of the magnetic field?

A. Clockwise

B. Anti-clockwise
C. Parallel to the current
D. Cannot be determined

Q.20 For a particle executing simple harmonic motion, which of the following statements is not correct?
A. Total energy is always directed toward a fixed point
B. Restoring force is always directed towards a fixed point
C. Restoring force is maximum at the extreme positions
D. Acceleration of the particle is maximum at the equilibrium position

Q.21 When a 2 kg body is suspended by a spring, the spring is stretched. If the body is pulled down slightly and released, it oscillates up and down. What force is applied on the body by the spring when it passes through the mean position?
A. Force equal to the gravity
B. Force equal to the pull
C. Conservative force
D. Force equal to the weight of the body

Q.22 Which alkyl halide has the highest reactivity for a particular alkyl group?
A. R-F　　　　**B.** R-Cl　　　　**C.** R-I　　　　**D.** R-Br

Q.23 Which of the following alloying element can be used to deoxidize steels?
A. Phosphorous　　　　**B.** Carbon
C. Cerium　　　　**D.** Selenium

Q.24 Which of the following terms refers to the amount of protein absorbed by the body from a food source?
A. Biological Value
B. Limiting Value
C. Reference pattern
D. None of the mentioned

Q.25 Laboratory diagnosis of Entamoeba histolytica depends on identification in the __________.
A. blood　　　　**B.** urine　　　　**C.** saliva　　　　**D.** stool

// Smart Answer Sheet //

Correct — Percentage of students who answered correctly. Skipped — Percentage of students who skipped.

Q.	Ans.	Correct / Skipped	Q.	Ans.	Correct / Skipped	Q.	Ans.	Correct / Skipped	Q.	Ans.	Correct / Skipped	Q.	Ans.	Correct / Skipped	Q.	Ans.	Correct / Skipped
1	A	52.5 % / 39.64 %	6	C	64.18 % / 32.97 %	11	D	82.58 % / 17.4 %	16	A	87.72 % / 11.22 %	21	D	10.64 % / 85.72 %			
2	A	56.2 % / 42.54 %	7	A	50.72 % / 47.98 %	12	B	63.91 % / 35.87 %	17	C	58.17 % / 37.4 %	22	C	65.15 % / 34.83 %			
3	A	17.84 % / 67.48 %	8	C	64.99 % / 32.7 %	13	B	87.61 % / 11.53 %	18	D	84.87 % / 13.66 %	23	C	57.3 % / 40.42 %			
4	C	82.87 % / 13.62 %	9	B	88.71 % / 10.93 %	14	D	52.25 % / 42.75 %	19	A	49.49 % / 49.11 %	24	A	83.71 % / 13.16 %			
5	B	59.97 % / 37.8 %	10	A	56.7 % / 37.04 %	15	D	69.25 % / 30.36 %	20	D	82.55 % / 13.85 %	25	D	47.5 % / 40.3 %			

//Hints and Solutions//

1. The size of the obstacle or aperture should be of the order of the wavelength of light used. Therefore, the size of an obstacle is not of the order of obstacle, or micrometer or nanometer.
Hence, the correct option is (A).

2. The rate of the reaction depends on the electron density in the ring and here in this case resonance is not favorable and the electronegativity dipole dominates. This slows down the reactivity of chlorobenzene.
Hence, the correct option is (A).

3. Potential gradient along the potentiometer wire,
$$= \frac{\text{potential difference along wire}}{\text{length of wire}}.$$
$$0.5 \times 10^{-3} = 1 \times \frac{50}{1000}$$
$$1 = 0.5 \times 10^{-3} \times \frac{1000}{50}$$
$$1 = \frac{1}{100}$$
So, $\dfrac{5}{(50+R)} = \dfrac{1}{100}$
$$R + 50 = 500$$
$$R = 450 ohms$$
Therefore, the resistance unplugged in the box is 450 ohms.
Hence, the correct option is (A).

4. The instantaneous current flowing in a transmission line, when measured using an ammeter, will give RMS current value. This value is 70.7% of the peak value. This is because, due to oscillations in AC, it is not possible to measure peak value. Hence to normalise, we consider current at any time in a line will be the RMS current.
Hence, the correct option is (C).

5. The third law of motion does not apply to skiing as in skiing we do not apply any force on the ground. The motion is caused by gravity and extremely less friction. In all the other cases, a force is applied on the ground or the other body, the reaction of which causes the motion.
Hence, the correct option is (B).

6. The value of gravitational constant was first experimentally determined by Henry Cavendish in the year 1798. It is also known as the Cavendish Gravitational Constant.
Hence, the correct option is (C).

7. If two bodies do not move along the same straight line path but lie in the same plane before and after the collision, the collision is said to be oblique or two dimensional collisions.
Hence, the correct option is (A).

8. When a conductor carries a certain value of current, the force developed in the conductor, the current in the conductor and the magnetic field in the conductor are mutually perpendicular to each other.
Hence, the correct option is (C).

9. A protein is a long chain of various amino acids which may or may not be needed by the body. Since proteins are the building blocks of the body, doing away with proteins cannot be done however taking proteins will harm the damaged kidney. In such cases, essential amino acids are ingested instead of taking in proteins. These essential amino acids are directly absorbed by the body. This allows the body to function normally and the pressure on the kidney is kept at the minimum.
Hence, the correct option is (B).

10. Closeness of two or more measurements is termed as precision. For example, if two measurements gives 3.1kg as output, then the measurement is said to be more precise.
Hence, the correct option is (A).

11. In the locomotive driving wheels and wheels of a moving car, then the total kinetic energy of the body is equal to the sum of kinetic energies of translation and rotation.

Hence, the correct option is (D).

12. Fluid Mechanics deals with the study of fluid at rest or in motion with or without the consideration of forces, Fluid Statics is the study of fluid at rest, Fluid Kinematics is the study of fluid in motion without consideration of forces and Fluid Dynamics is the study of fluid in motion considering the application forces.
Hence, the correct option is (B).

13. Internal energy corresponds to the mechanical energy of molecules. It is a state variable as it doesn't depend on the path taken. While heat is the energy in transit, so it is a path variable. Internal energy is a thermodynamic variable and is therefore macroscopic as thermodynamics deals with bulk systems.
Hence, the correct option is (B).

14. The stopping potential is directly proportional to the frequency of light. Hence, the stopping potential increases with an increase in the frequency of the incident light.
Hence, the correct option is (D).

15. Wavelength of de Broglie waves is given as:
$$\lambda = \frac{h}{p}.$$
As momentum is the same for all rays, all have the same wavelength λ.
Hence, the correct option is (D).

16. Alloys with two components are called binary alloy, while those with three components are called ternary alloy and alloys with 4 components are called quaternary alloy.
Hence, the correct option is (A).

17. There has been a decline of export of marine products to USA due to the emerging market there and the anti- dumping procedure by US government on many marine products. Hence both the mentioned points are correct.
Hence, the correct option is (C).

18. Leucocytes are involved in protecting body against infectious disease. They are produced in bone marrow. Leucocytes can squeeze through capillary walls and this is called as diapedesis.
Hence, the correct option is (D).

19. When the current flows into the page, the magnetic field is clockwise because of the right hand thumb rule, we orient our thumb into the page and our fingers curl in the clockwise direction.
Hence, the correct option is (A).

20. At the equilibrium position, the velocity of a particle in simple harmonic motion is maximum and consequently its acceleration is minimum.

Hence, the correct option is (D).

21. At the mean position, there is no acceleration in the body, hence the resultant force applied by the spring will be exactly equal to the weight of the body.

Hence, the correct option is (D).

22. Reactivity order for the alkyl halides towards Sn2 reaction is R-I>R-Br>R-Cl>R-F. This reactivity order reflects both the strength of the C–X bond, and the stability of $X^{(-)}$ as a leaving group, and leads to the general conclusion that alkyl iodides are the most reactive members of this functional class.

Hence, the correct option is (C).

23. Cerium, calcium, magnesium, manganese and titanium can be used to deoxidise steel.

Hence, the correct option is (C).

24. Biological Value (BV) refers to the amount of protein absorbed by the body from a food source. A protein is considered high bioavailable if it is easy to digest, absorb and make into other proteins.

Hence, the correct option is (A).

25. Laboratory diagnosis of Entamoeba histolytica depends on identification in the stools. Microscopic identification of cysts and trophozoites in the stool is the common method for diagnosing.

Hence, the correct option is (D).

Q.1 Match the following quantity with their SI units.

1. Electric Charge	a. Ohm
2. Electric Current	b. Volt
3. Electric Potential	c. Ampere
4. Electrical Resistance	d. Coulomb

A. 1-c, 2-d, 3-b, 4-a
B. 1-c, 2-b, 3-d, 4-a
C. 1-d, 2-c, 3-b, 4-a
D. 1-d, 2-c, 3-a, 4-b

Q.2 $[M^{-1} L^3 T^{-2}]$ are the dimensions of:
A. Gravitational constant
B. Gravitational potential energy
C. Gravitational potential
D. Gravitational intensity

Q.3 Keeping the speed of projection constant, the angle of projection is increased from $0°$ to $90°$. Then the horizontal range of the projectile:
A. Increases up to $45°$ and decreases afterwards.
B. Increases up to $60°$ and decreases later.
C. Increases up to $45°$ and remains unaltered thereafter.
D. Goes on increasing up to $90°$.

Q.4 An 800 kg car is moving at a speed of 90 km/h. It takes 5 s to stop after the brakes are applied. The force applied by the brakes will be_______.
A. 3000 N   **B.** 4000 N   **C.** 1000 N   **D.** 2000 N

Q.5 A coin is placed on a moving belt. The belt is suddenly stopped then coin will:
A. Stop suddenly with the belt
B. Continue moving for some time and then stops
C. Continue moving with a constant velocity
D. Continue moving with some acceleration

Q.6 Ranveer pulled a table cloth from a table without dislodging the dishes. This is due to:
A. Inertia   **B.** Impulse
C. Force   **D.** Momentum

Q.7 A rocket burns $0.4 kg$ of fuel per second and ejects out a gas with a velocity of $8 kms^{-1}$. Calculate the force exerted by the ejected gas on the rocket.
A. $2 \times 10^4 N$ **B.** $50 N$
C. $32 kN$ **D.** $3.2 kN$

Q.8 If simple harmonic motion is represented by $x = A\cos(\omega t + \varphi)$ then $'\varphi'$ is __________.
A. angular frequency   **B.** displacement
C. amplitude   **D.** phase constant

Q.9 The length of a second's pendulum is:
A. 140 cm   **B.** 70 cm
C. 100 cm   **D.** None of these

Q.10 Point of maximum positive displacement in a transverse wave is called:
A. Trough   **B.** Vertex   **C.** Apex   **D.** Crest

Q.11 Sound waves cannot travel in:
A. Air   **B.** Water   **C.** Vacuum   **D.** Steel

Q.12 A current of 0.5 A is drawn by a filament of an electric bulb for 20 minutes. The amount of electric charge that flows through the circuit is:
A. 1 C   **B.** 10 C   **C.** 600 C   **D.** 300 C

Q.13 The value of Coulomb's constant is _____ Nm^2/C^2.
A. 9×10^9 **B.** 6×10^6 **C.** 8×10^8 **D.** 7×10^7

Q.14 Which of the following statement regarding electric field lines is correct?
A. They can cross each other.
B. They can form a loop.
C. The magnitude of the electric field is minimum where the number of field lines is maximum.
D. They never cross each other.

Q.15 The value of R in the following circuit diagram will be:

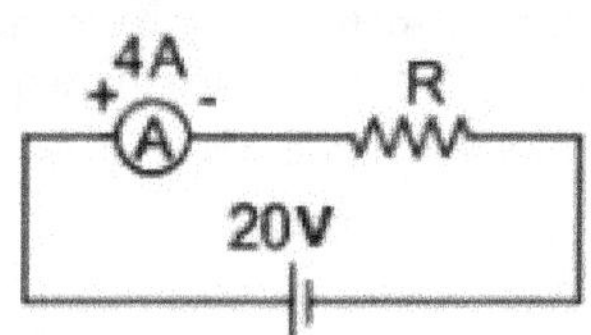

A. 5Ω **B.** 6Ω **C.** 8Ω **D.** 24Ω

Q.16 The power of a lens is $+2.5D$. What kind of lens is it and what is its focal length?
A. Convex lens, 40 cm
B. Concave lens, 100 cm
C. Convex lens, 50 cm
D. Concave lens, 40 cm

Q.17 Which of the following property is generally found in non-metals?
A. Ductility   **B.** Malleability
C. Conductivity   **D.** Brittleness

Q.18 If temperature of the gas is increased to three times, then its root mean square velocity become:
A. 3 times   **B.** 9 times
C. $\frac{1}{2}$ times   **D.** $\sqrt{3}$ times

Q.19 Which of the following is used as an antiseptic to sterilise wounds and syringes in hospitals?
A. Methanol   **B.** Propanol
C. Ethyl alcohol   **D.** Butanol

Q.20 Which of the following gas is evolved when ethanol reacts with sodium?

A. Oxygen   **B.** Chlorine
C. Hydrogen   **D.** Methane

Q.21 What are diseases like influenza, common cold and AIDS caused by?

A. Protozoan   **B.** Bacteria
C. Viruses   **D.** Worms

Q.22 _______ are the connective tissue that connects two bones to each other.

A. Tendons   **B.** Muscles
C. Cartilages   **D.** Ligaments

Q.23 The diagram shows the force field produced by a current-carrying wire. Name the force field.

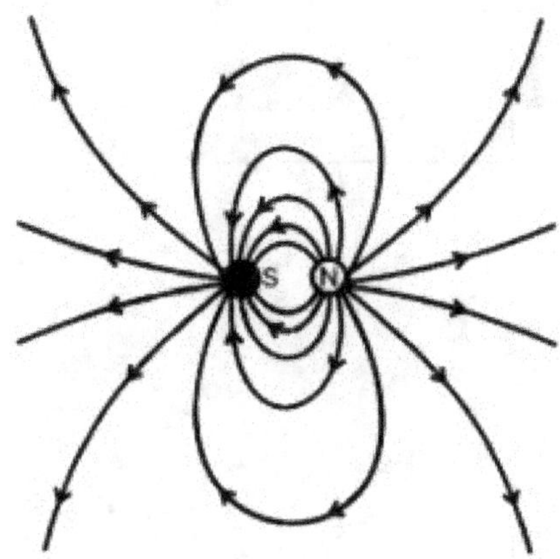

A. Electrostatic field
B. Magnetic field
C. Electromagnetic field
D. Static field

Q.24 A transformer is based on the principle of:

A. Mutual induction   **B.** Self induction
C. Ampere's law   **D.** Lenz's law

Q.25 GUI stands for:

A. Graph Use Interface
B. Graphical Universal Interface
C. Graphical User Interface
D. Graphical Unique Interface

// Smart Answer Sheet //

Correct — Percentage of students who answered correctly. **Skipped** — Percentage of students who skipped.

Q.	Ans.	Correct / Skipped	Q.	Ans.	Correct / Skipped	Q.	Ans.	Correct / Skipped	Q.	Ans.	Correct / Skipped	Q.	Ans.	Correct / Skipped	Q.	Ans.	Correct / Skipped
1	C	84.44 % / 11.14 %	6	A	76.32 % / 23.63 %	11	C	80.33 % / 12.97 %	16	A	89.27 % / 10.36 %	21	C	61.39 % / 32.05 %			
2	A	87.26 % / 12.31 %	7	D	89.4 % / 10.48 %	12	C	76.55 % / 12.52 %	17	D	85.59 % / 11.3 %	22	D	79.46 % / 18.24 %			
3	A	53.42 % / 30.73 %	8	D	78.24 % / 15.26 %	13	A	44.08 % / 50.64 %	18	D	78.1 % / 16.15 %	23	B	79.94 % / 19.02 %			
4	B	59.03 % / 32.86 %	9	C	88.6 % / 11.39 %	14	D	89.6 % / 10.37 %	19	C	88.89 % / 10.73 %	24	A	86.19 % / 11.02 %			
5	B	82.33 % / 16.78 %	10	D	44.93 % / 50.22 %	15	A	81.36 % / 12.06 %	20	C	80.43 % / 15.46 %	25	C	88.58 % / 10.9 %			

//Hints and Solutions//

1.

Quantity	SI Unit	Definition
Electric Charge	Coulomb (C)	Electric charge is the physical property of matter that causes it to experience a force when placed in an electromagnetic field.
Electric Current	Ampere (A)	It is the rate of flow of electric charge past a point or region.
Electric Potential	Volt (V)	It is the difference in electric potential between two points, which is defined as the work needed per unit of charge to move a test charge between the two points.
Electrical Resistance	Ohm (Ω)	The electrical resistance of an object is a measure of its opposition to the flow of electric current.

Hence, the correct option is (C).

2. The dimensional formula is defined as the expression of the physical quantity in terms of mass, length, time and ampere.

The magnitude of the gravitational force F is given by,

$$F = G\frac{M_1 M_2}{R^2}$$

Where, $G =$ universal gravitational constant, $M_1 =$ mass of 1st body, $M_2 =$ mass of 2nd body and $R =$ distance between the two bodies.

The above equation can be written as,

$$G = \frac{F \times R^2}{M_1 M_2}$$

Now,

Force $=$ mass $\times$ acceleration

Dimensional formula of force $(F) = [M] \times [LT^2] = [MLT^{-2}]$

Dimensional formula of radius $(R^2) = [L^2]$

Dimensional formula of radius $(M) = [M]$

Dimensional formula of universal gravitational constant $G = \frac{MLT^{-2} \times L^2}{M^2} = \frac{ML^3 T^{-2}}{M^2} = M^{-1}L^3 T^{-2}$

$\therefore$ The dimensional formula of universal gravitational constant G is $[M^{-1} L^3 T^2]$.

Hence, the correct option is (A).

3. The horizontal range of a projectile is given by,

$$R = \frac{u^2 \sin 2\theta}{g}$$

From the above equation it is clear that,

$$R \propto \sin 2\theta$$

From the above equation, it is clear that 2θ will increase till the value becomes one.

$$\sin 2\theta = 1$$

$$\Rightarrow \theta = \sin^{-1}\left(\frac{1}{2}\right)$$

$$\Rightarrow \theta = 45°$$

The horizontal range of the projectile increases up to $45°$ and then decreases afterwards.

Hence, the correct option is (A).

4. Given,

Initial velocity (u) = 90 km/h = 90$\times \frac{5}{18}$ = 25 m/s

Time taken to stop the car (t) = 5s

Final velocity (after stoping) (v) = 0 m/s

Mass of car (m) = 800 kg

Using, v = u + a t

0 = 25 + a × 5

So Acceleration (a) = $-\frac{25}{5}$ = - 5 m/s²

Force (F) = Mass (m) × Acceleration (a) = 800 × (-5) = - 4000 N

Negative sign show that the force acting is in opposite direction of the motion of the car.

Hence, the correct option is (B).

5. When a coin is moving with belt then coin has some velocity. If the belt stops moving suddenly then due to inertia of the coin, it will continue moving for some time and then stop due to the force of friction by the belt. Here force of friction by the belt act as an external force on the coin which stops the coin.

Hence, the correct option is (B).

6. When Ranveer pulled a table cloth from a table, at that time the dishes were at rest. Due to the inertia of rest, the dishes remain at rest because the cloths removed soon.

Hence, the correct option is (A).

7. Given,

Mass of a object $(m) = 0.4 kg,$

$\frac{velocity(u)}{time(t)} = 8 kms^{-1} = 8 \times 10^3 \ ms^{-1}$

According to Newton's second law of motion,

$$F = m\left(\frac{u}{t}\right)$$

$$\Rightarrow F = 0.4 \times 8 \times 10^3 = 3.2 \times 10^3 N = 3.2 kN$$

Hence, the correct option is (D).

8. Simple harmonic motion is represented by,

$$x = A\cos(\omega t + \varphi)$$

Where $A =$ amplitude, $\omega =$ Angular frequency, $x =$ Displacement and $\varphi =$ Phase constant

Hence, the correct option is (D).

9. Given,

$$T = 2 \text{ sec}$$

For a simple pendulum, the time period of swing of a pendulum depends on the length of the string and acceleration due to gravity.

$$T = 2\pi \sqrt{\frac{l}{g}}$$

The above formula is only valid for small angular displacements. Where, T = Time period of oscillation, l = length of the pendulum and g = gravitational acceleration

By squaring both side and rearranging we get,

$$l = \frac{T^2 \times g}{4\pi^2}$$

$$l = \frac{4 \times 9.8}{4 \times (3.14)^2} = 0.993 \text{ m} \approx 1 \text{ m} = 100 \text{ cm}$$

So, the length of second's pendulum is 99.3 cm or nearly 1 meter on earth surface.

Hence, the correct option is (C).

10. In a transverse waves particle of the medium vibrate up and down in the vertical direction whereas it is propagating along the horizontal direction. So, in a transverse wave, a crest is a part where particle rises from its mean position and has the maximum positive displacement whereas trough is a part where particle dips below mean position and has the maximum negative displacement.

Hence, the correct option is (D).

11. There are two types of waves Transverse and Longitudinal waves.

Transverse waves: The waves that produce vibrations in the medium in a direction perpendicular to their propagation (eg. Light).

Longitudinal waves: In these waves, the vibrations produced in a medium and their direction of propagation is the same.

The transverse waves can travel in a vacuum but the longitudinal waves require a medium to travel through. Sound waves are longitudinal in nature and therefore cannot travel in a vacuum.

From the above discussion, it is clear that the sound waves cannot travel in a vacuum.

Hence, the correct option is (C).

12. Given,

Current (I) = 0.5 A

Time (t) = 20 min = 20 × 60 sec = 1200 sec

Amount of electric charge (q) = current (I) × time (t) = 0.5 × 1200 = 600 C

Hence, the correct option is (C).

13. Coulomb's law in Electrostatics: It states that force of interaction between two stationary point charges is directly proportional to the product of the charges, and inversely proportional to the square of the distance between them and

acts along the straight line joining the two charges.

$$F \propto q_1 \times q_2$$

$$F \propto \frac{1}{r^2}$$

$$F = K \frac{q_1 \times q_2}{r^2}$$

Where $K = \dfrac{1}{4\pi\epsilon_0}$ constant called electrostatic force constant or Coulomb's Constant.

The value of K depends on the nature of the medium between the two charges and the system of units chosen.

From above it is clear that the constant in Coulomb's Law equation is $\dfrac{1}{4\pi\epsilon_0} = 9 \times 10^9 Nm^2/C^2$, where ε_0 is the permittivity of free space.

Hence, the correct option is (A).

14. If two lines will cross each other and we will take a tangents line on each curve at that point then we will get two directions of the electric field at that same point which is not possible. Since an electric field can have only one direction at a single point so the two electric field lines never cross each other.

Hence, the correct option is (D).

15. Given,

$$V = 20V \text{ and } I = 4A$$

According to ohm's law, $V = IR$

The above equation can be written for resistance as $R = \dfrac{V}{I} = \dfrac{20}{4} = 5\varOmega$

Hence, the correct option is (A).

16. As we know,

$$P = \frac{1}{f(m)} = \frac{100}{f(cm)}$$

Given,

Power of lens $(P) = +2.5D$

The power of a lens is given by,

$$f = \frac{100}{P} = \frac{100}{2.5} = 40 \text{ cm}$$

As the focal length is positive, therefore the lens is convex and has a focal length of 40 cm.

Hence, the correct option is (A).

17. Metals are malleable and ductile in nature whereas non-metals are neither malleable nor ductile, they are brittle. Brittleness is the ability of a material to break or shatter without significant deformation when under stress; the opposite of plasticity. For example, sudden breakage of cast iron job while hamming.

Hence, the correct option is (D).

18. The root mean square (rms) speed of any homogeneous gas sample is given by,

$$V_{rms} = \sqrt{\frac{3RT}{M}}$$

Here, M and R is constant, therefore

$$V_{rms} \propto \sqrt{T}$$

If the temperature is increased to 3 times, then V_{rms} is increased by $\sqrt{3}$ times.

Hence, the correct option is (D).

19. Ethanol is commonly known as Ethyl Alcohol. Its chemical formula is C_2H_5OH. Ethyl alcohol is used as an antiseptic to sterilise wounds and syringes in hospitals. Ethanol is a very good solvent. Many compounds that are insoluble in water are soluble in Ethyl Alcohol. It is used in many medicines, such as tincture iodine, cough syrups, etc. The melting point of Ethanol is −114° C and the boiling point is 78.37° C, which is very low with respect to water.

Hence, the correct option is (C).

20. Hydrogen gas is evolved when ethanol reacts with sodium.

$2Na + 2CH_3CH_2OH \ \square \ 2CH_3CH_2O–Na$ (Sodium ethoxide) $+ H_2(g)$

Alcohols react with sodium leading to the evolution of hydrogen. With ethanol, the other product is sodium ethoxide.

Hence, the correct option is (C).

21.

Agents	Diseases (Caused by)
Protozoan	• Malaria (spread by Anopheles mosquitoes, the Plasmodium parasite) • Amoebic dysentery (Entamoebahistolytica) • Sleeping sickness (Trypanosomabrucei)
Bacteria	• Whooping Cough (Borde tella pertussis) Diphtheria (Corynebacterium diphtheria) • Cholera (Vibrio cholera) • Leprosy (Mycobacterium leprae)
Viruses	• Chickenpox (Varicella-zoster virus) • Small Pox (Variola virus) • Common Cold (Rhinovirus) • AIDS, Acquired Immuno Deficiency Syndrome (Human Immunodeficiency Virus, HIV)
Worms	• Tapeworm (intestinal parasites) • Filariasis (by a thread) • Pinworm (by a small, thin, white roundworm called Enterobiusvermicularis)

Hence, the correct option is (C).

22. Ligaments are the connective tissue that connects two bones to each other. Ligaments are a short band of tough flexible connective tissues which connect two bones. Ligaments connect bones to other bones.

Hence, the correct option is (D).

23. The diagram shows the magnetic field produced by a current-carrying wire.

The magnetic field line starts from the North pole and ends at the south pole, it always makes a closed loop. It is formed by electric currents and magnets. The imaginary lines which represent the direction of the magnetic field are called magnetic field lines. The tangent at any point on the field lines gives the direction of the magnetic field vector at that point. Magnetic lines of force always emerge or start from the North Pole and terminate on the South Pole.

Hence, the correct option is (B).

24. A transformer is based on the principle of mutual induction.

When an electric current is passed through a coil changes with time, an emf is induced in the nearby coil then this phenomenon is called mutual induction.

Hence, the correct option is (A).

25. A Graphical User Interface is a computer interface that allows users to interact with a device through graphical elements such as pictures and animations, as opposed to text-based commands.

Hence, the correct option is (C).

Q.1 If $\begin{vmatrix} x & 2 \\ 18 & x \end{vmatrix} = \begin{vmatrix} 6 & 2 \\ 3x & 6 \end{vmatrix}$, then x is equal to:

A. 6 **B.** ±6 **C.** -6 **D.** 0

Q.2 What is the inverse of the matrix $A = \begin{pmatrix} \cos\theta & \sin\theta & 0 \\ -\sin\theta & \cos\theta & 0 \\ 0 & 0 & 1 \end{pmatrix}$:

A. $\begin{pmatrix} \cos\theta & -\sin\theta & 0 \\ \sin\theta & \cos\theta & 0 \\ 0 & 0 & 1 \end{pmatrix}$

B. $\begin{pmatrix} \cos\theta & 0 & -\sin\theta \\ 0 & 1 & 0 \\ \sin\theta & 0 & \cos\theta \end{pmatrix}$

C. $\begin{pmatrix} 1 & 0 & 0 \\ 0 & \cos\theta & -\sin\theta \\ 0 & \sin\theta & \cos\theta \end{pmatrix}$

D. $\begin{pmatrix} \cos\theta & \sin\theta & 0 \\ -\sin\theta & \cos\theta & 0 \\ 0 & 0 & 1 \end{pmatrix}$

Q.3 Find the equation of the curve with differential equation $(1 + y^2)dx = xydy$, and passing through $(1,0)$:

A. $x^2 - y^2 = 1$ **B.** $4x^2 - y^2 = 4$
C. $x^2 + y^2 = 1$ **D.** $4x^2 + y^2 = 4$

Q.4 Which of these is a second-order differential equation?

A. $y' + x = y^2$ **B.** $y'y'' + y = \sin x$
C. $y'''y'' + y = 0$ **D.** None of these

Q.5 Find the co-ordinates of in-centre of the triangle whose vertices are (0,6),(8,12) and (8,0):

A. $\left(\frac{16}{3}, 0\right)$ **B.** $(8,11)$ **C.** $(-4,3)$ **D.** $(5,6)$

Q.6 The modulus-amplitude form of $\sqrt{3} + i$, where $i = \sqrt{-1}$ is:

A. $2\left(\cos\frac{\pi}{3} + i\sin\frac{\pi}{3}\right)$

B. $2\left(\cos\frac{\pi}{6} + i\sin\frac{\pi}{6}\right)$

C. $4\left(\cos\frac{\pi}{3} + i\sin\frac{\pi}{3}\right)$

D. $4\left(\cos\frac{\pi}{6} + i\sin\frac{\pi}{6}\right)$

Q.7 What is $\frac{1}{\log_2 N} + \frac{1}{\log_3 N} + \frac{1}{\log_4 N} + \cdots + \frac{1}{\log_{100} N}$ equal to: $(N \neq 1)$

A. $\frac{1}{\log_{100!} N}$ **B.** $\frac{1}{\log_{99!} N}$ **C.** $\frac{99}{\log_{100!} N}$ **D.** $\frac{99}{\log_{99!} N}$

Q.8 What is $i^{1000} + i^{1001} + i^{1002} + i^{1003}$ equal to: (where $i = \sqrt{-1}$)

A. 0 **B.** i **C.** $-i$ **D.** 1

Q.9 $\int \frac{dx}{e^z + e^{-z}}$ equals:

A. $\log(e^x + e^{-x}) + c$ **B.** $\log(e^x - e^{-x}) + c$

C. $\tan^{-1} e^x + c$ **D.** $\tan^{-1} e^{-x} + c$

Q.10 If the sum of the infinite GP is $\frac{4}{3}$ and its first term is $\frac{3}{4}$ then its common ratio is:

A. $\frac{7}{16}$ **B.** $\frac{9}{16}$ **C.** $\frac{1}{9}$ **D.** $\frac{7}{9}$

Q.11 If α, β are the different complex numbers with $|\beta| = 1$, then find $\left|\frac{\beta - \alpha}{1 - \overline{\alpha}\beta}\right|$?

A. 3 **B.** 2 **C.** 1 **D.** 0

Q.12 In a class, 54 students are good in Hindi only, 63 students are good in Mathematics only and 41 students are good in English only. There are 18 students who are good in both Hindi and Mathematics. 10 students are good in all three subjects. What is the number of students who are good in either Hindi or mathematics but not in English?

A. 99 **B.** 107 **C.** 125 **D.** 130

Q.13 In a class, 54 students are good in Hindi only, 63 students are good in Mathematics only and 41 students are good in English only. There are 18 students who are good in both Hindi and Mathematics. 10 students are good in all three subjects. What is the number of students who are good in Hindi and Mathematics but not in English?

A. 18 **B.** 12 **C.** 10 **D.** 8

Q.14 How many four-digit numbers divisible by 10 can be formed using 1,5,0,6,7 without repetition of digits?

A. 24 **B.** 36 **C.** 44 **D.** 64

Q.15 If $\cos T = \frac{3}{5}$ and if $\sin R = \frac{8}{17}$, where T is in the fourth quadrant and R is in second quadrant, then $\cos(T - R)$ is equal to:

A. $\frac{77}{85}$ **B.** $\frac{13}{85}$ **C.** $-\frac{13}{85}$ **D.** $-\frac{77}{85}$

Q.16 The product of r consecutive positive integers, divided by $r!$ is:

A. A proper fraction **B.** Equal to r
C. A positive integer **D.** None of these

Q.17 If the ratio AM to GM of two positive numbers a and b is $5:3$, then $a:b$ is equal to:

A. $3:5$ **B.** $2:9$ **C.** $9:1$ **D.** $5:3$

Q.18 The number of non-zero integral solutions of the equation $|1 - 2i|^x = 5^x$ is:

A. 0 **B.** 1 **C.** 2 **D.** 3

Q.19 How many numbers between 100 and 1000 can be formed with the digits $5,6,7,8,9$, if the repetition of digits is not allowed?

A. 3^5 **B.** 5^3 **C.** 120 **D.** 60

Q.20 If the cardinality of a set A is 4 and that of a set B is 3, then what is the cardinality of the set $A \Delta B$?

A. 1

B. 5

C. 7

D. Cannot be determined

Q.21 In the expansion of $(1 + x)^{43}$ coefficients of $(2r + 1)^{th}$ and $(r + 2)^{th}$ terms are equal, then what is the value of r: $(\neq 1)$

A. 5   **B.** 14   **C.** 21   **D.** 22

Q.22 If $n = (2017)!$, then what is $\dfrac{1}{\log_2 n} + \dfrac{1}{\log_3 n} + \dfrac{1}{\log_4 n} + \cdots + \dfrac{1}{\log_{2017} n}$ equal to:

A. 0   **B.** 1   **C.** $\dfrac{n}{2}$ **D.** n

Q.23 If $n \in N$, then $121^n - 25^n + 1900^n - (-4)^n$ is divisible by which one of the following?

A. 1904   **B.** 2000   **C.** 2002   **D.** 2006

Q.24 What is the principal argument of $(-1 - i)$, (where $i = \sqrt{-1}$)?

A. $\dfrac{5\pi}{4}$ **B.** $-\dfrac{\pi}{4}$ **C.** $-\dfrac{3\pi}{4}$ **D.** $\dfrac{3\pi}{4}$

Q.25 If A + B + C = π, then what is sin (A + B) + sin C equal to?

A. 0   **B.** 2 sin C

C. cos C – sin C   **D.** None of the above

// Smart Answer Sheet //

Correct Percentage of students who answered correctly.   **Skipped** Percentage of students who skipped.

Q.	Ans.	Correct / Skipped	Q.	Ans.	Correct / Skipped	Q.	Ans.	Correct / Skipped	Q.	Ans.	Correct / Skipped	Q.	Ans.	Correct / Skipped	Q.	Ans.	Correct / Skipped
1	A	64.9 % / 33.02 %	6	B	67.55 % / 30.97 %	11	C	66.02 % / 33.83 %	16	C	83.01 % / 16.54 %	21	B	42.53 % / 56.98 %			/
2	A	60.69 % / 37.62 %	7	A	64.77 % / 32.87 %	12	C	56.13 % / 31.88 %	17	C	68.43 % / 31.16 %	22	B	62.91 % / 32.9 %			/
3	A	26.43 % / 67.49 %	8	A	57.85 % / 33.13 %	13	D	25.55 % / 72.75 %	18	A	42.94 % / 31.67 %	23	B	55.92 % / 35.45 %			/
4	B	69.17 % / 30.4 %	9	C	40.64 % / 45.98 %	14	A	80.92 % / 10.45 %	19	D	48.93 % / 32.71 %	24	C	64.19 % / 35.28 %			/
5	D	67.3 % / 32.2 %	10	A	55.92 % / 39.79 %	15	D	51.05 % / 30.03 %	20	D	88.94 % / 10.41 %	25	B	84.27 % / 11.42 %			/

//Hints and Solutions//

1. Given:
$$\begin{vmatrix} x & 2 \\ 18 & x \end{vmatrix} = \begin{vmatrix} 6 & 2 \\ 3x & 6 \end{vmatrix}$$
We have to find the value of x.
$$\Rightarrow x^2 - 36 = 36 - 6x \quad \left(\begin{bmatrix} a & b \\ c & d \end{bmatrix} = ad - bc\right)$$
$$\Rightarrow x^2 + 6x - 72 = 0$$
Using Shridharachaarye rule,
$$\Rightarrow x = \frac{-6 + \sqrt{6^2 + 4 \times 72}}{2}$$
$$= \frac{-6 \pm \sqrt{36(1+8)}}{2}$$
$$x = -3 \pm 9 = 6 \text{ or } -12$$
Hence, the correct option is (A).

2. We know that $A^{-1} = \dfrac{adj(A)}{|A|}$ .....(i)

Now,
$$|A| = \cos\theta(\cos\theta) - \sin\theta(-\sin\theta)$$
$$= \cos^2\theta + \sin^2\theta$$
$$= 1$$
Now,
$$AdjA = \begin{pmatrix} \cos\theta & -\sin\theta & 0 \\ \sin\theta & \cos\theta & 0 \\ 0 & 0 & 1 \end{pmatrix}$$
Putting the value in (i),
$$\therefore A^{-1} = \begin{pmatrix} \cos\theta & -\sin\theta & 0 \\ \sin\theta & \cos\theta & 0 \\ 0 & 0 & 1 \end{pmatrix}$$
Hence, the correct option is (A).

3. Given,
$$(1 + y^2)dx = xy\,dy$$
$$\Rightarrow \frac{2}{x}dx = \frac{2y}{1+y^2}dy \text{ ...(i)}$$
Let $t = 1 + y^2$
$$\Rightarrow dt = 2y\,dy \text{ .....(ii)}$$
integrating (i) and (ii),
Using $\Rightarrow \int \frac{2}{x}dx = \int \frac{dt}{t} + logc$
Therefore, $logx^2 = logct$
$$\Rightarrow x^2 = c(1 + y^2) \text{.....(i)}$$
Put $(x, y) = (1,0)$
$$\Rightarrow 1 = c(1 + 0)$$
$$\Rightarrow c = 1$$
Put $c = 1$ in (i),
So, the equation of the curve will be $x^2 - y^2 = 1$
Hence, the correct option is (A).

4. The order of a differential equation is the order of the highest order derivative.

So, $y''y' + y = sinx$ has order 2.

Hence, the correct option is (B).

5. Let, $A(x_1, y_1) = (0,6), B(x_2, y_2) = (8,12)$ and $C(x_3, y_3) = (8,0)$ be the vertices of triangle ABC.
Distance $= \sqrt{(X_1 - X_2)^2 + (Y_1 - Y_2)^2}$
Then, $c = AB$ for $(0,6)(8,12)$
$$= \sqrt{(0 - 8)^2 + (6 - 12)^2}$$
$$AB = 10$$
$b = CA$ for $(0,6)(8,0)$
$$= \sqrt{(0 - 8)^2 + (6 - 0)^2}$$
$$CA = 10$$
$a = BC$ for $(8,12)(8,0)$
$$= \sqrt{(8 - 8)^2 + (12 - 0)^2}$$
$$BC = 12$$
The co-ordinates of the in-centre are
$$\left(\frac{ax_1 + bx_2 + cx_3}{a+b+c}, \frac{ay_1 + by_2 + cy_3}{a+b+c}\right)$$
$$\Rightarrow \left(\frac{12 \times 0 + 10 \times 8 + 10 \times 8}{12 + 10 + 10}, \frac{12 \times 6 + 10 \times 12 + 10 \times 0}{12 + 10 + 10}\right)$$
$$\Rightarrow \left(\frac{160}{32}, \frac{192}{32}\right)$$
$$\Rightarrow (5,6)$$
Hence, the correct option is (D).

6. Modulus amplitude form of $(\sqrt{3} + i)$ is:
$$z = r(\cos\theta + isin\theta)$$
$$\Rightarrow rcos\theta = \sqrt{3}, rsin\theta = 1$$
$$\Rightarrow r^2(\cos^2\theta + \sin^2\theta) = 4$$
$$\Rightarrow r^2 = 4$$
$$\Rightarrow r = 2$$
$2cos\theta = \sqrt{3}$ and $2sin\theta = 1$
$$\Rightarrow cos\theta = \frac{\sqrt{3}}{2} \text{ and } sin\theta = \frac{1}{2}$$
$$\Rightarrow \theta = \frac{\pi}{6} \text{ and } \theta = \frac{\pi}{6}$$
$$\therefore z = 2\left(\cos\frac{\pi}{6} + isin\frac{\pi}{6}\right)$$
Hence, the correct option is (B).

7. $\dfrac{1}{log_2 N} + \dfrac{1}{log_3 N} + \dfrac{1}{log_4 N} + \cdots + \dfrac{1}{(log_{100} N)}$

Now we know that $\dfrac{1}{log_a b} = log_b a$
$$= log_N 2 + log_N 3 + log_N 4 + \cdots + log_N 100$$
$$= log_N(2.3.4 \ldots \ldots 100)$$
$$log_N(100!)$$
$$= \frac{1}{log_{100!} N}$$
Hence, the correct option is (A).

8. $i^{1000} + i^{1001} + i^{1002} + i^{1003}$
$$= i^{1000} + i^{1000} \cdot i + i^{1002} + i^{1002} \cdot i$$
$$= (i^2)^{500} + (i^2)^{500} \cdot i + (i^2)^{501} + (i^2)^{501} \cdot i$$
$$= (-1)^{500} + (-1)^{500} \cdot i + (-1)^{501} + (-1)^{501} \cdot i$$
$$= 1 + i - 1 - i$$
$$= 0$$
Hence, the correct option is (A).

9. $I = \int \dfrac{e^x}{e^x + e^{-x}} dx$

$I = \int \dfrac{e^x}{e^{2x} + 1} dx$

Let, $e^x = t$

$\Rightarrow e^x dx = dt$

$= \int \dfrac{1}{t^2 + 1} dt = \tan^{-1} t + c$

$\int \dfrac{e^x}{e^x + e^{-x}} dx = \tan^{-1} e^x + c$

Hence, the correct option is (C).

10. $S_\infty = \dfrac{a}{1 - r}$ where a' be the first term and r be the common ratio of GP.

$\therefore \dfrac{4}{3} = \dfrac{\frac{3}{4}}{1 - r}$

$\Rightarrow 1 - r = \dfrac{\frac{3}{4}}{\frac{4}{3}}$

$\Rightarrow r = 1 - \dfrac{\frac{3}{9}}{16}$

$\Rightarrow r = \dfrac{7}{16}$

Hence, the correct option is (A).

11. $\left| \dfrac{\beta - \alpha}{1 - \alpha\beta} \right|^2 = \left(\dfrac{\beta - \alpha}{1 - \overline{\alpha}\beta} \right) \left(\dfrac{\overline{\beta} - \overline{\alpha}}{1 - \alpha\overline{\beta}} \right)$

$\Rightarrow \left| \dfrac{\beta - \alpha}{1 - \alpha\beta} \right|^2 = \dfrac{\beta\overline{\beta} - \overline{\beta}\alpha - \alpha\beta + \alpha\overline{\alpha}}{(1 - \overline{\alpha}\beta)(1 - \alpha\overline{\beta})}$

$\Rightarrow \left| \dfrac{\beta - \alpha}{1 - \overline{\alpha}\beta} \right|^2 = \dfrac{|\beta|^2 - \overline{\beta}\alpha - \alpha\overline{\beta} + |\alpha|^2}{1 - \alpha\overline{\beta} - \overline{\alpha}\beta + |\alpha|^2 |\beta|^2}$

$\Rightarrow \left| \dfrac{\beta - \alpha}{1 - \alpha\beta} \right|^2 = \dfrac{|\alpha|^2 - \beta\overline{\alpha} - \alpha\overline{\beta} + 1}{1 - \alpha\overline{\beta} - \overline{\alpha}\beta + |\alpha|^2}, \quad [\because |\beta| = 1]$

$\Rightarrow \left| \dfrac{\beta - \alpha}{1 - \alpha\beta} \right| = 1$

Hence, the correct option is (C).

12.

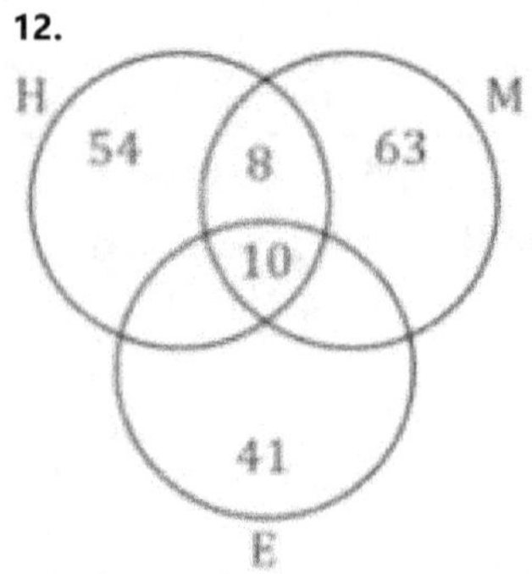

Let, H, M, E denote the set of students studying Hindi, Mathematics and English.

$n(H) + n(M) + n(H \cap M) - n(H \cap M \cap E)$ [

Excluding English]

$= 54 + 63 + 18 - 10$

$= 125$

Hence, the correct option is (C).

13.

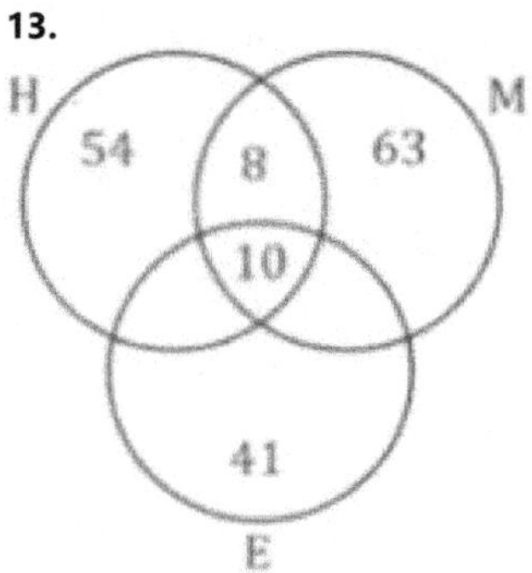

Let H, M, E denote the set of students studying Hindi, Mathematics and English.

$n(H \cap M) - n(H \cap M \cap E)$

$= 18 - 10$

$= 8$

Hence, the correct option is (D).

14. Four-digit numbers divisible by 10 using 1,5,0,6,7.

Divisibility by 10 $\rightarrow$ no. should end with zero

After fixing 'zero' at unit place, we are left with 4 numbers.

After placing any number at tens place we are left with '3' numbers.

After placing any number at tens and hundreds place.

Total $= 4 \times 3 \times 2$

$= 24$

Hence, the correct option is (A).

15. We have,

$\cos T = \dfrac{3}{5}$

$\sin T = \sqrt{1 - \cos^2 T}$

$\sin T = \sqrt{1 - \left(\dfrac{3}{5} \right)^2}$

$= \sqrt{1 - \dfrac{9}{25}}$

$= \sqrt{\dfrac{16}{25}} = -\dfrac{4}{5}$ (since T is in IV quadrant)

$\sin R = \dfrac{8}{17}$

$\cos R = \sqrt{1 - \sin^2 R}$

$\cos R = \sqrt{1 - \left(\dfrac{8}{17} \right)^2}$

$\cos R = \sqrt{1 - \dfrac{64}{289}}$

$= \sqrt{\dfrac{225}{289}} = -\dfrac{15}{17}$ (since R is in II quadrant)

Now,

$\because \cos(T - R) = \cos T \cos R + \sin T \sin R$

$= \dfrac{3}{5} \times \dfrac{-15}{17} + \dfrac{-4}{5} \times \dfrac{8}{17}$

$= \left[\dfrac{-45 - 32}{85} \right]$

$$= -\frac{77}{85}$$

Hence, the correct option is (D).

16. Consider r consecutive positive intergers,

$$n+1, \ldots\ldots, n+r-1, n+r$$

Then, $\dfrac{(n+1)\ldots(n+r)}{r!}$

$$= \frac{n!(n+1)\ldots\ldots(n+r)}{n!r!} = {}^{n+r}C_r$$

Which is a positive integer.

Hence, the correct option is (C).

17. $\dfrac{AM}{GM} = \dfrac{5}{3}$

$$\frac{\frac{a+b}{2}}{\sqrt{ab}} = \frac{5}{3}$$

$$\frac{a+b}{2\sqrt{ab}} = \frac{5}{3}$$

$$\frac{\frac{a}{b}+1}{2\sqrt{\frac{a}{b}}} = \frac{5}{3} \qquad \text{[divide numerator \& denominator by } b\text{]}$$

Let, $\dfrac{a}{b} = y$

$$\Rightarrow \frac{y+1}{2\sqrt{y}} = \frac{5}{3}$$

$$\Rightarrow 3y + 3 = 10\sqrt{y}$$

Squaring both sides,

$$\Rightarrow 9y^2 + 9 + 18y = 100y$$
$$\Rightarrow 9y^2 - 82y + 9 = 0$$
$$\Rightarrow 9y^2 - 81y - y + 9 = 0$$
$$\Rightarrow 9y(y-9) - 1(y-9) = 0$$
$$\Rightarrow (y-9)(9y-1) = 0$$
$$\Rightarrow y = \frac{1}{9} \text{ or } y = 9$$

i.e. $\dfrac{a}{b} = \dfrac{1}{9}$ or $\dfrac{a}{b} = \dfrac{9}{1}$

Hence, the correct option is (C).

18. Giving, $|1-2i|^x = 5^x$

We need to find the value of x for which should be an integer but not zero.

Let first find value of $|1-2i|$

$$\Rightarrow \begin{array}{l} |1-2i| = \sqrt{(1)^2 + (2)^2} = \sqrt{5} \\ \left[\because z = x + iy \Rightarrow |z| = \sqrt{x^2 + y^2}\right] \end{array}$$

So,

$$|1-2i|^x = 5^x$$

$$\Rightarrow \left(\sqrt{5}\right)^x = 5^x$$

$$\Rightarrow \left(\sqrt{5}\right)^x = \left(\sqrt{5}\right)^{2x}$$

Comparing powers,

$$\Rightarrow x = 2x$$

$$\Rightarrow x - 2x = 0$$

$$\Rightarrow -x = 0$$

$$\Rightarrow x = 0$$

Hence, the correct option is (A).

19. Number lying between 100 and 1000 formed by 3 digits.

And every digit have 5 option $(1,2,3,4,5)$ to select a number. But repetition is not allowed.

So, number $= {}^5P_3$

$$= \frac{5!}{(5-3)!}$$
$$= \frac{5!}{2!}$$
$${}^5P_3 = 60$$

Hence, the correct option is (D).

20. Since sets A and B are not known, the cardinality of the set $A\Delta B$ can not be determined.

Hence, the correct option is (D).

21. Given as:

$$(1+x)^{43}$$

As we know, the coefficient of the r term in the expansion of $(1+x)^n$ is ${}^nC_{r-1}$.

Therefore, the coefficients of the $(2r+1)$ and $(r+2)$ terms in the given expansion are ${}^{43}C_{2r+1-1}$ and ${}^{43}C_{r+2-1}$

For these coefficients to be equal, we must have,

$$\Rightarrow {}^{43}C_{2r+1-1} = {}^{43}C_{r+2-1}$$
$$\Rightarrow {}^{43}C_{2r} = {}^{43}C_{r+1}$$
$$\Rightarrow 2r = r+1 \text{ or } 2r + r + 1 = 43 \left[\text{since, } {}^nC_r = {}^nC_s \Rightarrow r = s \text{ (or) } r + s = n\right]$$
$$\Rightarrow 2r - r = 1 \text{ or } 3r + 1 = 43$$
$$\Rightarrow 3r = 43 - 1 \; r = 1$$
$$\Rightarrow r = 1 \text{ or } 3r = 42$$
$$\Rightarrow r = \frac{42}{3}$$
$$\Rightarrow r = 1 \text{ or } r = 14$$

$\therefore r = 14$ [since, value 1 gives the same term]

Hence, the correct option is (B).

22. If $n = (2017)!$

$$\frac{1}{\log_2 \pi} + \frac{1}{\log_3 n} + \cdots + \frac{1}{\log_{2017} n} \ldots\ldots\ldots\ldots \text{(i)}$$

Now we know that $\dfrac{1}{\log_n b} = \log_b a$

$\therefore$ We can rewrite (i) as, $\dfrac{1}{\log_2 n} + \dfrac{1}{\log_3 n} + \cdots + \dfrac{1}{\log_{2017} n}$

$$= \log_n 2 + \log_n 3 + \log_n 4 + \cdots + \log_n 2017$$
$$= \log_n(2.3.4\ldots\ldots 2017) \text{ as } [\log_a b + \log_a c = \log_a(b \times c)]$$

$\because n = (2017)!$

$\therefore \log_n(2.3.4\ldots.2017)$

$$= \log_{2017!}(2017)!$$

$= 1$

So,

$$\frac{1}{\log_2 n} + \frac{1}{\log_3 n} + \cdots + \frac{1}{\log_{2017} n} = 1$$

Hence, the correct option is (B).

23. $(121)^n - 25^n + 1900^n - (-4)^n$

For $n = 1$

$121 - 25 + 1900 - (-4)$

$= 121 - 25 + 1900 + 4$

$= 2025 - 25$

$= 2000$

Hence, the correct option is (B).

24. Given, $Z = -1 - i$

$$Z = r(\cos\theta + i\sin\theta)$$

Here, r is modulus and θ is argument.

$r\cos\theta = -1$ and $r\sin\theta = -1$

$\Rightarrow r^2 = 2$

$\Rightarrow r = \sqrt{2}$

Undefined control sequence therefore

$$\Rightarrow \cos\theta = \frac{-1}{\sqrt{2}}$$

$$\sqrt{2}\sin\theta = -1$$

$$\Rightarrow \sin\theta = -\frac{-1}{\sqrt{2}}$$

Here both $\cos\theta$ and $\sin\theta$ are negative.

So, θ lies in 3rd quadrant.

Argument $= -3\pi 4$

Hence, the correct option is (C).

25. As we know,
sin (π − θ) = sin θ
Given that:
A + B + C = π
⇒ A + B = π - C
Now,
sin (A + B) = sin (π -C)
Now put the value in given equation,
sin (A + B) + sin C
= sin (π − C) + sin C
= sin C + sin C (∵ sin (π − θ) = sin θ)
= 2 sin C
Hence, the correct option is (B).

Q.1 The value of the expression $\dfrac{4\sin 20 \sin 80 - 1}{\sin 10}$ is:

A. 0   **B.** 4   **C.** 1   **D.** 2

Q.2 If $\cos x + \cos y + \cos z = 0$ and $\sin x + \sin y + \sin z = 0$ then find the value of $\cos(x - y)$.

A. 1   **B.** $\frac{1}{2}$ **C.** $-\frac{1}{2}$ **D.** 0

Q.3 What is the value of $\left(1 + \cos\dfrac{\pi}{8}\right)\left(1 + \cos\dfrac{3\pi}{8}\right)\left(1 + \cos\dfrac{5\pi}{8}\right)\left(1 + \cos\dfrac{7\pi}{8}\right)$?

A. $\frac{1}{2}$ **B.** $\frac{1}{2} + \frac{1}{2\sqrt{2}}$

C. $\frac{1}{2} - \frac{1}{2\sqrt{2}}$ **D.** $\frac{1}{8}$

Q.4 Find the value of a for which $x + \sqrt{3x} + \dfrac{a^2}{4}$ is a perfect square.

A. $\sqrt{3}$ **B.** $2\sqrt{3}$ **C.** $3\sqrt{3}$ **D.** $4\sqrt{3}$

Q.5 If $x = 2 + 2^{\frac{2}{3}} + 2^{\frac{1}{3}}$, then what is the value of $x^3 - 6x^2 + 6x$?

A. 3   **B.** 2   **C.** 1   **D.** 0

Q.6 If $A = \begin{bmatrix} 2 & -3 \\ 0 & 1 \end{bmatrix}$ and $B = \begin{bmatrix} 1 & 2 \\ 3 & 0 \end{bmatrix}$ then $(B^{-1}A^{-1})^{-1}$ is equal to:

A. $\begin{bmatrix} 7 & 4 \\ 3 & 0 \end{bmatrix}$ **B.** $\begin{bmatrix} -7 & 4 \\ 3 & 0 \end{bmatrix}$

C. $\begin{bmatrix} -7 & 4 \\ 0 & 5 \end{bmatrix}$ **D.** $\begin{bmatrix} 4 & -7 \\ 3 & 0 \end{bmatrix}$

Q.7 Let p, q and r be three distinct positive real numbers. If $D = \begin{vmatrix} p & q & r \\ q & r & p \\ r & p & q \end{vmatrix}$, then which one of the following is correct?

A. $D < 0$ **B.** $D \le 0$ **C.** $D > 0$ **D.** $D \ge 0$

Q.8 If a, b, c are real numbers, then the value of the determinant $\begin{vmatrix} 1-a & a-b-c & b+c \\ 1-b & b-c-a & c+a \\ 1-c & c-a-b & a+b \end{vmatrix}$ is:

A. 0

B. $(a-b)(b-c)(c-a)$

C. $(a+b+c)^2$

D. $(a+b+c)^3$

Q.9 If $p + q + r = a + b + c = 0$, then the determinant $\begin{vmatrix} pa & qb & rc \\ qc & ra & pb \\ rb & pc & qa \end{vmatrix}$ equals:

A. 0

B. 1

C. $pa + qb + rc$

D. $pa + qb + rc + a + b + c$

Q.10 $\begin{vmatrix} a+b & b+c & c \\ b+c & c+a & a \\ c+a & a+b & b \end{vmatrix} = k \begin{vmatrix} a & b & c \\ b & c & a \\ c & a & b \end{vmatrix}$ then k is equal to:

A. 1   **B.** 2   **C.** 4   **D.** 6

Q.11 Focus of the parabola $y^2 - 8x + 6y + 1 = 0$ is:

A. (2, 0)   **B.** (1, -3)

C. (8, 0)   **D.** None of the above

Q.12 The two circles $x^2 + y^2 = r^2$ and $x^2 + y^2 - 10x + 16 = 0$ intersect at two distinct points. Then which one of the following is correct?

A. $2 < r < 8$ **B.** $r = 2$ or $r = 8$

C. $r < 2$ **D.** $r > 2$

Q.13 For a hyperbola $\dfrac{x^2}{16} - \dfrac{y^2}{9} = 1$ then its equation of directrix is:

A. $x = \frac{4}{5}$ **B.** $x = \frac{-4}{5}$ **C.** $x = \frac{16}{5}$ **D.** $x = \frac{17}{5}$

Q.14 The length of latus rectum of the ellipse $3x^2 + y^2 - 12x + 2y + 1 = 0$ is:

A. $2\sqrt{3}$ **B.** 12   **C.** $\frac{4}{\sqrt{3}}$ **D.** $\frac{3}{\sqrt{2}}$

Q.15 Find the radius of circle which passes through the points $(1,2)$ and $(3,4)$ and the centre lies on the straight line $y - 3x + 2 = 0$.

A. 3   **B.** $\sqrt{3}$ **C.** 5   **D.** $3\sqrt{2}$

Q.16 If the vectors $\hat{i} - x\hat{j} - y\hat{k}$ and $\hat{i} + x\hat{j} + y\hat{k}$ are orthogonal to each other, then what is the locus of the point (x, y)?

A. A parabola   **B.** An ellipse

C. A circle   **D.** A straight line

Q.17 If $\left|\vec{a}\right| = \sqrt{2}, \left|\vec{b}\right| = \sqrt{3}$ and $\left|\vec{a} + \vec{b}\right| = \sqrt{6}$, then $\left|\vec{a} - \vec{b}\right|$ equal to:

A. 1   **B.** 2   **C.** 3   **D.** 4

Q.18 The angle between the planes $2x + y + z = 7$ and $x - y + 2z = 9$ is:

A. 60°   **B.** 120°   **C.** 90°   **D.** 530°

Q.19 If a line makes $45°, 60°$ with the x-axis, y-axis respectively, then the angle made by that line with the z-axis is:

A. 75°   **B.** 45°   **C.** 60°   **D.** 30°

Q.20 Find the intercepts cut off by the plane $x + 2y - 4z = 8$.

A. $(1,2,4)$ **B.** $(1,2,-4)$

C. $(8,4,2)$ **D.** $(8,4,-2)$

Q.21 $\int \sqrt{2x + 3}\,dx$ is equal to:

A. $\dfrac{(2x+3)^{\frac{1}{2}}}{3} + c$ **B.** $\dfrac{(2x+3)^{\frac{3}{2}}}{2} + c$

C. $\dfrac{(2x+3)^{\frac{3}{2}}}{3} + c$ **D.** None of the above

Q.22 What is the value of $\int_{4}^{9} \dfrac{1}{\sqrt{x}}\,dx$?

A. 1 **B.** -2 **C.** 2 **D.** -1

Q.23 If $2x^3 - 3y^2 = 7$, what is $\dfrac{dy}{dx}$ equal to $(y \neq 0)$:

A. $\dfrac{x^2}{2y}$ **B.** $\dfrac{x}{2y}$

C. $\dfrac{x^2}{y}$ **D.** None of the above

Q.24 Let the average of three numbers be 16. If two of the numbers are 8 and 10, what is the remaining number?

A. -30 **B.** 18 **C.** 12 **D.** 30

Q.25 If A and B are two independent events with $P(A) = \dfrac{3}{5}$ and $P(B) = \dfrac{4}{9}$, then $P(A \cap B)$ equals:

A. $\dfrac{4}{15}$ **B.** $\dfrac{8}{45}$ **C.** $\dfrac{1}{3}$ **D.** $\dfrac{7}{12}$

// Smart Answer Sheet //

Correct — Percentage of students who answered correctly. **Skipped** — Percentage of students who skipped.

Q.	Ans.	Correct / Skipped	Q.	Ans.	Correct / Skipped	Q.	Ans.	Correct / Skipped	Q.	Ans.	Correct / Skipped	Q.	Ans.	Correct / Skipped	Q.	Ans.	Correct / Skipped
1	D	0 % / 100 %	6	B	3.45 % / 93.1 %	11	B	3.45 % / 93.1 %	16	C	0 % / 100 %	21	C	3.45 % / 93.1 %			
2	C	0 % / 100 %	7	B	3.45 % / 93.1 %	12	A	6.9 % / 93.1 %	17	B	3.45 % / 93.1 %	22	C	6.9 % / 93.1 %			
3	D	0 % / 100 %	8	A	0 % / 100 %	13	C	3.45 % / 93.1 %	18	A	6.9 % / 93.1 %	23	C	6.9 % / 93.1 %			
4	A	3.45 % / 93.1 %	9	A	6.9 % / 93.1 %	14	C	3.45 % / 93.1 %	19	C	0 % / 100 %	24	D	6.9 % / 93.1 %			
5	B	3.45 % / 93.1 %	10	A	3.45 % / 93.1 %	15	A	0 % / 100 %	20	D	0 % / 100 %	25	A	3.45 % / 93.1 %			

//Hints and Solutions//

1. As we know,

$2\sin x\sin y = \cos(x - y) - \cos(x + y)$

$4\sin20\sin80 - 1$

$= 2 \times (2\sin80\sin20) - 1$

$= 2 \times [\cos(80 - 20) - \cos(80 + 20)] - 1$

$= 2 \times [\cos60 - \cos100] - 1$

$= 2\cos60 - 2\cos100 - 1$

$= 2 \times \frac{1}{2} - 2\cos(90 + 10) - 1$

$= 1 - 2[-\sin10] - 1 \ [\because \cos(90 + \theta) = -\sin\theta]$

$= 2\sin10$

Now,

$\frac{4\sin20\sin80 - 1}{\sin10} = \frac{2\sin10}{\sin10} = 2$

Hence, the correct option is (D).

2. As we know,

$\sin^2 x + \cos^2 y = 1$

$\cos(x - y) = \cos x\cos y + \sin x\sin y$

Given,

$\cos x + \cos y + \cos z = 0$

$\Rightarrow \cos x + \cos y = -\cos z \ldots (1)$

$\sin x + \sin y + \sin z = 0$

$\Rightarrow \sin x + \sin y = -\sin z \ldots (2)$

Squaring and adding equation (1) and equation (2), we get

$(\cos x + \cos y)^2 + (\sin x + \sin y)^2 = (-\cos z)^2 + (-\sin z)^2$

$\Rightarrow \cos^2 x + \cos^2 y + 2\cos x\cos y + \sin^2 x + \sin^2 y + 2\sin x\sin y = \cos^2 z + \sin^2 z$

$\Rightarrow (\cos^2 x + \sin^2 x) + (\cos^2 y + \sin^2 y) + 2[\cos x\cos y + \sin x\sin y] = 1$

$\Rightarrow 1 + 1 + 2\cos(x - y) = 1$

$\Rightarrow 2\cos(x - y) = -1$

$\therefore \cos(x - y) = \frac{-1}{2}$

Hence, the correct option is (C).

3. $\left(1 + \cos\frac{\pi}{8}\right)\left(1 + \cos\frac{3\pi}{8}\right)\left(1 + \cos\frac{5\pi}{8}\right)\left(1 + \cos\frac{7\pi}{8}\right)$

$= \left(1 + \cos\frac{\pi}{8}\right)\left(1 + \cos\frac{3\pi}{8}\right)\left(1 + \cos\left(\pi - \frac{3\pi}{8}\right)\right)\left(1 + \cos\left(\pi - \frac{\pi}{8}\right)\right)$

$= \left(1 + \cos\frac{\pi}{8}\right)\left(1 + \cos\frac{3\pi}{8}\right)\left(1 - \cos\frac{\pi}{8}\right)\left(1 - \cos\frac{3\pi}{8}\right) (\because \cos(\pi - \theta) = -\cos\theta)$

$= \left(1 - \cos^2\left(\frac{\pi}{8}\right)\right)\left(1 - \cos^2\left(\frac{3\pi}{8}\right)\right)$

$(\because (a + b)(a - b) = a^2 - b^2)$

$= \sin^2\left(\frac{\pi}{8}\right) \times \sin^2\left(\frac{3\pi}{8}\right) (\because 1 - \cos^2\theta = \sin^2\theta)$

$= \left(\frac{1 - \cos\frac{\pi}{4}}{2}\right) \times \left(\frac{1 - \cos\frac{3\pi}{4}}{2}\right)$

We know that,

$\cos\frac{\pi}{4} = \frac{1}{\sqrt{2}}$ and $\cos\frac{3\pi}{4} = \frac{-1}{\sqrt{2}}$

$= \frac{1}{4}\left(1 - \frac{1}{\sqrt{2}}\right) \times \left(1 + \frac{1}{\sqrt{2}}\right) = \frac{1}{8}$

Hence, the correct option is (D).

4. Any quadratic equation $ax^2 + bx + c = 0$ is a perfect square if the discriminate (D) is zero, where $D = b^2 - 4ac$.

Given,

Equation, $x + \sqrt{(3x)} + \frac{a^2}{4} = 0$

Putting $x = y^2$, we get,

$y^2 + y\sqrt{3} + \frac{a^2}{4} = 0$

In order to be a perfect square,

$D = (\sqrt{3})^2 - \left(4 \times 1 \times \frac{a^2}{4}\right) = 0$

$\Rightarrow 3 - a^2 = 0$

$\Rightarrow a^2 = 3$

$\therefore a = \sqrt{3}$

Hence, the correct option is (A).

5. Given,

$x = 2 + 2^{\frac{2}{3}} + 2^{\frac{1}{3}}$

$\Rightarrow (x - 2) = \left(2^{\frac{2}{3}} + 2^{\frac{1}{3}}\right)$

Taking cube both the sides,

$x^3 - 8 - 6x^2 + 12x = 4 + 2 + 3 \times 2^{\frac{2}{3}} \times 2^{\frac{1}{3}}\left(2^{\frac{2}{3}} + 2^{\frac{1}{3}}\right)$

$\Rightarrow x^3 - 14 - 6x^2 + 12x = 6(x - 2)$

$\Rightarrow x^3 - 14 - 6x^2 + 12x - 6x + 12 = 0$

$\Rightarrow x^3 - 6x^2 + 6x = 2$

Hence, the correct option is (B).

6. Given,

$A = \begin{bmatrix} 2 & -3 \\ 0 & 1 \end{bmatrix}$ and $B = \begin{bmatrix} 1 & 2 \\ 3 & 0 \end{bmatrix}$

$\Rightarrow (B^{-1} A^{-1})^{-1} = (A^{-1})^{-1}(B^{-1})^{-1}$

$(\because (AB)^{-1} = B^{-1} A^{-1})$

$= AB \ (\because (A^{-1})^{-1} = A)$

$= \begin{bmatrix} 2 & -3 \\ 0 & 1 \end{bmatrix} \times \begin{bmatrix} 1 & 2 \\ 3 & 0 \end{bmatrix}$

$= \begin{bmatrix} (2 \times 1) + (-3 \times 3) & (2 \times 2) + (-3 \times 0) \\ (0 \times 1) + (1 \times 3) & (0 \times 2) + (1 \times 0) \end{bmatrix}$

$= \begin{bmatrix} -7 & 4 \\ 3 & 0 \end{bmatrix}$

Hence, the correct option is (B).

7. $D = \begin{vmatrix} p & q & r \\ q & r & p \\ r & p & q \end{vmatrix}$

$= p(qr - p^2) - q(q^2 - pr) + r(pq - r^2)$

$= pqr - p^3 - q^3 + pqr + pqr - r^3$

$= 3pqr - (p^3 + q^3 + r^3)$

As we know,

Arithmetic mean (AM) $\geq$ Geometric mean (GM)

Now, AM of p^3, q^3 and $r^3 = \dfrac{p^3 + q^3 + r^3}{3}$

Now, AM of p^3, q^3 and $r^3 = (p^3 \times q^3 \times r^3)^{\frac{1}{3}} = pq$

Therefore,

$\dfrac{p^3 + q^3 + r^3}{3} \geq pqr$

$\Rightarrow p^3 + q^3 + r^3 \geq 3pqr$

$\Rightarrow 3pqr - (p^3 + q^3 + r^3) \leq 0$

$\therefore D \leq 0$

Hence, the correct option is (B).

8. Let $\Delta = \begin{vmatrix} 1-a & a-b-c & b+c \\ 1-b & b-c-a & c+a \\ 1-c & c-a-b & a+b \end{vmatrix}$

Applying $C_2 \to C_2 + C_3$, we get

$\Delta = \begin{vmatrix} 1-a & a & b+c \\ 1-b & b & c+a \\ 1-c & c & a+b \end{vmatrix}$

Applying $C_1 \to C_1 + C_2, C_3 \to C_3 + C_2$, we get

$\Delta = \begin{vmatrix} 1 & a & a+b+c \\ 1 & b & b+c+a \\ 1 & c & c+a+b \end{vmatrix}$

Taking common $a + b + c$ from C_3, we get

$\Delta = (a+b+c) \begin{vmatrix} 1 & a & 1 \\ 1 & b & 1 \\ 1 & c & 1 \end{vmatrix}$

We know that if two columns of a determinant are identical, the value of the determinant is zero.

$\therefore \Delta = 0$

Hence, the correct option is (A).

9. Let $\begin{vmatrix} pa & qb & rc \\ qc & ra & pb \\ rb & pc & qa \end{vmatrix} = R_1$

Expanding R_1

$= pa(ra \times qa - pb \times pc) - qb(qc \times qa - pb \times rb) + rc(qc \times pc - ra \times rb)$

$= pa\left(a^2qr - p^2bc\right) - qb\left(q^2ac - b^2pr\right) + rc\left(c^2pq - r^2ab\right)$

$= a^3pqr - p^3abc - q^3abc + b^3pqr + c^3pqr - r^3abc$

$= pqr(a^3 + b^3 + c^3) - abc(p^3 + q^3 + r^3)$

Now we know that,

$a^3 + b^3 + c^3 = 3abc,$ if $a + b + c = 0$

$= pqr(3abc) - abc(3pqr)$

$= 0$

Hence, the correct option is (A).

10. Given,

$\begin{vmatrix} a+b & b+c & c \\ b+c & c+a & a \\ c+a & a+b & b \end{vmatrix} = k \begin{vmatrix} a & b & c \\ b & c & a \\ c & a & b \end{vmatrix}$

Let $\Delta = \begin{vmatrix} a+b & b+c & c \\ b+c & c+a & a \\ c+a & a+b & b \end{vmatrix}$

Apply $C_2 \to C_2 - C_3$, we get

$= \begin{vmatrix} a+b & b & c \\ b+c & c & a \\ c+a & a & b \end{vmatrix}$

Apply $C_1 \to C_1 - C_2$, we get

$= \begin{vmatrix} a & b & c \\ b & c & a \\ c & a & b \end{vmatrix}$

Now,

$\begin{vmatrix} a+b & b+c & c \\ b+c & c+a & a \\ c+a & a+b & b \end{vmatrix} = k \begin{vmatrix} a & b & c \\ b & c & a \\ c & a & b \end{vmatrix}$

$\Rightarrow \begin{vmatrix} a & b & c \\ b & c & a \\ c & a & b \end{vmatrix} = k \begin{vmatrix} a & b & c \\ b & c & a \\ c & a & b \end{vmatrix}$

$\Rightarrow k = 1$

Hence, the correct option is (A).

11. Given,

$y^2 - 8x + 6y + 1 = 0$

$\Rightarrow y^2 + 6y + 9 - 9 - 8x + 1 = 0$

$\Rightarrow (y + 3)^2 - 8x - 8 = 0$

$\Rightarrow (y + 3)^2 = 8x + 8$

$\Rightarrow (y + 3)^2 = 8 (x + 1)$

Let new coordinate axes be X and Y.

Here X = x + 1 and Y = y + 3

$\Rightarrow Y^2 = 4aX$

Now comparing with above equation,

$\therefore 4a = 8$

$\Rightarrow a = 2$

Focus: (a, 0)

X = a and Y = 0

$\Rightarrow x + 1 = 2$ and $y + 3 = 0$

$\Rightarrow x = 1$ and $y = -3$

$\therefore$ focus of parabola is (1, -3).

Hence, the correct option is (C).

12. Given,

Circles are $x^2 + y^2 = r^2$ and $x^2 + y^2 - 10x + 16 = 0$.

Let center of two circles are C_1 and C_2 and radius are r_1 and r_2.

$C_1 = (0,0)$ and $r_1 = r$

$C_2 = (5,0)$ and $r_2 = \sqrt{5^2 + 0^2 - 16} = 3$

Now,

$$C_1 C_2 = \sqrt{(5-0)^2 + (0-0)^2} = 5$$

When two circles will intersect at two points,

$$r_1 - r_2 < C_1 C_2 < r_1 + r_2$$
$$\Rightarrow r - 3 < 5 < r + 3$$

$$\therefore 2 < r < 8$$

Hence, the correct option is (A).

13. Given,

$$\frac{x^2}{16} - \frac{y^2}{9} = 1$$

Compare with standard equation, we get

$$a^2 = 16 \text{ and } b^2 = 9$$

Eccentricity $e = \sqrt{1 + \frac{b^2}{a^2}} = \sqrt{1 + \frac{9}{16}} = \sqrt{\frac{16+9}{16}} =$

$$\sqrt{\frac{25}{16}} = \frac{5}{4}$$

Now, equation of directrix,

$$x = \pm \frac{a}{e} = \pm \frac{4}{\left(\frac{5}{4}\right)} = \pm \frac{16}{5}$$

Hence, the correct option is (C).

14. As we know,

Standard Equation of ellipse is $\dfrac{x^2}{a^2} + \dfrac{y^2}{b^2} = 1$.

Length of latus rectum $= \dfrac{2b^2}{a}$, when $a > b$ and $\dfrac{2a^2}{b}$, when $a < b$

Given,

$$3x^2 + y^2 - 12x + 2y + 1 = 0$$
$$\Rightarrow 3(x^2 - 4x + 4) - 12 + (y^2 + 2y + 1) = 0$$
$$\Rightarrow 3(x-2)^2 - 12 + (y+1)^2 = 0$$
$$\Rightarrow 3(x-2)^2 + (y+1)^2 = 12$$
$$\Rightarrow \frac{3(x-2)^2}{12} + \frac{(y+1)^2}{12} = 1 \text{ (Divide by } 12)$$
$$\Rightarrow \frac{(x-2)^2}{4} + \frac{(y+1)^2}{12} = 1$$
$$\Rightarrow \frac{(x-2)^2}{2^2} + \frac{(y+1)^2}{(2\sqrt{3})^2} = 1$$

$$\therefore a^2 = 2^2 \text{ and } b^2 = (2\sqrt{3})^2$$

Here $a < b$

So, length of latus rectum $= \dfrac{2a^2}{b}$

$$= \frac{2(4)}{2\sqrt{3}}$$
$$= \frac{4}{\sqrt{3}} \text{ units}$$

Hence, the correct option is (C).

15. As we know,

Distance between two points (x_1, y_1) and (x_2, y_2) is given by

$$d = \sqrt{(x_2 - x_1)^2 + (y_2 - y_1)^2}$$

Centre lies on the line $y - 3x + 2 = 0$.

Let $x = h$

$$\Rightarrow y = 3h - 2$$

So the center is of the form $(h, 3h - 2)$.

Distance of centre from $(1,2)$ and $(3,4)$ will be equal.

$$\Rightarrow (h-1)^2 + (3h - 2 - 2)^2 = (h-3)^2 + (3h - 2 - 4)^2$$
$$\Rightarrow h^2 - 2h + 1 + 9h^2 - 24h + 16 = h^2 - 6h + 9 + 9h^2 - 36h + 36$$
$$\Rightarrow -26h + 17 = -42h + 45$$
$$\Rightarrow 16h = 28$$
$$\Rightarrow h = \frac{7}{4}$$
$$\therefore y = \frac{21}{4} - 2 = \frac{13}{4}$$

So, the centre is $\left(\frac{7}{4}, \frac{13}{4}\right)$.

Now, radius will be distance from any point (say $(1,2)$) to the center of circle $\left(\frac{7}{4}, \frac{13}{4}\right)$.

$$\therefore r^2 = \left(1 - \frac{7}{4}\right)^2 + \left(2 - \frac{13}{4}\right)^2$$
$$= \left(-\frac{3}{4}\right)^2 + \left(\frac{-5}{4}\right)^2$$

Hence, the correct option is (A).

16. Given,

$\hat{\imath} - x\hat{\jmath} - y\hat{k}$ and $\hat{\imath} + x\hat{\jmath} + y\hat{k}$ are orthogonal to each other.

$\hat{\imath} - x\hat{\jmath} - y\hat{k}$ and $\hat{\imath} + x\hat{\jmath} + y\hat{k}$

$$\Rightarrow (\hat{\imath} - x\hat{\jmath} - y\hat{k}) \cdot (\hat{\imath} + x\hat{\jmath} + y\hat{k}) = 0$$
$$\Rightarrow 1 - x^2 - y^2 = 0$$
$$\Rightarrow x^2 + y^2 = 1$$

So, it is a circle.

Hence, the correct option is (C).

17. Given,

$$\left|\vec{a}\right| = \sqrt{2}, \left|\vec{b}\right| = \sqrt{3} \text{ and } \left|\vec{a} + \vec{b}\right| = \sqrt{6}$$

As we know,

$$\left|\vec{a} + \vec{b}\right|^2 + \left|\vec{a} - \vec{b}\right|^2 = 2\left(\left|\vec{a}\right|^2 + \left|\vec{b}\right|^2\right)$$

$$\Rightarrow (\sqrt{6})^2 + \left|\vec{a} - \vec{b}\right|^2 = 2 \times \left[(\sqrt{2})^2 + (\sqrt{3})^2\right]$$

$$\Rightarrow \left|\vec{a} - \vec{b}\right|^2 = 4$$

$$\therefore \left|\vec{a} - \vec{b}\right| = 2$$

Hence, the correct option is (B).

18. The acute angle θ between two planes $a_1 x + b_1 y + c_1 z = d_1$ and $a_2 x + b_2 y + c_2 z = d_2$ is given by the formula,

$$\cos\theta = \frac{a_1 a_2 + b_1 b_2 + c_1 c_2}{\sqrt{(a_1^2 + b_1^2 + c_1^2)(a_2^2 + b_2^2 + c_2^2)}}$$

Given,

$$2x + y + z = 7 \text{ and } x - y + 2z = 9$$

That means,

$a_1 = 2, \, b_1 = 1, c_1 = 1$ and $a_2 = 1, \, b_2 = -1, c_2 = 2$

Using the above formula for angle θ,

$\cos\theta = \dfrac{2\times 1 + 1\times(-1) + 1\times 2}{\sqrt{(2^2+1^2+1^2)(1^2+(-1)^2+2^2)}} = \dfrac{3}{\sqrt{6\times 6}} = \dfrac{3}{6} = \dfrac{1}{2}$

$\Rightarrow \theta = 60°$

Hence, the correct option is (A).

19. Given,

A line makes $45°, 60°$ with the x-axis, y-axis.

Therefore, $\alpha = 45°$ and $\beta = 60°$

Let γ is the angles made by the line with the z-axis.

As we know that,

$\cos^2\alpha + \cos^2\beta + \cos^2\gamma = 1$

$\Rightarrow \cos^2 45° + \cos^2 60° + \cos^2\gamma = 1$

$\Rightarrow \left(\dfrac{1}{\sqrt{2}}\right)^2 + \left(\dfrac{1}{2}\right)^2 + \cos^2\gamma = 1$

$\Rightarrow \dfrac{1}{2} + \dfrac{1}{4} + \cos^2\gamma = 1$

$\Rightarrow \cos^2\gamma = 1 - \dfrac{3}{4} = \dfrac{1}{4}$

$\Rightarrow \cos\gamma = \pm\left(\dfrac{1}{2}\right)$

$\therefore \gamma = 60°$ or $120°$.

Hence, the correct option is (C).

20. As we know,

The intercept form of the plane is given by,

$\dfrac{x}{a} + \dfrac{y}{b} + \dfrac{z}{c} = 1$

Where a is the x-intercept and b is the y-intercept and c is the z-intercept.

Given,

$x + 2y - 4z = 8$

$\Rightarrow \dfrac{x}{8} + \dfrac{2y}{8} - \dfrac{4z}{8} = 1$

$\Rightarrow \dfrac{x}{8} + \dfrac{y}{4} + \dfrac{z}{-2} = 1$

As we know that,

Intercept form of the plane is given by,

$\dfrac{x}{a} + \dfrac{y}{b} + \dfrac{z}{c} = 1$

So, the intercepts cut off by the given plane are $(a, b, c) = (8, 4, -2)$

Hence, the correct option is (D).

21. Given,

$\int x^n dx = \dfrac{x^{n+1}}{n+1} + c$

$I = \int \sqrt{2x+3}\, dx$

Let $2x + 3 = t^2$

Differenating with respect to x, we get

$2dx = 2tdt$

$\Rightarrow dx = tdt$

Now,

$I = \int \sqrt{t^2} \times tdt$

$= \int t^2 dt$

$= \dfrac{t^3}{3} + c$

$= \dfrac{(2x+3)^{\frac{3}{2}}}{3} + c$

Hence, the correct option is (C).

22. $\int \dfrac{1}{\sqrt{x}} dx = \int x^{-\frac{1}{2}} dx$

$= \dfrac{x^{-\frac{1}{2}+1}}{-\frac{1}{2}+1} + C$

$= 2\sqrt{x} + C$

$\therefore \int_4^9 \dfrac{1}{\sqrt{x}} dx = [2\sqrt{x}]_4^9 = 2[\sqrt{9} - \sqrt{4}] = 2(3 - 2) = 2$

Hence, the correct option is (C).

23. Given,

$2x^3 - 3y^2 = 7$

Differentiating w.r.t. x, we get

$6x^2 - 6y\dfrac{dy}{dx} = 0$

$\Rightarrow x^2 - y\dfrac{dy}{dx} = 0$

$\Rightarrow \dfrac{dy}{dx} = \dfrac{x^2}{y}$

Hence, the correct option is (C).

24. Mean of $'n'$ observations $= \dfrac{\text{Sum of observations}}{n}$

Here $n = 3$

Let the third number is x.

$\therefore 16 = \dfrac{x+8+10}{3}$

$\Rightarrow x + 18 = 48$

$\Rightarrow x = 30$

Hence, the correct option is (D).

25. Given,

$P(A) = \dfrac{3}{5}$ and $P(B) = \dfrac{4}{9}$

Since A and B are independent events: $P(A \cap B) = P(A) \times P(B)$

$\Rightarrow P(A \cap B) = \dfrac{3}{5} \times \dfrac{4}{9} = \dfrac{4}{15}$

Hence, the correct option is (A).

Q.1 The value of $\dfrac{\tan 60°}{\cot 30°}$ is equal to:

A. 0 **B.** 1 **C.** 2 **D.** 3

Q.2 If $\cos X = \dfrac{2}{3}$ then $\tan X$ is equal to:

A. $\dfrac{5}{2}$ **B.** $\sqrt{\dfrac{5}{2}}$ **C.** $\sqrt{\dfrac{5}{4}}$ **D.** $\dfrac{2}{\sqrt{5}}$

Q.3 If $^nP_r = 3024$ and $^nC_r = 126$ then find n and r.

A. 9,4 **B.** 10,3 **C.** 12,4 **D.** 11,4

Q.4 Consider a dice with the property that that probability of a face with n dots showing up is proportional to n. The probability of face showing 4 dots is?

A. $\dfrac{1}{7}$ **B.** $\dfrac{5}{42}$ **C.** $\dfrac{1}{21}$ **D.** $\dfrac{4}{21}$

Q.5 Find median and mode of the messages received on 9 consecutive days $15,11,9,5,18,4,15,13,17$.

A. 13,6 **B.** 13,18 **C.** 18,15 **D.** 15,16

Q.6 Forces F_1 and F_2 act on a point mass in two mutual perpendicular directions. The resultant force on the point mass will be:

A. $F_1 + F_2$ **B.** $F_1 - F_2$
C. $\sqrt{F_1^2 + F_2^2}$ **D.** $F_1^2 + F_2^2$

Q.7 The area of a parallelogram whose adjacent sides are represented by the vectors $a = -\hat{i} - 2\hat{j} - 3\hat{k}$ and $b = -\hat{i} + 2\hat{j} - 3\hat{k}$ is:

A. $\sqrt{14}$ **B.** $\sqrt{6}$ **C.** $\dfrac{49}{36}$ **D.** $4\sqrt{10}$

Q.8 Let A and B be two finite sets such that n(A) = 20, n(B) = 28 and n(A ∪ B) = 36, find n(A ∩ B).

A. 12 **B.** 13 **C.** 14 **D.** 15

Q.9 A and B are two sets having 3 elements in common. If $n(A) = 5, n(B) = 4$, then $n(A \times B)$ is equal to:

A. 0 **B.** 9 **C.** 15 **D.** 20

Q.10 What is the degree of the differential equation

$$\left(\frac{d^3y}{dx^3}\right)^{\frac{3}{2}} = \left(\frac{d^2y}{dx^2}\right)^2 ?$$

A. 1 **B.** 2 **C.** 3 **D.** 4

Q.11 The fifth term of an AP of n terms, whose sum is $n^2 - 2n$, is:

A. 5 **B.** 7 **C.** 8 **D.** 15

Q.12 What is $C(n,r) + 2C(n, r - 1) + C(n, r - 2)$ equal to:

A. $C(n + 1, r)$ **B.** $C(n - 1, r + 1)$
C. $C(n, r + 1)$ **D.** $C(n + 2, r)$

Q.13 If $z = -2 + 5i$ then $z^2 + 4z + 30$ is:

A. 1 **B.** 0 **C.** 2 **D.** 4

Q.14 If the line $y = x + k$ is a normal to the parabola $y^2 = 4x$ then find the value of k.

A. -3 **B.** 3 **C.** 2 **D.** -2

Q.15 The value of k which makes $f(x) = \begin{cases} \sin x, & x \neq 0 \\ k, & x = 0 \end{cases}$ continuous at $x = 0$, is:

A. 2 **B.** 1 **C.** -1 **D.** 0

Q.16 The period of $f(x) = \sin\dfrac{\pi x}{2} + 2\cos\dfrac{\pi x}{3} - \tan\dfrac{\pi x}{4}$ is:

A. 6 **B.** 3 **C.** 4 **D.** 12

Q.17 The number of commutative binary operations that can be defined on a set of 2 elements is:

A. 8 **B.** 6 **C.** 4 **D.** 2

Q.18 Find the 4th term in the expansion of $(x - 2y)^{12}$.

A. $-1760x^9y^3$ **B.** $1760x^9y^3$
C. $-1760x^8y^9$ **D.** $-1999x^9y^3$

Q.19 The co-efficient of y in the expansion of $(y^2 + c/y)^5$ is?

A. $10c^3$ **B.** $20c^3$ **C.** $10c$ **D.** $20c$

Q.20 For what value of x, the matrix A is singular? $A = \begin{bmatrix} 3 - x & 2 & 2 \\ 2 & 4 - x & 1 \\ -2 & -4 & -1 - x \end{bmatrix}$

A. $x = 0,2$ **B.** $x = 1,2$ **C.** $x = 2,3$ **D.** $x = 0,3$

Q.21 The area of a triangle with vertices $(-3,0), (3,0)$ and $(0, k)$ is 9 sq units. then the value of k will be:

A. 9 **B.** 3 **C.** -9 **D.** 6

Q.22 In the given figure O is the centre of the circle and $\angle PQR = 40°$, find the measure of $\angle POR$.

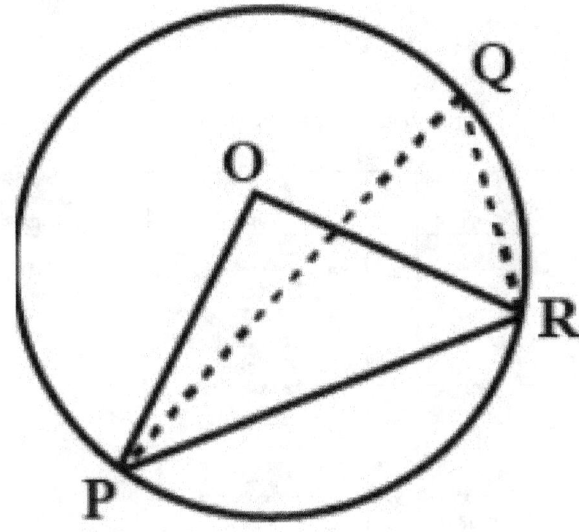

A. 80°   **B.** 60°   **C.** 50°   **D.** 40°

Q.23 If O is the centre of the circle and $\triangle AOB$ is an equilateral triangle, then the measure of $\angle ACB$ is:

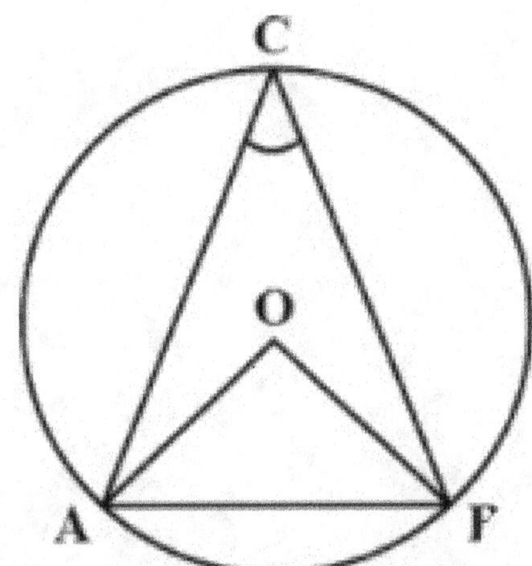

A. 60°   **B.** 30°   **C.** 90°   **D.** 75°

Q.24 If $f(x) = x\cos x$, then $f'(0) =$?

A. −1   **B.** 0   **C.** 1   **D.** ∞

Q.25 If $f(x) = x\sin x$, then $f'(0) =$?

A. −1   **B.** 0   **C.** 1   **D.** ∞

// Smart Answer Sheet //

Correct — Percentage of students who answered correctly. **Skipped** — Percentage of students who skipped.

Q.	Ans.	Correct / Skipped	Q.	Ans.	Correct / Skipped	Q.	Ans.	Correct / Skipped	Q.	Ans.	Correct / Skipped	Q.	Ans.	Correct / Skipped	Q.	Ans.	Correct / Skipped
1	B	76.6 % / 12.61 %	6	C	78.34 % / 20.58 %	11	B	55.83 % / 42.29 %	16	D	81.79 % / 16.3 %	21	B	49.51 % / 42.19 %			
2	C	69.27 % / 30.44 %	7	D	57.89 % / 37.45 %	12	D	87.02 % / 12.86 %	17	D	59.74 % / 35.5 %	22	A	80.25 % / 16.06 %			
3	A	43.13 % / 32.39 %	8	A	84.19 % / 15.79 %	13	A	40.18 % / 32.86 %	18	A	77.55 % / 10.2 %	23	B	89.28 % / 10.39 %			
4	D	85.12 % / 13.83 %	9	D	89.61 % / 10.21 %	14	A	80.5 % / 17.18 %	19	A	87.78 % / 10.13 %	24	C	85.86 % / 13.2 %			
5	B	87.49 % / 11.68 %	10	C	53.64 % / 41.28 %	15	D	78.94 % / 14.28 %	20	D	79.83 % / 18.44 %	25	B	84.26 % / 14.23 %			

//Hints and Solutions//

1. $\tan 60° = \sqrt{3}$ and $\cot 30° = \sqrt{3}$

So, $\dfrac{\tan 60°}{\cot 30°} = \dfrac{\sqrt{3}}{\sqrt{3}} = 1$

Hence, the correct option is (B).

2. By trigonometry identities, we know:
$$1 + \tan^2 x = \sec^2 x$$
And $\sec X = \dfrac{1}{\cos X} = \dfrac{1}{\left(\frac{2}{3}\right)} = \dfrac{3}{2}$

So,
$$1 + \tan^2 X = \left(\dfrac{3}{2}\right)^2 = \dfrac{9}{4}$$
$$\tan^2 X = \dfrac{9}{4} - 1 = \dfrac{5}{4}$$
$$Tan X = \sqrt{\dfrac{5}{4}}$$

Hence, the correct option is (C).

3. $\dfrac{^nP_r}{^nC_r} = \dfrac{3024}{126}$

$^nP_r = \dfrac{n!}{(n-r)!}$

$^nC_r = \dfrac{n!}{(n-r)! \times r!}$

So, $\left[\dfrac{n!}{(n-r)!}\right] \div \left[\dfrac{n!}{(n-r)! \times r!}\right] = 24$

$24 = r!$

So, $r = 4$

Now, $^nP_4 = 3024$

$\dfrac{n!}{(n-4)!} = 3024$

$n(n-1)(n-2)(n-3) = 9.8.7.6$

$n = 9$

Hence, the correct option is (A).

4. $P(n)$ is proportional to n where $n = 1,2,3,\dots 6$ is random variable.

$P(n) = kn$
$P(1) + P(2)\dots.P(6) = 1$
$K(1 + 2 + 3 + 4 + 5 + 6) = 1$
$K = \dfrac{1}{21}$

So, $P(4) = 4 K = \dfrac{4}{21}$

Hence, the correct option is (D).

5. Arranging the terms in ascending order
$4,5,9,11,13,14,15,18,18$

Median is $\dfrac{(n+1)}{2}$ term as $n = 9$ (odd)

$= \dfrac{(9+1)}{2} = \dfrac{10}{2} = 5^{th}$ term which is 13,

Median is 13

Mode $= 18$ which is repeated twice.
Hence, the correct option is (B).

6. We know that resultant,
$$R = \sqrt{A^2 + B^2 + 2AB\cos\theta}$$
$$\therefore R = \sqrt{F_1^2 + F_2^2 + 2F_1F_2\cos 90}$$
$$= \sqrt{F_1^2 + F_2^2}\,[\cos 90^0 = 0]$$

Hence, the correct option is (C).

7. Area of parallelogram $= |a \times b|$
$$= \begin{vmatrix} \hat{\imath} & \hat{\jmath} & \hat{k} \\ -1 & -2 & -3 \\ -1 & 2 & -3 \end{vmatrix}$$
$$= |\hat{\imath}(6 + 6) - \hat{\jmath}(3 - 3) + \hat{k}(-2 - 2)| = |12\hat{\imath} - 4\hat{k}|$$
$$= \sqrt{12^2 + 4^2} = 4\sqrt{10}$$

Hence, the correct option is (D).

8. Using the formula n(A ∪ B) = n(A) + n(B) - n(A ∩ B)

Then n(A ∩B) = n(A) + n(B) - n(A ∪B)

= 20 + 28 - 36

= 48 - 36

n(A ∩ B) = 12

Hence, the correct option is (A).

9. Given, $n(A) = 5, n(B) = 4$ and A and B have 3 elements in common.
$$n(A \times B)$$
$$= n(A)n(B)$$
$$= 5 \times 4$$
$$n(A \times B) = 20$$
Hence, the correct option is (D).

10. We have, $\left(\dfrac{d^a y}{dx^2}\right)^{\frac{3}{2}} = \left(\dfrac{d^2 y}{dx^2}\right)^2$

Squaring both the sides, we get,
$$\left(\dfrac{d^3 y}{dx^3}\right)^3 = \left(\dfrac{d^2 y}{dx^2}\right)^4$$

Here highest derivative is $\left(\dfrac{d^3 y}{dx^3}\right)^3$.

$\therefore$ Degree $=$ power of $\left(\dfrac{d^3 y}{dx^3}\right)^3 = 3$

Hence, the correct option is (C).

11. Given,
Sum of n terms of an $AP = n^2 - 2n$

$\therefore$ Sum of first 5 terms $(S_5) = 5^2 - 2 \cdot (5)$
$$= 25 - 10 = 15$$
Similarly,

Now, Sum of first 4 terms $(S_4) = 4^2 - 2 \cdot (4)$
$$= 16 - 8 = 8$$

$\therefore$ The fifth term of an $AP(T_5) = S_5 - S_4$ ...(Using $T_n = S_n - S_{n-1}$)
$$= 15 - 8$$

$T_5 = 7$

Hence, the correct option is (B).

12. Given,

$^nC_r + 2\,^nC_{(r-1)} + \,^nC_{r-2}$

$= \,^nC_r + \,^nC_{(r-1)} + \,^nC_{(r-1)} + \,^nC_{(r-2)}$

Using, $^nC_r + \,^nC_{(r-1)} = \,^{(n+1)}C_r$

$= (n+1)C_r + (n+1)C_{(r-1)}$

Again using $^nC_r + \,^nC_{(r-1)} = \,^{(n+1)}C_r$

$= (n+2)C_r$

Hence, the correct option is (D).

13. Given,

$z = -2 + 5i$

$\Rightarrow z + 2 = 5i$

Squaring both sides, we get,

$(z+2)^2 = (5i)^2$

$\Rightarrow z^2 + 4z + 4 = -25$

$\Rightarrow z^2 + 4z + 29 = 0$

Now, adding (1) both sides, we get,

$\therefore z^2 + 4z + 30 = 1$

Hence, the correct option is (A).

14. Given equation:

$y = x + k$.....(i)

Equation of normal of parabola $= y = mx - 2am - am^3$.....(ii)

On comparing (i)and (ii),

$m = 1, a = 1$

put value in (ii),

$y = x - 2 - 1$

$y = x - 3$.....(iii)

Compare the equation (i)and (iii),

$k = -3$

Hence, the correct option is (A).

15. $f(x)$ is Continuous at $x = 0$

$\Rightarrow \lim_{x \to 0^+} f(x) = \lim_{x \to 0^-} f(x) = f(0)$

$\Rightarrow \lim_{x \to 0^+} \sin x = \lim_{x \to 0^-} \sin x = k$

$\Rightarrow \lim_{h \to 0} \sin(0 + h) = \lim_{h \to 0} \sin(0 - h) = k$

$\Rightarrow k = 0$

Hence, the correct option is (D)

16. Period of $\sin \dfrac{\pi x}{2}$ is $\dfrac{2\pi}{\pi/2} = 4 = T_1$

Period of $\cos \dfrac{\pi x}{3}$ is $\dfrac{2\pi}{\pi/3} = 6 = T_2$

Period of $\tan \dfrac{\pi x}{4}$ is $\dfrac{\pi}{\pi/4} = 4 = T_3$

Period of f is $=$ L.C.M. of $T_1, T_2, T_3 = 12$

Hence, the correct option is (D).

17. The number of commutative binary operations on a set of n elements is $n^{\frac{n(n-1)}{2}}$.

Therefore, Number of commutative binary operations on a set of

2 elements $= 2^{\frac{2(2-1)}{2}}$

$= 2^1$

$= 2$

Hence, the correct option is (D).

18. It is known that $(r + 1)$ th term (T_{r+1}) in the binomial expansion of $(a + b)^n$ is given by,

$T_{r+1} = \,^nC_r a^{n-r} b^r$

Thus the 4th term in the expansion of $(x + 2y)^{12}$,

$T_4 = T_{3+1} = \,^{12}C_3 (x)^{12-3}(-2y)^3 = (-1)^3 \frac{12!}{3!9!} \cdot x^9 \cdot (2)^3 \cdot y^3$

$= -\dfrac{12.11.10}{3.2} \cdot (2)^3 x^9 y^3 = -1760 x^9 y^3$

Hence, the correct option is (A).

19.

$\left(y^2 + c/y\right)^5 = \,^5C_0\left(\frac{c}{y}\right)^0 (y^2)^{5-0} + \,^5C_1\left(\frac{c}{y}\right)^1 (y^2)^{5-1}$

$+ \ldots + \,^5C_5\left(\frac{c}{y}\right)^5 (y^2)^{5-5}$

$= \sum_{r=0}^{5} \,^5C_r \left(\frac{c}{y}\right)^r (y^2)^{5-r}$.....(i)

We need cofficient of $y \Rightarrow 2(5 - r) - r = 1$

$\Rightarrow 10 - 3r = 1$

$\Rightarrow r = 3$

put $r = 3$ in (i),

$= \,^5C_3 \left(\frac{c}{y}\right)^3 (y^2)^2$

$= \,^5C_3 c^3 y$

So, cofficient of $y = \,^5C_3 \cdot c^3$

$= 10c^3$

Hence, the correct option is (A).

20. $A = \begin{bmatrix} 3 - x & 2 & 2 \\ 2 & 4 - x & 1 \\ -2 & -4 & -1 - x \end{bmatrix}$

If the matrix is singular, its determinant has to be zero.

$\Rightarrow (3 - x)[(4 - x)(-1 - x) + 4] - 2[2(-1 - x) + 2] + 2[-8 + 2(4 - x)] = 0$

$\Rightarrow (3 - x)[-4 - 4x + x + x^2 + 4] - 2[-2 - 2x + 2] + 2[-8 + 8 - 2x] = 0$

$\Rightarrow (3 - x)[x^2 - 3x] + 4x - 4x = 0$

$\Rightarrow (3 - x)x(x - 3) = 0$

$\Rightarrow x = 0, 3$

Hence, the correct option is (D).

21. We know that,

Area of a triangle with vertices $(a_1, y_1), (x_2, y_2)$ and (x_3, y_3) is given by,

$$\Delta = \frac{1}{2}\begin{vmatrix} x_1 & y_1 & 1 \\ x_2 & y_2 & 1 \\ x_3 & y_3 & 1 \end{vmatrix}$$

$$\therefore \Delta = \frac{1}{2}\begin{vmatrix} -3 & 0 & 1 \\ 3 & 0 & 1 \\ 0 & k & 1 \end{vmatrix}$$

Expanding along R_1

$$9 = \frac{1}{2}[-3(-k) - 0 + 1(3k)]$$
$$\Rightarrow 18 = 3k + 3k = 6k$$
$$\therefore K = \frac{18}{6} = 3$$

Hence, the correct option is (B).

22. We know, the angle subtended by an arc of a circle at the centre is double the angle subtended by it at any point on the remaining part of the circle.

So, in given circle,

$$\angle POR = 2\angle PQR$$

Therefore $\angle POR = 2 \times 40° = 80°$

Hence, the correct option is (A).

23. Given,

O is the center of the circle and $\triangle AOB$ is an equilateral triangle.

Thus, $\angle AOB = 60^0$

We know that the angle at the center of the circle is twice the angle at the circumference subtended by the same arc.

Thus, $\angle AOB = 2\angle ACB$
$$\Rightarrow 60 = 2\angle ACB$$
$$\Rightarrow \angle ACB = \frac{60}{2}$$
$$\Rightarrow \angle ACB = 30^0$$

Hence, the correct option is (B).

24. $f(x) = x\cos x$

As we know that $D(uv) = uv' + vu'$

So, $f'(x) = x(-\sin x) + \cos x(1)$
$$= -x\sin x + \cos x$$

By putting $x = 0$, we have

$$f'(0) = 0 + \cos(0) \ (\because \cos(0) = 1)$$
$$= 1$$

Hence, the correct option is (C).

25. $f(x) = x\sin x$

As we know that,

$$D(uv) = uv' + vu'$$

So,

$$f'(x) = x(\cos x) + \sin x(1)$$
$$= x\cos x + \sin x$$

By putting $x = 0$, we have

$$f'(0) = 0 + \sin(0) \ (\because \sin(0) = 1)$$
$$= 0$$

Hence, the correct option is (B).

Sectional Test 10

Q.1 Which city has been chosen by the Union of European Football Associations (UEFA) as a replacement of St Petersburg for the Champions League 2022 ?

[Delhi Forest Guard, 2021]

A. Paris   **B.** Brussels   **C.** London   **D.** Munich

Q.2 Who has been appointed as the new chairman of the International Aluminium Institute (IAI) on 6 June 2022?
A. Swarup Kumar Saha
B. Miles Prosser
C. Ben Kahrs
D. Satish Pai

Q.3 Raja Rammohan Roy was not connected with:
A. The abolition of Sati
B. Widow remarriage
C. The Promotion of English
D. Sanskrit education

Q.4 In ______, a major upheaval took place that shook the foundation of British Rule and is often referred to as the 'First War of Independence.
A. 1856   **B.** 1875   **C.** 1947   **D.** 1857

Q.5 In which year did the Khilafat Movement start?
A. 1922   **B.** 1923   **C.** 1919   **D.** 1921

Q.6 Hirakund Dam is located in which state?
A. Bihar   **B.** Orissa
C. Maharashtra   **D.** Punjab

Q.7 Which of the following is the largest delta in the world?
A. Indus River Delta
B. Danube Delta
C. Ganges-Brahmaputra Delta
D. Amazon Delta

Q.8 Which is the longest tributary river in India?
A. Beas   **B.** Ganga   **C.** Ravi   **D.** Yamuna

Q.9 'Matki' is a popular folk dance of which of the following states?
A. Assam   **B.** Madhya Pradesh
C. Bihar   **D.** Rajasthan

Q.10 Which of the following folk dances belongs to Punjab?
A. Giddha Dance   **B.** Akiri Dance
C. Monyo Asho   **D.** Loor Dance

Q.11 Which of the following is a well-known place for Chikankari embroidery?
A. Ranchi   **B.** Lucknow
C. Raipur   **D.** Indore

Q.12 Which festival marks the beginning of the Tibetan New Year?
A. Saga Dawa festival   **B.** Ongkor festival
C. Losar festival   **D.** Shoton festival

Q.13 Who has won the 2020 Dayton Literary Peace Prize's lifetime achievement award?
A. Alice Munro   **B.** Margaret Atwood
C. Jane Austen   **D.** J. K. Rowling

Q.14 Which of the following has bagged the best drama series honour at the 48th International Emmy Awards?
A. She   **B.** Delhi Crime
C. Mirzapur   **D.** Crime Patrol

Q.15 Ishwar Pandey is related to which of the following sports?
A. Hockey   **B.** Football
C. Cricket   **D.** Badminton

Q.16 ______ was the world's first female astronaut.
A. Svetlana Savitskaya
B. Valentina Tereshkova
C. Sally Ride
D. Judith Resnik

Q.17 Who is known as the 'Milkman of India'?
A. RS Sodhi   **B.** Norman Borlaug
C. GH Wilster   **D.** V Kurien

Q.18 Calcium deficiency in old age leads to which disease?

[UPTET Social Studies, 2019]

A. Osteoporosis   **B.** Anaemia
C. Osteomalacia   **D.** Rickets

Q.19 If MUSIC is coded SZWLE, then how is CANOE coded?
A. LSWER   **B.** FGSE   **C.** IFRRG   **D.** RGFIS

Q.20 In a certain code language "PRINCE" is written as "356987". In that code language, how will "NICE" be written?

[UP Police Sub Inspector, 2017]

A. 8965   **B.** 9687   **C.** 9876   **D.** 7896

Q.21 Direction: From the given alternatives, select the word which CANNOT be formed using the letters of the given word.
FEARLESS
A. GRASS   **B.** RESEAL
C. LESSER   **D.** ERASE

Q.22 Direction: From the given alternatives, select the word which CANNOT be formed using the letters of the given word.
CREATIVITY
A. VARIETY   **B.** ACTIVE
C. VERIFY   **D.** REACT

Q.23 Direction: Choose the correct alternative from the given ones that will complete the series.

72, 78, 90, 110, 140, ___

A. 172   **B.** 182   **C.** 185   **D.** 144

Q.24 Direction: A series is given with one term missing. Select the correct alternative from the given ones that will complete the series.

1, 5, 14, 30, 55, ?

A. 88   **B.** 91   **C.** 72   **D.** 65

Q.25 What is the full form of "BRICS"?

A. Bangladesh, Romania, Indonesia, Cambodia, and South Africa

B. Botswana, Rwanda, Ivory Coast, Croatia, and South Africa

C. Bangladesh, Romania, India, Cambodia, and South Africa

D. Brazil, Russia, India, China, and South Africa

// Smart Answer Sheet //

Correct Percentage of students who answered correctly.   **Skipped** Percentage of students who skipped.

Q.	Ans.	Correct / Skipped	Q.	Ans.	Correct / Skipped	Q.	Ans.	Correct / Skipped	Q.	Ans.	Correct / Skipped	Q.	Ans.	Correct / Skipped	Q.	Ans.	Correct / Skipped
1	A	46.28 % / 37.53 %	6	B	76.69 % / 19.84 %	11	B	86.27 % / 13.47 %	16	B	87.64 % / 10.44 %	21	A	51.97 % / 46.99 %			
2	D	44.61 % / 33.51 %	7	C	45.11 % / 32.64 %	12	C	51.71 % / 33.67 %	17	D	89.79 % / 10.18 %	22	C	81.57 % / 10.49 %			
3	D	88.0 % / 11.75 %	8	D	85.54 % / 10.78 %	13	B	84.42 % / 10.21 %	18	A	51.68 % / 31.19 %	23	B	67.43 % / 31.87 %			
4	D	42.97 % / 31.77 %	9	B	42.33 % / 48.56 %	14	B	89.91 % / 10.08 %	19	C	56.97 % / 37.81 %	24	B	86.63 % / 11.28 %			
5	C	80.66 % / 19.18 %	10	A	78.54 % / 14.1 %	15	C	80.4 % / 11.5 %	20	B	55.48 % / 43.68 %	25	D	66.88 % / 31.95 %			

//Hints and Solutions//

1. Russia was stripped of hosting the Champions League final by UEFA on 25 Feb 2022 with St. Petersburg replaced by Paris after Russia's invasion of Ukraine. France last hosted the Champions League final 16 years ago, when Barcelona beat Arsenal in the 2006 final.

Hence, the correct option is (A).

2. Satish Pai has been appointed as the new chairman of the International Aluminium Institute (IAI) on 6 June 2022.

The International Aluminium Institute (IAI), the only body representing the global primary aluminium industry, has announced the appointment of Satish Pai as its new Chairman. He is the Managing Director of Hindalco Industries, one of the world's largest integrated producers of aluminium.

Hence, the correct option is (D).

3. Raja Rammohan Roy was not connected with Sanskrit education. Raja Rammohan Roy is considered the prophet of socio-religious movements in India. Raja Rammohan Roy is the father of the Indian renaissance. He founded a reform association known as the Brahmo Sabha in Calcutta. Later Brahma Sabha was known as Brahma Samaj.

- He began campaigns against the practice of Sati and abolished Sati from India. Sati was banned in 1829.
- Raja Rammohan Roy argued in favour of widow re-marriage.
- Raja Rammohan Roy was keen to spread the knowledge of Western education in India.

Hence, the correct option is (D).

4. The revolt of 1857 started on 10th May when the Company's Indian soldiers at Meerut rebelled.

- It is also called the Sepoy Mutiny by the British.
- It is now also known as the 'First War of Independence' against the British rulers.
- The main event which became the immediate cause of the war was the refusal of the Sepoys to use the grease-covered cartridges (greased with the fat of pig and cow) on January 23, 1857.

Hence, the correct option is (D).

5. The Khilafat Movement started in the year 1919.

- The Ali Brothers—Mohammad Ali and Shaukat Ali—launched an anti-British movement in 1919.
- The movement was for the restoration of the Khilafat Movement.
- Maulana Abul Kalam Azad also led the movement.
- It was supported by Mahatma Gandhi and INC.
- On October 17, 1919, 'Khilafat Day' was celebrated.

Hence, the correct option is (C).

6. Hirakud Dam is located in Orissa. Hirakud Dam is built across the Mahanadi river about 15 km. Its height is 61m.

Sir Hawthorne Lavish founded the Hirakud Dam when he was the Governor of Orissa. Pandit Jawaharlal Nehru laid the first batch of concrete on 12 April 1948.

Hence, the correct option is (B).

7.

- Ganges-Brahmaputra Delta is the largest delta in the world.
- The deposition of sediment that is carried by a river created a landform called a river delta.
- The Ganges Delta also called Sunderban Delta is situated in the Bengal region of the Indian subcontinent and also in Bangladesh. The delta surface area of some 100.000 km^2.
- The Ganges Delta is formed by three major rivers the Ganga, the Brahmaputra, and the Megna river. Ganges Delta is also one of the most fertile regions in the world.

Hence, the correct option is (C).

8. The Yamuna is the longest tributary of the River Ganga. It does not directly fall into the sea. The major states through which the river flows are Uttarakhand, Delhi, Himachal Pradesh, Haryana, and Uttar Pradesh.

Hence, the correct option is (D).

9. Matki dance form has been developed by nomadic tribes in Madhya Pradesh. Performed using a "small pitcher" is a folk dance originating from central India known as the "Matki Dance". This "pitcher dance" belongs to the state of Madhya Pradesh, and is mainly performed in the Malwa region.

Hence, the correct option is (B).

10. Giddha dance is a folk dance of Punjab. Giddha, a traditional pastoral dance performed by women of the Punjab, India, and Pakistan at festival times and at the sowing and reaping of the harvest. Patterned on a circle, it is notable for the bodily grace of the women's movements (especially of the arms and hands) and for the charming melody that accompanies it. It is a dance style that is very colourful and is now copied in all regions of the world. This dance is usually performed by women on festive or social occasions. The dance is accompanied by rhythmic clapping and the aged ladies in the background sing a typical traditional folk song.

Hence, the correct option is (A).

11. The Chikankari embroidery is a traditional embroidery style from Lucknow. It is one of Lucknow's best-known textile decoration styles. Chikan is a delicate and artfully done hand embroidery on a variety of textile fabrics like muslin, silk, chiffon, organza, net, etc. White thread is embroidered on cool, pastel shades of light muslin and cotton garments. The market for local chikan is mainly in Chowk, Lucknow.

Hence, the correct option is (B).

12. Losar festival marks the beginning of the Tibetan New Year. The Losar festival is celebrated with great zeal and fervour in the Lahaul Valley of Himachal Pradesh. It is also known as a festival of happiness and prosperity. The celebrates the Ladakhi or Tibetan New Year.

Hence, the correct option is (C).

13. Margaret Atwood has won the 2020 Dayton Literary Peace Prize's lifetime achievement award. The award celebrates literature's power to foster peace, social justice and global understanding. Atwood is a prolific writer of poetry, fiction, nonfiction, essays, comic books. Atwood published her first book of poetry, Double Persephone, in 1961.

Hence, the correct option is (B).

14. Netflix's India Original series "Delhi Crime", helmed by Indian-Canadian director Richie Mehta, has bagged the best drama series honour at the 48th International Emmy Awards. The series deconstructs the case of the 23-year-old physiotherapy intern who was abducted and gang-raped in a moving bus on the night of December 16, 2012. The show was released in the year 2019.

Hence, the correct option is (B).

15.

- Ishwar Chand Pandey is a former Indian cricketer who played for Madhya Pradesh.
- He was a right-arm medium-fast bowler who was the leading wicket-taker of the 2012-13 Ranji Trophy.
- He played for India A and was selected in the Indian Test and ODI squads for the New Zealand tour of 2014.
- He was bought by the Chennai Super Kings in the 2014 IPL auction for Rs 1.5 crores and was bought by Rising Pune Supergiants in the 2016 and 2017 editions of IPL.
- Ishwar Pandey was born in Rewa, Madhya Pradesh.

Hence, the correct option is (C).

16. On 16 June 1963, Soviet Cosmonaut Valentina Tereshkova became the first woman to travel into space. Valentina Tereshkova was the first female cosmonaut and the first and youngest woman to have flown in space with a solo mission on the Vostok 6 in 1963.

Hence, the correct option is (B).

17.

- Mr. V. Kurien was an Indian engineer and entrepreneur who was regarded as the architect of India's "White Revolution".
- He is also known as the 'Milkman of India'.
- The revolution associated with a sharp increase in milk production in the country is called the White Revolution in India also known as Operation Flood.
- He received numerous honours, chief among them the Ramon Magsaysay Award for community leadership (1963) and the World Food Prize (1989).

Hence, the correct option is (D).

18. Calcium deficiency occurs at any stage. It can result in rickets, osteoporosis, and osteopenia. Osteoporosis occurs at later stages of life and is a disease in which bone becomes more fragile and more likely leading to fractures.

Hence, the correct option is (A).

19. The logic is :

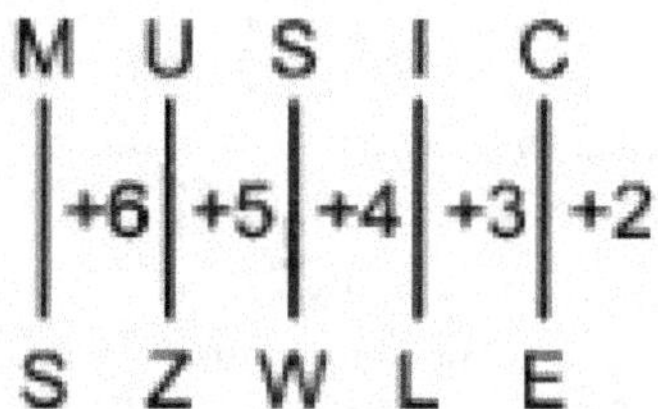

Similarly,

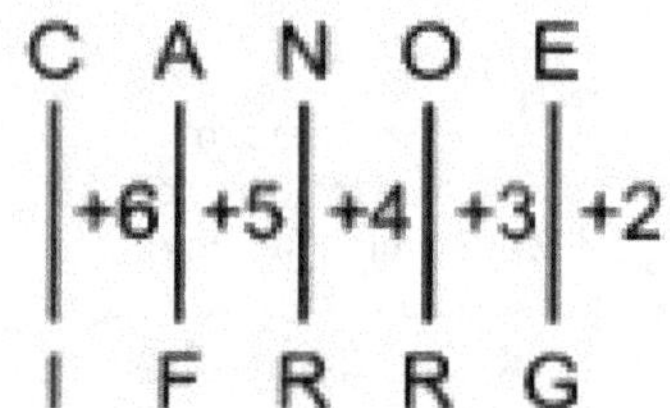

Therefore, CANOE will be coded as IFRRG.

Hence, the correct option is (C).

20. In a certain code:

Words	P	R	I	N	C	E
Codes	3	5	6	9	8	7

In the same way,

Words	N	I	C	E
Codes	9	6	8	7

Therefore, In that code language "NICE" will be written as 9687.

Hence, the correct option is (B).

21. GRASS – FEARLESS (Cannot be formed because G is missing)

RESEAL – FEARLESS (Can be formed)

LESSER – FEARLESS (Can be formed)

ERASE – FEARLESS (Can be formed)

Hence, the correct option is (A).

22. VARIETY – CREATIVITY (Can be formed)

ACTIVE – CREATIVITY (Can be formed)

VERIFY – CREATIVITY (Cannot be formed because F is missing)

REACT – CREATIVITY (Can be formed)

Hence, the correct option is (C).

23. The pattern followed here is as below:

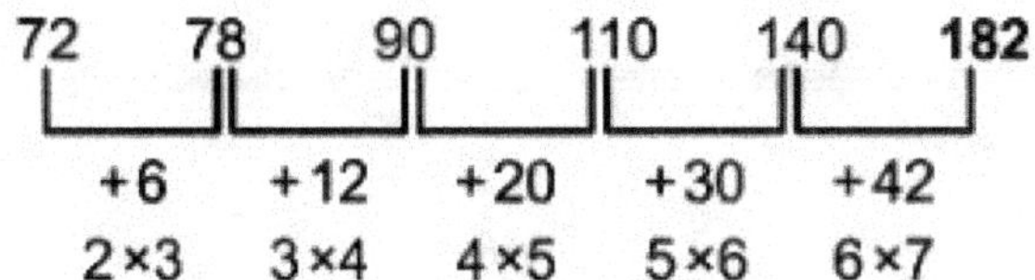

$$72 \quad 78 \quad 90 \quad 110 \quad 140 \quad 182$$

$$+6 \quad +12 \quad +20 \quad +30 \quad +42$$

$$2\times3 \quad 3\times4 \quad 4\times5 \quad 5\times6 \quad 6\times7$$

Hence, the correct option is (B).

24. The logic is :

$1 + 2^2 = 5$

$5 + 3^2 = 14$

$14 + 4^2 = 30$

$30 + 5^2 = 55$

$55 + 6^2 = 91$

Hence, the correct option is (B).

25. The full form of "BRICS" is Brazil, Russia, India, China, and South Africa.

BRICS is an acronym for the powerful grouping of the world's leading emerging market economies, namely Brazil, Russia, India, China, and South Africa. The BRICS mechanism aims to promote peace, security, development, and cooperation. BRICS countries have individually emerged to assume new economic rankings.

Hence, the correct option is (D).

Q.1 Who has been appointed as a director in the Prime Minister's Office (PMO) in August 2022?

A. Shweta Singh

B. Ravi Kumar

C. Ruchi Mishra

D. Anoop Kumar Pathak

Q.2 Which edition of Chartered Accountant's Day was observed on 1 July 2022?

A. 70th **B.** 72th **C.** 74th **D.** 76th

Q.3 Which of the following ruler was the founder of Khilji Dynasty?

A. Mubarak Khilji

B. Jalaluddin Firuz Khilji

C. Malik Kafur

D. Alauddin Khilji

Q.4 In which of his movements Gandhiji went on a hunger strike for the first time?

A. Kheda Satyagraha

B. Ahmedabad mill strike

C. Champaran Satyagraha

D. Non-Cooperation Movement

Q.5 Bangladesh has a land border with________.

A. only India **B.** India and Myanmar

C. India and Bhutan **D.** India and China

Q.6 Which of the following dams is located in Karnataka?

A. Tungabhadra Dam **B.** Gandhi Sagar Dam

C. Srisailam Dam **D.** Mullaiperiyar Dam

Q.7 The number of spokes in the 'Chakra' in the Indian National Flag is:

A. 40 **B.** 24 **C.** 22 **D.** 20

Q.8 In a certain code language, GAME is written as FHZBLNDF then BLUE will be?

A. BBLMDFTV **B.** CDMNTVFG

C. ACKMTVDF **D.** ACZXVWNP

Q.9 Direction: From the given alternatives find the word which can be formed from the letters used in the given word.
SUBJECTIVELY

A. STYLISE **B.** VISIBLY

C. JIVIEST **D.** JUSTICE

Q.10 Direction: A series is given with one term missing. Select the correct alternative from the given ones that will complete the series.
8, 13, 23, 38, 58, 83, ?

A. 113 **B.** 97 **C.** 131 **D.** 63

Q.11 'Statue of Liberty' is the National Emblem of:

A. UK **B.** USA

C. Germany **D.** Russia

Q.12 K. Sanjita Chanu is related to which of the following sports?

A. Chess **B.** Cricket

C. Tennis **D.** Weightlifting

Q.13 Direction: In the following question, select the number which can be placed at the sign of question mark $(?)$ from the given alternatives.

4	6	5	16
9	8	3	21
5	8	7	?

A. 18 **B.** 21 **C.** 23 **D.** 27

Q.14 What is the currency of Egypt?

A. Euro **B.** Pound **C.** Dollar **D.** Dinar

Q.15 Penalty stroke is used in which of the following given game?

A. Football

B. Field hockey and Football

C. Baseball

D. Rugby

Q.16 Zooter is used in which game?

A. Cricket **B.** Cycling

C. Football **D.** Badminton

Q.17 Who is the author of the book 'My Seditious Heart'?

A. Salman Rushdie **B.** Amitav Ghosh

C. Arundhati Roy **D.** Chetan Bhagat

Q.18 Which of the following books was written by Leo Tolstoy?

A. Moby Dick **B.** War and Peace

C. Odyssey **D.** Ulysses

Q.19 ________ was the first person to isolate methane gas. He discovered that methane mixed with air could be exploded using an electric spark.

A. William Thomson **B.** William Crookes

C. Louis Pasteur **D.** Alessandro Volta

Q.20 Who first discovered that the earth revolves around the sun?

A. Newton **B.** Dalton

C. Copernicus **D.** Einstein

Q.21 Where is Karni Mata temple situated?

A. Jodhpur **B.** Bikaner **C.** Karauli **D.** Baran

Q.22 The famous painting 'Satyam Shivam Sundaram' was the creation of____.

A. Mahendranath Singh

B. Vishwanath Mehta

C. Nand Kishore Sharma

D. Sivnandan Nautiyal

Q.23 Which dance festival is performed by Khasi tribe people?

A. Nongkrem   **B.** Jatara

C. Cherav   **D.** Bihu

Q.24 Sultan Muhammad Ghori who defeated Prithviraj III in 1192 was a ruler from _____.

A. Afghanistan   **B.** Persia

C. Iran   **D.** Egypt

Q.25 If HOCKEY means HPENID, then find the code for CGYOCZ.

A. CICUKJ   **B.** CHARGE

C. ABHFYS   **D.** None of these

// Smart Answer Sheet //

Correct — Percentage of students who answered correctly.　　**Skipped** — Percentage of students who skipped.

Q.	Ans.	Correct / Skipped	Q.	Ans.	Correct / Skipped	Q.	Ans.	Correct / Skipped	Q.	Ans.	Correct / Skipped	Q.	Ans.	Correct / Skipped	Q.	Ans.	Correct / Skipped
1	A	80.37 % / 10.87 %	6	A	82.54 % / 15.97 %	11	B	58.99 % / 38.85 %	16	A	64.07 % / 32.12 %	21	B	87.79 % / 11.5 %			
2	C	88.36 % / 11.56 %	7	B	87.02 % / 12.68 %	12	D	57.02 % / 32.89 %	17	C	45.66 % / 30.65 %	22	D	66.07 % / 31.26 %			
3	B	57.85 % / 41.84 %	8	C	62.99 % / 34.33 %	13	B	85.99 % / 13.1 %	18	B	43.54 % / 54.86 %	23	A	83.92 % / 10.47 %			
4	B	86.09 % / 13.78 %	9	D	89.17 % / 10.73 %	14	B	81.49 % / 11.7 %	19	D	68.96 % / 30.0 %	24	A	41.29 % / 31.02 %			
5	B	78.53 % / 10.98 %	10	A	53.72 % / 41.43 %	15	B	78.61 % / 20.48 %	20	C	79.03 % / 10.87 %	25	B	84.82 % / 11.21 %			

//Hints and Solutions//

1. Indian Foreign Service (IFS) officer Shweta Singh was on 2 August 2022 appointed as a director in the Prime Minister's Office (PMO).

- She is a 2008-batch IFS officer.
- The Appointments Committee of the Cabinet (ACC) approved Singh's appointment for a period of three years from the date of her joining.

Hence, the correct option is (A).

2. 74th edition of Chartered Accountant's Day was observed on 1 July 2022.

The day is celebrated by Institute of Chartered Accountants of India (ICAI). ICAI was established by the Parliament of India in 1949. It is the second-largest accounting and statutory body across the globe. In India, ICAI is the only licensing and regulatory body for the financial audit and accounting profession.

Hence, the correct option is (C).

3. Jalaluddin Firuz Khilji was the founder of the Khilji Dynasty.

He killed the last descendent of the Slave Dynasty and then he declared himself the sultan of Delhi sultanate at the age of 70 years.

Jalaluddin Khilji was killed by his nephew and son-in-law Alauddin Khilji who succeeded him and became the new King.

Hence, the correct option is (B).

4. Gandhiji went on a hunger strike for the first time during the Ahmedabad mill strike.

Gandhiji went on a hunger strike for the first time in March 1918 in support of the workers of Ahmedabad. There was a dispute between mill owners and labourers over the 'plague bonus'. Impressed by the movement, the mill owners agreed to give 35 percent of the bonus to the workers.

Hence, the correct option is (B).

5. Bangladesh has a land border with India and Myanmar.

India shares a 4,096-km-long border with Bangladesh.

It is the fifth-longest land border in the world.

India shares its longest boundary with Bangladesh.

Bangladesh touches Assam, Tripura, Mizoram, Meghalaya, and West Bengal.

Hence, the correct option is (B).

6.

- Tungabhadra Dam is constructed on the Tungabhadra river in Karnataka.
- Srisailam Dam is located in Andhra Pradesh.
- Gandhi Sagar Dam is located in Madhya Pradesh.
- Mullaiperiyar Dam is located in Kerala.

Hence, the correct option is (A).

7. The Ashoka Chakra should have 24 spokes that are uniformly spaced in the Indian National Flag. The Ashoka Chakra was selected as a depiction of Dharma. The size of the Ashoka Chakra was not defined in the Flag code. The Ashoka Chakra is in a Navy-blue colour on the white stripe of the flag.

Hence, the correct option is (B).

8. The pattern for the code is as follows,

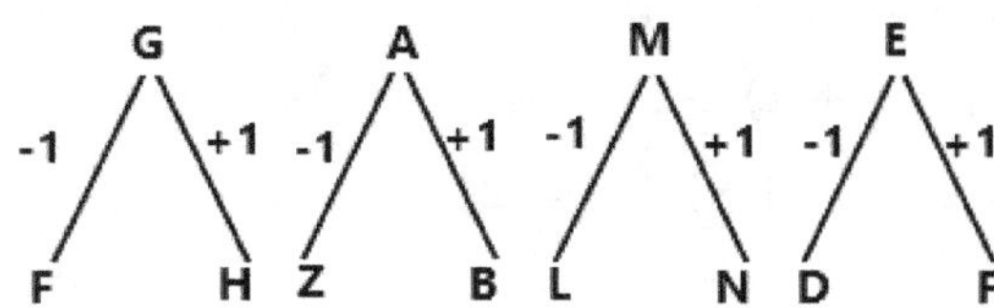

Each letter of the given word is replaced by its adjacent letters.

Similarly,

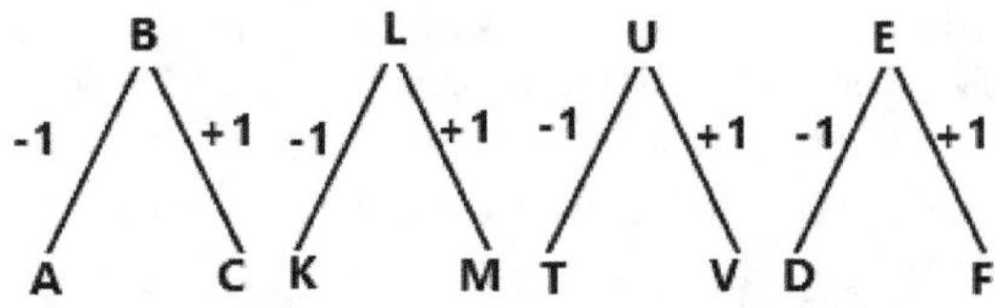

Therefore, BLUE is coded as ACKMTVDF.

Hence, the correct option is (C).

9. JUSTICE → can be formed.

STYLISE → Only single S is present in SUBJECTIVELY. So, cannot be formed.

VISIBLY → Only single I is present in SUBJECTIVELY. So, cannot be formed.

JIVIEST → Only single I is present in SUBJECTIVELY. So, cannot be formed.

Hence, the correct option is (D).

10. The pattern followed here is:

$8 + 5 = 13$

$13 + 10 = 23$

$23 + 15 = 38$

$38 + 20 = 58$

$58 + 25 = 83$

Similarly,

$83 + 30 = 113$

Hence, the correct option is (A).

11. The Statue of Liberty stands in Upper New York Bay, a universal symbol of freedom. Originally conceived as an emblem of the friendship between the people of France and the U.S. and a sign of their mutual desire for liberty.

Hence, the correct option is (B).

12. K. Sanjita Chanu is a weightlifting player from India. He won a gold medal in the 48 kg category of the weightlifting event at the 2014 Commonwealth Games in Glasgow. He lifted a total of 173 kg, with 77 in snatch and 96 in clean and jerk. She hails from Kakching district in Manipur.

Hence, the correct option is (D).

13. The logic here is as follows,

First row: $(4 + 6 + 5) + 1 = 16$

Second row: $(9 + 8 + 3) + 1 = 21$

Similarly,

Third row: $(5 + 8 + 7) + 1 = 21$

Hence, the correct option is (B).

14.

- The currency of Egypt is the Egyptian Pound which is divided into 100 piastres. It is abbreviated as LE which means livre egyptienne (French for Egyptian pound).
- Cairo is the capital of Egypt and Arabic is its official language.
- Abdel Fattah el-Sisi is the present President of the Arab Republic of Egypt.

Hence, the correct option is (B).

15.

- A penalty stroke is the most severe penalty given in field hockey and football.
- It is predominantly awarded when a foul has prevented a certain goal from being scored or for a deliberate infringement by a defender in the penalty circle.
- Other terms associated with field hockey are Artificial turf, Attacker, Breakaway, Corner flag etc.

Hence, the correct option is (B).

16. Zooter is used in Cricket. A Zooter is a special type of ball throwing that has little or no spin at all. Australian player Shane Warne is famous for using Zooter in his cricket career.

Hence, the correct option is (A).

17. Arundhati Roy is the author of the book 'My Seditious Heart'. Arundhati Roy is also the author of "The God of Small Things", which won the Man Booker Prize in 1997. The God of Small Things became the biggest-selling book by a non-expatriate Indian author.

Hence, the correct option is (C).

18. War and Peace is a novel written by Russian author Leo Tolstoy. The novel describes the impact of the French invasion of Russia through the stories of 5 Russian families. It was first produced serially from 1865 to 1867. The complete book was produced in 1869.

Hence, the correct option is (B).

19. Alessandro Volta was the first person to isolate methane gas. He discovered that methane mixed with air could be exploded using an electric spark. He is also known for inventing electric batteries and discovering contact electricity.

Hence, the correct option is (D).

20. Nicolaus Copernicus was an astronomer and mathematician who was the first to discover that the earth revolves around the sun giving birth to the heliocentric model in which the sun is at the center of the universe.

Hence, the correct option is (C).

21.

- Karni Mata is the Kuldevi of Charan and Rathore of Bikaner.
- She is also called the incarnation of Jogmaya, the goddess of mice and Jagat Mata.
- Her temple is in Deshnok Bikaner, whose foundation was laid by Karni Mata herself.
- The original temple of Karni Mata was built by King Jai Singh.
- The present grand appearance of this temple was given by Maharaja Surat Singh.
- Most of the rats are found in this temple, so the temple is also called the temple of rats.

Hence, the correct option is (B).

22. The famous painting 'Satyam Shivam Sundaram' was the creation of Sivnandan Nautiyal. Satyam Shivam Sundaram is a Sanskrit phrase that has a significant meaning in the Indian Upanishads. Satyam Shivam Sundaram is used to show respect and devotion to Lord Shiva.

Hence, the correct option is (D).

23.

- Nongkrem dance festival is an annual festival of the Khasi tribe of Meghalaya.
- Ka Pomblang Nongkrem dance is popularly known as Nongkrem dance.
- The celebration goes on for five days and is commonly celebrated in the period of November.
- The festival is celebrated during Autumn in Smit, which is the social focus of the Khasi Ŏhills.
- This indigenous dance festival is celebrated in order to honor the powerful Goddess Ka Blei Synshar for blessing the people of the community with a good harvest and prosperity.
- The Syiem of Khyrim along with the high priest performs the Pemblang ceremony.
- During the Nongkrem dance festival, traditional dance is performed by the young men and women of the Khasi tribe.
- The dance performed by the men is known as "Ka Shad Mastieh".

- The dance performed by the women is known as "Ka Shad Kynthei".

Hence, the correct option is (A).

24. Sultan Muhammad Ghori was of Iranian descent who ruled over the Ghor region of present-day central Afghanistan. The Second Battle of Tarian (Taraori) was fought between Muhammad Ghori and Prithviraj Chauhan. The battle took place in 1192 A.D near Train. In this battle, Prithviraj Chauhan was defeated by Muhammad Ghori.

Hence, the correct option is (A).

25. The pattern followed here is,

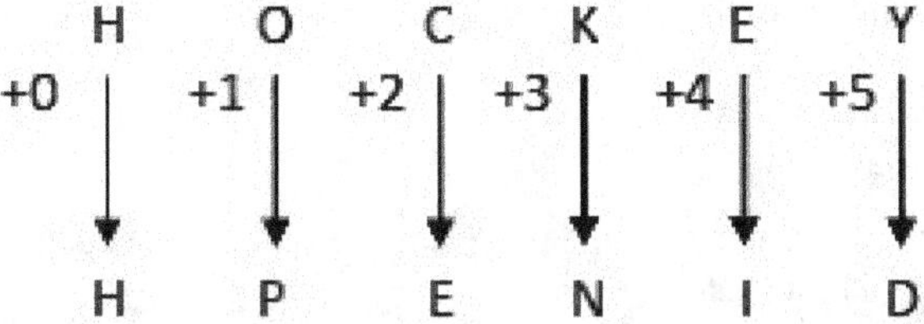

Similarly,

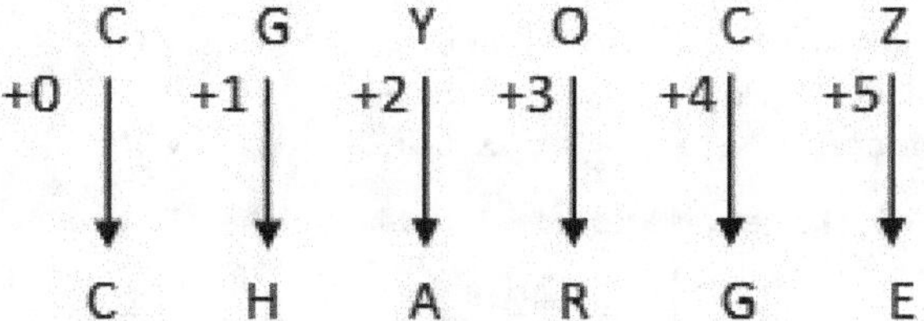

Therefore, the code for CGYOCZ is CHARGE.

Hence, the correct option is (B).

Q.1 Which Formula One racing driver won the British F1 Grand Prix on 3 July 2022?

A. Lewis Hamilton
B. Sergio Perez
C. Carlos Sainz
D. Max Verstappen

Q.2 How many hi-tech libraries will be built in the villages of Haryana?

A. 500 **B.** 700 **C.** 900 **D.** 1000

Q.3 Allahabad Pillar Inscription gives a detailed account of the reign of which king?

A. Chandragupta Maurya
B. Kanishka
C. Samudra Gupta
D. Ashoka

Q.4 Who was the first Gupta ruler to adopt the title of Maharajadhiraja?

A. Chandragupta I
B. Chandragupta II
C. Samudragupta
D. Srigupt

Q.5 Massanjore Dam lies on which river?

A. Haldi River
B. Jaldhaka River
C. Mayurakshi River
D. Damodar River

Q.6 Which meridian or longitude is also termed as the Standard Meridian of India?

A. 27°30'E **B.** 27°30'W **C.** 82°30'W **D.** 82°30'E

Q.7 Which plateau is situated between the Aravalli and Vindhya mountain ranges?

A. Plateau of Deccan
B. Plateau of Meghalaya
C. Plateau of Malwa
D. Plateau of Chhotanagpur

Q.8 'Ganga Sagar Mela' is celebrated on the occasion of Makar Sankranti from 13 to 15 January every year in:

A. Uttar Pradesh
B. West Bengal
C. Bihar
D. Uttarakhand

Q.9 Ghumot was declared as the Heritage musical instrument of which state?

A. Goa
B. Gujarat
C. Rajasthan
D. Jharkhand

Q.10 The Hornbill Festival is one of the important festivals celebrated in ________.

A. Arunachal Pradesh
B. Nagaland
C. Mizoram
D. Meghalaya

Q.11 Who among the following is/was a famous Tabla player?

A. TN Krishnan
B. Bhimsen Joshi
C. Alla Rakha
D. Hariprasad Chaurasia

Q.12 Manisha Gulyani is related to which of the following dance form?

A. Kathak
B. Kuchipudi
C. Bharatanatyam
D. Odissi

Q.13 Who were the first Indian to translate the Mahabharata into English?

A. Kisari Mohan Ganguly
B. Pandit Ram Awatar Sharma
C. Vallabhacharya
D. TA Saraswati

Q.14 Which of the following prominent leaders wrote the book 'Citizen Delhi: My Life, My Times'?

A. Sheila Dikshit
B. Arvind Kejriwal
C. Harsh Vardhan
D. Arun Jaitley

Q.15 Tiger Woods is associated with:

A. Formula 1 racing
B. Tennis
C. Fencing
D. Golf

Q.16 A Snickometer is associated with which of the following sports?

A. Tennis **B.** Cricket **C.** Hockey **D.** Football

Q.17 In a certain code, 'HUNTER' is coded as 'UHNTRE'. How is 'MANAGE' coded in that code?

A. MAANGE
B. EGNAAM
C. AMNAEG
D. MNAAEG

Q.18 In a certain code, 'FINGER' is written as '852369' and 'IGNORE' is written as '532796'. How is 'FOREIGN' written in that code?

A. 8795362 **B.** 8795632 **C.** 8967532 **D.** 8796532

Q.19 Direction: Complete the series.

38, 35, 34, 31, 30, ___

A. 24 **B.** 25 **C.** 28 **D.** 27

Q.20 Direction: Complete the series.

4, 4, 8, 24, 96, ...

A. 448 **B.** 493 **C.** 461 **D.** 480

Q.21 Direction: In the following question, select the word which cannot be formed using the letters of the given word. PREDICAMENT

A. DICE **B.** MATE **C.** TEAM **D.** RAIL

Q.22 Blood groups were discovered by:

A. Landsteiner
B. William Harvey
C. Weismann
D. Morgan

Q.23 Insulin was discovered by:

A. Frederick Banting
B. Edward Jenner

C. Ronald Ross　　　　**D.** S.A. Wakesman

Q.24 How many Asiatic Lions are there in the State Emblem of India?

A. 3　　　　**B.** 4　　　　**C.** 5　　　　**D.** 2

Q.25 Who is the author of the book "I do what I do"?

A. Pranab Mukherjee　　　　**B.** Raghuram G Rajan

C. Urjit Patel　　　　**D.** Jagdish Prakash

// Smart Answer Sheet //

Correct — Percentage of students who answered correctly. **Skipped** — Percentage of students who skipped.

Q.	Ans.	Correct / Skipped	Q.	Ans.	Correct / Skipped	Q.	Ans.	Correct / Skipped	Q.	Ans.	Correct / Skipped	Q.	Ans.	Correct / Skipped	Q.	Ans.	Correct / Skipped
1	C	60.89 % / 36.31 %	6	D	43.29 % / 37.8 %	11	C	86.38 % / 12.48 %	16	B	48.79 % / 37.49 %	21	D	53.47 % / 43.72 %			
2	D	47.09 % / 47.22 %	7	C	42.98 % / 47.5 %	12	A	48.76 % / 40.68 %	17	C	78.74 % / 10.53 %	22	A	44.54 % / 44.99 %			
3	C	68.78 % / 30.29 %	8	B	60.03 % / 31.63 %	13	A	43.05 % / 40.5 %	18	D	65.44 % / 33.47 %	23	A	45.72 % / 45.69 %			
4	A	48.74 % / 39.83 %	9	A	61.84 % / 35.74 %	14	A	66.49 % / 32.55 %	19	D	78.55 % / 20.41 %	24	B	61.96 % / 31.8 %			
5	C	41.42 % / 35.48 %	10	B	89.64 % / 10.25 %	15	D	54.19 % / 39.84 %	20	D	76.71 % / 17.59 %	25	B	42.54 % / 41.84 %			

//Hints and Solutions//

1. Ferrari's Carlos Sainz won his career's first Formula One race on 3 July 2022 with a victory at the British Grand Prix.

Red Bull's Sergio Perez and Mercedes' Lewis Hamilton finished second and third respectively. Championship leader Max Verstappen finished seventh. Sainz has moved up to fourth in the 2022 Driver standings.

Hence, the correct option is (C).

2. Haryana Development and Panchayat Minister Devendra Singh Babli said that one thousand hi-tech libraries would be built in the villages as a pilot project in the state. Addressing a public meeting during the 'Madhur Milan Program' organized at Kheri Raiwali village of Kaithal district, the ministers said that the youth of rural areas will be able to make their future bright by taking education according to the present requirement from these libraries. Along with this, work is also going on to build 1000 gyms in villages to encourage youth towards sports and keep them away from drugs.

Hence, the correct option is (D).

3. Samudra Gupta court poet and minister Harisena composed the Allahabad pillar Inscription or Prayag Prasasti. The Pillar was an Ashokan Pillar erected by Ashoka six centuries before him. This Inscription is a eulogy of Samudra Gupta and mentions the conquests of Samudra Gupta and the boundaries of the Gupta Empire. As per this inscription, Samudra Gupta defeated 9 kings in the North, 12 Kings in the South, reduced all the Atavika states to vassalage.

Hence, the correct option is (C).

4. Chandragupta I was the first ruler of the Gupta dynasty to adopt the title of Maharajadhiraja. Chandragupta I was a son of the Gupta king Ghatotkacha, and a grandson of the dynasty's founder Gupta, both of whom are called Maharaja in the Allahabad Pillar inscription. He was also the father of Samudragupta, his next successor.

Hence, the correct option is (A).

5. Massanjore Dam is a hydropower generating dam over the Mayurakshi River located at Massanjore near Dumka in the state of Jharkhand, India. It is also called Canada Dam. The Massanjore dam across the Mayurakshi was commissioned in 1955. Massanjore dam is about 38 kilometres upstream from Siuri in West Bengal.

Hence, the correct option is (C).

6. 82°30′E meridian or longitude is also termed as the Standard Meridian of India. The standard meridian of India is east of the Greenwich Meridian. Indian Standard time has a time offset of UTC+05:30. Greenwich Mean Time (GMT) is the mean solar time at the Royal Observatory in Greenwich.

Hence, the correct option is (D).

7. The Plateau of Malwa is situated between the Aravalli and Vindhya mountain ranges. Malwa Plateau, plateau area in central north India. It is bounded to the north by the plateau of Madhya Bharat and Bundelkhand Upland, to the east and south by the Vindhya Range and to the west by the plains of Gujarat.

Hence, the correct option is (C).

8. Ganga-Sagar Mela is one of such festival of India celebrated on the occasion of Mankar Sankranti, during 13th – 15th January every year in West Bengal, which draws thousands of pilgrims from all over the world. The hosting state of West Bengal organizes this fair with great pride and devout. The pilgrims take a holy dip in the water of the River Ganga in the morning while worshipping Lord Surya.

Hence, the correct option is (B).

9. Ghumot was declared as the Heritage musical instrument of Goa. Ghumot is a specially designed earthen pot in which the skin of the monitor lizard is made tightly at the mouth of the earthen pot. It was banned by the forest department of Goa due to the skin of a lizard being the main component. It is widely played during Ganesh Chaturthi aarties.

Hence, the correct option is (A).

10. Hornbill Festival is one of the most important festivals of Nagaland. It takes place from 1st to 7th December every year. It is done by the Naga Troops.

Hence, the correct option is (B).

11. Ustaad Allarakha Qureshi popularly known as Alla Rakha was an Indian tabla player who specialized in Hindustani classical. He was a frequent accompanist of sitar player Ravi Shankar and was largely responsible for introducing Tabla to the western audience.

Hence, the correct option is (C).

12. Manisha Gulyani is a very famous Kathak dancer from India. She is a disciple of Pt. Girdhari Maharaj, an ICCR Kathak artist and teacher cum performer for ICC centres abroad.

Hence, the correct option is (A).

13. Kisari Mohan Ganguly was the first to translate the Mahabharat into English from Sanskrit.

Kisari Mohan Ganguli was an Indian translator known for being the first to provide a complete translation of the Sanskrit epic Mahabharata in English. His translation was published as The Mahabharata of Krishna-Dwaipayana Vyasa Translated into English Prose between 1883 and 1896.

Hence, the correct option is (A).

14. Sheila Dikshit wrote the book 'Citizen Delhi: My Life, My Times'. The book was published on 10 February 2018. Sheila Dixit was known as the longest-serving Chief Minister of Delhi for a period of 15 years.

Her books are:

- Citizen Delhi: My Times, My Life
- Dilli Meri Dilli: Before and After 1998

Hence, the correct option is (A).

15. Eldrick Tont Tiger Woods is an American professional golfer. He is tied for first in PGA Tour wins and ranks second in men's major championships and also holds numerous golf records. Woods is widely regarded as one of the greatest golfers, and one of the most famous athletes of all time.

Hence, the correct option is (D).

16. Snickometer is the name of a computer and camera system used in Cricket matches. This technology is used in televised cricket matches to graphically show the video of the ball passing the bat at the same time as the audio of any sounds at the time. It is only used to give the television audience more information and to show if the ball did or did not actually hit the bat.

Hence, the correct option is (B).

17. The logic is:

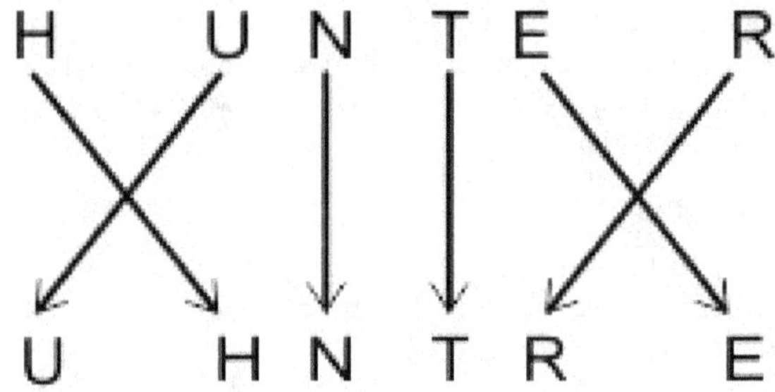

Similarly,

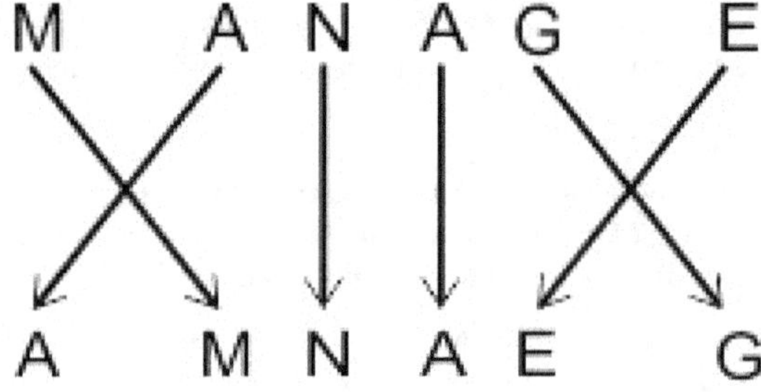

Hence, the correct option is (C).

18. Combining the 2 words and their depictions in sequence, we can infer the following representation of letters:

F	I	N	G	E	R
8	5	2	3	6	9
I	G	N	O	R	E
5	3	2	7	9	6

So, from the above table, FOREIGN can be represented as,

F	O	R	E	I	G	N
8	7	9	6	5	3	2

Hence, the correct option is (D).

19. The logic is:

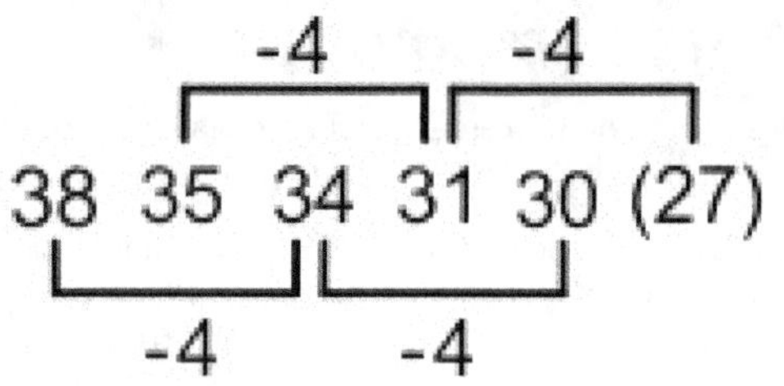

Hence, the correct option is (D).

20. The logic here is,

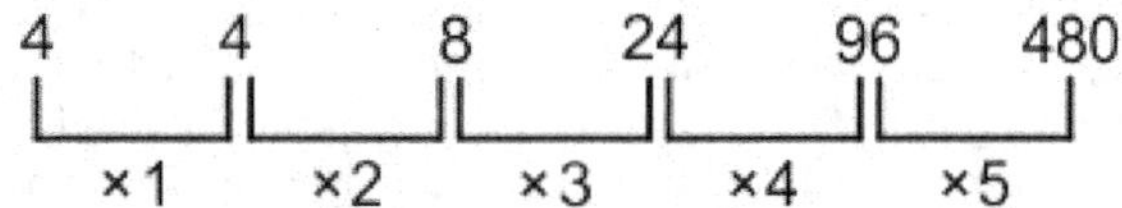

Hence, the correct option is (D).

21. 1) DICE → PREDICAMENT → can be form.

2) MATE → PREDICAMENT → can be form.

3) TEAM → PREDICAMENT → can be form.

4) RAIL → PREDICAMENT → cannot be form as there is no letter L.

Hence, the correct option is (D).

22. The ABO blood group system is widely credited to have been discovered by the Austrian scientist Karl Landsteiner, who identified the O, A, and B blood types in 1900. He was awarded the Nobel Prize in Physiology or Medicine in 1930 for his work.

Hence, the correct option is (A).

23. Frederick Banting was a Canadian medical scientist, doctor and Nobel laureate noted as one of the main discoverers of insulin. In 1923 Banting and John James Rickard Macleod received the Nobel Prize in Medicine, becoming the youngest recipient of the Nobel Prize in Physiology/Medicine.

Hence, the correct option is (A).

24. The national emblem is an adaptation of the Lion Capital, originally found atop the Ashoka Column at Sarnath, established in 250 BC. The capital has four Asiatic lions—symbolising power, courage, pride and confidence—seated on a circular abacus. The abacus has sculptures of a bull, a horse, a lion and an elephant.

Hence, the correct option is (B).

25.

- I do what I Do is a non-fiction book authored by Raghuram Rajan.
- Mr. Rajan is an economist and former Governor of the Reserve Bank of India.
- This book is published by Harper Collins India in 2017.
- The book is a collection of speeches delivered by Rajan during his tenure as the Governor of the Reserve Bank of India along with his views on the economic and political context prevalent at that time.
- The book was released on September 5, 2017.

- It became one of the best-selling books of that time.

Hence, the correct option is (B).

// Notes //

// Notes //

www.ingramcontent.com/pod-product-compliance
Lightning Source LLC
Chambersburg PA
CBHW081307130726
47998CB00010B/2962